MUSLIM

Other Books by Hank Hanegraaff

Has God Spoken?:
Memorable Proofs of the Bible's Divine Inspiration

Resurrection

The Farce of Evolution

The Creation Answer Book

Christianity in Crisis:
21st Century

Counterfeit Revival

The Prayer of Jesus:
Secrets to Real Intimacy with God

The Covering:
God's Plan to Protect You from Evil

The Heart of Christmas

The Complete Bible Answer Book, Collector's Edition

The Apocalypse Code:
Find Out What the Bible Really Says About the
End Times and Why It Matters Today

MUSLIM

WHAT YOU NEED TO KNOW ABOUT THE WORLD'S FASTEST-GROWING RELIGION

HANK HANEGRAAFF

W PUBLISHING GROUP

AN IMPRINT OF THOMAS NELSON

Muslim

© 2017 Hank Hanegraaff

Published in Nashville, Tennessee, by W Publishing Group, an imprint of Thomas Nelson.

Thomas Nelson titles may be purchased in bulk for educational, business, fund-raising, or sales promotional use. For information, please e-mail SpecialMarkets@ThomasNelson.com.

Unless otherwise noted, Scripture quotations are taken from the Holy Bible, New International Version®, NIV®. © 1973, 1978, 1984, 2011 by Biblica, Inc.® Used by permission of Zondervan. All rights reserved worldwide.

Scripture quotations marked NKJV are from the New King James Version®. © 1982 by Thomas Nelson. Used by permission. All rights reserved.

Scripture quotations marked ESV are from the ESV® Bible (The Holy Bible, English Standard Version®). © 2001 by Crossway, a publishing ministry of Good News Publishers. Used by permission. All rights reserved.

Scripture quotations marked NASB are from New American Standard Bible®. © 1960, 1962, 1963, 1968, 1971, 1972, 1973, 1975, 1977, 1995 by The Lockman Foundation. Used by permission.

Italics in Bible quotations indicate the author's emphasis.

Unless otherwise noted, all Qur'an quotations are from the Yusuf Ali translation: Abdullah Yusuf Ali, *The Meaning of the Holy Qur'an*, tenth ed. (Beltsville, MD: Amana, 1999, 2001).

Qur'an quotations marked *Study Quran* are taken from *The Study Quran: A New Translation and Commentary*, ed. Seyyed Hossein Nasr (New York: HarperOne, 2015).

Qur'an quotations marked *Hilali-Khan* are taken from *The Noble Quran*, trans. Muhammad Taqi-ud-Din Al-Hilali and Muhammad Muhsin Khan (Riyadh, Kingdom of Saudi Arabia: Dar-us-Salam). Online at www.noblequran.com/translation/.

Qur'an quotations marked *Sahih International* are taken from Saheeh International, The Qur'an: English Meanings and Notes (Riyadh, Kingdom of Saudi Arabia: Al-Muntada Al-Islami Trust, 2001–2011; Jeddah: Dar Abul-Qasim Publishing House, 1997–2001).

Qur'an quotations marked *Shakir* are taken from *The Holy Qur'an*, trans. M. H. Shakir (New York: Tahrike Tarsile Qur'an, Inc., 1983). Online at quod.lib.umich.edu/k/koran/.

Qur'an quotations marked *Arberry* are taken from *The Koran Interpreted*, trans. Arthur J. Arberry (New York: Macmillan & Co., 1955).

Qur'an quotations marked *Malik* are taken from *English Translation of the Meaning of Al-Qur'an: The Guidance for Mankind*, trans. Muhammad Farooq-i-Azam Malik (Houston: Institute of Islamic Knowledge, 1997).

Qur'an quotations marked *Majestic* are taken from *The Majestic Qur'an: An English Rendition of Its Meanings*, 4th ed., trans. Ali Ozek, Nureddin Uzunoglu, Tevfik R. Topuzoglu, Mehmet Maksutoglu (Chicago: Nawawi Foundation; London: Ibn Khaldun Foundation, 2000).

Qur'an quotations marked *Pickthall* are taken from *The Meaning of the Glorious Koran*, trans. Mohammad Marmaduke Pickthall (New York: New American Library, n.d.).

Italics in Qur'an quotations indicate the author's emphasis and bracketed text is his own. Parenthetical insertions are by the translator.

Q stands for Qur'an in parenthetical references.

Concerning citations to *ahadith*, since they do not have a standardized referencing system, when possible, I've restricted citations to the numbering system of the English translations at Center for Muslim-Jewish Engagement, University of Southern California, www.usc.edu/org/cmje/religious-texts/hadith/. *Sahih al-Bukhari* translated by M. Muhsin Khan; *Sahih Muslim* translated by Abdul Hamid Siddiqui; *Sunan Abu-Dawud* translated by Ahmad Hasan.

Unless otherwise indicated, all cited URLs were last accessed in March 2017.

ISBN 978-0-7852-1603-2 (eBook)

ISBN 978-0-7852-1660-5 (IE)

Library of Congress Control Number: 2017910353

ISBN 978-0-7852-1602-5 (HC)

Printed in the United States of America

17 18 19 20 21 LSC 10 9 8 7 6 5 4 3 2 1

I gratefully dedicate this book to Jack Countryman who has taught me by word and example what it means to love my Lord, my family, and my craft. With him I pray, "Lord, please don't ever put me on the bench."

CONTENTS

CONTENTS

FOREWORD

The Bible Answer Man Becomes
the Qur'an Answer Man

Long renowned as the Bible Answer Man, Hank Hanegraaff has gained
a well-deserved reputation for thoroughness of research, honesty of
evaluation, and clarity of thought. In *Muslim: What You Need to Know About
the World's Fastest Growing Religion*, he now becomes the Qur'an Answer
Man, directing his considerable analytical powers to the religion of Islam, a
study that world events are daily making more timely, important, and necessary for every Christian to undertake.

In the years that I have devoted to calling attention to the nature and
magnitude of the global jihad threat, I have encountered many people who
have told me that it isn't necessary to know what's in the Qur'an and Islamic
teaching: all we need to know is that there are Muslims who are trying to kill
us, and we need to stop them. Indeed, under Barack Obama that was essentially the policy of the US government. In 2011, the Obama administration
directed intelligence and law enforcement agencies to make no mention of
Islam or jihad in connection with terrorism, and Obama himself repeatedly
proclaimed that Islam was a religion of peace and tolerance. The Obama
administration's primary counterterror initiative was called "Countering
Violent Extremism" and took great pains to say nothing at all about Islam.

Denial and willful ignorance were the least of that program's problems.

The worst aspect of it was that it was doomed to failure, for it is an adage as old as warfare itself that no war is won without knowing one's enemy. Voluntarily abandoning any effort to understand the ideology, motives, and goals of the enemy was a recipe for defeat, and thus it came as no surprise that during the eight years of the Obama administration, the global jihad advanced on all fronts. Muslim Brotherhood-linked organizations became entrenched at the highest levels of the US government, the Islamic State (ISIS) established a caliphate in Iraq and Syria over an expanse of territory larger than the size of Great Britain, and jihad massacres became an ever more common feature of daily life in Europe and North America.

Muslim contains the antidote to all that. Organizing the book around the word *Muslim* as an acronym, Hanegraaff offers an astonishing breadth and depth of material, from the Qur'an's martial verses and the bloody career of Muhammad, the prophet of Islam, to the inherently political, authoritarian, and supremacist character of Islamic law; as well as the numerous errors of fact and logic in the Qur'an; its contradictions of numerous Christian doctrines (which may come as a surprise to naïve Christians who prate about the "three Abrahamic faiths" and believe that "interfaith dialogue" will prove a cure for jihad terror and Muslim persecution of Christians); the meaning and importance of the caliphate and the Levant region for Muslims; and much more.

The most important section of this book is organized around one of Hank's trademark acronyms exploring the Islamic misapprehensions of the Deity of Christ, Original Sin, the Canon, the Trinity, the Resurrection, the Incarnation, the New Creation, and Eschatology. Hanegraaff concludes: "The end of the matter is this. We have laid the straight stick of essential Christian DOCTRINE next to the Islamic counterfeit and by contrast have observed its crookedness. The deity of Christ is denied as he is rendered the mere 'slave of Allah.' Original sin is recast as an original slip—a mere bout of forgetfulness. The divine canon is usurped by the factual errors, faulty ethics, and feigned eloquence of the Qur'an. The incomprehensible Trinity is commandeered by a morally defective unitarian imposter. Resurrection—the greatest feat in human history—is demoted to mere fantasy, and incarnation is demeaned as blasphemy. The scintillating truth that 'if anyone is in Christ he is a new creation' is negated by a capricious Allah.

And eschatology—the thread that weaves the tapestry of Scripture into a harmonious pattern—is ignominiously sullied by the sensual enticements of a largely incoherent Islamic eschatological charade."

That is indeed the heart of the matter: in the global Islamic jihad, the Western world, built on the Christian faith, is facing not just a threat of violence and subversion but also a challenge to Christianity and to the West's very social order, built upon Judeo-Christian principles.

Yet the churches have been notably slow, not only to meet this challenge but even to recognize it as such. While Muslim groups are making concerted efforts to convert young Christians to Islam and place them on the road to jihad—and some of the foremost international jihad leaders have been young American men of Christian backgrounds (the Taliban's John Walker Lindh, al-Qaeda's Adam Gadahn, ISIS' John Georgelas)—Christian leaders of all denominations have been notably remiss: there is no significant effort anywhere to equip young Christians to meet the challenge of Islamic proselytizing and answer the arguments that Muslim preachers adduce.

The seriousness of this omission is compounded by the fact that Islam shares a feature common to many spiritual counterfeits: a simplicity and directness that seem to contrast favorably with what can appear to be Christianity's complexity and difficulty (indeed, one of the favorite tactics of Muslim proselytizers is to attack the doctrine of the Trinity as illogical and therefore false and evidence of the falsity of Christianity as a whole).

Hank Hanegraaff shows in *Muslim*, however, that Islam's simplicity and superficial clarity dissolve, upon closer inspection, into a chaos of self-contradiction, illogic, and absurdity, featuring doctrines borrowed from Christianity, severely misunderstood, and twisted beyond recognition to form part of the incoherence that is Islamic theology. One notorious example of this is the depiction of Jesus in the Qur'an and Hadith (traditions of Muhammad): Jesus is born of a virgin, called the Word of God, speaks from the cradle, performs miracles as a child, is sinless, and will return at the end of the world. None of this is said of Muhammad, yet Muhammad is held to be the greater prophet, indeed, the "seal of the prophets."

This oddity is a byproduct, of course, of the Islamic appropriation of Christian doctrines that the borrowers, at best, only dimly understood. But few are aware of the patchwork and inconsistent character of Islamic doctrine, as even most Christians who enter into dialogue with Muslims are anxious not to cause offense by drawing attention to uncomfortable truths.

Muslim, once again, is the antidote. Islamic doctrine does dissolve into chaos upon a closer inspection, and here is that closer inspection. Islam does contain teachings that incite violence and pose a direct threat, not just to the safety of non-Muslims but also to the ultimate survival of governments that are not constituted according to the strictures of Islamic law. As Hanegraaff demonstrates, Islam is waging and has been waging for fourteen hundred years, perpetual war against non-Sharia governments.

The overall picture is not as comforting as the one someone may get from listening to those who preach "Peace! Peace!" when there is no peace, but Hank Hanegraaff has never been one to shy away from the facts when they were not politically correct or easy to follow, and he does not shy away now. Above all, he shows in *Muslim* that the resistance to the global jihad is a spiritual battle, and in that battle Christians have the most formidable and potent weapon of all at their disposal: the truth.

The conflict between Islam and the West is not going to die down or fade away. The Islamic doctrines upon which it is based, as Hanegraaff shows, are going to continue to cause conflict on an ever-increasing scale. But now at last, with *Muslim*, Christians can equip themselves and others to withstand in the evil days that are sure to come and, having done all, to stand firm on the truth of Christ.

For that, we all owe Hank Hanegraaff an immense debt of gratitude.

—Robert Spencer
Director of Jihad Watch and author of New York Times bestsellers *The Politically Incorrect Guide to Islam (and the Crusades)* and *The Truth About Muhammad* as well as the more recent *The Complete Infidel's Guide to Free Speech (and Its Enemies)* and *Confessions of an Islamophobe*

INTRODUCTION

Allah will grant Islam victory in Europe—without
swords, without guns, without conquests.
—MU'AMMAR GADHAFI[1]

During the thirty-third anniversary of the overthrow of the shah of Iran, I was afforded the opportunity to speak at the University of Tehran and Allameh Tabataba'i University. As I waited to board a United Emirates flight from Dubai to Tehran, I was captivated by the sight of an elderly Iranian man. His son engaged me in polite conversation, telling me that his father was now one hundred years old.

On the plane I sat next to Mojdeh, an accomplished Persian woman with two master's degrees. After pleasant conversation she graciously offered me assistance should I need it while in Iran. As I deplaned, I was kissed by two Muslim men and heard the word *salaam* (peace).

The following morning I met Fatima, a translator whose countenance quite literally lit up the room. She seemed amused when I told her that I had not ventured out of the hotel and assured me that I could walk the streets of Tehran in the middle of the night with complete confidence. She was right. For the next five nights I walked the streets of Tehran (sometimes very late at night) and was routinely greeted with smiles and acts of kindness.

In short, without exception, the Persians I encountered in Iran were extraordinarily hospitable. My encounters emphasize the distinction between individual Muslims and the religion of Islam. *Many Muslims are peaceful and tolerant; however, the history of Islam demonstrates conclusively that it is not a peaceful and tolerant religion.*

Islam is the only significant religious system in the history of the human race with a sociopolitical structure of laws that mandate violence against the infidel. This graphic global reality makes Islam a religious ideology espousing terrorism as a permanent policy rather than as a temporary expedient.[2] Such is historical reality, from the early seventh-century Medina massacres to the 9/11 twenty-first century Manhattan massacre and beyond.

The current narrative is that to tell the truth in this regard is tantamount to radicalizing Muslims and exacerbating hostilities that may otherwise lie dormant. A common refrain has reverberated throughout the West: "Islam is not our adversary." These were precisely the words spoken by Hillary Clinton in the wake of the Paris terrorist attacks back in November of 2015.[3] The Clinton refrain harmonizes well with that of George W. Bush, who on September 20, 2001, pronounced the teachings of Islam "good and peaceful." Bush went on to say, "terrorists are traitors to their own faith, trying, in effect, to hijack Islam itself."[4]

Barack Obama went further, noting that the United States and Muslims worldwide "share common principles—principles of justice and progress; tolerance and the dignity of all human beings." Not only so, said Obama, but "throughout history, Islam has demonstrated through words and deeds the possibilities of religious tolerance and racial equality."[5]

Former secretary of state John Kerry was equally emphatic. "The real face of Islam is a peaceful religion based on the dignity of all human beings." Lest anyone mistake his meaning, Kerry proceeded to underscore his deep conviction that "Muslim communities are advocating for universal human rights and fundamental freedoms, including the most basic freedom to practice one's faith openly and freely."[6] What Kerry said as secretary of state under Obama is little different from what Condoleezza Rice said as secretary of state under Bush. The president, said Rice, wants to make "very, very clear" that "Islam stands for peace and stands for nonviolence."[7]

Many other examples could be cited, including former prime minister Tony Blair, who voiced anger toward anyone who described terrorists, such as Osama bin Laden, as *Islamic*: "It angers me, as it angers the vast majority of Muslims, to hear bin Laden and his associates described as Islamic terrorists. They are terrorists pure and simple. Islam is a peaceful and tolerant religion and the acts of these people are wholly contrary to the teachings of the Koran."[8] Blair noted that his convictions regarding Islam did not arise in a vacuum. Unlike a vast majority of non-Muslim politicians and pundits, he made clear that he had actually read the Qur'an![9]

But is Islam really a peaceful and tolerant religion? This question does not lend itself to a simplistic answer. To begin with, we should note that the word *Islam*, derived from the root *s-l-m*, means "submission (to the will of Allah)." As the venerable Muslim scholar Abdullah Yusuf Ali rightly conveys in his widely respected translation of the Qur'an, "The Religion before Allah is Islam [*l-is'lāmu*] (submission to His Will)" (3:19).[10] Thus, when Muhammad instructed devotees to fight "the People of the Book, until they pay the *Jizya* with willing submission, and feel themselves subdued" (Q 9:29),[11] he was clearly communicating that submission to Allah meant fighting Christians and Jews to the point of surrender or death. And as Allah makes plain in the very next ayah (verse), waging war against "People of the Book" was not necessitated by self-defense but by what he perceived as the falsity of their Judeo-Christian traditions.

Therefore, it is fair to note that Islam is not a religion in the sanitized Western sense. It is an all-encompassing sociopolitical legal matrix that has bred a worldview antagonistic to anything but itself.[12] Again, there may be millions of peaceful and tolerant Muslims, but that hardly means that Islam is a peaceful and tolerant religion.

To determine whether it is or is not requires an objective, open-minded look at Islamic history. This includes unbiased consideration of historical realities ranging from the seventh-century poetess Asma bint Marwan, who Muhammad murdered for a poetic slight,[13] to the twenty-first century Dutch filmmaker Theo van Gogh, murdered by Mohammed Bouyeri for artistically objecting to the subjugation of women.[14]

While cultural elites seek to censor such communal consideration, Islamic sources are more than candid. Muhammad's earliest biographer, Ibn Ishaq,[15] is illustrative of the Islamic sources that chronicle the killings of hundreds of Qurayza Jews forced to kneel in trenches filled with bodies and blood before being brutally beheaded by the apostle: "The apostle went out to the market of Medina (which is still its market today) and dug trenches in it. Then he sent for them and struck off their heads in those trenches as they were brought out to him in batches." Ishaq forthrightly chronicles that the number of Jews slaughtered "were 600 or 700 in all, though some put the figure as high as 800 or 900."[16] Moreover, as the Qur'an makes clear, in addition to those who Muhammad slew, many others (in context, wives and children) he "made prisoners" (Q 33:26).

Within five years of his murderous mayhem, Muhammad would succumb to a raging fever.[17] Islamic killings, however, have continued unabated. Scarcely two years after his death (632), Muslim hordes massacred multiple thousands of Christians in Syria. A year later they massacred monks in the monasteries of Mesopotamia.[18] During the next three hundred years, Islamic imperialists succeeded in subjugating two-thirds of the Christian world—including Palestine, where Christ was born; Egypt, where monasticism was birthed; and Asia Minor, where the early Christian church first flourished.[19]

By the Middle Ages the Muslim menace had become so acute that despite the Schism of 1054,[20] Emperor Alexius of Constantinople implored the Western pontiff to come to the aid of the beleaguered Eastern church. Thus it was that in 1095, Pope Urban II formulated the first Christian crusade. While historical revisionists have cynically recast crusades as imperialistic ventures, that was hardly the intent.[21] In any case, the relief spelled by Christian crusaders was short-lived. In 1244, Muslims regained Christian holy sites, murdered thousands in Caesarea, put thousands more to the sword in Antioch, and sold tens of thousands into slavery. With the dawn of the fourteenth century, the crusades had become history; the Muslim horror had not.[22]

In India Muslim shah Jahan (1593–1666), builder of the Taj Mahal, murdered thousands near Calcutta and offered multitudes more Islam or death. As noted by historian Serge Trifkovic, "The massacres perpetrated by Muslims in India are unparalleled in history, bigger in sheer numbers than the Holocaust, or the massacre of the Armenians by the Turks; more extensive even than the slaughter of the South American native populations by the invading Spanish and Portuguese."[23]

In considering whether Islam is good and peaceful, the Ottoman

Empire begs consideration. While it reached its zenith in the sixteenth century, its most notable atrocities are of recent vintage. Consider the mass extermination of Armenians as well as the death of Christianity in Asia Minor—both twentieth-century Muslim mass murders. We rightly remember Adolf Hitler's genocidal mania but have regrettable amnesia respecting Abdul Hamid II, who initiated his ethnic cleaning policies at the turn of the century by systematically slaughtering 300,000 Armenians. By the time World War 1 broke out, the Muslim leadership of Turkey had committed itself to eliminating the whole of the Christian population—their "Turkey only for the Turks" mantra morphed into massacre with the ethnic cleansing of one and a half million Christians. Among the most noteworthy casualties was extermination of the historic city of Smyrna. Conquering Turks went house to house murdering, looting, pillaging, and raping. All told, by 1923, three and a half million Christians had been exterminated.[24]

One of them was the Bishop of Smyrna, Metropolitan Chrysostomos. On September 9, 1922, the "Butcher of Ionia" spat on Chrysostomos before turning him over to a Muslim mob. They tore out his eyes and dragged him by his beard through the streets of the Turkish Quarter. "Every now and then, when he had the strength to do so, he would raise his right hand and bless his persecutors, repeating, 'Father, forgive them.' A Turk got so furious at this gesture that he cut off the Metropolitan's hand with his sword. He fell to the ground and was hacked to pieces by the angry mob. The carnage culminated in the burning of Smyrna."[25]

Other tragedies cry out for consideration—including the grotesque martyrdom of scores of Christian clergymen during the Armenian Genocide. One was tied and cut to pieces while still breathing. Another dowsed in oil and burned alive. A third, tortured for forty-one days before being put to death. Yet another buried alive. Many other such atrocities could be cited, including a bishop who had horseshoes nailed to his feet before his body was slashed to pieces. Beheadings were so rampant that grieving Greek women carried baskets filled with the severed heads of their loved ones.[26] Ironically, it was Hitler who cynically anticipated the collective amnesia of the modern world. "I have given orders to my Death Units to exterminate without mercy or pity, men, women, and children belonging to the Polish speaking race," he said. "*After all, who remembers the extermination of the Armenians?*"[27]

Indeed, who remembers the Qurayza Jews butchered at the hands of Muhammad, the massacres in India, the horrors exacted on humanity at the hands of the Ottoman Turks, or for that matter the indignity in November 2015 when, during a moment of silence in remembrance of the Paris massacre, Muslim soccer fans in Istanbul booed or broke out in chants, including *Allahu Akbar, Allahu Akbar, Allahu Akbar*?[28] Who remembers earlier that year when Muslim militants in Syria tried to force two Christian women and six Christian men to convert to Islam? Upon their refusal, the women were brutally raped before being beheaded alongside the men. The same day militants cut off the fingertips of a twelve-year-old boy in a failed attempt to force his Christian father to convert.[29] When the father refused the forced conversion, he was tortured and subsequently crucified in adherence to the Qur'anic command: "I will cast terror into the hearts of those who disbelieve. Therefore strike off their heads and strike off every fingertip of them" (Q 8:12 *Shakir*). Who, for that matter, remembers Jacques Hamel, who on July 26, 2016, was brutally beheaded in the north of France while dispensing the body and blood of Christ?[30]

Is Islam a religion of peace and tolerance? Permit the Qur'an and the consensus in tandem with the *ahadith* and history to answer for you.[31] In the meantime, carefully consider another historical reality. Islam has not only advanced by the sword but continues to advance through migration without assimilation, "as a python swallows its prey—slowly, with a long digestion."[32] The frog slowly boiled in water may be legend. This, however, is all too real.

While Western politicians may be in denial, the late Libyan leader Mu'ammar Gadhafi was not. In an address to throbbing thousands memorialized on Al Jazeera television, he boasted of the millions of Muslims already in Europe. This, he said, is a certain sign that "Allah will grant Islam victory in Europe—without swords, without guns, without conquests. The fifty million Muslims of Europe will turn it into a Muslim continent within a few decades." And fifty million Muslims is just the beginning. When Allah adds Turkey to the European Union, "there will be one hundred million Muslims in Europe," Gadhafi went on to say; "Europe is in a predicament, and so is America. They should agree to become Islamic in the course of time or else declare war on the Muslims."[33]

Gaddafi's words should not be cavalierly brushed aside. He was sadistic, but hardly stupid. Though raping hundreds of teenagers in specially built sex dungeons,[34] he understood better than most that Europe is swiftly moving in the direction of self-extinction—a death wish born out of birth control, abortion, euthanasia, same-sex-sexuality, transgenderism, and so forth. In other words, in nations such as Britain and Belgium, the native-born culture is dying out, and a rapidly multiplying Muslim culture is filling the vacuum. Europe is now dependent not only on foreign fossil fuels but also on foreign fertility.[35]

That is no doubt what Gaddafi had in mind. A civilization that is becoming Islamic demographically will inevitably succumb to Islam politically as well. No need to fly airplanes into buildings when, with patience, those same buildings can be yours. Think back to when Muslims renamed Constantinople Istanbul and replaced the cross adorning Hagia Sophia with a crescent. Had Gadhafi lived to see more than one million immigrants being admitted into Germany by Angela Merkel—dubbed by *Time* "Chancellor of the Free World"[36]—he would no doubt have proudly donned the prophetic mantle.

Merkel is the face of a nation in which the death rate exceeds the birth rate.[37] Though she herself is the eldest of three children, she has no children of her own. And like few others she knows the consequences of a nation losing its native workforce. As far back as 1960, Germany brought in Turks to satisfy labor shortages. But that was then, this is now. In September 2015 Merkel struck an arrangement to usher Syrian refugees through Austria into Germany. Not just hundreds or several thousand but hundreds of thousands. *Time* notes that as "refugees keep coming—nearly a million so far, with no end in sight" many Germans began questioning Merkel's mindset. Her "bluff confidence—'We can handle this!'—is running up against the exhaustion of the volunteers."[38] Moreover, in the wake of the Paris terrorist attacks,[39] a good portion of the German population has awakened to the danger of migration sans assimilation.

Not so American politicians, who seem largely asleep to the selfsame realities. They are strangely unwilling to welcome Syrian refugees into their own homes but more than willing to welcome millions of immigrants into a nation already submerged in debt approaching twenty trillion dollars.[40]

Why worry about immigrants they will never personally clothe and feed, or debt that can be passed on to their children and grandchildren?

Gadhafi understood full well what Western politicians seem blithely unaware of. From the fall of Constantinople, the Ottoman Empire advanced steadily into Europe—their sights set on the wealth of Austria and Germany. Had it not been for the leadership of Poland's King Jan Sobieski, who on September 11, 1683, halted the Muslim menace at the gates of Vienna, Europe might have already been renamed Eurabia.[41] On September 11, 2001, the Western world faced yet another such moment of truth. This time no Jan Sobieski arrived on the scene fully understanding that the destiny of the West hung in the balance. Instead, obsessively self-loathing Western elites such as Merkel pontificate that "Islam belongs to Germany"[42] and vicariously to the best of the West.

In a *Wall Street Journal* article aptly titled "It's the Demography, Stupid: The Real Reason the West Is in Danger of Extinction," political pundit Mark Steyn notes that immediately following September 11 prominent Western leaders from Canadian prime minister Jean Chrétien to American president George W. Bush rushed to pay homage at Islamic mosques. While "the get-me-to-the-mosque-on-time fever died down," it nevertheless "set the tone for our general approach to these atrocities. The old definition of a nano-second was the gap between the traffic light changing in New York and the first honk from a car behind. The new definition is the gap between a ter-rorist bombing and the press release from an Islamic lobby group warning of a backlash against Muslims."[43]

Steyn went on to note that "in most circumstances, it would be consid-ered appallingly bad taste to deflect attention from an actual 'hate crime' by scaremongering about a purely hypothetical one."[44] Former US attorney general Loretta Lynch underscored Steyn's supposition. Whatever her per-sonal predilections following the terrorist attack in San Bernardino, her first public posturing was not to mourn the deaths of innocent Americans but rather to stage an appearance with a Muslim advocacy group to mouth what she designated her "greatest fear"—that of Muslims and mosques being unjustly implicated by the deeply held Islamic convictions of shooters Sayed Farook and Tashfeen Malik.[45]

All this leads back to the question at hand. Are such acts of terrorism a function of a hijacked religion, or is this what we should expect from authentic Islam? Does Obama's assurance that Muslims worldwide share his principles—"principles of justice and progress; tolerance and the dignity of all human beings"—fit the facts? Is Tony Blair correct in pontificating that the acts of terrorists are wholly contrary to the teachings of the Qur'an? Moreover, how should the current US president, Donald Trump, respond to Islam during his tenure as leader of the free world?

Is it possible to attribute the reality of millions of peace-loving Muslims to a sort of cognitive dissonance that allows them to enjoy their teachings and traditions despite the bloody history in which they were forged? Could it be that what they wish were true about their religion isn't actually so?

And what is the responsibility of authentic Christians to use the socioreligious deviations of Islam as springboards or opportunities to communicate the grace and truth that only Christ can bring to the human heart?

To answer such questions necessitates understanding the world's fastest-growing religion. To misapprehend the facts in an age of Islamic terrorism and expansionism is a price no one can afford to pay. To remember the details, I've codified them around the acronym **M-U-S-L-I-M**.

MUHAMMAD: FROM RAGS TO RICHES TO RADICALIZATION

Every Muslim, without exception, is committed to the *shahada*—"There is no god but Allah, and Muhammad is the Messenger of Allah." As such, we begin our odyssey through the acronym MUSLIM by taking a close look at the life and legacy of Islam's quintessential man. Muhammad, according to the most authoritative Muslim sources, married a six-year-old girl and consummated the marriage when she was but nine. In arguably the greatest of his conquests, he had a Jewish man beheaded, took his wife as booty, and, after having her beautified, forced on her his bed. Moreover, his every stratagem of war paved the way for what fourteen centuries later would be the fastest-growing pseudo-religious cult in the world.

Unreliable Revelations: The Emperor Has No Clothes

In chapter 2, we disclose that while Islam relies on a multitude of revelations, only the Qur'an is considered to be the eternally existent word of Allah. Muslims regard it as uncreated and unalterable—without error, having ethics beyond question, and eloquent above anything the world has ever known. In reality, the emperor has no clothes. *Unreliable Revelations* populate Qur'anic pages—including an overt denial of the crucifixion of Christ. Faulty ethics are similarly egregious. Incredible but demonstrable, the Qur'an sanctions murder, adultery, stealing, false testimony, and coveting. Moreover, Qur'anic elegance is but feigned. The arrangement of the Qur'an is wearisome, its prophetic prowess unspectacular, and its sophistication grossly overstated.

Sharia Is State and State Is Sharia

Chapter 3 uncloaks the oppression of sharia. Here we come face-to-face with the reality that Islam is not a religion in the Western sanitized sense of the word. Instead, it is a comprehensive socioeconomic-political juggernaut riding on the rails of sharia. *Sharia is state and state is sharia* sums it up suitably. In Islam there simply is no distinction between sharia and state. This is particularly troubling in that sharia has enshrined inequality for women as a core value. Sharia does not afford women, unlike men who can have up to four spouses, the same right. Moreover, while sharia allows a husband to beat his spouse, there is no such provision for a wife. Nor can a woman initiate a divorce. Only men can do so, and that with relative ease. Furthermore, sharia mandates *proactive* and *perpetual* war against Jews and Christians: *"First invite them to Islam, then invite them to pay the jizya (tax on Kafirs). If they reject conversion and the jizya, then attack them."*[46] The consensus of sharia law, in concert with the will of Allah, mandates war as a *"religious duty, because of the universalism of the Muslim mission and (the obligation to) convert everybody to Islam either by persuasion or by force."*[47] Finally, we make plain that inhabitants of Western civilization need not wonder what life would be like under sharia. They have already experienced it. In Spain. During what cultural elites describe as "the Golden Age of Islam," sharia dictated virtually every aspect of public and private life. Far from a portrait of Muslims, Jews, and Christians living in the midst of an Andalusian "paradise," non-Muslims were subject to the severity of sharia. Their choice was simple: *shahada*, *subjugation*, or *sword*.

LEVANT: CROSSROADS OF WORLD HISTORY

During the fourth section of the journey, we travel to the Levant for a closer look at the land-bridge linking three continents (Europe, Asia, and Africa). The Levant set the stage for some of the principal events in history, is the source of two great monotheistic religions, and supplied the foundations for a third. Thus, it is rightly described as the crossroads of world history. Levant, essentially the western rim of the Fertile Crescent, boasts Jerusalem as its epicenter. For Jews, the destruction of the Jerusalem temple brought an end to the age of sacrifice. Judaism now largely finds expression in Torah study rather than temple sacrifice. Various Jewish traditions are grateful to have a democratic ally in the Middle East but believe the sanctity of Jewish life trumps the sanctity of Jewish land. For Christians, the Levant continues to have historical and archaeological significance but no longer fuels an eschatological mandate. From the time of Jerusalem's destruction to the time that Christianity became the official religion of the Roman Empire, Jerusalem did not play a major role in world history until Constantine transformed it into a destination point for Christian pilgrimages. Early Christians had no interest in rebuilding the temple in that the death and resurrection of Jesus superseded its significance. Thus, under Christian control, Temple Mount became little more than a garbage dump. Islamic aggression changed all that. In the seventh century, Jerusalem was captured by Caliph Omar and became a major focus in the Islamic world. When Omar arrived at Temple Mount, he was shocked to find it but a rubbish heap. He ordered it cleared and built the Al-Aqsa mosque at its southern end. The Dome of the Rock was later built on or about the place where the Jewish temples had previously stood. Temple Mount continues to have transcendent significance for

Islam. It is at once the place where God called Abraham to sacrifice Ishmael and the place to which Buraq, a mulish beast with a human head and the tail of a peacock, transported Muhammad during his infamous Night Journey. The Dome, bedecked by eighty kilograms of gold, is now the Levant's most recognizable landmark. The message reflecting from its gilded dome is unmistakable—Islam is the culmination of Judaism and Christianity, and Muhammad is the climax of the prophets.

ISLAMIC STATE: RETURN OF THE CALIPHATE

Chatper 5 highlights the return of the caliphate and with it a brutal caliph named Abu Bakr al-Baghdadi. Baghdadi renamed himself Abu Bakr, in honor of the first caliph and favored father-in-law of Muhammad, and Baghdadi, in honor of Baghdad, famed capital of the Abbasid dynasty widely considered to have been the quintessential caliphate of the Islamic empire. Islamic State as a moniker is not only emblematic of a twenty-first-century terror network but is indicative of the way of Muhammad. Dressed in a black robe and turban harkening back to the garb donned by Muhammad during his subjugation of Mecca, Baghdadi declared the "establishment of the religion—a Book that guides and a sword that supports."[48] The return of the caliphate is supported by numerous cobelligerents including Saudi Arabia. Former Democratic senator Bob Graham bravely dubbed the Islamic State "a product of Saudi ideals, Saudi money, and Saudi organizational support."[49] Nevertheless, Western elites have continued to portray sharia-subservient states, including Saudi Arabia, as peace-loving allies in the fight against terrorism. Worse still, Western governments, along with academic institutions and media outlets, have proven themselves cobelligerents in exporting a false narrative respecting the religious tenets that animate the Islamic State. Whether the Islamic State will succeed in its murderous mission to expand the caliphate or be supplanted by an even more dangerous ideological child remains to be seen. What we do know is this: the caliphate abolished by Mustafa Kemal Atatürk in 1924 has returned with a vengeance—and that in the midst of a crumbling post-Christian culture.

Major Muslim Misapprehensions

Finally, during the last and arguably most significant part of our journey, we examine major Muslim misapprehensions that compromise, confuse, or outright contradict essential Christian **D-O-C-T-R-I-N-E**. As contrast is the mother of clarity, we lay the straight stick of essential truth next to the Islamic counterfeit and make clear its crookedness. Major Muslim misapprehensions begin with the mother of all errors—failure to apprehend the **D**eity of Christ. In grave misapprehension, Islam renders Jesus Christ a mere slave of Allah; **O**riginal Sin is recast an original slip—a mere bout of forgetfulness; the divine **C**anon is subverted by the factual errors, faulty ethics, and feigned eloquence of the Qur'an; the incomprehensible **T**rinity is usurped by a morally defective unitarian imposter; **R**esurrection—the greatest feat in human history—is demoted to mere fantasy, and **I**ncarnation is demeaned as blasphemy; the scintillating truth that anyone in Christ is a **N**ew Creation is negated by a capricious Allah; and **E**schatology—the thread that weaves the tapestry of Scripture into a harmonious pattern—is ignominiously sullied by the sensual enticements of a largely incoherent Islamic eschatological charade.

We now journey into the world's fastest-growing religion with an in-depth look at the man revered by all authentic Muslims as the quintessential model of humanity.

Muhammad

Unreliable Revelations

Sharia Is State, and State Is Sharia

Levant

Islamic State

Major Muslim Misapprehensions

CHAPTER 1

MUHAMMAD

From Rags to Riches to Radicalization

You can deny Allah, but you cannot deny the Prophet![1]
—MUHAMMAD IQBAL, "SPIRITUAL FATHER" OF PAKISTAN

ove of the Prophet runs like blood in the veins of [the Muslim] community," intoned the iconic Muslim philosopher-poet Muhammad Iqbal,[2] "You can deny Allah, but you cannot deny the Prophet!"[3] He is venerated as the Truth, the Exalted, the Forgiver, the Raiser of the Dead, the Chosen of God, the Seal of the Prophets, the Mediator, the Shining Star, the Justifier, and the Perfect One. Hundreds more titles are afforded him, including Peace of the World and Glory of the Ages.[4] Of one thing we can be certain. *All* Muslims are deeply devoted to the life and practice of Muhammad—there is *no* exception.[5]

Muhammad Al-Ghazali (d. 1111), widely considered the most influential Muslim other than Muhammad himself, pronounced that the key to happiness was "to imitate the Messenger of God in all his coming and going, his movements and rest, in his way of eating, his attitude, his sleep and his talk."[6] Annemarie Schimmel, the venerable Harvard scholar, agreed. In her classic book *And Muhammad Is His Messenger: The Veneration of the Prophet in Islamic Piety*, she notes that the *imitatio Muhammadi* ("the imitation of Muhammad"), with its attention to the minute details of daily life, has given the Muslim community remarkable uniformity of behavior. "Wherever one may be, one knows how to behave when entering a house, which formulas of greeting to employ, what to avoid in good company, how to eat, and how to travel. For centuries Muslim children have been brought up in these ways."[7]

All this underscores a salient truth: one cannot comprehend Islam apart from comprehending Muhammad. He is said to be of noble birth, graceful form, perfect intellect, the model of humility, and the exemplar of all humanity.[8] And he is revered as the greatest of the prophets[9]—greater than Moses or Abraham; greater than Joseph or John; greater than Jesus of Nazareth.[10] All this from a man whose first forty years are spectacularly unremarkable.

Muhammad was born in Mecca six centuries after the birth of Christ and died in Medina in his sixty-second year (AD 570–632).[11] His father Abd'Allah died before he was born; his mother Amina shortly thereafter. At age six he was passed on to a grandfather who died three years later. At nine he was dispatched to his uncle Abu Talib and then to the wealthy widow Khadija, whom Muhammad married at age twenty-five. Thereafter, he went on to a life of mystic meditations.

Not until age forty was there so much as a hint that Muhammad would become progenitor of what is now the fastest-growing religion on earth.[12] Three nights paved the pathway toward its birth. Ten years forged the pattern for its next fourteen centuries.

NIGHT OF DESTINY

Muhammad's night of destiny began in epic fashion. In a cave at Mount Hira a presence materialized clutching a cloth covered with characters. With force so great that he feared for his life, the mysterious presence pressed him to "Read!" Twice he experienced an acute fear of death. Upon the third, he submitted.

> Read in the name of thy Lord who created,
> Who created man of blood coagulated.

Read! Thy Lord is the most beneficent,
Who taught by the pen,
Taught that which they knew not unto men.[13]

The rhyme so distressed Muhammad that he thought in his heart,

> Woe is me *poet or possessed*—Never shall Quraysh [the pagan ruling tribe of Mecca] say this of me! I will go to the top of the mountain and throw myself down that I may kill myself and gain rest. So I went forth to do so and then when I was midway on the mountain, I heard a voice from heaven saying, "*O Muhammad! Thou art the apostle of God and I am Gabriel.*" As he lifted his sights to the heavens he saw a being standing astride the horizon and heard the words, "*O Muhammad! Thou art the apostle of God and I am Gabriel.*"[14]

Upon hearing these words a second time, he aborted thoughts of suicide, returned to Khadija, "sat by her thigh," and poured out his dread.[15] Two possibilities pressed him: "poet or possessed." Khadija was convinced of a third. He was neither poet nor possessed, he was "*the* prophet."[16] Despite her conviction, Muhammad remained unconvinced. For years he battled doubt.[17] Was he truly a prophet and a poet or was he truly possessed?

At times his uncertainty was so acute that he once again began contemplating suicide.[18] In time, confidence that he was a prophet prevailed over the conviction that he was possessed. As such, Muhammad chose life—and during the next two decades changed the trajectory of human history. During the first ten years, he exercised the role of prophet; during the final ten, that of political tyrant. One ten he spent in Mecca; the other ten, Medina.

The decade in Mecca proved difficult. Khadija's conversion came easy—as did the conversions of Muhammad's adopted son Zayd, his ten-year-old cousin Ali, and future father-in-law Abu Bakr.[19] Gaining converts among Quraysh, keepers of the Ka'bah, proved much more difficult. They had every reason to reject Muhammad's monotheistic message and little reason to receive it. Mecca was the place of pilgrimage for polytheistic tribes throughout the Arabian Peninsula.[20] And pilgrimages brought profits.

As did the sale of gods and goods. Predictably, persecution ensued. As did doubt. Mercifully, Gabriel materialized to revivify the beleaguered prophet.

NIGHT JOURNEY

According to Islamic tradition, Muhammad's night of destiny was not the first time he'd experienced the angel. Before the death of his mother, when he was not yet five years of age, he lay prostrate in the desert sand, his chest slashed open from throat to stomach. Gabriel removed his heart, scrubbed out the black clot with the water of Zamzam,[21] and restored him to life.[22] Now at age fifty, Muhammad experienced Gabriel a third time as he lay prostrate near the sacred mosque in Mecca, his heart removed and lying in a golden bowl.[23] Cleansed with Zamzam water, he mounted a mulish beast with a human head and the tail of a peacock. So it was that in the company of Gabriel, Muhammad embarked upon a night journey that will forever live in infamy.

Buraq was no ordinary beast. His stride reached toward the horizon and with sudden swiftness brought Muhammad "from the Sacred Mosque to the Farthest Mosque" (Q 17:1). Upon Muhammad's arrival at Masjid Al-Aqsa in Jerusalem,[24] Gabriel presented him with a life-altering choice—milk or wine. The prophet wisely selected milk, thereby choosing right over wrong, good over evil—a straight path ascending to the heavens over the crooked path leading to hell. With his beast securely tethered to a ring embedded in the mosque, Muhammad embarked upon a magical mystery tour.

Ascending from a sacred stone, he traveled upward toward seven heavens. The gates to the first level opened, and he found himself standing face-to-face with the father of all humanity. Adam proceeded to venerate Muhammad as the greatest of all his descendants.[25] Muhammad next ascended to a second level where he exchanged greetings with John and Jesus—two of many prophets who had made straight the path before him. The ascent continued to a third heaven, where he encountered Joseph, son of Jacob—a man whose beauty was remarkable. After meeting Idris (Enoch), the personification of truth, on level four, Muhammad ascended to level five where he met Aaron, who, in concert with those in the levels below, professed faith in Muhammad's prophetic calling. The sixth level of heaven brought with it a flood of tears—mighty Moses weeping upon the realization that his rival would cause more to enter paradise than those who had followed Moses. Yet all of this was but prelude to that which was yet to come.

At the final level of heaven, the apostle of Allah met Abraham, who, through Ishmael, had fathered the Arabs, built the Ka'bah, and placed within it a black stone that had fallen from the sky. Moreover, in the seventh heaven Muhammad beheld a facsimile of the earthly Ka'bah replete with seventy thousand angels circumambulating it as they had been doing for millions of years. As Muhammad made his way past Bayt al-Ma'mur ("the Much-Frequented House"),[26] he came upon Sidrat al-Muntaha, a lote tree at the uppermost boundary of the highest heaven.[27] Its fruits were like crocks, its leaves like elephant ears, and out of its roots followed the four rivers of earth.

It was then that he began moving into previously uncharted territory—into a space that neither man nor angel had ever attained. Slipping from *heaven* into the *hereafter*, he found himself standing in the very presence of Allah. Whether Muhammad actually saw Allah is hotly debated among the Muslim faithful.[28] What is not in dispute is that Allah onerously prescribed fifty daily prayers for the prophet and his progeny.

With the mission deemed complete, Muhammad began a descent through the sixth heaven, where Moses unexpectedly instructed him to ascend back into the hereafter in order to bargain for prayer reduction. Allah relented. The number was reduced to forty. As Muhammad descended through the sixth heaven once more, he was enjoined to negotiate a further reduction. The process continued until the prayer package had been reduced to five. Though Moses importuned further reduction, Muhammad resolutely refused. Rather than return to the throne room of Allah once more, he descended through the heavens and miraculously emerged back in the sands of the Great Mosque of Mecca.[29]

There he began to tell devotees of his encounters with Adam, Abraham, and Allah. Though the majority found it all too fantastical, Abu Bakr exuded, "If the messenger of God said it is so, then so it is!"[30] Thus it was that from that day to this, Abu Bakr became known as Al-Siddiq—"the foremost believer."[31]

While tales of the night of destiny and night journey convinced some to turn Muslim, the majority simply turned off. "During the season of pilgrimage, the Quraysh posted guards along the roads into Mecca, to inform every visitor that Muhammad was a dangerous sorcerer who did not speak for his neighbors and tribespeople, and should be shunned."[32] Many flesh-and-blood family members also became fervent opponents, including Abu Lahab, his paternal uncle.[33] To make matters worse, Khadija (his first disciple) and uncle Abu Talib (his faithful defender) both died during the year of the night journey (619).[34]

As things began to unravel precipitously in Mecca, something magical was happening two hundred miles to the north. In 620, six men from Yathrib pledged allegiance to Muhammad in a narrow valley called Aqaba on the outskirts of Mecca.[35] The following year (621), on the occasion of the pagan pilgrimage, a group of twelve disciples acknowledged Muhammad as their prophet in what became known as Al-Aqaba's first pledge.[36] The year thereafter (622) things took on an even brighter hue.

In the second pledge of Aqaba, seventy-three men and two women from Yathrib vowed to protect Muhammad as they would their own families in return for the promise of paradise. "Testify that I am Allah's Messenger and protect me as you would yourselves, your children, and your wives," the prophet murmured. "What is in it for us?" they replied. "Paradise," whispered Muhammad. "Upon this, our Holy Prophet declared, 'Choose twelve individuals from among yourselves who will stand by me in every matter as the representatives of their tribes.'"[37]

Scarcely three months after the second pledge, Muhammad embarked upon a night flight (called the *Hijra*) that would mark his final decade on the planet and fourteen centuries of planetary history.

Night Flight

In concert with the pledges of Aqaba, Muhammad encouraged Meccan devotees to migrate to the land of his twelve disciples. Thus it was that in the dead of a September night, Muhammad and his *muhajirun* (emigrants) stole out of Mecca and began the *Hijra* (flight) that marked the birth of Islam.[38]

From 622 forward, their destination would no longer be known as Yathrib but as Medinnet el Nebi—the city of the prophet. In Mecca, Muhammad had been a marginalized prophet; in Medina he became a political monarch who, in a mere ten years, transformed the Arabian Peninsula.

Muhammad proved a cunning diplomat. He highlighted Islamic commonalities with those described in the Qur'an as People of the Book. First, he emphasized concord between his monotheism and that of Jews and Christians.[39] Furthermore, he highlighted Moses as the quintessential Jewish prophet.[40] And, finally, in concert with Jewish and Christian sensibilities, he mandated that devotees pray in the direction of Jerusalem.[41]

As Muhammad progressively gained political power and prestige, all of that changed. In time he received messages from Allah claiming that People of the Book holding Jesus to be the Son of God were guilty of the unforgiveable sin of *shirk* (Q 4:116).[42] In addition, he began emphasizing the primacy of Abraham, who allegedly dwells in the seventh level of heaven, over Moses on level six and Jesus whose abode is on the second to the lowest level.[43] Moreover, Muhammad feigned a message from Allah, forever changing the direction of prayer from Jerusalem to Mecca (Q 2:142–49).[44]

More ominous still, Muhammad began receiving revelations that would submerge the Arabian Peninsula in blood.

NEXUS OF EVIL

As noted by the acclaimed Sufi writer Stephen Schwartz, "Angelic communications continued for two years before the Prophet began sharing them widely."[45] During the following decade (612–622), Muhammad became increasingly vocal. Said Ibn Ishaq, the Meccans "had never known anything like the trouble they had endured from this fellow; he had declared their mode of life foolish, insulted their forefathers, reviled their religion, divided the community, and cursed their gods."[46]

The next ten years (622–632) brought far more than curses. During those years, Muhammad graduated from a war of words to a war of weapons. In 623, he drew first blood.

AD 623: First Murder in Muslim History

When ye meet the Unbelievers (in fight), smite at their necks.
—Q 47:4

In Mecca, Muhammad's first wife, Khadija, had showered him with wealth. In Medina, Muhammad was not afforded the same luxury. Thus, he faced the daunting challenge of finding alternate sources to fund his new religion. The solution came in the form of a Qur'anic revelation sanctioning terrorist attacks. "When ye meet the Unbelievers (in fight), smite at their necks" (47:4).

With new revelation in hand, Muhammad mandated the practice of raiding Meccan caravans. His first raid was a standoff. The second was only slightly more successful. It marked the first shot fired in the "cause of Allah"[47] but brought with it neither blood nor booty. The next four raids were similarly unspectacular. On the seventh try the Muslims finally cashed in. They recorded the first murder in Muslim history ("Wāqid shot 'Amr b. al-Ḥaḍramī with an arrow and killed him"[48]) and took the spoils of war back to their base in Medina.

The first Muslim murder raised serious concerns throughout the Arabian Peninsula. The Quraysh were shocked that anyone, much less a fellow tribesman, would so coldheartedly kill and plunder during the sacred month of Rajab. The Jews were equally outraged and "turned this raid into an omen against the apostle." Even "their Muslim brethren reproached them for what they had done," fearing that Allah would turn such gratuitous evil against them.[49]

Again, however, "God relieved the Muslims of their anxiety in the matter" via divine revelation.[50] "They ask you about war in the Sacred Month. Tell them: 'Fighting in this month is a heinous offence; but to prevent from the path of Allah, to deny Him, to prevent access and expel His worshippers from the Sacred Mosque is a more severe crime, since mischief is worse than killing in His sight'" (Q 2:217 *Malik*).[51]

With conscience thus salved, Muhammad and the Muslim raiders moved into a year that brought with it the infamous Battle of Badr.

AD 624: From Trembling Prophet to Political Tyrant

O Prophet! Urge the believers to war; if there are twenty patient
ones of you they shall overcome two hundred, and if there are
a hundred of you they shall overcome a thousand of those who
disbelieve, because they are a people who do not understand.
—Q 8:65 SHAKIR

As the articulate apologist for the apostle of Allah, Stephen Schwartz has aptly noted, "Muslims view the Battle of Badr as a major event in human history and believe Muhammad's forces were favored by divine assistance, including the help of angels"[52] that outnumbered Muhammad's army by a score of three to one. Five hundred angels fought for Muhammad under the command of Gabriel and five hundred more under the command of the archangel Michael.[53]

As with the raid that took place during the sacred month of Rajab, the Battle of Badr took place during a sacred month. This time, the month of Ramadan. As a large Meccan caravan loaded with loot was making its way along the coastal route from Syria to Mecca, Muhammad struck with lethal force. Abu Jahl, "the main force behind the Quraysh army's encounter with the Muslims,"[54] proved no match for the apostle and his band of men and angels. He won the battle decisively.[55]

But with the spoils of war came significant challenges, including how to justify murdering his Meccan kin, how to divide up the booty, and how to motivate men to risk martyrdom in the cause of an unproven prophet and a fledgling faith. The first problem was solved through a Qur'anic revelation saying, "It is not ye who slew them; it was Allah: When thou threwest (a handful of dust), it was not thy act, but Allah's" (8:17). The second, through a revelation which said, "Out of all the booty that ye may acquire (in war), a fifth share is assigned to Allah—and to the Messenger" (Q 8:41)—thus, leaving four-fifth to the rest of the marauders. The third challenge was solved by promising those who died a paradise replete with houris (*ḥūr*)—voluptuous women "with beautiful, big, and lustrous eyes—like unto Pearls" (Q 56:22–23). Said Schwartz:

At Badr the Prophet also exhorted his troops by promising direct entry into Paradise for martyrs on the battlefield. Their reward was to include the company of eternal servants and "dark-eyed" or "large-eyed" girls. These virginal lovers are described in *Qur'an* as "immortal youths with bowls and ewers and a cup of purest wine (that will neither pain their heads nor take away their reason); with fruits of their own choice and flesh of fowls that they relish."[56]

The Battle of Badr proved decisive in yet another way. At Badr, Muhammad made complete his transition from trembling prophet to political tyrant. In Mecca, the day after the night journey, Abu Jahl jeered the prophet.[57] In Medina, the day after the Battle of Badr, the prophet—turned political tyrant—sneered as the severed head of Jahl was thrown before him.[58]

Jahl's beheading would become the signature of Islamic terror from that day forward.

AD 625: Exile and Execution at the Pleasure of the Prophet

I will instill terror into the hearts of the Unbelievers: smite ye above their necks and smite all their fingertips off them.
—Q 8:12

Islamic terror manifests in many ways. Beheading is one of them. Cutting off fingertips, another. As noted in the Yusuf Ali translation of the Qur'an, when a person's hands are "put out of action, he is unable to wield his sword or lance or other weapon, and easily becomes a prisoner."[59]

Despite such brutal measures, Muhammad was not always successful on the field of battle. A year after victory in the Battle of Badr, Muhammad lost to the Meccans at Mount Uhud. Schwartz points out that combat at Uhud was even fiercer than at Badr. The prophet "was struck down by a sword blow" and "a tremor of shock rolled across the battlefield." Some Muslims fled, other men fought on ferociously. "Believing their prophet had died, men rushed to follow him into death's outstretched arms, that the virgins of Paradise might delight in granting them their favors. But Muhammad regained his footing and led his detachment to safety on the heights of Mount Uhud. The Quraysh had won the contest of arms, but the survival of the Prophet had turned defeat into a moral victory for the Muslims."[60]

From that day forward, those following Muhammad's example fought on with carnal lust. The plunder of the Meccan caravan outside of Medina had provided substantial wealth. Now Muslims sought wealth from within as well. Realizing that one Jewish tribe (Qaynuqa) was at odds with two others (Qurayza and Nadir), they seized the vulnerability, deporting the tribe and taking their property and possessions as plunder.[61] The Jews who were exiled lived. Many who remained did not.[62]

Asma bint Marwan, said to be a Jewish poet, was among those who died. She reviled the Muslims for following a man whose violence and conduct she found deplorable. "Do you expect good from him after the killing of your chiefs?" Upon hearing her rebuke, Muhammad said, "Who will rid me of Marwān's daughter?" That very night, Umayr "went to her house and killed her. In the morning he came to the apostle and told him what he had done and he said, 'You have helped God and His apostle, O Umayr!' When he asked if he would have to bear any evil consequences the apostle said, 'Two goats won't butt their heads about her.'"[63]

Despite Muhammad's portrayal of Asma's murder as helping God, the esteemed early twentieth-century Muslim biographer Muhammad Husayn Haykal rightly portrayed its ghastly horror. In *The Life of the Noble Prophet Muhammad*, he explained that "Umayr ibn 'Awf attacked her during the night while she was surrounded by her children, one of whom she was nursing."[64] Tragically, Asma was but one of many who were executed at the pleasure of Muhammad.[65] And the Qaynuqa were but the first to be exiled. Shortly after their exile he would banish the Jewish tribe of Nadir as well.[66] Having seized the property and possessions of two Jewish tribes, Muhammad and the Muslims were exceedingly rich.

In the coming years they would become exceedingly ruthless as well.

AD 626: Convenient Revelations on Marriage and Divorce

When Zayd had dissolved (his marriage) with her, with the necessary (formality), We joined her in marriage to thee: in order that (in

future) there may be no difficulty to the Believers in (the matter of)
marriage with the wives of their adopted sons, when the latter have
dissolved with the necessary (formality) (their marriage) with them.
—Q 33:37

As Muhammad accumulated wealth so, too, he accumulated wives—and in the most unusual ways. Following the death of Khadija when he was fifty, Muhammad married a six-year-old girl named Aisha and consummated his marriage with her when she was nine.[67] In addition to Khadija and Aisha, Muhammad accumulated additional wives and sex slaves, one of whom refused to marry the prophet after being subjected to the beheading of her husband.[68] Most notable among them was his cousin Zaynab, who, in accordance with Allah's decree, was divorced from her husband in the year 626.[69]

Muhammad's marriage to Zaynab is interesting on a number of levels. First, as underscored by the Muslim organization Islam's Women, "The prophet (peace and blessings be upon him) suggested to his cousin Zaynab that he had decided to get her engaged to Zayd bin Harithah, his adopted son." This was not a matter for discussion or dispute. Allah had spoken through the prophet, and that was the end of the matter: "'It is not for a believer, man or woman, when Allah and His Messenger have decreed a matter that they should have any option in their decision. And whoever disobeys Allah and His Messenger, he has indeed strayed in a plain error' [33:36 *Hilali-Khan*]."[70]

Furthermore, says Islam's Women, "Arabs thought it was wrong for a man to marry the widow or divorcee of his adopted son. Allah wanted to abolish this uncivilized custom, so He sent the Angel Jibril [Gabriel] to tell the Prophet (peace and blessings be upon him) in secret that Zaynab would one day be his wife." Thus, "the decision had been made in the heavens by Allah" that Zaynab was to divorce Zayd and marry Muhammad. "'When Zayd had accomplished his desire from her (i.e., divorced her), We gave her to you in marriage, so that [in the future] there may be no difficulty to the believers in respect of (the marriage of) the wives of their adopted sons when the latter have no desire to keep them. And Allah's Command must be fulfilled' [33:37 *Hilali-Khan*]."[71]

Finally, "Zaynab used to say very proudly to the other Mothers of the Believers that her marriage had been performed not by her family but by Allah above the Heavens with His beloved Prophet (peace and blessings be upon him). When the hypocrites criticized the Prophet (peace and blessings be upon him) for this marriage, Allah replied, 'There is no blame on the Prophet (peace and blessings be upon him) in that which Allah has made legal for him' [33:38 *Hilali-Khan*]."[72]

The thought that immediately comes to mind is, *how convenient.* Whenever Muhammad wanted the unusual (i.e., to marry his cousin, wife of his son-in-law) a command came from heaven to sanction it.[73] Examples populate the pages of the Qur'an. In Qur'an 4:3, Muhammad received a revelation from God allowing men to "marry women of your choice, two, or three, or four." But in Qur'an 33:50, he receives a divine sanction to marry "*any* believing woman who dedicates her soul to the Prophet if the Prophet wishes to wed her." Thus, while other Muslim men were permitted to marry up to only four wives, Allah provided Muhammad with a divine exception to marry to his heart's desire. Even his favored wife, Aisha, seemed to recognize the pattern, saying to Muhammad, "I feel that your Lord hastens in fulfilling your wishes and desires."[74] Also troubling is the fact that the Qur'an allows men to beat their wives in order that they might "return to obedience" (Q 4:34 *Hilali-Khan*).[75]

Male-perpetrated beatings and empowerment, however, pale by comparison to the macabre beheadings and enslavements awaiting the last of the Jewish tribes.

AD 627: Year of the Jewish Holocaust

Those of the people of the Book who aided [the unbelievers]—Allah did take them down from their strongholds and cast terror into their hearts, (so that) some ye slew, and some ye made prisoners.
—Q 33:26

The night that Muhammad fled to Medina, three Jewish tribes prospered there. Half a decade later, all three would be either evicted or eradicated. The Qaynuqa and Nadir largely escaped with their lives; the Qurayzah were not nearly as fortunate. As Yusuf Ali notes in his Qur'anic commentary, "The men of the Qurayẓah were slain: the women were sold as captives of war: and their lands and properties were divided among the Muhājirs."[76]

The murder of the Qurayzah will forever live in infamy. Even told from a thoroughly Muslim perspective, the details are dreadful. After the apostle had designated the Qurayzah "brothers of monkeys," Allah began to "cast terror into their hearts."[77] The account as told by Muhammad's earliest biographer in a tome titled *The Life of Muhammad* is as gripping as it is gruesome. "The apostle went out to the market of Medina (which is still its market today) and dug trenches in it. Then he sent for them [Qurayzah Jews] and struck off their heads in those trenches as they were brought out to him in batches." Ibn Ishaq goes on to say that the number of Jews slaughtered by Muhammad "were 600 or 700 in all, though some put the figure as high as 800 or 900."[78]

Yet this was only the beginning of horrors. After "the apostle had made an end of them," he summoned the chief of the banished Nadir tribe. With "hands bound to his neck by a rope," his "head was struck off."[79] Thereafter, the prophet exacted vengeance on two women—one was beside herself with hysteria and the other, beautiful. The prophet's wife Aisha tells the story of the first woman in the following manner:

> "She was actually with me and was talking with me and laughing immoderately as the apostle was killing her men in the market when suddenly an unseen voice called her name. 'Good heavens,' I cried, 'what is the matter?' 'I am to be killed,' she replied. 'What for?' I asked. 'Because of something I did,' she answered. She was taken away and beheaded. 'Ā'isha used to say, 'I shall never forget my wonder at her good spirits and her loud laughter when all the time she knew that she would be killed.'"[80]

The second woman suffered a fate worse than death. The apostle exchanged some of the captive women for horses and weapons but held back this beauty for himself. According to his biographer, "The apostle had proposed to marry her and put the veil on her, but she said: 'Nay, leave me in your power, for that will be easier for me and for you.'"[81] She had seen the murder of her husband and wanted no part of a man whose hands were stained by blood. Thus, she resolutely chose the horrors of sexual servitude over the hideousness of marital misery.

When she was captured, her repugnance for the prophet was matched only by "repugnance towards Islam." How that all changed remains shrouded in mystery. Ishaq does tell us this much: "The apostle put her aside and felt some displeasure. While he was with his companions he heard the sound of sandals behind him and said, 'This is Tha'laba b. Sa'ya coming to give me the good news of Rayḥāna's acceptance of Islam' and he came up to announce the fact. This gave him pleasure."[82] Reading between the lines, the word *compulsion* comes to mind. All Medina, including Rayhana, now served at the pleasure of Muhammad.

The prophet now set his sights on the world.

AD 628: Treacherous Treaties

Truly did Allah fulfil the vision for His Messenger: Ye shall enter the Sacred Mosque, if Allah wills, with minds secure, heads shaved, hair cut short, and without fear.

—Q 48:27

Muhammad had mastered Medina. But his vision was to be master of Mecca as well. As noted by Yusuf Ali in his translation of the Qur'an, "The Prophet had had a dream that he had entered the Sacred Mosque at Makkah, just before he decided on the journey which resulted in the Treaty of Ḥudaybīyah."[83] By this treaty, said Yusuf Ali, "the door was then opened for the free spread of Islam throughout Arabia and thence through the world."[84]

The Treaty of Hudaybiyyah was a pact between the Muslims and the Meccans signed in March 628 at the western edge of the city of Mecca in a place called Hudaybiyyah.[85] The agreement involved a ten-year cease-fire and would permit the Muslims the privilege of circumambulating the pagan Ka'bah the following year (629). The treaty was unpopular among the Muslims. But Muhammad knew what he was doing.

Hudaybiyyah set the pattern for the spread of Islam from then to now.

The formula was straightforward. If you have military superiority, use it for conquest. If not, sign a treaty. As such, when the twentieth-century Muslim Yasser Arafat was criticized for making concessions to Israel, he quelled the angst by referring to Hudaybiyyah. "This agreement [the Oslo Accords], I am not considering it more than the agreement which had been signed between our Prophet Muhammad and Quraish [in Mecca]."

Arafat went on to say that "Caliph Omar had refused this agreement and considered it *Sulha Dania* [a despicable truce]. But Muhammad [peace be upon him] had accepted it and we are accepting now this [Oslo] peace accord."[86] Mortimer Zuckerman, then editor-in-chief of *U.S. News & World Report,* understood Arafat's allusion to Hudaybiyyah better than most. "The Israelis have a historic question," wrote Zuckerman. "Is Arafat a true peacemaker, or does he believe his own rhetoric when he echoes the doctrine of the prophet Muhammad of making treaties with enemies while he is weak, violating them when he is strong?"[87] When the Council on American-Islamic Relations (CAIR) realized that Zuckerman was on to them, all hell broke loose. CAIR's constituency made such a racket that the magazine felt obligated to redact Zuckerman's observations.[88]

Hudaybiyyah is likely the way many Muslims today view the Iran nuclear deal. As with Muhammad, Ayatollah Khamenei is well aware of his present weaknesses. If and when he becomes strong, he may well find a convenient pretext for violating the agreement. Of course, if all else fails, there's always the Shi'a dogma of *taqiyya* (religious dissimulation).[89]

AD 629: The Prize of Arabia

And He made you heirs of their lands, their houses, and
their goods, and of a land which ye had not frequented
(before). And Allah has power over all things.
—Q 33:27[90]

As with Arafat, the followers of Muhammad viewed the Treaty of Hudaybiyyah as a sign of weakness. The Quraysh of Mecca and Jews of Khaybar were similarly persuaded. Both lived to regret their miscalculations. Muhammad first fixed his sights on Khaybar. Mecca would be later.

Following Hudaybiyyah, Muhammad began an epic march toward the prize of Arabia. English historian Edward Gibbon put it this way:

> Six days' journey to the north-east of Medina, the ancient and wealthy town of Chaibar was the seat of the Jewish power in Arabia: the territory, a fertile spot in the desert, was covered with plantations and cattle, and protected by eight castles, some of which were esteemed of impregnable strength.[91]

Though the Jews of Khaybar were the best suited for war in all of Arabia, the Muslim hordes quickly overwhelmed seven of its eight citadels. While initially taxing Muslim determination, in the end, the eighth fell just as the others had.

The conquest of Khaybar proved a milestone in Islamic history. It afforded Muhammad immeasurable wealth, superior weaponry, and some of the finest women in all Arabia. One of them was Safiya, whom he married shortly after the torture and murder of her husband, Kinana, chief of the Khaybar. Kinana had had custody of the treasure of the Nadir tribe but had refused to confess its whereabouts. Muhammad said to one of his men, "'Torture him until you extract what he has,' so he kindled a fire with flint and steel on his chest until he was nearly dead. Then the apostle delivered him to Muhammad bin Maslama and he struck off his head."[92]

With Kinana dead, Muhammad had Safiya "beautified and combed" and "passed the night with her in a tent."[93] The rest of the women of Khaybar he "distributed among the Muslims."[94] When the surrounding cities heard what had been done in Khaybar, they were terrified. Ishaq provides the commentary: "When the apostle had finished with Khaybar, God struck terror to the hearts of the men of Fadak when they heard what the apostle had done to the men of Khaybar. They sent to him an offer of peace on condition that they should keep half of their produce." Muhammad accepted their terms, and "Fadak became his private property."[95]

Muhammad continued his conquest of territories and tribes until the fall of 629, at which time he returned his gaze to Mecca. He had left the city during the night flight in 622; seven years later he would reenter in broad daylight. He fled Mecca a persecuted prophet. He returned a powerful political leader sporting an entourage of some two thousand Muslims. He kissed the black stone, ritually walked around the Ka'bah seven times, and prepared to marry Maymuna.

However, on the third day, the Quraysh came to him saying, "Your time is up, so get out from us." Muhammad answered them saying, "How would it harm you if you were to let me stay and I gave a wedding feast among you."[96] The Meccans would have none of it and ordered him out of their city.

This they would never do again!

AD 630: Mecca Redivivus

Indeed, We have given you, [O Muhammad], a clear conquest that
Allah may forgive for you what preceded of your sin and what
will follow and complete His favor upon you and guide you to a
straight path and [that] Allah may aid you with a mighty victory.
—Q 48:1–3 SAHIH INTERNATIONAL

Following the conquest of Khaybar, Muhammad no longer had any need or room for the Treaty of Hudaybiyyah. He was now the most prosperous and powerful lord in all Arabia. And so, in January 630, he marched toward Mecca with an army of ten thousand seasoned warriors. Knowing that they were no match for the Muslim might, the Meccans submitted without a fight.

Scarcely a month earlier Muhammad had been ordered to leave Mecca. Now even Abu Sufyan, the most powerful man in the whole of Mecca, lived at the mercy of the master. Muhammad addressed him in ominous tone, *"'Woe to you, Abu Sufyan. Is it not time for you to realize that there is no God but the only God?'* Abu Sufyan answered: 'I do believe that.' Muhammad then said to him: *'Woe to you, Abu Sufyan. Is it not time for you to know that I am the apostle of God?'* Abu Sufyan answered: 'By God, O Muhammad, of this there is doubt in my soul.' The 'Abbas who was present with Muhammad told Abu Sufyan: *'Woe to you! Accept Islam and testify that Muhammad is the apostle of God before your neck is cut off by the sword.'"* Thus compelled, Sufyan submitted. "He professed the faith of Islam and became a Muslim."[97]

Others did not fare as well. When Ibn Khatal was found clinging to the curtains of the Ka'bah, the prophet said, "Kill him."[98] Thus, Abu Barzah "ripped open his belly."[99] Ishaq notes that Khatal "had two singing-girls Fartanā and her friend who used to sing satirical songs about the apostle, so he ordered that they should be killed with him."[100] One was murdered; the other ran away and was later spared.

Like the satirist, Abdullah, son of Sa'd, fortuitously escaped the sword. Muhammad had ordered his execution because "he had been a Muslim and used to write down revelation; then he apostatized and returned to Quraysh."[101] When he was brought before Muhammad, the apostle "kept silent," intending that one of his companions would "get up and strike off his head!" Muhammad's men, however, were confused about his intentions. One of them asked, "Why didn't you give me a sign, O apostle of God?" Muhammad "answered that a prophet does not kill by pointing."[102]

Muhammad killed as he willed. Some he spared; others he executed in gruesome fashion. When the killings abated, Muhammad considered the Ka'bah. He "encompassed it seven times on his camel touching the black stone with a stick which he had in his hand." Thereafter, "he ordered that all the idols which were round the Ka'ba should be collected and burned with fire and broken up."[103] From that day forward, the apostle would be its only idol and Islam its only ideology.

Infidels would be banished from its soil, and to experience it would become the desire of every Muslim heart.

AD 631: Sura of the Sword

Fight and slay the Pagans wherever ye find them, and seize them, beleaguer them, and lie in wait for them in every stratagem (of war).
—Q 9:5

The year 631 marked Muhammad's final foray. The inhabitants of Arabia had been subjected to the Islamic state—the world now beckoned. Thus, he set out with an army toward Tabuk. The prophet had in "mind (the idea of threatening the) Christians of Arabia in Syria and those of Rome."[104] This comports well with Ibn Kathir's commentary on the famed sura of the sword: *"slay the polytheists wherever you find them"* (Q 9:5 *Majestic*).

Do not wait until you find them. Rather, seek and besiege them in their areas and forts, gather intelligence about them in the various roads and fairways so that what is made wide looks ever smaller to them. This way, they will have no choice, but to die or embrace Islam.[105]

Though no adversary appeared when he and his thirty thousand arrived in Tabuk, Muhammad's desert journey set the pattern for the rest of Islamic history. As noted Islamic expert Robert Spencer has well said, "Not long after Muhammad's death, the Muslims invaded the Byzantine Empire—fired up by Muhammad's promise that 'the first army amongst my followers who will invade Caesar's city [Constantinople] will be forgiven their sins.'[106] In 635, just three years after Muhammad died, Damascus, the city where Saint Paul was heading when he experienced his dramatic conversion to Christianity, fell to the invading Muslims." Two years later, "Antioch, where the disciples of Jesus were first called 'Christians' (Acts 11:26), fell." And shortly thereafter, "it was the unhappy task of Sophronius, the patriarch of Jerusalem, to hand over the city to the conquering Umar."[107]

From the fall of Jerusalem to the present, the world has known jihad. Muhammad's trail of terror is the legacy of Islam. He migrated to Medina but never assimilated. After reaching critical mass, he "slew the pagans," taking their houses and lands; he later "seized" Mecca and made it the centerpiece of his conquests; and he "beleaguered" the cities of Arabia, taking their women and their wealth as his private property. His "every stratagem of war" paved the way for what fourteen centuries later would be the most prolific pseudo-religion in the world (see Q 9:5).

But like every other man, he would soon face his own mortality.

AD 632: First and Final *Hajj*

> *And proclaim to mankind the Hajj (pilgrimage). They will come*
> *to you on foot and on every lean camel, they will come from every*
> *deep and distant (wide) mountain highway (to perform Hajj).*
> —Q 22:27, HILALI–KHAN

In March 632, Muhammad would make his first and final *hajj*.[108] Hordes from all over the Arabian Peninsula descended upon the city of the prophet, eager to participate in *hajj* under the sway of the master. Muhammad and his wives departed Medina for Mecca with an entourage of thirty thousand who would hear his final religious directive. "Today, those who disbelieve have despaired of prevailing against your religion, so don't fear them but fear me. Today I have perfected for you your religion and have completed my grace upon you, and have chosen Islam [submission] for you as your religion [Q 5:3]."[109]

What Muhammad did in Mecca became the pattern for all Muslims to emulate from that day forth.

> The apostle completed the *hajj* and showed men the rites, and taught them what God had prescribed as to their *hajj*, the station, the throwing of stones, the circumambulation of the temple, and what He had permitted and forbidden. It was the pilgrimage of completion and the pilgrimage of farewell because the apostle did not go on pilgrimage after that.[110]

In the months following the *hajj*, Muhammad's past came back to bite him with a vengeance. Khaybar had been his greatest victory; now it threatened to be his greatest defeat. After dividing the women among his men, he had taken one and was poisoned by another. The noted Muslim historian al-Tabari (d. 923) explained:

> When the Messenger of God rested from his labor, Zaynab bt. al-Ḥārith, the wife of Sallām b. Mishkam, served him a roast sheep. She had asked what part of the sheep the Messenger of God liked best and was told that it was the foreleg. So she loaded that part with poison, and she poisoned the rest of the sheep, too. Then she brought it. When she set it before the Messenger of God, he took the foreleg and chewed a bit of it, but he did not swallow it. With him was Bishr b. al-Barā' b. Ma'rūr, who, like the Messenger of God, took some of it; Bishr, however, swallowed it, while the Messenger of God spat it out, saying, "This bone informs me that

it has been poisoned." [Thereafter, he asked Zaynab what had led her to poison him. She replied,] "How you have afflicted my people is not hidden from you. So I said, 'If he is a prophet, he will be informed; but if he is a king, I shall be rid of him.'"[111]

Bishr died that very day. Muhammad was not as fortunate. As noted by Aisha, then still in her teens, "The Prophet in his ailment in which he died, used to say, 'O 'Aisha! I still feel the pain caused by the food I ate at Khaibar, and at this time, I feel as if my aorta is being cut from that poison.'"[112]

From then until the time of his death, he suffered mightily with headaches and recurring fever.[113] Seeing his calamity and knowing whom he favored, the other wives graciously waived their turns with the prophet. Thus it was that on June 8, 632, Muhammad died in the lap of Aisha and was buried beneath her floor.[114]

Since the homicide of Muhammad is frought with intrigue, I devote the appendix to the matter (see pp. 185–88). In sum, the Sunnis believe Muhammad was poisoned by the Jewess Zaynab; while Shi'as are convinced he was poisoned by two of his wives (Aisha, daughter of Abu Bakr, and Hafsa, daughter of Umar).

Today, fourteen hundred years after his death, all Muslims—without exception—swear allegiance to the life and legacy of Muhammad. They laud him as the chosen of God, the Seal of the Prophets. The mere mention of his name, whether in conversation or debate, is appended by the words *peace be upon him*. Yet like all the other greats in history, his grave is evidence that the living know that they will die.

Consider Cyrus the Great. He was the embodiment of a kingdom of bronze that would rule over all the earth. Yet despite the most celebrated edict in the history of humanity and an empire that was not eclipsed until the time of the Romans, Cyrus was dead scarcely nine years after overwhelming Babylon, glory of the Chaldeans.[115]

Or consider Alexander the Great. He, too, is immortalized in the annals of human history. When Darius III offered him the entirety of the Persian Empire west of the Euphrates in return for peace, he responded in bloody pursuit. At the apex of power, however, Alexander went the way of all flesh.

One month shy of his thirty-third birthday, he who wept because there were no more kingdoms to conquer was dead.[116]

Antiochus, the Old Testament antichrist, like Cyrus and Alexander before him, ruled the world with an iron fist. As chief villain of the Greco-Syrian Empire, he mercilessly trampled his foes underfoot. He crucified the Jews of Jerusalem for resisting his hellenizing advances and in superhuman arrogance declared himself the incarnation of Zeus. Yet barely three years after he had accomplished his mission to desecrate the temple fortress, abolish the daily sacrifice, and set up the abomination that causes desolation, the Syrian beast was dead.[117]

Muhammad is hardly the exception. He founded the world's fastest-growing religiopolitical cult and brutally subjected the Arabian Peninsula to tyrannical terror. In the greatest of his conquests, he had a Jewish man beheaded, took his wife as booty, had her beautified, and then forced on her his bed. He promised his men either earthly goods or an eternity in the graces of houris. However, like Antiochus, scarcely three years after he had slaughtered the Jews of Khaybar, he was dead in the arms of a woman he married at age six.

How different the life of Jesus Christ! He elevated females to ontological equality with men[118] and taught all his followers the principles of a kingdom that would never end.[119] He commanded devotees to love their enemies and pray for those who persecuted them.[120] He instructed adherents to turn the other cheek[121]—to be peacemakers rather than makers of war.[122] When a disciple struck a soldier with his sword, Jesus said to him, "Put your sword in its place, for all who draw the sword will die by the sword."[123] He defended the downtrodden and condemned the self-righteous.[124] Above all, he set the ultimate moral example by dying so that others might live.[125]

The distance between mere mortals, like Cyrus, Alexander, Antiochus, and Muhammad, and the One who said, "I am the way and the truth and the life"[126] is that of an unbridgeable chasm. Likewise, the difference between the unreliable revelations of Islam and the certain revelations of Christianity is the distance of infinity. Not only does the prophetic prowess of the Bible elevate it far above the Qur'an, but as new archaeological nuggets are uncovered, the trustworthiness of Scripture is further illumined. Flawless ethics and factual evidence demonstrate the Bible to be divine rather than merely human in origin. Faulty ethics, factual errors, and feigned eloquence demonstrate that the Qur'an is devoid of divine sanction.

One is built on solid rock, the other on the shifting sands of unreliable revelations.

CHAPTER 2

UNRELIABLE REVELATIONS

The Emperor Has No Clothes

They killed him not, nor crucified him, but
so it was made to appear to them.

—Q 4:157

Islam relies on a multitude of revelations. But only one is considered to be the eternally existent word of Allah, channeled through his chosen prophet six centuries after the crucifixion of Christ. It is considered to be uncreated and unalterable, without error, having ethics beyond question, and eloquent above anything the world has ever experienced.[1]

The Qur'an comprises 114 suras (chapters), some revealed in Mecca, others in Medina. Meccan suras feature Muhammad as God's final prophet —a prophet greater than all the prophets who came before him. They begin with the account of Allah's creation of Adam "out of a (mere) clot of congealed blood" (96:2) and progress to the night of destiny in which Muhammad discovers that he has been called to be Allah's messenger (although the *shahada* by which Muslims are saved—"There is no god but God; Muhammad is the messenger of God"—is not found in the Qur'an, it can be pieced together through the collation of various passages). Also included in the Meccan suras is Muhammad's famed night journey "from the Sacred Mosque to the Farthest Mosque" (17:1), as well as accounts of subordinate prophets that he meets along the way. While the names of these prophets—Jesus, Abraham, Moses, and so on—remain unchanged, the narrative of their lives and practices is radically altered from earlier biblical accounts.

In contrast to the suras of Mecca, the Medinan suras are less prophetic and more political. Jews and Christians are rendered *persona non grata*. "O ye who believe! Take not the Jews and the Christians for your friends and protectors; they are but friends and protectors to each other. And he amongst you that turns to them (for friendship) is of them" (5:51). Moreover, the penalty for disbelief in this life may be "execution, or crucifixion, or the cutting off of hands and feet from opposite sides, or exile from the land" (5:33). Muhammad also presents persuasive predictive pictures of the pleasures that await Muslims who are willing to die for the cause of the prophet. They are showered with wealth, "bracelets of gold and pearls" (22:23); enjoy "rivers of wine" (47:15); and indulge in endless celestial sex with beautiful women, "whom no man or Jinn before them has touched" (55:56).

To make sense of the Qur'an (recited revelations), Muslims employ traditions (unrecited revelations) such as the *sirah* (biographies of Muhammad) and the *hadith* (narratives).[2] "Together, the *Sirah* and the *Hadith*, comprising Muhammad's oral commentaries, remarks, and teachings, make up the *Sunna*, or 'example' provided by the prophet. From the *Sunna* is derived the essential body of faith, morals, and doctrine on which Islam is based."[3] But only the Qur'an is considered infallible. And that in Arabic alone.

Esteemed Arabic expert W. St. Clair Tisdall put it this way:

[Muhammad] heard Gabriel reading aloud or reciting in a voice distinctly audible to him every single word of the Qur'an, according as it was inscribed on the "Preserved Tablet" in heaven. Arabic is held to be the language of heaven and of the angels, and hence in the Qur'an we have the very words, as well as the Word, of God Himself. Words, metaphors, reflections, narratives, style, all are wholly and entirely of Divine origin.[4]

The claim, of course, is self-evidently false. Far from being divine, the Qur'an is clearly human in origin.

> It breathes the air of the desert, it enables us to hear the battle-cries of the Prophet's followers as they rushed to the onset, it reveals the working of Muhammad's own mind, and shows the gradual declension of his character as he passed from the earnest and sincere though visionary enthusiast into the conscious impostor and open sensualist.[5]

In sharp contrast to the Holy Bible, the Qur'an is replete with *faulty ethics* and riddled with *factual errors*. Moreover, as we will see, the Qur'anic claim, "If the whole of mankind and Jinns were to gather together to produce the like of this Qur'an they could not produce the like thereof, even if they backed up each other with help and support" (17:88), is but *feigned eloquence*.

Faulty Ethics

Jesus, demonstrably God in human flesh, gave the world two great commandments. "Love the Lord your God with all your heart and with all your soul and with all your mind," and "love your neighbor as yourself" (Mark 12:30–31). The Qur'anic God violates both with reckless abandon.

The first great commandment is violated through the remaking of the one eternal holy and majestic God, revealed in three centers of consciousness, into a being that not only misapprehends basic grammatical constructs but cannot so much as apprehend irrefutable historical realities. In this vein, Allah grossly imagines that, with respect to the Son of God, the word *begotten* presupposes sexual reproduction[6] rather than special relationship,[7] and he thoroughly misapprehends the Trinity—supposing that Mary is God[8] and the Holy Spirit the angel Gabriel.[9] Moreover, against the weight of history and evidence, Allah denies the crucifixion of Jesus Christ.[10]

Allah's violation of the second great commandment is even more blatant. As such, he sanctions murder, adultery, stealing, false testimony, and coveting.

You Shall Murder

You shall not murder.

—EXODUS 20:13

In stark contrast to the God of the Bible, the Qur'anic Allah commands murder—and in grotesque and horrifying fashion. Of his more than one hundred murderous commands, three immediately spring to mind.

The first is that of Amr son of al-Hadrami, a member of Muhammad's own tribe. This murder (the first in Muslim history) deeply troubled Muslim raiders in that it took place during the sacred month of Rajab. Allah, however, "relieved the Muslims of their anxiety in the matter,"[11] saying, "Mischief is worse than killing."[12]

Furthermore, Islamic terrorist attacks are directly mandated by Allah, who spoke to Muslim devotees saying, "When ye meet the Unbelievers (in fight), smite at their necks" (Q 47:4).[13] No one took the command of Allah more literally than did Muhammad, who in 627 beheaded six hundred–plus Jews in Medina.[14]

Finally, we should note that murder is not only permitted by Allah but also prescribed by Allah. "Fighting is *prescribed* upon you, and ye dislike it. But it is possible that ye dislike a thing which is good for you, and that ye love a thing which is bad for you. But Allah knoweth, and ye know not" (Q 2:216). Far from a vice, then, murder is rendered a virtue. Nor can the command of Allah be misunderstood as mere self-defense. In context, the murderous commands of Allah were given in order to motivate Muslims in their task of raiding Meccan caravans.[15]

You Shall Commit Adultery

You shall not commit adultery.

—EXODUS 20:14

Adultery is rampant within Islam. Shi'a Muslims have even crafted a dogma called *mut'ah* as a means for having sex without the encumbrance of permanent marriage.[16] *Mut'ah* marriages typically range from a few hours to several days. They serve as a convenient option for unmarried Shiite Muslims who desire sex without commitment. Crucial components of *mut'ah* include a "bridal gift" paid in cash and a commitment to stay single for at least two menstrual cycles after the *mut'ah* contract expires.[17]

Adultery, however, is hardly limited to *mut'ah*. From the beginning, Allah has provided all Muslims with the divine sanction of having adulterous sex with captured females—"those whom your right hands possess" (Q 4:24). In Khaybar, for example, Muhammad had one of his men torture and kill a Jew and shortly thereafter engaged in sex with his widow. The rest of the female captives he distributed among his Muslim warriors.[18]

Furthermore, Allah is so deeply committed to the principle of sexual slavery that he recapitulates his adulterous commands on multiple occasions. On one occasion, he tells his prophet it is "lawful to you your wives, to whom you have paid their *Mahr* (bridal money given by the husband to his wife at the time of marriage), and those (captives or slaves) whom your right hand possesses—whom Allah has given to you" (Q 33:50 *Hilali-Khan*). On another occasion, he tells Muslim men that they should "abstain from sex, except with those joined to them in the marriage bond, or (the captives) who their right hands possess" (Q 23:5–6). And, in Qur'an 70, he makes crystal clear that adulterous relationships are limited to female slaves and captives. Those who go beyond that, he deems "transgressors" (70:30–31).[19]

Finally, Allah provides for what in polite society would be considered adulterous polygamy. In Qur'an 4:3, Allah permits Muslims to "marry women of your choice, two, or three, or four." Ironically, in Qur'an 33:50, Allah provides Muhammad with a divine sanction to marry "any believing woman who dedicates her soul to the Prophet if the Prophet wishes to wed her." Thus, while other men were only permitted to marry up to four wives, Allah provided Muhammad with a divine exception for his marriage to at least a dozen women.[20]

You Shall Steal

You shall not steal.

—EXODUS 20:15

First, as Allah makes clear, Muslims *are* permitted to steal—but only from unbelievers. If a Muslim steals from another Muslim, he mandates amputation—"As to the thief, male or female, cut off his or her hands" (Q 5:38). Those who reject Allah's explicit commands are designated "unbelievers" and "hypocrites," and their "abode is Hell" (Q 66:9).

Furthermore, Allah commands Muslims not only to steal but also to relish the process. "*Enjoy* what ye *took*," for it is "lawful and good" (Q 8:69). And Allah's directives are not merely relegated to petty theft; they entail grand theft as well. After casting terror into the hearts of People of the Book, he advises Muslims to steal "their houses, and their goods" (Q 33:26–27).

Finally, it is important to grasp the expansive nature of Allah's promises. Stealing in the beginning encompassed only the booty of Meccan caravans. Later on, Muslims were empowered to steal whole cities, such as Khaybar. And in the end, Allah promises that theft by the sword will yield a caliphate encompassing the entire earth.[21] Allah's incentives are always the same. Four fifths belong to Muslim hordes, the final fifth to Allah and to his Muslim herald: "Whatever ye take as spoils of war, lo! a fifth thereof is for Allah, and for the messenger" (Q 8:41 *Pickthall*).[22]

You Shall Give False Testimony Against Your Neighbor

You shall not give false testimony against your neighbor.
—Exodus 20:16

In his famed Cairo University speech, Barack Obama quoted Allah's words as channeled through the Qur'an. "The Holy Koran teaches that whoever kills an innocent, it is as if he has killed all mankind. And the Holy Koran also says whoever saves a person, it is as if he has saved all mankind." Obama went on to say, "Islam is not part of the problem in combating violent extremism—it is an important part of promoting peace."[23]

As a self-proclaimed student of history, Obama surely knew that this was *taqiyya* (religious dissimulation) plain and simple. He took a text out of context and used it as a pretext for peace, when in reality the Qur'an intends to communicate something very different. In context, Allah is paraphrasing the

God of the Jewish Talmud and is doing so to make a larger point—namely, that the murder, the crucifixion, or the mutilation of Jews is warranted in that disbelief is tantamount to mischief.

As readers of the Qur'an know all too well, the verse following the one misquoted by Obama says this:

> The punishment of those who wage war against Allah and His messenger and strive to make mischief in the land is only this, that they should be murdered or crucified or their hands and their feet should be cut off on opposite sides or they should be imprisoned; this shall be as a disgrace for them in this world, and in the hereafter they shall have a grievous chastisement. (5:33 *Shakir*)[24]

Furthermore, what Obama did in Cairo is repeated again and again by radical Muslim organizations such as the Council on American-Islamic Relations (CAIR). Following the Muslim murders in Paris at the offices of Charlie Hebdo and at a Jewish supermarket, Osama Al-Qasem modified the words of Qur'an 5:32 and disregarded the very next verse altogether.[25] CAIR spokespersons have mastered the art of telling the truth, but not the whole truth, with the intention to mislead (*kitman*). Their goal is always the same—to conceal from disbelievers dogmas they would otherwise find abhorrent.

Finally, the Qur'an overtly teaches that Allah is the master of *makr* or deception. As Qur'an 3:54 and 8:30 put it, "Allah (is the) best (of) the deceivers" (literal translation). Perhaps even more troubling from the perspective of Islam is that, as Qur'an 7:99 makes plain, even devout Muslims need to be wary of Allah's deceptions. As the venerable Muslim translator Muhammad Pickthall rendered it, "None deemeth himself secure from Allah's scheme save folk that perish." Ironically, numerous Qur'anic translators use deception in order to make the word *makr* appear benign.[26]

Before moving on, allow me to emphasize that there are likely millions of devout Muslims who could not so much as imagine trodding the path of *taqiyya*. In concert with multitudes of non-Muslims, they likely regard the religious dissimulation tactics of Muslim organizations like CAIR to be cringeworthy at best.

You Shall Covet

You shall not covet your neighbor's house. You shall not covet
your neighbor's wife, or his male or female servant, his ox
or donkey, or anything that belongs to your neighbor.
—EXODUS 20:17

The God of the Bible condemns coveting in no uncertain terms. In sharp contrast, the God of the Qur'an commends it. When David, king of Israel, coveted Uriah's wife and took her for his own, God sent the prophet Nathan to pronounce judgment upon him.[27] When Muhammad, prophet of Allah, coveted his neighbor's wife—as in Zaynab, wife of his adopted son Zayd—Allah sent the prophet a message saying, "there is no blame on the Prophet (SAW) in that which Allah has made legal for him" (Q 33:38 *Hilali-Khan*).

Furthermore, as I have previously noted, the God of Islam permitted Muhammad to lust after all the wealth and women of the Arabian Peninsula.[28] He coveted not only wives but also male and female slaves, oxen, donkeys, and anything else he could get his hands on. Had a true biblical prophet done such a thing, he would have been severely chastised by the God of Abraham, Isaac, and Jacob, as were David and Solomon.[29]

Finally, the depravity of Allah is seen in that he permitted Muslims to have sexual relations with any "(captives) whom their right hands possess" (Q 23:5–6).[30] As a direct result of Allah's many Qur'anic assertions, sexual slavery was widely practiced and considered perfectly normal by Muhammad and his men. Covetedness in Islam is so pervasive that Muslim men are permitted by Allah to engage in the practice of polygamy (Q 4:3).

The faulty ethics of the Qur'anic Allah extend even further still. In Qur'an 4:34, Allah exhorts Muslim men to "scourge"[31] their wives in order that they might "return to obedience."[32] This Qur'anic directive is so unpalatable to Western sensibilities that some Muslim translators change the phrase *scourge them* to *beat them*. Abdullah Yusuf Ali goes as far as gratuitously to add the word *lightly*, though no such qualification exists in the original Arabic.[33]

When we compare the personal morality of Muhammad with that of Jesus, the difference is remarkable. The Qur'an exhorts Muhammad to ask "forgiveness for thy fault" (Q 40:55). Conversely, Jesus' ethics regarding every aspect of life—including his treatment of women—was so unimpeachable that he could rightly ask, "Can any of you prove me guilty of sin?" (John 8:46; see also 2 Corinthians 5:21; 1 John 3:5).

FACTUAL ERRORS

As the Qur'an is riddled by faulty ethics, so, too, it is replete with factual errors—none worse than its denial of the crucifixion of Christ. This Qur'anic denial chronicled in sura 4:157 is explicit and emphatic: *"They killed him not, nor crucified him*, but so it was made to appear to them, and those who differ therein are full of doubts, with no (certain) knowledge, but only conjecture to follow, for *of a surety they killed him not."* Allah's contention that Christ was not crucified is, of course, factually false.

Crucifixion

The fatal suffering of Jesus Christ as recounted in the New Testament is one of the most well-established facts of ancient history. Even in today's modern age of scientific enlightenment, there is a virtual consensus among New Testament scholars—*both conservative and liberal*—that Jesus died on a Roman cross and that he was buried in the tomb of Joseph of Arimathea and that his death drove his disciples to despair.[34]

While Allah contends that Christ was not crucified, the evidence clearly points in a different direction. Christ's fatal torment began in the Garden of Gethsemane after the emotional Last Supper. There he experienced a medical condition known as hematidrosis—tiny capillaries in his sweat glands ruptured, mixing sweat with blood.[35]

After being arrested by the temple guard, he was mocked, beaten, and spat upon. The next morning, battered, bruised, and bleeding, he was stripped and subjected to the brutality of Roman flogging—a whip replete with razor-sharp bones and lead balls reduced his body to quivering ribbons of bleeding flesh.

As Jesus slumped into the pool of his own blood, soldiers threw a scarlet robe across his shoulders, thrust a scepter into his hands, and pressed sharp thorns into his scalp. Thereafter, a heavy wooden beam was thrust upon his bleeding body, and he was led away to "the place of the skull" (Matthew 27:33). There, in the form of a cross, he experienced excruciating physical torment—the word *excruciate* (literally, "out of the cross") coined to convey its horror.

At "the place of the skull," Roman soldiers drove thick seven-inch iron spikes through Christ's hands and feet. In the ensuing hours Jesus experienced cycles of joint-wrenching cramps, intermittent asphyxiation, and excruciating pain as his lacerated body moved up and down against the rough timber of the cross with every breath he tried to take.

As the chill of death crept through his body, Jesus cried out, "My God, my God, why have you forsaken me?" (Matthew 27:46). And in that anguished cry is encapsulated the greatest agony of all. For on the cross Christ bore the sin and suffering of all humanity. And then with his passion complete, Jesus gave up his spirit.

Shortly thereafter, a Roman legionnaire drove his spear through the fifth intercostal space between the ribs, upward through the pericardium and into Christ's heart. Immediately, there rushed forth blood and water, demonstrating conclusively that Jesus had suffered fatal torment. As Isaiah prophesied, "He was pierced for our transgressions, he was crushed for our iniquities" (Isaiah 53:5). Or in the words of the apostle Paul, "Christ died for our sins according to the Scriptures" (1 Corinthians 15:3).

Recent archaeological discoveries not only corroborate the Bible's description of Roman crucifixion but also authenticate the biblical details surrounding the trial that led to his death. Excavations at the ruins of an ancient Herodian theater at Caesarea—the Roman capital of Judea—uncovered a first-century inscription confirming Pilate as the Roman governor during the epoch in which Christ was tried and crucified.[36] Many similar proofs can be forwarded, including the discovery of a burial chamber dating back to the first century that validates the biblical assertion that Caiaphas was the high priest who presided over the religious trials that led to crucifixion.[37]

As with archaeologists, ancient historians—such as Flavius Josephus, a Jew writing at the pleasure of the Romans—testify to the historical reality of Christ's crucifixion.[38] Cornelius Tacitus, widely deemed the greatest first-century historian of the ancient Roman Empire, provides reliable corroborating testimony.[39] And as with Josephus and Tacitus, Gaius Suetonius Tranquillus, best known for his biography *The Twelve Caesars*, lends reliable external evidence to the validity of a crucified Christ.[40]

Additionally, both liberal and conservative New Testament scholars agree that the body of the crucified Christ was buried in the private tomb of Joseph of Arimathea.[41] One final point should be made. The Qur'anic denial of Christ's crucifixion has led to a host of other errors as well. From a Muslim perspective, Jesus was never crucified and, thus, never resurrected. Instead, in Islam, God made someone look like Jesus, and the look-alike was mistakenly crucified in his place. The notion that Judas was made to look like Jesus has been popularized in Muslim circles by a late medieval invention titled *The Gospel of Barnabas*.[42]

This, of course, is no small matter. Like the denial of Christ's crucifixion, the Muslim denial of his resurrection is tantamount to tearing the heart out of the historic Christian faith. But as is the case with his fatal torment, Islam is dead wrong in denying his resurrection. The apostles did not merely propagate Christ's teachings; they were absolutely certain that he had appeared to them in the flesh. In 1 Corinthians 15:3–7 the apostle Paul reiterated a Christian creed that scholars of all stripes conclude can be dated to mere months after Messiah's murder. This creed, which unambiguously affirms Christ's post-resurrection appearances, is free from legendary contamination and ultimately grounded in eyewitness testimony.[43]

One of the most amazing post-resurrection appearances involves James. Before Christ's appearances, James was embarrassed by all that Jesus represented. Afterward, he was willing to die for the notion that his relative was God.[44] The question that inevitably arises is this: What would it take for someone to willingly die for the notion that one of his family members was God? The answer is nothing other than the post-resurrection appearances of Messiah.

What happened as a result of the resurrection is unique in human history. In the span of a few hundred years, a small band of seemingly insignificant believers succeeded in turning an entire empire upside down. While it is conceivable that they would have faced torture, vilification, and even cruel deaths for what they fervently believed to be true, it is inconceivable that they, like their Lord, would have been willing to die for what they knew to be a lie. If their testimony was not true,[45] there was no possible motive for them to say otherwise.[46]

Denial of Christ's crucifixion is certainly enough to discount the Qur'an as a wholly human invention. But there's more. Much, much, more.

Trinity

In Muhammad's day, if human reproduction was considered at all, it was considered quite simple—for all practical purposes, little more than what the Qur'an describes as reproduction via an unsophisticated clot of blood.[47] Moreover, no seventh-century man could have possibly imagined subatomic particles—much less the atomic energy that can be generated by splitting atoms. Indeed, the negotiation of complex treaties to ensure that humanity does not vaporize itself in a nuclear holocaust facilitated by the splitting of atoms would have been considered laughable fourteen centuries ago.

In similar fashion an ineffable God who created the universe *ex nihilo* would have been incomprehensible to Muhammad. It has always been the Christian contention that genuine revelation is the necessary precondition for understanding. Reason alone is simply insufficient. No matter how keen a man's eyesight, he can see nothing if confined to pitch-black darkness. As light is axiomatic to seeing, so revelation is needed for knowing.[48]

Just as Muhammad could not have comprehended the complex tapestry of matter, he could not conceive of a complex trinitarian deity. Nor, for that matter, can anyone else. While we can *apprehend* what God has disclosed of himself, we cannot *comprehend* the God who spoke and the universe leapt into existence. God is indeed ineffable. This is precisely why Christians bow before God's self-revelation, while Muslims use fallible reason to remake God in their own image.

C. S. Lewis said it well: "It is simple religions that are the made-up ones."[49] He may have had in mind the thoroughly made-up religion of Islam. "If Christianity was something we were making up, of course we could make it easier. But it is not. We cannot compete, in simplicity, with people who are inventing religions. How could we? We are dealing with Fact. Of course anyone can be simple if he has no facts to bother about."[50]

The Christian concept of God is anything but simplistic. What we *apprehend* we cannot fully *comprehend*. Even in eternity we will continue to grow in apprehension of an infinite, incomprehensible, ineffable deity who has condescended to reveal his tri-unity to mortals. In short, his revelation is threefold: (1) there is but one God; (2) the Father is God, the Son is God, and the Holy Spirit is God; (3) Father, Son, and Holy Spirit are eternally distinct.

First, there is only one God. Christianity is not polytheistic but fiercely monotheistic. "'You are my witnesses,' declares the LORD, 'and my servant whom I have chosen, so that you may know and believe me and understand that I am he. *Before me no god was formed, nor will there be one after me*'" (Isaiah 43:10).

Secondly, in hundreds of Scripture passages, the Father, Son, and Holy Spirit are each declared to be the true God. As a case in point, the apostle Paul said that, "there is but one God the Father" (1 Corinthians 8:6). The Father, speaking of the Son, says, "Your throne, O God, will last for ever and ever" (Hebrews 1:8). And when Ananias "lied to the Holy Spirit," Peter pointed out that he had "not lied just to human beings but to God" (Acts 5:3–4).

Thirdly, the Father, Son, and Holy Spirit are eternally distinct. Scripture clearly portrays subject-object relationships between Father, Son, and Holy Spirit. For example, the Father and the Son love one another, speak to each other, and together send the Holy Spirit.[51] Additionally, Jesus proclaims that he and the Father are two distinct witnesses and two distinct judges (John 8:14–18). If Jesus were himself the Father, his argument would have been not only irrelevant but fatally flawed; and, if such were the case, he could not have been truely God.

It is important to note that when Christians speak of one God, they are referring to the nature or essence of God. Moreover, when they speak of persons, they are referring to personal self-distinctions within the Godhead. Put another way, we hold to one *What* and three *Whos*.[52]

All of this is a far cry from the pathetic caricature of God posited by the Qur'anic Allah. It is not merely that he denies the doctrine of the Trinity. He misapprehends and distorts it. In mulish misconception or malicious misrepresentation, he recasts the Trinity as Father, Mary, and Jesus. While the

Qur'anic language isn't exactly fluid, it is instructive to try to get a handle on Allah's convoluted refutation of the Trinity:

> They are unbelievers who say, "God is *the Third of Three*." No god is there but One God. If they refrain not from what they say, there shall afflict those of them that disbelieve a painful chastisement. Will they not turn to God and pray His forgiveness? God is All-forgiving, All-compassionate. The Messiah, son of Mary, was only a Messenger; Messengers before him passed away; his mother was a just woman; they both ate food. Behold, how We make clear the signs to them; then behold, how they perverted are! (Q 5:73–75 *Arberry*)[53]

To begin with, we should note that Allah seems to think that Christians (whom he deems unbelievers) hold that God is "the third of three." This, of course, is patently false. Christians in concert with Jews and Muslims hold that there is only one God. The book of Deuteronomy contains the most significant prayer (Hebrew Shema) of Old Testament Judaism: "Hear, O Israel: The LORD our God, the LORD is one" (6:4). And when the teachers of the law asked Jesus, "Of all the commandments, which is the most important?" Jesus answered, "The most important one is this: 'Hear, O Israel, the Lord our God, the Lord is one'" (Mark 12:28–29).

Furthermore, if Allah is indeed God he should have been well aware that Christians believe that Messiah is not merely a man who "ate food" but rather the God-man who created the very food he ate. The apostle Paul said:

> The Son is the image of the invisible God, the firstborn over all creation. *For in him all things were created*: things in heaven and on earth, visible and invisible, whether thrones or powers or rulers or authorities; all things have been created through him and for him. He is before all things, and in him all things hold together. (Colossians 1:15–17)

Finally, to suppose, as does Allah, that Christians think Mary is the third member of the triune Godhead is to completely misconstrue the biblical concept of Trinity. It would be one thing for a seventh-century Muslim such as Muhammad to be mistaken in this matter; it is quite another to imagine that an all-knowing Allah could have made such an elementary error in a book that is supposed to have existed from all eternity[54]—a book that was given to answer the assertion that God is "He and Jesus and Mary."[55]

While there are various ways to interpret Qur'anic assertions respecting the status of Mary, this much is inviolate. No orthodox Christian would so much as contemptate elevating Mary to the status of God. Christians rightly venerate Mary, but worship is strictly forbidden. If the Bible is clear about anything, it is that *Theotokos* ("Mother of God") is a human servant of God (certainly not a wife or partner), fully submitted to being transformed by Christ her Savior (see Luke 1:48). (For further discussion, see Major Muslim Misapprehensions, pages 156ff.)

Holy Spirit

As if denial of the Crucifixion and the Trinity were not error enough, Allah demonstrates complete and utter cluelessness with respect to the Christian doctrine of the Holy Spirit. Far from Mary being the third person of the triune God, the Holy Spirit is clearly identified in Scripture as the third person of the Trinity. After Ananias lied to the Holy Spirit in the book of Acts, Peter said to him, *"You have not lied just to to human beings but to God"* (5:3–4).[56] Allah's factual errors respecting the Holy Spirit are so acute they eliminate him from any serious claim to divinity.

In contrast to Allah, those familiar with the Holy Spirit know that he—not Mary—is not only the third person in the Trinity, but he also inspired true prophets to speak true words of God. As the apostle Peter put it, "Above all, you must understand that no prophecy of Scripture came about by the prophet's own interpretation of things. For prophecy never had its origin in the human will, but prophets, though human, spoke from God as they were carried along by the Holy Spirit" (2 Peter 1:20–21).[57]

Indeed, every major decision of the embryonic Christian church was made under the guidance, direction, and move of the Holy Spirit. And as the early church began to grow, early Christians began to grasp what Jesus had in mind when he said, "It is for your good that I am going away. Unless I go away, the Advocate will not come to you; but if I go, I will send him to you" (John 16:7). Indeed, the Advocate, the Counselor, the Helper—the

Holy Spirit—was directly involved in every notable advancement of the Christian church. For example, when the apostles in Jerusalem heard that Samaria had accepted the life and truth of Christ, they sent Peter and John to place their hands on them so that they might receive the Holy Spirit (Acts 8:14–17). In the church at Antioch the Holy Spirit revealed to the believers that Barnabus and Saul should be set apart as apostles to the Gentiles (Acts 13:2).[58] And it is the Holy Spirit who "intercedes for God's people in accordance with the will of God" (Romans 8:27).

In short, contrary to Allah, Christians do not worship Mary as the third person of the Trinity; rather they worship the precious Holy Spirit—the third center of consciousness within the only immutable God. While Mary is rightly venerated by believers, worship belongs to God alone. The Holy Spirit alone is the one who empowers us to "understand what God has freely given us" (1 Corinthians 2:12).

Furthermore, we should note that the Qur'anic God makes the elementary error of confusing the Holy Spirit with the angel Gabriel, who dictated the Qur'an to Muhammad over a period of approximately twenty-three years. As the fundamentalist Muslim organization Submission.org correctly notes, "The Holy Spirit in the Quran is clearly defined as the angel Gabriel who has been the angel-messenger between The Almighty God and the human beings." As this web entry goes on to explain, the "Arabic Quran calls him; 'Ruhhil-Qudus' (Holy Spirit), 'Ruuhanaa' (Our Spirit), 'Ruuhul-'Amiin' (The Honest Spirit) and 'Al-Ruh'' (The Spirit). Thus, when reading the verses in the Quran, the whole Quran, we see that Gabriel is the Holy and Honest Bearer of Revelations. We learn from 2:97 that these references are indeed talking about Gabriel."[59] The Submission Muslims conclude their article with these words: *"The 'Holy Spirit' in the Quran refers to the angel Gabriel and has nothing to do with Trinity or part of a Trinity. Trinity is denounced in the strongest language in the Quran."*[60]

Abdullah Yusuf Ali made the Qur'anic connection between the Holy Spirit and Gabriel equally clear in a footnote in his notable English translation. "The title of the Angel Gabriel, through whom the revelation came down," is none other than "the Holy Spirit" (see Q 16:102).[61]

From a Christian perspective, equating the Holy Spirit with Gabriel is sheer blasphemy. The Holy Spirit is God and should never be confused with an angel that God created. Moreover, God, and God alone, is the infallible agent of divine revelation. In stark contrast to an erroneous Qur'an, the Bible is without error.[62] In evidence, the archaeologist's spade has piled up proof upon proof for the people, places, and particulars inscribed on the parchment and papyrus of the biblical manuscripts.[63]

Finally, even if we were to grant that the Holy Spirit was an angel, he most certainly was not the angel Gabriel (Jibril). What Muhammad originally suspected is far more likely to be true—namely, that he was possessed by an evil spirit (jinn). As such, when he was told, "Read in the name of thy Lord who created, who created man of blood coagulated" (see Q 96:1–2),[64] the apparition that spoke to him was more likely than not jinn, not Jibril. In point of fact, it took a great deal of persuasion by his first wife Khadija to convince Muhammad that his encounter may have been divine as opposed to demonic in origin.[65]

As credible Muslim sources make clear, Muhammad's first inclination following what he believed must surely have been an encounter with the jinn was to leave the caves of Hira and "go to the top of the mountain and throw myself down that I may kill myself and gain rest."[66] Though thoughts of suicide eventually abated, Muhammad continued to battle doubt and depression in the years that followed—plagued by the notion that he was possessed by jinn.[67]

Fears of demonic possession were later compounded by what is popularly referred to as the "satanic verses." In essence, these Qur'anic verses refer to an episode in the life of Muhammad during which he compromised the missive of a unitarian God with pagan polytheistic verses. The essence of the story as chronicled by Al-Tabari, one of Islam's greatest historians, is as follows. "When the Messenger of God saw how his tribe turned their backs on him and was grieved to see them shunning the message he had brought to them from God, he longed in his soul that something would come to him from God which would reconcile him with his tribe." His longing found satisfaction in a divine revelation in which Allah spoke to the prophet saying, "Have you thought upon al-Lāt and al-'Uzzā and Manāt?"[68]

Not only did the words of Allah please Muhammad's enemies, they appeased his enthusiasts as well.

The Muslims, having complete trust in their Prophet in respect of the messages which he brought from God, did not suspect him of error, illusion, or mistake. When he came to the prostration, having completed the sūrah, he prostrated himself and the Muslims did likewise, following their Prophet, trusting in the message which he had brought and following his example.[69]

Gabriel, however, was less than pleased that the Muslims, in tandem with pagans, had prostrated themselves before female gods. He "came to the Messenger of God and said, 'Muhammad, what have you done? You have recited to the people that which I did not bring to you from God, and you have said that which was not said to you.'"[70] Thankfully, Allah was not equally exercised. He informed Muhammad that "Satan cast words into his recitation (*umniyyah*)" and "God abrogates what Satan casts" (Q 22:52).[71] Thus, God absolved Muhammad of his polytheistic pronouncement and "cancelled the words which Satan had cast on his tongue."[72]

Al-Tabari, of course, was not alone in chronicling Muhammad's trek into polytheism. Muhammad's earliest Muslim biographer, Ibn Ishaq, gave a similar report, which concludes with Allah assuring Muhammad that he would "annul what Satan has suggested" and swap the satanic suras with more suitable ones. "When the annulment of what Satan had put upon the prophet's tongue came from God, Quraysh said: 'Muhammad has repented of what he said about the position of your gods with Allah, altered it and brought something else.'"[73]

The "something else" brought by Muhammad is now encapsulated in the revised verses of Qur'an 53:19–23. Verses in which "Lāt, and 'Uzzā, and another, the Third (goddess), Manāt" are rendered "but names which ye have devised," names that "follow nothing but conjecture." As such, the satanic verses are now rendered but a momentary polytheistic lapse during which Muhammad prostrated himself before three of the pagan gods of the Arabian polytheistic pantheon.[74]

The satanic verses are of great consequence to Muslims. If Satan cast words upon Muhammad's tongue on one occasion and caused him to fear being possessed by the jinn on another, it follows that the prophet of Allah may well have been demonically deluded during other recitations as well.

Thus, when Salman Rushdie, an author who grew up in a nominal Muslim environment, published a novel titled *The Satanic Verses*, all hell quite literally broke loose.[75]

There is no telling how much mayhem resulted because of Rushdie's book. Muslims the world over engaged in bombings, book burnings, and blatant bullying. *Time* reported:

> Iranian spiritual leader Ayatullah Ruhollah Khomeini publicly condemned the Indian-British author to death, putting a $1 million bounty on his head (an Iranian assassin would get $3 million, Khomeini promised). [And] Venezuelan officials threatened anyone who owned or read the book with 15 months of prison. Japan fined anyone who sold the English-language edition, and a Japanese translator was subsequently stabbed to death for his involvement with the book.[76]

If Christians behaved like Muslims, they would have long ago issued a fatwa against the Qur'an. Its faulty ethics are abominable, and its factual errors ample. Against the weight of history and evidence, Allah blindly denies the historicity of Christ's crucifixion, mocks and misconstrues the Trinity, and confuses the third person of the divine Godhead with either Jibril or jinn.

These are serious errors. But silly errors litter the pages of the Qur'an as well. For example, the Qur'an contends that human beings are "created from an ejected fluid, that issues from between the spine and the ribs" (Q 86:6–7 *Majestic*). This is plain wrong. Sperm cells originate in the testes. For Muhammad to have gotten this wrong is one thing; for Allah, quite another. Muslim protestations in this regard are at best humorous.[77]

Another example involves Alexander the Great. Alexander, who died one month shy of his thirty-third birthday, is rendered an elderly Muslim a thousand years before Islam was even invented (see Q 18:83–98).[78] In like fashion, Pharaoh threatens his magicians with crucifixion long before crucifixion was invented by the Persians and later popularized by the Romans (see Q 7:124).[79] Clearly, factual errors render the Qur'an a thoroughly human concoction.

We now turn to the third significant matter—that of *feigned eloquence*.

Feigned Eloquence

Many years ago there was an emperor who pined for the finest clothing in the land. The finest fabrics. The most exquisite patterns. The brightest colors. In time, two swindlers appeared who feigned the ability to weave the most beautiful garments of all time. "Not only were their colors and patterns uncommonly fine, but clothes made of this cloth had a wonderful way of becoming invisible to anyone who was unfit for his office, or who was unusually stupid."[80] The emperor paid the swindlers a large sum of money and they set up two looms and pretended to weave the finest piece of clothing in history. The clerics of the kingdom, of course, could not see the clothing, but fearing for their lives, they feigned admiration for the elegance of the emperor's new clothes. In time the emperor donned his new garment and with pomp and ceremony led a procession through the streets of the kingdom. All the subjects in the land feigned admiration for the elegance of his clothing not wanting anyone to suspect that they were infidels or unusually stupid. And then, suddenly, the unimaginable happened. A child too young to know the score blurted, "The emperor has no clothes!" The father quickly chastened the child, and so the pretense continued.

The Emperor's New Clothes by Hans Christian Andersen aptly illustrates the feigned eloquence of the Qur'an. As with feigned modesty or feigned humility, feigned eloquence is not real; it is imaginary. When Allah says, "If the whole of mankind and Jinns were to gather together to produce the like of this Qur'an they could not produce the like thereof, even if they backed up each other with help and support" (17:88),[81] the elegance he boasts of is no more real than were the emperor's new clothes. Qur'anic arrangement is atrocious, its prophecies unspectacular, and its elegance grossly overstated.

Atrocious Arrangement

The nineteenth-century Scottish essayist and social historian Thomas Carlyle wryly remarked that "The Mahometans [followers of Muhammad] regard their Koran with a reverence which few Christians pay even to their Bible."[82] Yet the difference between the two can hardly be overstated. The Bible is a majestic literary tapestry arranged with desirable coherence, decipherable chronology, and discernible context. By comparison, Qur'anic arrangement is discombobulated, disjointed, and disorganized.

Though Carlyle expressed considerable admiration for Muhammad, his disdain for Allah's Qur'anic arrangement was palpable. "I must say, it is as toilsome reading as I ever undertook. A wearisome confused jumble, crude, incondite; endless iterations, long windedness, entanglement; most crude." And still he was not done. The Qur'an, said Carlyle, was published "without any discoverable order as to time or otherwise—merely trying, as would seem, and this not very strictly, to put the longest chapters first. The real beginning of it, in that way, lies almost at the end: for the earliest portions were the shortest. Read in its historical sequence it perhaps would not be so bad." As is, it is written "as badly as almost any book ever was!"[83]

Furthermore, Islamic expert Robert Spencer has appropriately said:

> For a book that provokes so many charges that readers are taking it out of context, the Qur'an is remarkably decontextualized. Although it retells many biblical stories (usually in slightly altered form), in its over-all form it lacks the chronological arrangement of the Old Testament historical books or even the rough temporal movement of the Gospels. Instead, its 114 chapters (*suras*) are arranged by length from the longest to the shortest; the biblical stories and other narratives are distributed haphazardly throughout the book.[84]

Spencer goes on to explain how the first revelation Muhammad received from Allah is not near the front of the Qur'an but ninety-six chapters into the book, and chapter titles have little or nothing to do with the content therein.

> Most of the chapters—"The Cow" (sura 2), "The Spider" (sura 29), "Smoke" (sura 44)—take their name from an apparently randomly chosen element of the chapter itself, one that does not necessarily have any particular importance. Only a few chapters, such as "The Spoils of War" or "Booty" (sura 8), bear titles that actually summarize their contents.[85]

Finally, it is interesting to note that Allah, and Allah alone, takes credit for the atrocious arrangement of Qur'anic passages. It would surely be forgivable for Muhammad—in the midst of "battles with the Koreish and Heathen, quarrels among his own people, backslidings of his own wild heart"[86]—to produce a disjointed narrative devoid of arrangement and internal coherence. But Allah? One would think not! Yet it is Allah, and he alone, who claims credit for producing the Qur'an in "well-arranged stages" (Q 25:32; see also 75:17).

Of one thing we can be certain—despite myriad Muslim apologists seeking to convince the gullible that the arrangement of the Qur'an is of surpassing beauty—the emperor has no clothes!

Prophetic Pretense

As with the arrangement of the Qur'an, its prophetic pretenses should not go unchallenged. It's "crookedness" is readily apparent when laid next to the "straight stick" of biblical brilliance. The Bible is replete with prophecies that could not have been fulfilled through chance, good guessing, or deliberate deceit. Such prophecies provide powerful proof that God has spoken. "I told you these things long ago; before they happened I announced them to you so that you could not say, 'My images brought them about; my wooden image and metal god ordained them'" (Isaiah 48:5). Or in the words of Jesus, "I have told you now before it happens, so that when it does happen you will believe" (John 14:29).

For example, Daniel, writing six centuries before the advent of Christ, was empowered by almighty God to do what the Muslim Allah could not so much as conceive of. With awesome precision he predicted a succession of nations from Babylon through the Median and Persian empires, to the persecution and suffering of the Jews under the second-century Greco-Syrian beast Antiochus IV Epiphanes, including the despot's desecration of the Jerusalem temple, his untimely death, and freedom for the Jews under Judas Maccabaeus.[87]

Moreover, the Bible is filled with prophecies identifying Jesus as the only one who can emerge through the doorway of Old Testament prophecy. One thing is certain. Jesus had to be a Jew. Not just any Jew. He had to be the Jewish descendant of Israel's quintessential king—through Jesse by way of Judah and in the lineage of Jacob. God sovereignly directed the course of human history from the woman Eve who was deceived, to the woman Mary who conceived. (For more on prophecy, see Major Muslim Misapprehensions on pages 147ff.)

In sharp contrast, prophecies validating the divine origin of the Qur'an are conspicuous by their absence. What's more, even the prophecies that are feigned by Muslim apologists as evidence of Qur'anic eloquence are vastly inferior to biblical counterparts. Three examples in particular establish the unbridgeable chasm between the brilliance of biblical prophecy and the pretense of that which is feigned in the Qur'an. First and foremost is the Qur'anic prophecy that Muhammad would return to Mecca.

Qur'an 48. "Truly did Allah fulfill the vision for His messenger: Ye shall enter the Sacred Mosque, if Allah wills, with minds secure, heads shaved, hair cut short, and without fear" (48:27). To begin with, this prophecy is very different from biblical prophecy. At best, it is a self-fulfilling prophecy. Something Muhammad said he would do, did, and did within a year or so.[88] This is far different from the luminescence of biblical prophets such as Daniel, writing six centuries before Christ, and by the power of almighty God predicting a succession of nations from Babylon to the Babe of Bethlehem.

Furthermore, this feigned prophetic eloquence is qualified by the phrase, "if Allah wills." In other words, "If I will," Muhammad *will* return to Mecca. And "If I *do not* will," Muhammad will not return to Mecca. As such, Qur'an 48:27 is unfalsifiable and worthless as an apologetic for the Qur'an's prophetic prowess. If Muhammad returns to Mecca, it is true; and if he does not, it is equally true. Besides, if Allah is truly an omniscient being, he would have no need whatsoever to qualify this prediction.

Finally, what is interesting about this Qur'anic prophecy is that shortly after Allah's prediction that Muhammad would return to Mecca, Muhammad tried to return to Mecca, and failed. Thereafter, he signed the Treaty of Hudaybiyyah, which all but guaranteed his return the following year.[89]

Bottom line, there is nothing spectacular about the self-fulfilling prediction that Muhammad would return to Mecca.

Qur'an 30. Another prophecy frequently cited in feigned evidence for Qur'anic eloquence is 30:1–5. Not only is this prophecy singularly unspectacular, but the language used by Allah is pedestrian at best:

Alif Lam Mim. The Roman Empire has been defeated—in a land close by: But they, (even) after (this) defeat of theirs, will soon be victorious— within a few years. With Allah is the Decision, in the Past and in the Future: On that day shall the Believers rejoice—with the help of Allah. He helps whom He will, and He is Exalted in Might, Most Merciful.

As with the previous prophecy, Allah's prediction here is but feigned eloquence. In what by any standard seems to be stilted prose, he predicts that after Rome is defeated (in an unspecified land) it will soon be victorious (in an unspecified number of years). Interestingly, in the notes of his Qur'anic translation, Muslim apologist Yusuf Ali argues that "a few years" (biḍ') designates "a period of from three to nine years."[90] However, as revered Muslim biographer Al-Tabari rightly observes, the Roman victory did not, in fact, fall within this time frame.[91] While it would be imprudent to interject myself into intramural Muslim debates, the overall point seems unassailable—namely, Allah's predictive prowess here is hardly miraculous.

Furthermore, variant readings of this passage exist in early Qur'anic manuscripts.[92] Thus, there is considerable question among Arabic linguists as to whether the text predicts further defeat or predicts further victory for the Romans. The beauty from a biblical perspective is that the wealth of biblical manuscripts empowers textual critics to ferret out copyist errors, allowing the autographs (originals) to emerge unscathed. The blight for Muslim scholarship is that textual criticism is strongly denounced under the guise that the Arabic Qur'an is a flawless rendition of a Mother manuscript housed somewhere in the seventh heaven.

Finally, Allah's prophecies are rendered even more unspectacular in that there is a very small window between the prophecy and its purported fulfillment. In the "Muhammad will return to Mecca" prophecy, only a year or so is in play, and in this one no more than a decade. How different the eloquence and exactness of biblical prophecies. For example, seven hundred years before Jesus was born, the prophet Micah prophesied that the birthplace of Messiah would be Bethlehem (Micah 5:2). Not just any Bethlehem, but Bethlehem Ephrathah on the outskirts of Jerusalem. Had Jesus been born anywhere other than Bethlehem Ephrathah, Micah's prophecy and consequently the whole of biblical prophecy would have been disqualified.

In sharp contrast, Allah's prophecies are rightly relegated to good guessing, common sense, or worse.

Qur'an 7. Thus far we have unmasked the feigned eloquence of two Qur'anic pseudo-prophecies. But there is a third. It involves Allah's assertion that long before he disclosed the Qur'an to Muhammad as the mother of all revelations, he divulged the coming of Muhammad—"the last and greatest of the Messengers of Allah"[93]—through the medium of the Christian Scriptures. Or, as Allah put it in Qur'an 7:157, "In *the Law* and *the Gospel.*"

In evidence that Allah had foretold the coming of Muhammad in the Law, Muslim apologists such as Yusuf Ali point to Deuteronomy 18 where God promises Moses that he will raise up "a Prophet *like you from among their brethren,* and will put My words in His mouth, and He shall speak to them all that I command Him."[94] However, as should be self-evident, the words *like you* and *from among their brethren* do not point to the coming of Muhammad but rather toward a line of prophets culminating in Messiah.[95] In fact, in his poignant and powerful proclamation at the portico of Solomon, Peter points back to these very words in evidence of Messiah as the last and greatest messenger of God (Acts 3:22–23).

In feigned confirmation that Allah had foretold the coming of Muhammad in the Gospel, Yusuf Ali points to John 14:16, in which Jesus tells his disciples, the Father "will give you another Helper [*parákletos*], to be with you forever" (ESV). Said Ali: "The Greek word *Paraclete* [*parákletos*] which the Christians interpret as referring to the Holy Spirit is by our Doctors taken to be *Periclyte* [*periklutós*], which would be the Greek form of Aḥmad [Muhammad; literally, Praised One]."[96] This, too, is self-evidently absurd.

First, archaeologists have now uncovered almost six thousand Greek New Testament manuscripts and not one of them renders *parákletos* as *periklutós*![97]

Furthermore, a quick look at the immediate context identifies the helper as the Holy Spirit. For as Christ goes on to tell his disciples,

"He [the Father] will give you another Helper, to be with you forever, even the Spirit of truth, whom the world cannot receive, because it neither sees him nor knows him. You know him, for he dwells *with* you and will be *in* you." (John 14:16–17 ESV)

Obviously, Muhammad was not *with* the disciples, nor was he *in* them.

Finally, as Jesus promised, the helper was to come in a matter of days, not in a matter of centuries (Acts 1:5).[98] (For further detail, see Major Muslim Misapprehensions on pages 154–55.)

Exaggerated Elegance

At this point, we have demonstrated that the arrangement of the Qur'an is atrocious (a wearisome confused jumble) and its prophetic prowess singularly unspectacular. As we will now demonstrate—its elegance, too, is grossly overstated. This is particularly so in that Allah makes the boast that the "Qur'an is not such as can be produced by other than Allah." In other words, no one but the transcendent Creator of all things could so much as imagine producing a book of such surpassing elegance. It is "a confirmation of (revelations) that went before it, and a fuller explanation." And to those who say, "*He [Allah] forged it?*" Allah has a challenge: "*Bring then a Sūrah like unto it, and call (to your aid) anyone you can, besides Allah, if it be ye speak the truth!*" (Q 10:37, 38).

Speaking the truth requires little more than to repeat with emphasis: *The emperor has no clothes!* To begin with, the notion that the Arabic Qur'an is an elegant and perfectly preserved copy of the "Mother of the Book" housed in the heavens is unadulterated nonsense. Truth be told, there never was an original copy of the Qur'an.

Since "contrast is the mother of clarity,"[99] it is profitable to contrast transmission of the Qur'an with that of the Bible. Early on, in the religio-political history of Islam, Uthman (third of the "rightly guided caliphs") commissioned the burning of variant versions of the Qur'an to establish a singular authorized version.[100] From then till now, discovery of manuscripts that survived the burning are not only not cherished, they're censored. The entire smoldering mess would have been unnecessary had there been a perfectly preserved copy to begin with.

By way of contrast, there was never a time in the ecclesiastical history of the New Testament that any person or group could determine its contents.

Instead, its books were written at various times and then copied and distributed. By the time anyone did obtain centralized power, the copies had long been buried in the sands of time.[101] While there is no such thing as a "Mother of the Book" in Christianity, we have something more—a treasure trove of manuscripts. The beauty from a biblical perspective is that the wealth of manuscripts empowers textual critics to credibly sort out copyist errors so that the autograph may emerge. (For further detail, see Major Muslim Misapprehensions on pages 141–44.)

Furthermore, as has been well documented, the elegance of the Qur'an is undermined by its grammatical imperfections. In his book *Twenty-Three Years: The Life of the Prophet Mohammad*, twentieth-century Muslim scholar Ali Dashti wrote:

> The Qor'ān contains sentences which are incomplete and not fully intelligible without the aid of commentaries; foreign words, unfamiliar Arabic words, and words used with other than the normal meaning; adjectives and verbs inflected without observance of the concords of gender and number; illogically and ungrammatically applied pronouns which sometimes have no referent; and predicates which in rhymed passages are often remote from the subjects. These and other such aberrations in the language have given scope to critics who deny the Qor'ān's eloquence. . . .
>
> More than one hundred Qor'ānic aberrations from the normal rules and structure of Arabic have been noted. Needless to say, the commentators strove to find explanations and justifications of these irregularities. Among them was the great commentator and philologist Mahmud oz-Zamakhshari [1075–1144], of whom a Moorish author wrote: "This grammar-obsessed pedant has committed a shocking error. Our task is not to make the readings conform to Arabic grammar, but to take the whole of the Qor'ān as it is and make Arabic grammar conform to the Qor'ān."[102]

Understandably, Dashti did not have the temerity to publish his observations during his own lifetime.

Finally, the supposed elegance of the Qur'an is undermined by a multitude of errors. One poignant example should suffice. It involves the well-circulated story of Jesus fashioning birds out of clay, breathing life into them and watching them fly away while yet a child of five. "I make for you out of clay, the figure of a bird, and breath into it, and it becomes a bird by Allah's leave: and I heal those born blind, and the lepers, and I quicken the dead, by Allah's leave; and I declare to you what ye eat, and what ye store in your houses. Surely therein is a Sign for you if ye did believe" (Q 3:49).

What is particularly noteworthy about this confabulated Qur'anic account is that it is a muddy mixture of truth and error. The reference to Christ's healing "those born blind and the lepers" as well as "quickening the dead" are consistent with the New Testament Gospels. The legendary bird tale, however, comes from a late gnostic gospel known as the Infancy Gospel of Thomas.[103] This same gospel portrays a vengeful Christ child killing another child that "dashed against his shoulder." Thereafter, Jesus struck the child's parents with blindness for saying to Joseph, "Thou that hast such a child canst not dwell with us in the village: or do thou teach him to bless and not to curse: for he slayeth our children."[104]

The point that should not be missed here is that the Muslim Allah cannot tell the difference between a questionable gnostic account and a legitimate Gospel account. Moreover, the character of Jesus as portrayed in the gnostic gospels is a far cry from the Jesus of the Bible. One is petulant. The other is perfect. How anyone, much less one who claims to be divine, can mistake the elegance of the Gospels with the boorishness of the gnostics is a mystery. It is likewise a mystery that anyone paying attention can remain convinced of Qur'anic elegance.

In sum, the Qur'an is clearly an unreliable revelation. It prostitutes the Bible, denies the deity of Christ, misrepresents the Trinity, repudiates the cross, and more. It is replete with faulty ethics, riddled with factual errors, and its eloquence is but feigned. Samuel Zwemer, a longtime Christian missionary in Arabia, said it best:

> Islam thrives only by its denial of the authority of the Scriptures, the deity of our Lord, the blessedness of the Holy Trinity, the cruciality and significance of the cross (nay, its very historicity), and the preeminence of Jesus Christ as King and Savior. And this great denial is accompanied

by the assertion of the authority of another book, the Koran, the eclipse of Christ's glory by another prophet, even Mohammed, and the substitution of another path to forgiveness and holiness for the way of the cross. These denials and assertions are imbedded in the Koran and are the orthodox belief of all who know anything of their religion.[105]

CHAPTER 3

SHARIA IS STATE, AND STATE IS SHARIA

Congress shall make no law respecting an establishment
of religion, or prohibiting the free exercise thereof; or
abridging the freedom of speech, or of the press; or
the right of the people peaceably to assemble, and to
petition the Government for a redress of grievances.
—FIRST AMENDMENT TO THE CONSTITUTION
OF THE UNITED STATES OF AMERICA

In his introduction to the *Encyclopedia of Islamic Law*, Professor Kevin Reinhart of Dartmouth College notes that "Islamic law has formed the spine of Islam throughout its history. It has given Muslims a sense of unity and recognition in cultures as heterogeneous as the Chinese and the African, the Soviet and the American. Its results, particularly in the realm of day-to-day morality, have impressed such diverse figures as Martin Luther and Edward Lane."[1]

Professor Reinhart was right to highlight Luther and Lane as being *impressed* by sharia (law of Allah), and wrong to leave the impression that they were positively impressed. Luther was anything but. Writing at a crucial juncture during the long and torturous struggle between Islam and Europe, Luther described Muhammad's Qur'an as "a foul and shameful book."[2]

The law of Allah, said Luther, is tantamount to the law of the sword.

> It is commanded in their law, as a good and divine work, that they shall rob and murder, devour and destroy more and more those that are round about them; and they do this, and think that they are doing God service. Their government, therefore, is not a regular rulership, like others, for the maintenance of peace, the protection of the good, and the punishment of the wicked, but a rod of anger and a punishment of God upon the unbelieving world.[3]

Luther was particularly sickened by sharia's impact on women. "Mohammed's Koran thinks nothing of marriage, but permits everyone to take wives as he will." Luther went on to declare that the law of Allah subjected women to the indignities of being "bought and sold like cattle. Although there may be some few who do not take advantage of this law, nevertheless this is the law and anyone can follow if he will."[4]

Edward Lane, Britain's beloved nineteenth-century Middle Eastern scholar, was not as negative toward the law of Allah as was Luther, but he was nevertheless nonplussed by "the tax that is taken from the free non-Muslim subjects of a Muslim government whereby they ratify the compact that assures them protection, as though it were compensation for not being slain."[5] On most other counts, he loved Egyptian culture. Though his research on Muslim women was significantly hindered by the sharia mandate on gender segregation, sharia culture permitted him to buy a little girl whom he would later make his wife. As noted by biographer Jason Thompson, when Lane departed Egypt, "he was accompanied by a little girl named Nefeeseh whom either he or his friend Robert Hay purchased in the Cairo slave market."[6]

As diverse as Luther and Lane were with respect to sharia, both highlight aspects of the law of Allah that are hugely problematic for civilization at large. Lane's writing reveals a worldview in which non-Muslims are subjected to paying a poll tax (*jizya*) as "compensation for not being slain," as well as a reminder of their inferior status. "Fight those who believe not in

Allah nor the Last Day, nor hold that forbidden which hath been forbidden by Allah and His Messenger, nor acknowledge the Religion of Truth, from among the People of the Book, until they pay the *Jizya* with willing submission, and feel themselves subdued" (Q 9:29).

For his part, Luther reminds us that the law of Allah advances not so much by word as by sword. "Fight and slay the Pagans wherever ye find them, and seize them, beleaguer them, and lie in wait for them in every stratagem (of war)" (Q 9:5). His indignation for the law of Allah respecting women should be ours as well. Not only does sharia sanction polygamy (Q 4:3), but it sanctions the possession of women as sex slaves (Q 33:50).

Sharia is ultimately rooted and grounded in the words of Allah and, as such, is unalterable. Disputes over interpretation are resolved by "the record of the Prophet Muhammad's normative action (*sunnah*) as recorded in the manifold volumes of *hadith*."[7] Sharia or divine Islamic law embodies the will of God for every aspect of society. As such, there is no real distinction between sharia and state. Sharia is state and state is sharia. In the words of Muslim enthusiast Karen Armstrong, "Like the religion of the very first *ummah* [Muslim community], the philosophy, law and spirituality of Islam were profoundly political."[8]

Sharia governs virtually everything, from personal conduct to how you worship, as well as legal matters and national governance. As the articulate ex-Muslim Ayaan Hirsi Ali has noted, sharia "is exacting and punishment-centered. It prescribes what to do with unbelievers, both infidels and those who stray from the faith. It even contains rules on what types of blows are permissible when a husband beats his wife."[9] And as Allah is not subject to adaptation, neither is sharia. "We put thee on the (right) Way of Religion: so follow thou that (Way) [sharia], and follow not the desires of those who know not" (Q 45:18).

In her book, *Cruel and Usual Punishment*, Egyptian-born author Nonie Darwish explained what it was like to grow up in Egypt under sharia law:

> For the first thirty years of my life, I lived as a virtual slave. I was a bird
> in a cage; a second-class citizen who had to watch what I said even to
> my close friends. Under Islamic law I had to live in a gender-segregated

environment and always be aware that the legal and social penalty for 'sin' could end my life.[10]

Darwish went on to explain that sharia "deals with all aspects of day-to-day life, including politics, economics, banking, business law, contract law, marriage, divorce, child rearing and custody, sexuality, sin, crime, and social issues. It makes no distinction between public and private life, treating all aspects of human relations as governable by Allah's law. The Sharia laws are based on the Qur'an and hadiths (sayings and example of the Prophet) as well as centuries of debate, interpretation, and precedent."[11] Said Darwish: "It allows a woman seen without a headdress to be flogged, punishes rape victims, and calls for beheading for adultery. I never questioned or challenged it—or dared to even think about its validity."[12]

While many today seek to find commonalities between sharia and Mosaic law, the contrast could not be starker. Though an avowed atheist, Hirsi Ali fairly noted the differences:

> Moses imparts a great many laws, governing everything from the removal of boundary stones to the muzzling of oxen, to prohibitions against marrying one's stepmother, to the punishment of stoning for the crime of idolatry. The difference is that no one invokes these passages in modern-day jurisprudence, and their prescribed punishments have long since been set aside. If there is one set of rules that is "timeless" in the Jewish Torah and the Christian Bible, it is the Ten Commandments, a relatively short list of prohibitions on killing, stealing, adultery, and so on.[13]

What's more, the aim of Mosaic law was to shape a compassionate, consistent, nondiscriminatory populace in which people trump possessions.

> There need be no poor people among you, for in the land the LORD your God is giving you to possess as your inheritance, he will richly bless you, if only you fully obey the LORD your God and are careful to follow all these commands I am giving you today. (Deuteronomy 15:4–5)

Even a cursory overview of Mosaic initiatives should suffice to moderate modern superiority complexes: do not be tightfisted but give generously and every seventh year forgive your debtors their debts (Deuteronomy 15); reserve the seventh year of the planting cycle for the poor among you (Exodus 23); leave the margins around your fields unharvested so that the needy are not deprived of food (Leviticus 19); exempt the poor from interest payments (Leviticus 25); every third year you must dedicate your Levitical tithe to the poor (Deuteronomy 14). In short, Israel was adjured to remember the harsh conditions of her own captivity in Egypt so that she would not likewise abuse the alien, the poor, or the downtrodden in her midst.[14]

Sharia, by contrast, demands a significantly different disposition toward foreigners and infidels. "Muhammad (SAW) is the Messenger of Allah, and those who are with him are severe against disbelievers, and merciful among themselves" (Q 48:29 *Hilali-Khan*). Why? Because from the perspective of sharia law, Jews, Christians, and pagans are inferior people. "Verily, those who disbelieve (in the religion of Islam, the Qur'an and Prophet Muhammad (peace be upon him)) from among the people of the Scripture (Jews and Christians) and *Al-Mushrikun* [idolaters] will abide in the Fire of Hell. They are the worst of creatures" (Q 98:6 *Hilali-Khan*).

Furthermore, as Hirsi Ali rightly notes, Mosaic law is time bound as opposed to timeless. And in contrast to the expansionism of sharia, Mosaic law was geographically bounded. It was for a particular people at a particular time in history.[15] Mosaic law is fulfilled in Jesus while in sharia, Muhammad is the last and greatest of the prophets. Unlike Muhammad, Jesus never commanded beheading infidels and oppressing women. Rather, he rightly elevated women[16] and taught his disciples that the meek would inherit the earth (Matthew 5:5).

Finally, while sharia applies to all people, in all places, at all times, Mosaic law has long since been abrogated. As such, it is more than a little messed up for pundits such as Barack Obama to say that Leviticus "suggests that slavery is all right and eating shellfish is an abomination."[17] To read anachronistic modern meanings into the Ancient Near Eastern word *slave* is hardly enlightened. In the New World a *slave* may have been a commodity or property denuded of rights and privileges. Not so in ancient Israel. There a *slave* was akin to a *subject* or a *servant*. As such, when a Christian calls herself a slave or bondservant of Christ, we do not for a moment mistake her meaning. While we would never call a modern presidential aid a slave, an ancient Israelite vassal king, with all the pomp and circumstance of monarchy, could so be designated. In other words, in ancient Israel *slavery* denoted subordination and social standing.[18]

Obama's mischaracterizations regarding shellfish are more subtle but equally misleading. He is right in suggesting that Leviticus characterizes the eating of shellfish as "an abomination." He is wrong in isolating this injunction from its historical context. The distinction between clean and unclean foods symbolized the difference between that which was holy and that which was unholy within the context of an ancient theocratic form of government. Consequently, from a New Testament perspective, it is as morally appropriate to eat shellfish as it is to eat steak.[19]

I would be remiss here if I did not explicitly address another canard raised ad nauseam ad infinitum by those who inappropriately put Mosaic law on the same footing as sharia.

> If a man happens to meet a virgin who is not pledged to be married and rapes her and they are discovered, he shall pay the girl's father fifty shekels of silver. He must marry the girl, for he has violated her. He can never divorce her as long as he lives. (Deuteronomy 22:28–29)

This, according to cultural elites, is nothing short of barbaric. In truth, however, the Mosaic law is hardly about letting a rapist off easy. If the woman was not engaged, the rapist was spared for the sake of the woman's security. Having lost her virginity, she would have been deemed undesirable for marriage—and in the culture of the day, a woman without a father or husband to provide for her faced a life of abject poverty, destitution, and social ostracism. As such, the rapist was compelled to provide for the rape victim for as long as he lived. Thus, far from barbaric, the law was a cultural means of protection and provision.

Additionally, there was precedent under Mosaic law for the victimized woman not to marry the victimizer if her father determined that she could be provided for in a more suitable manner (Exodus 22:16–17). Thus, the law was not designed to force the rape victim into an unbearable marriage, but to secure her future and that of her children. Neither then nor now is there a perfect resolution for a woman who has been violated through the horror of rape. Indeed, if we are completely satisfied by any earthly solution—even the death penalty—our moral sensibilities are seriously skewed. Ultimately, only eternity will make all wrongs right.[20]

The point here is that in place of reading anachronistic prejudices into Mosaic law, we would be well served to read the Bible synergistically. Just as former Speaker of the House Nancy Pelosi had no hope of comprehending the provisions of the Affordable Care Act apart from reading its two thousand–plus pages, so we do no justice to Mosaic law without careful consideration of its complexities. We can no more read New World realities into ancient Near Eastern legalities than we can read Mosaic legalities into New Testament realities.[21]

By contrast, sharia is considered by Muslims to be as valid today as it was fourteen centuries ago. To gain a perspective on what creeping sharia is like in the modern world, one need look no further than Brunei (Southeast Asia). In 2014, the Sultan of Brunei, Hassanal Bolkiah, announced his plans to impose sharia in three phases.

The first phase includes "fines and prison sentences for 'crimes' such as pregnancies outside of wedlock, propagating religions other than Islam, and not attending mandatory Friday prayers." The second phase includes "floggings and cutting off of hands for property offenses" and the third "stoning, for offenses like adultery, abortion, homosexuality/sodomy, and even blasphemy." All of this, said the Sultan, is to cohere to "Allah's command as written in the Qur'an."[22]

What Brunei is imposing on its citizens is standard fare in Muslim countries. Even conversion from Islam to Christianity, according to modern-day sharia, is punishable by beheading, hanging, or stoning. Lest anyone think that this is *radical* Islam, consider that of the more than one-and-a-half billion Muslims worldwide, a majority affirms the principles and precepts of sharia. Or as Hirsi Ali has well said, "Sharia has spread to a point where it has found near-universal acceptance across the Muslim world."[23]

The Pew Research Forum report titled "The World's Muslims: Religion, Politics and Society" documents that "solid majorities in most of the countries surveyed across the Middle East and North Africa, sub-Saharan Africa,

South Asia and Southeast Asia favor the establishment of sharia, including 71% of Muslims in Nigeria, 72% in Indonesia, 74% in Egypt and 89% in the Palestinian territories."[24] That's some fifty million Nigerian Muslims; a hundred and fifty million Indonesians; sixty million Egyptians; and another four million Palestinians. And that's just Nigeria, Indonesia, Egypt, and Palestine. The Pew report "includes data on every nation with a Muslim population of more than 10 million except Algeria, China, India, Iran, Saudi Arabia, Sudan, Syria and Yemen."[25] It is plausible to assume that similar proportions of people in those majority Muslim countries not surveyed also support sharia. Thus, it is safe to say that most Muslims worldwide want sharia—more than eight hundred million.[26] And, as we will now see, no demographic is more adversely affected by sharia than women.

WOMEN

No president in the history of America understood Islam better than Barack Obama. He quotes from the Qur'an with ease and fluidity and, having grown up in a Muslim context, has far more than an academic understanding of Islamic faith and practices and has had a tremendous impact on the modern Western narrative. At Cairo University, Obama noted that "as a student of history," he is in a unique position to understand "civilization's debt to Islam." With soaring rhetoric he articulated the progress that the world has experienced during Islam's fourteen centuries. And he noted that "throughout history, Islam has demonstrated through words and deeds the possibilities of religious tolerance and racial equality."[27]

Given his deeply held convictions concerning sharia's contributions to tolerance and equality, Obama is understandably distressed by those who fail to share his perspective on Islam. Speaking from a mosque in Baltimore, Maryland, he decried "distorted media portrayals" of Islam and news reports of terrorism in the wake of Muslim massacres. "I've had mothers write and say, 'my heart cries every night,' thinking about how her daughter might be treated at school. A girl from Ohio, 13 years old, told me, 'I'm scared.' A girl from Texas signed her letter 'a confused 14-year-old trying to find her place in the world.'" Obama insists we know the facts. "For more than a thousand years, people have been drawn to Islam's message of peace." Fact is, at least according to Obama, that "the very word itself, Islam, comes from *salam*—peace."[28]

The Qur'an, of course, does not define the word *Islam* as "peace."[29] And many who have experienced sharia first-hand do not share Obama's enthusiasm. This is particularly the case with women. While his heart aches for how Muslim girls are treated in school, their hearts ache for how girls are treated in sharia. What Obama lauds as a wonderful system of law and life, they loath as systematic oppression. Hirsi Ali is a classic case in point. In a chapter titled "Shackled by Sharia," she explained the horror of sharia for women:

> No group is more harmed by sharia than Muslim women. [Indeed,] women are considered under the code to be worth at most "half a man." Sharia subordinates women to men in a multitude of ways: the requirement of guardianship by men, the right of men to beat their wives, the right of men to have unfettered sexual access to their wives, the right of men to practice polygamy, and the restriction of women's legal rights in divorce cases, in estate law, in cases of rape, in court testimony, and in consent to marriage. Sharia even states that women are considered naked if any part of their body is showing except for their face and hands, while a man is considered naked only between his navel and his knees.[30]

As a student of history, Obama understands all of this and more. He is also well aware that Muslim women in the West are in no position to expose what many may consider hypocrisy. As Nonie Darwish made plain, Muslim women who complain about the inequities of sharia suffer untold consequences:

> The Qur'an, various hadiths, and Sharia all prescribe severe punishment for the rebellious woman. [She] can be beaten by her husband and ordered by the Sharia court to never leave the home without his permission in *beit al taa*, meaning "house of obedience," a practice that amounts to house arrest.[31]

When Darwish wrote about sharia law, she was not blowing smoke. Like Obama, she grew up in a Muslim context. What for Obama is tolerant, for Darwish was terrifying. From her vantage point, the thirteen-year-old girl who wrote to the president had a right to be scared. Scared not only because the then most powerful man in the world considered Islam enlightened but also because of what she would be subjected to under its legalities:

> A Muslim woman who commits adultery is to be stoned to death; unmarried girls who have sex must be flogged; women's testimony in court is half the value of a man; women get half the inheritance of a man; there is no community property between husband and wife; if a woman is killed, her indemnity money is half the indemnity money of a man; if her family follows Shafi'i law, then her clitoris must be removed at a young age—that is female castration in order for the man to make sure her sexual appetite is suppressed; she needs her guardian's permission for marriage or else it is void; she needs her husband's or male relative's permission for travel; she must cover all her body except her face and hands. . . .
>
> [In short,] while Islam claims respect for the woman's body, the laws do not support that claim. Sharia stones women for adultery, but men are not stoned for rape—such inequity contradicts any claims of Islam's honor of women.[32]

Indeed, inequity is the essence of the matter. Plainly put, sharia subjugates women in virtually every dimension of their lives.

Adultery

A hundred years ago Theodore Roosevelt, twenty-sixth president of the United States, spoke of the profundity of the Bible:

> Every thinking man, when he thinks, realizes what a very large number of people tend to forget, that the teachings of the Bible are so interwoven and entwined with our whole civic and social life that it would be literally, I do not mean figuratively, I mean literally impossible for us to figure to ourselves what that life would be if these teachings were

removed. We would lose almost all the standards by which we now judge both public and private morals; all the standards toward which we, with more or less of resolution, strive to raise ourselves.[33]

Modern perceptions of the Bible are markedly different. In a book titled *The Audacity of Hope: Thoughts on Reclaiming the American Dream*, Obama demonstrates remarkable disdain for the Christian Bible. Leviticus "suggests that slavery is all right" and Deuteronomy "suggests stoning your child if he strays from the faith," wrote Obama.[34] The implication of Obama's assertions is hard to mistake: Plainly put, the Bible is littered with significant error. No God worthy of worship would teach that slavery is okay. And no parent in his right mind would stone a child who strays from the faith.

The real danger here is a failure to apprehend the biblical text. Far from extolling the virtues of slavery, the Bible denounces slavery as sin. The New Testament goes so far as to put slave traders in the same category as murderers, adulterers, perverts, and liars (1 Timothy 1:10). And as previously noted, in the Old Testament, slavery was sanctioned due to economic realities rather than racial or sexual prejudices. While Scripture recognizes the reality of slavery, it never promotes the practice of slavery. In fact, Obama knows that it was the application of biblical principles that ultimately led to the overthrow of slavery, both in ancient Israel and in the United States of America.

To suggest that the Bible teaches parents to stone a child who strays from the faith is an equally disturbing mischaracterization of Deuteronomy. Its legal remedies are prescribed within the context of a theocracy—not modern times. As even the most cursory perusal of context makes plain, the son in question (not child) is morally culpable of extravagantly wicked behavior that threatens the health and safety of the entire community. The prescribed punishment was hardly for adolescent dissipation but adult degeneracy. Further, ratification by the elders precluded a precipitous judgment on the part of the parents. Thus, the standard of evidence prescribed by Mosaic law exceeds that of modern jurisprudence. For Obama to claim the moral high ground over the Bible is the height of duplicity. Particularly in that he has personally sanctioned the systematic slaughter of innocent *children* in the second or third trimester of fetal development[35]—children who clearly deserve protection rather than capital punishment![36]

All of this is hugely relevant to the matter at hand. In a story concerning Jesus handed down through the centuries by word of mouth, the teachers of the law brought a woman to Jesus who, to paraphrase Obama, had "strayed from the faith." They reminded Jesus that the law of Moses commanded stoning such women. Jesus replied, "If any one of you is without sin, let him be the first to throw a stone at her" (John 8:7). These words are consistent with the central message of Scripture in that Jesus both forgives and bears the punishment of sin.[37]

The contrast between Jesus and Muhammad could not be starker. In *Sahih Muslim*, a pregnant woman from Ghamid was brought to Muhammad. After she had confessed adultery, she begged the prophet for purification. Instead, after she had given birth to her child, he had her stoned. "She was put in a ditch up to her chest and he [Muhammad] commanded people and they stoned her."[38] This passage from *Sahih Muslim* is completely consistent with the central message of Muhammad. Speaking from the plain of Arafa during his final pilgrimage to Mecca, he said to devotees: "The adulterer must be stoned."[39]

Umar, Islam's second caliph, augmented the stoning edict of Muhammad saying, "Verily Allah sent Muhammad (may peace be upon him) with truth and He sent down the Book upon him, and the verse of stoning was included in what was sent down to him."[40] In keeping with Muhammad's example, sharia law does not permit a pregnant adulteress to be stoned, "until she gives birth and the child can suffice with the milk of another."[41] The only fornication that Muhammad permitted was that between a Muslim man and one of his slaves.[42]

Hirsi Ali tells the horrifying story of a thirteen-year-old girl in Somalia who was found guilty of adultery after reporting that she had been raped by three men. Unlike the thirteen-year-old girl from Ohio who told Obama that she was scared because someone might scorn her, Aisha Ibrahim Duhulow—named after the prophet Muhammad's nine-year-old wife—was dragged, screaming and flailing, into a stadium in Kismayo to be stoned:

> It took four men to bury her up to her neck in the hole. Then fifty men spent ten minutes pelting her with rocks and stones. After ten minutes had passed, there was a pause. She was dug out of the ground and two nurses

examined her to see if she was still alive. Someone found a pulse and breathing. Aisha was returned to the hole and the stoning continued.[43]

Following the sharia stoning, "a local sheik told a radio station that Aisha had provided evidence, confirmed her guilt, and 'was happy with the punishment under Islamic law.'"[44]

The tragic reality is that the practice of rape is inextricably bound to Muhammad's own personal conduct. It is difficult to imagine that Safiya voluntarily spent the night with Muhammad in his tent after he had brutally tortured and killed her husband Kinana. And in keeping with his example, the other women captives were raped and marketed as chattel.[45]

Beatings

Sahih al-Bukhari, one of the most trusted sources in Islam, recounts the plight of an abused woman who came to Muhammad and begged him to halt her husband's brutal beatings. Her skin was so badly bruised that it was green. Instead of putting a stop to the beatings, Muhammad afforded her a taste of prophetic wisdom. For wife beating to cease, all a woman need do is submit to her husband's sexual desires. Aisha was not so easily satisfied. The horrendous agony suffered by the unnamed woman prompted her to exclaim, "I have not seen any woman suffering as much as *the believing women. Look! Her skin is greener than her clothes!*"[46]

Aisha herself was no stranger to spousal abuse. She spoke openly about the pain she experienced when Muhammad the prophet of Allah struck her. As *Sahih Muslim* relates the occasion, it was Aisha's turn to spend the night with Allah's messenger. After perceiving that she had fallen asleep, the prophet got up and left the house. Aisha covered her head, put on her veil, tightened her waist wrapper and followed him. Being spooked by her shadow, Muhammad returned to the house. While Aisha was able to get back to bed before he arrived, her heavy breathing betrayed her. After confessing that she had indeed left the house without his permission, the prophet of Allah disciplined his young wife. "He struck me on the chest which caused me pain."[47]

Like Muhammad, Allah approves of wife beating. Long before Muhammad was born, he told Job to take a "green branch" and "beat" his wife with it (Q 38:44 *Shakir*).[48] Allah's reasoning was clear and unmistakable. If a man feared that his wife may desert him, he should first refuse to sleep with her. If that didn't do the trick, Allah prescribes scourging the rebellious woman. "As for those from whom ye fear rebellion, admonish them and banish them to beds apart, and scourge them" (Q 4:34 *Pickthall*). Commenting on this seminal verse, the distinguished Shafii scholar al-Tabari said that if disobedient wives "refused to repent, then tie them up in their homes and beat them until they obey Allah's commands toward you."[49]

Reliance of the Traveller: A Classic Manual of Islamic Sacred Law explicates the subtleties of sharia: "When a husband notices signs of rebelliousness in his wife (whether in words, as when she answers him coldly when she used to do so politely, or he asks her to come to bed and she refuses)," the first recourse is to warn the wife. "The warning could be to tell her, 'Fear Allah concerning the rights you owe to me,' or it could be to explain that rebelliousness nullifies his obligation to support her and give her a turn amongst other wives, or it could be to inform her, 'Your obeying me is religiously obligatory.'"[50]

If all such measures fail to bring the rebellious woman back to bed, sharia, in concert with the practice of Muhammad and the will of Allah, prescribes a beating—but only within limits. The husband "may not bruise her, break bones, wound her, or cause blood to flow."[51] In all, sharia mandates three basic steps—and if all else fails, a fourth: (1) Admonition, (2) Not sleeping in bed with her, and (3) If keeping from her is ineffectual, it is permissible for him to hit her. And if this fails to root out the rebellion, the fourth and final step may involve divorce.[52]

It should be emphasized that in order to appease Western sensibilities some English versions of the Qur'an gratuitously insert the adverb *lightly* to modify the verb *beat*. In point of fact, the adverb *lightly* simply does not appear in the original Arabic text. Moreover, it should go without saying that there are no circumstances in which it is ever permissible for a man to beat his wife—lightly or otherwise. Nor should sexual intimacy ever be forced.

Intimacy between a man and a woman has been aptly likened to the mysterious parable of Christ and his church. The husband is the image of Christ; the wife the image of the church. As Christ is sufficient to our every need, a husband is commanded to fulfill the needs of his wife. Unlike the Qur'an, the biblical notion of submission does not invoke a husband beating his wife but rather a husband sacrificing his rights for the sake of his wife.

> Husbands, love your wives, just as Christ loved the church and gave himself up for her to make her holy, cleansing her by the washing with water through the word, and to present her to himself as a radiant church, without stain or wrinkle or any other blemish, but holy and blameless. (Ephesians 5:25–27)

The husband is thus called to fulfill his wife—to understand her needs and to fill them. To esteem her satisfaction as greater than his own. To love his wife as his own body. "After all, no one ever hated their own body, but they feed and care for their body, just as Christ does the church" (Ephesians 5:29). A wife, likewise, is to fulfill the needs of her husband.

> The husband should fulfill his marital duty to his wife, and likewise the wife to her husband. The wife does not have authority over her own body but yields it to her husband. In the same way, the husband does not have authority over his own body but yields it to his wife. (1 Corinthians 7:3–4)

In the words of Thomas Aquinas,

> the man should give to his wife her conjugal rights, namely, with his own body through carnal union, and likewise the wife to her husband, because in this matter they are judged equal. Hence the woman was not formed from the feet of the man as a servant, nor from the head as lording it over her husband, but from the side as a companion.[53]

To fail to do so is called fraud, "because one is taking away what belongs to another."[54]

Nowhere in this equation is there a place for plural wives. And nowhere is there a place for beating. Christ must be the model. Certainly not Muhammad.

Captives

In August 2014, two months after the fall of Mosul, the second-largest city in Iraq, Muslim fighters captured Yazidi villages on the southern flank of Mount Sinjar in northern Iraq. *New York Times* foreign correspondent Rukmini Callimachi vividly described the horrors that unfolded in the aftermath of the conquest:

> Adolescent boys were told to lift up their shirts, and if they had armpit hair, they were directed to join their older brothers and fathers. In village after village, the men and older boys were driven or marched to nearby fields, where they were forced to lie down in the dirt and sprayed with automatic fire.[55]

What happened to women and children might truly have been worse. As chronicled in the Islamic State online recruitment tool *Dabiq*, "After capture, the Yazidi women and children were then divided according to the Sharī'ah amongst the fighters of the Islamic State who participated in the Sinjar operations, after one fifth of the slaves were transferred to the Islamic State's authority to be divided."[56]

Captives were sent "to Syria or to other locations inside Iraq, where they were bought and sold for sex." One of the captives, a twelve-year-old Yazidi child, was raped by a devout Muslim fighter who "took the time to explain that what he was about to do was not a sin. Because the preteen girl practiced a religion other than Islam, the Quran not only gave him the right to rape her—it condoned and encouraged it."[57] Sadly, the little girl is just one of thousands.

In December 627, fourteen hundred years prior to the time that the Yazidi captives were raped and murdered in Iraq, Muhammad and his fighters invaded the villages of the prosperous Banu Mustaliq Jewish tribe on the shores of the Red Sea between Jeddah and Rabigh. As chronicled in *Sahih al-Bukhari*, "The Prophet had suddenly attacked Bani Mustaliq without warning while they were heedless and their cattle were being watered at the places of water. Their fighting men were killed and their women and children were taken as captives."[58] As with the Yazidis, the Jewish men and boys murdered by Muhammad and his Muslim hordes were spared the unthinkable atrocities their loved ones were about to suffer. In accordance with the law of Allah, many were raped, others sold as chattel.

Though the Yazidi and Mustaliq atrocities bookend nearly fourteen hundred years of Islamic history, their treatment of female captives was virtually identical. Why? Because, as chronicled in *Dabiq*, what the Islamic State does in the twenty-first century is an authentic application of the teachings and practices of their prophet:

> Saby (taking slaves through war) is a great prophetic Sunnah containing many divine wisdoms and religious benefits, regardless of whether or not the people are aware of this. The Sīrah is a witness to our Prophet's (sall-allāhu 'alayhi wa sallam) raiding of the kuffār [unbelievers]. He would kill their men and enslave their children and women. The raids of the beloved Prophet (sallallāhu 'alayhi wa sallam) convey this to us. Ask the tribes of Banī al-Mustaliq, Banī Quraydhah, and Hawāzin about this.[59]

Sad to say, the claims of *Dabiq* correspond to reality. They are highlighted in both the unalterable law of Allah and the life and teachings of Muhammad, as embodied in the Sunnah and Sīrah:

> Enslaving the families of the kuffār and taking their women as concubines is a firmly established aspect of the Sharī'ah that if one were to deny or mock, he would be denying or mocking the verses of the Qur'ān and the narrations of the Prophet (sallallāhu 'alayhi wa sallam), and thereby apostatizing from Islam.[60]

According to sharia, women (and little girls) who are captives of war can be raped by their Muslim captors—and that according to one of the most trusted Muslim sources of all time. In *Sahih Muslim*, two of Muhammad's warriors discuss the proper way to engage in sex with the captives of Mustaliq:

> "We went out with Allah's Messenger (may peace be upon him) on the expedition to the Bi'l-Mustaliq and took captive some excellent Arab women; and we desired them, for we were suffering from the absence

of our wives, (but at the same time) we also desired ransom for them. So we decided to have sexual intercourse with them but by observing 'azl (withdrawing the male sexual organ before emission of semen to avoid conception). But we said: We are doing an act whereas Allah's Messenger is amongst us; why not ask him? So we asked Allah's Messenger (may peace be upon him), and he said: It does not matter if you do not do it, for every soul that is to be born up to the Day of Resurrection will be born."[61]

Here we have Muslim men practicing *coitus interruptus* because pregnant captives were not saleable ("we desired ransom for them"). And instead of telling his men that they shouldn't be raping their captives, Muhammad tells them that *coitus interruptus* is unnecessary because "every soul that is to be born up to the Day of Resurrection will be born." In other words, everything is theistically predetermined by Allah; therefore, there is no need to worry about getting your possessions pregnant and losing the desired ransom.

More appalling still is that the sanction for raping captives comes directly and specifically from Allah. Again and again he commands Muslim men to "guard their chastity, *except* with their wives *and the* (*captives*) whom their right hands possess—for (then) they are not to be blamed" (Q 70:29–30).[62] And, as noted in the classic manual of Islamic sacred law, *Reliance of the Traveller*, "When a child or a woman is taken captive, they become slaves by the fact of capture, and the woman's previous marriage is immediately annulled."[63]

This is precisely what happened to a beautiful young Jewish woman named Bara who was captured during Muhammad's massacre in Mustaliq. Bara's marriage to Musab Safwan was annulled, her name was changed to Juwayrah, and she was added to Muhammad's stable of wives and concubines.[64]

The Islamic State is right:

Enslaving the families of the kuffār and taking their women as concubines is a firmly established aspect of the Sharī'ah that if one were to deny or mock, he would be denying or mocking the verses of the

Qur'ān and the narrations of the Prophet (sallallāhu 'alayhi wa sallam), and thereby apostatizing from Islam.[65]

To justify the precepts of Allah and the behavior of his prophet, Muslim apologists invariably point to the Jewish treatment of female captives within the context of Old Testament theocratic law. Differences, however, are palpable. If, as was the case with Muhammad, an Israelite saw among the captives a beautiful woman and desired her, he must first allow her a months' time to lament the loss of land and loved ones. Furthermore, unlike Muhammad and his men, the Israelite was not permitted to have sex with a captive apart from marriage. Finally, under no circumstance was he permitted to sell her for ransom (see Deuteronomy 21:10–14).

More to the point, can anyone imagine Jesus saying or doing what Muhammad said or did? In a first-century culture in which women were relegated to the lowest rung of the socioeconomic ladder, Jesus elevated women to complete ontological equality with men.[66] And far from treating captives as chattel, the apostle Paul, who considered himself a bond-slave of Jesus, said, "There is neither Jew nor Gentile, neither slave nor free, nor is there male and female, for you are all one in Christ Jesus. If you belong to Christ, then you are Abraham's seed, and heirs according to the promise" (Galatians 3:28–29).

Far from being chattel, women were cherished by Christ.

Divorce

In a stunning chapter on marriage and divorce, Nonie Darwish displays an Egyptian Muslim marriage contract. The visual is more than disturbing. In the center of the contract is a section in which the bride is obligated to describe the *"condition of virginity,"* and the groom *"declares that he has no other wife or he has other wives as follows"*:[67]

Wife No 1-Name _____

Address _____ / _____ / _____

Wife No 2-Name _____

Address _____ / _____ / _____

Wife No 3-Name   _____

Address   _____ / _____ / _____

If all the blank spaces are filled out, the bride-to-be has an idea of what she is getting into. On the other hand, if one or more entries are blank, she knows that her husband-to-be has not yet exhausted all his options. The contract virtually screams, "You can be replaced." "It may be, if he divorced you (all), that Allah will give him in exchange Consorts better than you" (Q 66:5).

More daunting still is the process for getting a divorce:

> Under Shariah laws, instant, final divorce is the right of the husband only. And all it requires is to repeat the words "I divorce you" three times. Actually, verbalizing it is not even required. He can hold up a thumb and two fingers as he says it. He can also do it by sticky note, by leaving a message on an answering machine, and now, say the scholars, by e-mail or text messaging, thus bringing the seventh-century desert code of instantly getting rid of a wife into the twenty-first century. Sharia places no restraints on a man's divorcing his wife or wives, and no reason is required.[68]

For Darwish this is hardly humorous.

> Theoretically, he can get rid of his four wives and start a new cycle with four new wives plus 'slave wives.' There is even a law that states that final divorce takes place even if the husband divorces while intoxicated, under the influence of narcotics, or in pain of disease—or even in a joke.[69]

The possibility of a husband divorcing his wife "under the influence" or in anger or haste, and subsequently changing his mind gave rise to another disturbing Islamic fundamental. Here's how the classic manual of Islamic sacred law words it:

> When a free man has pronounced a threefold divorce, the divorced wife is unlawful for him to remarry until she has married another husband

in a valid marriage and the new husband has copulated with her, which at minimum means that the head of his erect penis fully enters her vagina.[70]

And just when you thought it couldn't get worse! Think about it. According to Islamic law, for reconciliation and remarriage to take place, a divorcée is forced to consummate a transitional marriage with a surrogate husband, be divorced again, and then, in humiliating fashion, return to her former husband who can, on a whim, dispense with her again. Such sharia insanity gave rise to the perverse phenomenon of overnight husbands. As Robert Spencer aptly put it, "After a husband has divorced his wife in a fit of pique, these men will 'marry' the hapless divorcee for one night in order to allow her to return to her husband and family."[71]

In sharia everything is definitively skewed in the favor of men. Only a man can initiate divorce; a man can regain custody of children after a woman completes the taxing task of nurturing them through the challenging prepubescent years—and if she should reject Islam, all bets are off.

> Many a Western woman married to a Muslim man has awakened one morning to find that her husband has disappeared with the children, taking them back to Iran, Saudi Arabia, or whatever his country of origin. He is perfectly within his rights to do so under Islamic law, and getting the children back is often impossible for these distraught mothers.[72]

The more you study the subject of divorce sharia style, the more a sense of uncleanness overwhelms you. Allah goes so far as to prescribe a husband's responsibilities in divorcing a prepubescent child. In other words, he sanctions divorcing a little girl who hasn't even had her period! "If you are in doubt concerning those of your wives who have ceased menstruating, know that their waiting period shall be three months. The same shall apply to those who have not yet menstruated" (Qur'an 65:4).[73] Had he wanted, Muhammad could have divorced Aisha either before or after she began menstruating.

Equally disturbing is the fact that organizations such as the Los Angeles-based Muslim Women's League had the temerity to pontificate that "Spiritual equality between men and women in the sight of God is not limited to purely spiritual, religious issues, but is the basis for equality in all temporal aspects of human endeavor."[74] Or as Egyptian Dr. Nawal el-Saadawi put it, "Our Islamic religion has given women more rights than any other religion has, and has guaranteed her honour and pride."[75]

This, of course, is politically correct propaganda.

Equality

What has been demonstrated thus far is that equality is conspicuous by its absence in Islam. This reality is forever enshrined in the inalterable words of Allah as well as in the practices of Muhammad, whom all Muslims (male and female) are bound to follow.

There is an exception. Allah allowed Muhammad many more wives than he allowed other men. In Sura 4:3 Allah, via Gabriel, told Muhammad that Muslim men may *"marry women of your choice, two, or three, or four"* whereas, in Sura 33:50 Allah provided Muhammad with divine sanction to marry *"any* believing woman who dedicates her soul to the Prophet if the Prophet wishes to wed her."

Contrary to Muslim apologists, Allah's decrees enshrine inequality. Unlike men, who can have up to four wives, Allah does not afford women the option to *"marry men of your choice, two, or three, or four."* Moreover, while Allah allows a husband to beat his wife, there is no Qur'anic provision for a wife to beat her husband. Nor can she initiate a divorce. Only men can do so, and that with relative ease.

All of this is tragic enough. But imagine, being referred to as *tilth.* "Your women are a tilth [field] for you (to cultivate) so go to your tilth as ye will" (Q 2:223 *Pickthall*).[76] In a blatant show of inequality, a man has unrestrained access to his wife's body. *Reliance of the Traveller: A Classic Manuel of Islamic Sacred Law* leaves little room for leeway: "It is obligatory for a woman to let her husband have sex with her immediately"—unless she is physically unable to endure it.[77] Or as Muhammad proffers, "the marriage vow most rightly expected to be obeyed is the husband's right to enjoy the wife's vagina,"[78] and should she refuse, "the angels send their curses on her till morning."[79]

Plainly put, there is no equality for women sorrowfully shackled by sharia.

WAR

Is Islam a religion of peace? Barack Obama left no doubt. Speaking from a mosque that once symbolized jihad, he argued that the word *Islam* itself means peace.[80] Madeline Albright, secretary of state under president Bill Clinton, was equally emphatic. "It cannot be said too often that Islam is a religion of peace."[81] This remarkable refrain was not relegated to any particular party or platform. It is chorused by George W. Bush[82] and former Secretary of State Colin Powell[83] and across the pond by British Prime Ministers Tony Blair[84] and David Cameron.[85] The words are repeated with predictable uniformity and appended by the platitude that Islamic terrorists have hijacked a religion of peace.

In concert with a chorus of voices declaring Islam to be peace not war, Islamic scholar Varun Soni, dean of religious life at the University of Southern California (USC), argues that the war as delineated by Islamic law is *internal* not *external*. On an Oprah series watched the world over, Soni claimed that "what jihad *actually* represents is an internal struggle, the battle that's raging in our own heart. And all of our religious traditions talk about that internal struggle. In that respect, jihad isn't just a Muslim idea but it's a reality of the human condition."[86]

Soni's contentions are seemingly buttressed by Gallup. "One thing is clear," said Gallup's International Bureau Chief Richard Burkholder. "Across the Ummah—Islam's global community of believers—the concept of *jihad* is considerably more nuanced than the single sense in which Western commentators invariably invoke the term." In asking the question, *"Jihad—holy war, or internal spiritual struggle?"* a majority of those polled said that *jihad* had "*no* explicit militaristic connotation at all."[87]

Had Ayaan Hirsi Ali participated in the Gallup poll when she was a teenager in Kenya, she might well have agreed:

> Every prayer, every veil, every fast, every acknowledgment of Allah signaled that I was a better person or at least on the path to becoming one. [This is] how jihad is generally first presented to most young Muslims—a manifestation of the inner struggle to be a good Muslim. It's a spiritual struggle, a path toward the light. But then things change.

Gradually, jihad ceases to be simply an inner struggle; it becomes an outward one, a holy war in the name of Islam by an army of glorious "brothers" ranged against the enemies of Allah and the infidel.[88]

Sharia confirms Hirsi Ali's contention. "*Jihad* means to war against non-Muslims, and is etymologically derived from the word *mujahada*, signifying warfare to establish the religion."[89] While sharia acknowledges that the greater jihad is "spiritual warfare against the lower self (nafs),"[90] most of sharia law is devoted to prescribing what it means to wage *war against non-Muslims*:

> The scriptural basis for jihad, prior to scholarly consensus . . . is such Koranic verses as: (1) "Fighting is prescribed for you" (Koran 2:216); (2) "Slay them wherever you find them" (Koran 4:89); (3) "Fight the idolaters utterly" (Koran 9:36); and such hadiths as the one related by Bukhari and Muslim that the Prophet (Allah bless him and give him peace) said: "I have been commanded to fight people until they testify that there is no god but Allah and that Muhammad is the Messenger of Allah, and perform the prayer, and pay zakat.[91] If they say it, they have saved their blood and possessions from me, except for the rights of Islam over them. And their final reckoning is with Allah"; and the hadith reported by Muslim, "To go forth in the morning or evening to fight in the path of Allah is better than the whole world and everything in it."[92]

I should emphasize here that these words are taken verbatim from *Reliance of the Traveller: A Classic Manual of Islamic Sacred Law* authored by Ahmad ibn Naqib al-Misri (AD 1302–1367) and endorsed by top modern-day Islamic scholars, including Dr. Taha Jabir al-'Alwani of the International Institute of Islamic Thought, and certified by the Sunni Muslim world's oldest and most prestigious institution of higher Islamic learning, Al-Azhar University (Cairo).[93] Moreover, since sharia ordinances find their origin in the Qur'an and the *Sunna* (*sira* and *ahadith*)—the words of Allah and the life and practices of Muhammad—they are not subject to change or alteration over time.

Clearly then, it is not the dark night of the soul that predominates sharia; it is the sharp edge of the sword. We do well to remember that Muhammad, the itinerant Meccan preacher, converted fewer than two hundred people by means of the word. Conversely, Muhammad, the Medinan warlord, conscripted more than a hundred thousand by means of the sword. Moreover, in the fourteen centuries that followed his death, Islamic warfare against the *kafirs* (unbelievers) has claimed the lives of at least a quarter of a billion non-Muslims—sixty million of whom were followers of Christ.[94]

There is no mistaking the centrality of violent jihad in sharia. When a devotee of Muhammad asked, "'What is the best deed?' he replied, 'To believe in Allah and His Apostle (Muhammad).' The questioner then asked, 'What is the next (in goodness)? He replied, 'To participate in Jihad (religious fighting) in Allah's Cause.'"[95] Some calculate as many as "35,213 Qur'an verses, hadiths, sharia laws, and various Muslim scriptures commanding and encouraging killing, violence, war, annihilation, corporal punishment, hatred, boycott, humiliation, and subjugation aimed mainly against non-Muslims."[96] What can be said with certainty is that thousands of such violent jihadist injunctions can be found in the authoritative Muslim sources.

In essence, the world, according to sharia, is divided into two domains, the house of Islam (*dar al-Islam*) and the house of war (*dar al-harb*)—those who already live under sharia, and those who are predestined to sharia subjection. And this is not radical Islam; it is just plain run-of-the-mill Islam. In evidence, *Dictionary of Islam* defines jihad (from the Arabic *jahada* meaning struggle or striving) as "a religious war with those who are unbelievers in the mission of Muhammad. It is an incumbent religious duty, established in the Qur'ān and in the Traditions as a divine institution, and enjoined specially for the purpose of advancing Islām and of repelling evil from Muslims."[97] And David Cook, renowned professor of religious studies at Rice University, further explained,

"Warfare with spiritual significance" is the primary and root meaning of the term as it has been defined by classical Muslim jurists and legal scholars and as it was practiced by Muslims during the premodern period. This meaning is sustained in the standard definition given in the new edition of the *Encyclopedia of Islam*: "In law, according to general doctrine and in historical tradition, the *jihad* consists of military action with the object of the expansion of Islam and, if need be, of its defense." This terse summary of Muslim law and history is the standard, scholarly one.[98]

Myriad non-Muslim dictionaries define jihad in similar fashion. *The American Heritage Dictionary* (fourth edition) delineates jihad as "A Muslim holy war or spiritual struggle against infidels;" the *Oxford Dictionary of Current English*, "A war or struggle against unbelievers;" and the online *Merriam-Webster Learner's Dictionary*, "a war fought by Muslims to defend or spread their beliefs."[99]

Sharia describes jihad as "a communal obligation,"[100] the objective of which is to invite infidels (Jews, Christians, et al.) "to enter Islam in faith and practice" or else pay "the non-Muslim poll tax (jizya)." If infidels neither convert nor pay, war is prescribed. "'Fight those who do not believe in Allah and the Last Day and who forbid not what Allah and His messenger have forbidden—who do not practice the religion of truth, being of those who have been given the Book—until they pay the poll tax out of hand and are humbled' (Koran 9:29)."[101]

What should be plain to all with eyes wide open is that the consensus of Muslim jurisprudence (the four Sunni schools of sharia Shafii, Hanafi, Hanbali, and Maliki—and the dominant Shi'a Sharia school Jafari) mandate holy war in the name of Allah as a moral imperative.[102] As the pioneering Maliki legal scholar Ibn Khaldun (1332–1406) put it, "In the Muslim community, the holy war is a religious duty, because of the universalism of the Muslim mission and (the obligation to) convert everybody to Islam either by persuasion or by force."[103]

This jihadi prescription was personified by the life of Muhammad, but tragically did not end there. In 633—the year following his death—Abu Bakr, first Muslim caliph, waged jihad on the Fertile Crescent,[104] the North African Coast, and parts of the Persian and Christian Greek Roman Empires. In 634, Umar, the second caliph, continued the pattern of expansion by the sword. He not only succeeded in subduing the entire Arabian Peninsula but looted central Syria as well.[105] In 635, Muslim warriors conquered Damascus as well as Pella,[106] which had provided refuge for Christians who had heeded Christ's warning to flee "when you see Jerusalem being surrounded by armies" prior to the destruction of Jerusalem in AD 70 (Luke 21:20).[107]

In 636, Muslim armies captured substantial sections of Iraq and "in a great battle in 637 at al-Qadisiyah (modern Kadisiya) in southern Iraq, the Sasanians [Persians] were decisively broken, opening the rich alluvial lands of Iraq to occupation by the armies of the Believers."[108] In and around 638, Jerusalem itself, epicenter of the Levant, fell victim to the Muslim juggernaut. The subjugation of the holy city solidified Islamic control of Palestine, from 638 to the time of the first crusade (1099). Muslims advanced into Egypt in 639 and, in 640, captured the city of Babylon (near modern Cairo). In 641, the major Christian Greek Roman city of Caesarea fell to Muslim aggression. Alexandria succumbed in 642 and, in 643, all of Armenia. And that was but the first decade following the death of Muhammad.

According to *The Oxford History of Islam,*

> by the mid-650s the Believers ruling from Medina had loose control over a vast area stretching from Yemen to Armenia and from Egypt to eastern Iran. And from various staging centers in this vast area, the Believers were organizing raids into areas yet further afield: from Egypt into Libya, North Africa, and Sudan; from Syria and northern Mesopotamia into Anatolia; from Armenia into the Caucasus region; from lower Mesopotamia into many unconsolidated districts in Iran and eastward toward Afghanistan and the fringes of Central Asia.[109]

Darío Fernández-Morera has rightly noted that primary Muslim and Christian chronicles are in concert with archaeology:

> In the second half of the seventh century, the Islamic Caliphate's armies from Arabia and the Middle East swept through North African coastal areas held by the Christian Greek Roman Empire (usually referred to as the Byzantine Empire). North Africa had been largely Christian territory since at least the early fourth century. This was the land of Tertullian (ca. 160–ca. 225) and Saint Cyprian (ca. 200–258) of Carthage, Saint

Athanasius of Alexandria (ca. 296–373), and Saint Augustine of Hippo (354–430).[110]

During the first half of the eighth century, Islamic forces crossed the Strait of Gibraltar, conquering Spain. Thereafter, they sacked Bordeaux in the southwest of France, burning churches along the way. "This time, however, the Islamic invaders were beaten. In what has become known as the Battle of Tours (or Battle of Poitiers, October 10, 732), a Frankish army led by the Franks' Christian leader (and de facto ruler), Charles Martel, defeated the Islamic forces."[111] The Islamic juggernaut would not seriously threaten Europe again

> until Muslim Turks defeated the Serbians at Kosovo in 1389 and captured Constantinople on May 29, 1453 (thus completing their destruction of the Christian Greek Roman Empire and the subjection of the Christian Greeks, which would last for four hundred years), and then moved through the Balkans to defeat the Hungarians at Móhacs in 1526 (fourteen thousand Hungarian soldiers were slain, and with the heads of prisoners, including those of seven bishops, the Turks built a mound as a warning to Christians who dared to resist) and finally reached the gates of Vienna in 1529 (Battle of the Siege of Vienna) and again in 1683 at the momentous Battle of the Gates of Vienna.[112]

September 11 of that year proved decisive in world history. Within mere decades of the death of Muhammad, the jihadi juggernaut had conquered Egypt, breadbasket of the ancient classical Christian world, as well as Syria, its brain.[113] By 711, Arab armies had defeated the king of Spain and, in less than ten years, controlled most of its territory. And if Jan Sobieski had not halted Muslim expansionism at the gates of Vienna on September 11, 1683, the whole of Europe would have fallen to Islam as well.[114]

As horrifying as Muslim atrocities themselves is the modern bent on refashioning fourteen centuries of Islamic history. Andalusia, in particular, has been recast as the golden age of Islam.[115] An age characterized by tolerance, multiculturalism, diversity, and peace. Barack Obama is effusive: "Islam has a proud tradition of tolerance. We see it in the history of Andalusia and Córdoba during the Inquisition."[116]

And he is not alone. Politicians, professors, and pundits of all stripes echo his sentiment. David Levering Lewis, two-time Pulitzer Prize winner and Julius Silver Professor of History at New York University, enthusiastically highlights Islam's "proud tradition of tolerance" by contrasting it with a narrative of Christian intolerance. In the Middle Ages two antipodal Europes emerged, said the professor, "one [Muslim Europe] secure in its defenses, religiously tolerant, and maturing in cultural and scientific sophistication; the other [Christian Europe] an arena of unceasing warfare in which superstition passed for religion and the flame of knowledge sputtered weakly."[117]

The former president, along with assorted professors and pundits, is hell-bent on presenting Islamic jihad as mental not martial. Thus, they recast Andalusia as a paradise in which Muslims lived in peaceful and tolerant harmony alongside Christians and Jews. This narrative is no longer the stuff of ivory tower elites. It has filtered down through all levels of society.

In his must-read volume *The Myth of the Andalusian Paradise: Muslims, Christians, and Jews under Islamic Rule in Medieval Spain*, Fernández-Morera lamented:

> Houghton Mifflin's *Across the Centuries* teaches children that *jihad* is an "inner struggle" that urges the faithful to "do one's best to resist temptation and overcome evil."[118] This view of *jihad* is now taught in many schools in the United States.[119] The publically funded and produced BBC hagiographic documentary *The Life of Muhammad* (2011), regularly broadcast by educational television stations in England and the United States, makes this claim as well.[120]

With tongue firmly planted in cheek, Fernández-Morera rightly exposes the absurdity of the narrative:

> It is certainly possible that, for centuries, the medieval Muslim scholars who interpreted the sacred Islamic texts, as well as Muslim military

leaders (including perhaps Muhammad himself when he led his armies into battle against infidels unwilling to submit), misunderstood (unlike today's experts in Islamic studies) the primarily peaceful and "defensive" meaning of "*jihad*," and that, as a result of this mistake, Muslim armies erroneously went and, always defensively, conquered half the known world. Or perhaps these conquering Muslim armies were, somehow, merely "exerting" themselves "to resist temptation and overcome evil."[121]

Putting satire aside, what should be self-evident to anyone interested in truth is that when the Maliki school of sharia, prevalent in medieval Spain, defines jihad, it does not do so in the context of "spiritual inner struggle" but rather as a holy war against the infidel.[122] In like fashion, Al-Shafii, who studied under Malik, delineates jihad as outward aggression, as do the Hanafi and Hanbali schools of sharia.[123] As such, rulers of the Andalusian paradise routinely beheaded prisoners of war and displayed the severed heads of victims as symbols of brutality and strength.

Fernández-Morera cites the tenth-century ruler Abd al-Rahman III, the first Andalusian Umayyad to proclaim himself caliph, as a classic case in point. Al-Rahman ordered the religious establishment in the mosques of Spain to read what follows to Muslim devotees:

Persecute them by all means available, send them your spies, make an effort to know their secrets and when it is clear that someone belongs to them [those who attack the Qur'an and the *ahadith*] write to the Caliph a list with their names, location, names of the witnesses against them and their accusations so that one may order to have them brought to the gate of al-Sudda and punished in their capital.[124]

Christian persecution in the Andalusian paradise was particularly hellish. The well-documented slaughter of Friday, March 2, 939, is but one noteworthy example. On that day one hundred Christians arrived at the Aljama mosque of Córdoba at the conclusion of Friday prayer, so that the Muslim faithful could witness the judgment of Allah in full bloom. "All the prisoners, one by one, were decapitated in his presence and under his eyes, in plain sight of the people, whose feelings against the infidels Allah alleviated, and they showered their blessings on the Caliph."[125]

Al-Rahman's decapitations were trumped only by mass crucifixions, and yet he was neither the most intolerant nor the most insidious. Muslim rulers martyred multitudes who, according to conscience, converted to Christianity. Students of history are all too familiar with the Martyrs of Córdoba who were brutally murdered for testifying to the divinity of Christ. Among myriad murderous Muslim magistrates was the notorious al-Mansur ("The Victorious") who "carried out nearly sixty successful *jihads* and ordered that the dust on his clothes be collected after each expedition against the hated Christians so that he could be buried under that glorious dust when he died."[126]

The question that begs an answer in light of the terror and intolerance exacted upon Christians by such well-known tyrants is why historically literate politicians such as Obama continue to peddle the myth of an Andalusian paradise. As Fernández-Morera notes, "It can hardly be explained by linguistic ignorance, since the primary medieval Latin, Spanish, Arabic, and Hebrew sources required for a good general understanding of Islamic Spain have been translated into accessible Western languages such as Spanish, French, English, and German, in some cases more than once."[127]

What it may be explained by is "what economists call 'stakeholder interests and incentives,' which affect the research of academics in the humanities no less and perhaps even more than those in the sciences."[128] There may be other significant factors in play as well:

Perhaps it has to do with what psychologists call "motivated blindness," which inhibits an individual's ability to perceive inconvenient data. Perhaps it has to do with the "innocence of intellectuals." Perhaps it is simply the result of shoddy research by a number of university professors repeated by many journalists. Or perhaps since the eighteenth-century Enlightenment the critical construction of a diverse, tolerant, and happy Islamic Spain has been part of an effort to sell a particular cultural agenda, which would have been undermined by the recognition of a multicultural society wracked by ethnic, religious, social, and political conflicts that eventually contributed to its demise—a multicultural society held together only by the ruthless power of autocrats and clerics.[129]

Perhaps what is really in play is a serious case of Christophobia. How else can one explain President Obama's gratuitous comparison of the Islamic State's current terrorism tactics with the "terrible deeds" committed by Christians during "the Crusades and the Inquisition"[130]—all the while failing to note that atrocities committed during the Crusades and Inquisition were despite Christian values, not because of them.

And as Obama must have surely known, in contrast to the Crusades, the atrocities committed by Muslims during fourteen centuries of jihad were directly mandated by Islamic law. Thus, if the brutality of the Islamic State is to be compared with anything, it would rightly be compared to crucifixions and beheadings during the Spanish inquisitions of al-Rahman.

Crusade historian Thomas Madden documents that after centuries of jihad, Muslims had "taken all of North Africa, the Middle East, Asia Minor, and most of Spain. In other words, by the end of the eleventh century the forces of Islam had captured two-thirds of the Christian world. Palestine, the home of Jesus Christ; Egypt, the birthplace of Christian monasticism; Asia Minor, where St. Paul planted the seeds of the first Christian communities: These were not the periphery of Christianity but its very core." Thus, "as far as unprovoked aggression goes, it was all on the Muslim side. At some point what was left of the Christian world would have to defend itself or simply succumb to Islamic conquest."[131]

In his classic monograph, *The Crusades, Christianity, and Islam*, Jonathan Riley-Smith underscored the transcendent distinction between jihad, as mandated by sharia, and just war theory, as delineated by centuries of Christian theology:

For more than 2,000 years of Western history, violence, whether expressed in warfare, armed rebellion, or the employment of force as a state sanction, and whether holy or merely licit, has required three criteria to be considered legitimate. First, it must not be entered into lightly or for aggrandizement, but only for a legally sound reason, which has to be a reactive one. Second, it must be formally declared by an authority recognized as having the power to make such a declaration. Third, it must be waged justly.[132]

In stark contrast, sharia mandates proactive and perpetual war against Jews and Christians: "First invite them to Islam, then invite them to pay the jizya (tax on Kafirs). If they reject conversion and the jizya, then attack them."[133] The consensus of Muslim jurisprudence, in concert with the will of Allah, mandates war as a "religious duty, because of the universalism of the Muslim mission and (the obligation to) convert everybody to Islam either by persuasion or by force."[134] Thus, when asked what to do with the crosses and sacred books of Christians defeated in jihad, Malik, one of the four principle figures of sharia, answered, "The [gold] crosses must be broken up before being distributed [as booty to the Muslim warriors] but one must not distribute them directly. As for their sacred books, one must make them disappear."[135]

In sum, the Islamic wars mandated by sharia, like imperialist and fascist wars, are not only unjust and illegitimate, they are a plague on the landscape of humanity.

WESTERN CIVILIZATION

Christians and Jews do not have to wonder what life in Western civilization might be like under sharia. They have already experienced it—in Spain. "From the conquest in 711, to its reduction to the small kingdom of Granada after 1248, to its final demise in 1492, religion was the law, and therefore Islam was the law."[136] During what is described as "the golden age of Islam," sharia dictated virtually every aspect of public and private life. Thus, in the Andalusian paradise there was no separation between sharia and state.[137]

Muslim clerics meticulously micromanaged virtually every aspect of human behavior, including . . .

whether donkey's milk should be drunk, or whether objects or water touched by Christians could be used for ritual purposes, or whether a

Muslim was allowed to wipe his hands on his socks after an ablution, or whether one could enter a mosque after eating garlic, or what hand should be used for eating and drinking, or what the correct punishment should be for having intercourse with one's wife during Ramadan, or the proper blood cost of a cut-off penis or testicle, or whether children should be allowed to enter a mosque (they should not).[138]

In this—the golden age of Islam—musical instruments were strictly forbidden. So was singing.[139] As stipulated by Andalusian law: "It is not lawful for you to deliberately listen to all of a falsehood nor to take pleasure in listening to the words of a woman who is not lawful for you nor to listen to musicians and singers."[140]

Where music and singing did exist in Andalusia, it did so not because of sharia stipulations but in spite of them. Had Islam prevailed in Western Europe, there would be "no Gregorian chant; no polyphony; no organs (which developed as part of Roman Catholic church music); no vocal and instrumental masses of Victoria, Bach, Mozart, and Beethoven; no symphonies; no operas; no great composers; and no jazz."[141]

Also unlawful in Islam were the artistic representations of human bodies—much less their dissection. Therefore, it was not Muslims who paved the path toward modern medical achievements but Western thinkers like the Belgian physician Andreas Vesalius, who not only broke new ground in the art and science of dissection but, in doing so, also advanced the accurate depiction of internal bodily organs. The plain fact is that Western civilization thrived on intellectual traditions that made medical and mathematical advancements feasible. Islam did not.[142]

As far as freedom of religion is concerned it simply did not exist. Much like in Saudi Arabia or Iran today, Christians under the control of sharia were not permitted to celebrate faith in the public square. The display of crosses and the ringing of church bells were strictly forbidden. And woe to anyone who dared proclaim that Jesus was divine or Muhammad a false prophet: "Whoever blasphemes against Allah or his Messenger, be he a Muslim or an unbeliever, must be killed, and the opportunity to repent must not be given to him."[143] In Córdoba (specially singled out by President Obama as the quintessence of tolerance), "Maliki authority Uthman Ibn

Kinana (d. 802) asserted that a ruler could choose what kind of punishment to administer for blasphemy, either beheading or crucifixion."[144]

Far from a portrait of Muslims, Jews, and Christians living in the midst of a peaceful Andalusian paradise of tolerance, non-Muslims were subjugated by the severity of sharia. The choice was simple: *shahada*, *subjugation*, or *sword*. Moreover, as Fernández-Morera has accentuated, lost in today's politically correct rhetoric is the tragic reality that Christians (and Jews) in medieval Spain

> *were by definition a subaltern group, a fourth- or fifth-class marginalized people in a hierarchical society*, and that they were the victims of *an extortion system, the* dhimma, *that gave them the choice that gangsters give to their victims: pay to be protected, or else.* [To suggest] that Christians might be "content" with their status in Spain, Greece, or elsewhere under medieval Islamic rule is even more preposterous than saying that American blacks might be "content" with their second-class citizenship under the tolerant white hegemony in certain areas of the United States prior to the twentieth-century civil rights movement, or perhaps even with their treatment by slave owners in the American South before the War of Secession, who often "made them part of the family."[145]

Were it not for Christian discontent with the trappings of Spanish sharia—including their extortion as *dhimmis*, treatment of women, and rank intolerance of anything other than doctrinaire Islam—there would have been no reconquest. And were there no reconquest, Spain today would more resemble North Africa or Iran than the Netherlands or Italy.

Indeed, if it were not for Christian resistance and reconquest, Spain simply would not—could not—have recaptured the richness of its heritage.

> After the Muslim occupation in the eighth century, it took many years for Christian Spain to develop the greatness of its own medieval Christian culture, with its rich lyric and narrative poetry, and its powerful Romanesque and Gothic architecture and sculpture. The process continued through the Renaissance and the Catholic Counter-Reformation, and culminated in the "Spanish Golden Age."[146]

The great danger today is that the reconquest of Spain is in real danger of being undone by a false narrative repeated again and again—a narrative that seeks to convince the uninitiated that the real golden age of Spain was Islamic as opposed to Christian. No one is more convinced than the former prime minister of Great Britain, Tony Blair, who said, "The standard-bearers of tolerance in the early Middle Ages were far more likely to be found in Muslim lands than in Christian ones."[147]

Former Republican presidential candidate Carly Fiorina is even more effusive in her espousal of medieval Islam. In her considered judgment, Islamic civilization from the year 800 to 1600 was "the greatest in the world." She claims Islam was responsible for keeping safe the treasuries of past knowledge alive and calls Islamic leadership enlightened: "It was leadership that harnessed the full capabilities of a very diverse population—that included Christianity, Islamic, and Jewish traditions. This kind of enlightened leadership—leadership that nurtured culture, sustainability, diversity and courage—led to 800 years of invention and prosperity."[148]

Of course, Blair and Fiorina are not alone. An endless number of modern politicians, professors, and pundits seem bent on perpetuating this narrative. Former president Barack Obama, for one, waxes eloquent regarding the "proud tradition of tolerance" and ominously warns Westerners against "impeding Muslim citizens from practicing religion *as they see fit.*" In Obama's world, impeding the religio-sociopolitical practices of Islam is nothing less than a manifestation of rank hostility: And "we can't disguise *hostility* towards any religion behind the pretence of liberalism."[149]

Behind the rhetoric of Obama lurks the ever-present specter of censorship. To question "the proud tradition" of sharia is now considered "hostility." And to impede "Muslim citizens from practicing religion *as they see fit*" is characterized as Islamophobia.[150] If consistent with his own dogmatism, Obama would have little tolerance for those who question the right of a Muslim man to hit a rebellious wife who refuses to allow him "*full lawful sexual enjoyment of her person.*" Why? Because in accordance with sharia ordinances, "*it is permissible for him to hit her if he believes that hitting her will bring her back to the right path.*"[151]

Ironically, what is in question now is no longer the hostility of the husband but the hostility of those who have the hubris to question the hostility of the husband hitting his wife. Obama could not have said it more clearly. Islam has a proud religious tradition that Muslims must be allowed to practice in the West *as they see fit*.

The problem with the premise, of course, is that Islam is far more than a religion. It is a comprehensive socioeconomic-political juggernaut riding on the rails of sharia. Moreover, it is a system of law and practices that, as Carly Fiorina maintains, has produced the greatest civilization in the history of the world. "The reach of this civilization's commerce extended from Latin America to China, and everywhere in between."[152] It is a civilization, said Fiorina, that was driven by invention:

> Its architects designed buildings that defied gravity. Its mathematicians created the algebra and algorithms that would enable the building of computers, and the creation of encryption. Its doctors examined the human body, and found new cures for disease. Its astronomers looked into the heavens, named the stars, and paved the way for space travel and exploration.[153]

And still she is not done. "When other nations were afraid of ideas, this civilization thrived on them, and kept them alive. When censors threatened to wipe out knowledge from past civilizations, this civilization kept the knowledge alive, and passed it on to others."[154] Put another way, when Western Europe was mired in the backward environs of the Dark Ages, it was the sharia culture that enlightened the world. In the Fiorina fairytale, Western civilization effectively lost touch with Greek philosophy and Roman learning. Were it not for the broadmindedness of sharia, the backwardness of Western Europe would have cast a dark shadow on progress and enlightenment.

This narrative, of course, is self-evidently false, as professor Thomas F. Bertonneau so eloquently elucidated:

> In the spasm of western Islamophilia that followed the terrorist attacks of 2001, the myth of medieval Muslim learnedness and medieval European illiteracy gained strong new power for the Left whose acolytes have disseminated it with vigor from their ensconcement in the colleges

and universities. Facts might have dispelled the myth had anyone cared to notice them. For one thing, Europeans never lost contact with the Byzantine Greeks, who blithely went on being scholarly classicists until Mehmet II bloodily vanquished Constantinople in 1453, slaughtering the literate elites and forcing the peasantry to submit to Allah.[155]

Far from being a bridge transmitting ancient erudition and knowledge westward, Islam has always posed a significant barrier. Were it not for the translation work of Aramean and Christian Arabs, the heritage of Athens and Jerusalem would most surely have died on the altar of sharia dogmatism. As documented by the venerable French historian Sylvain Gouguenheim, sharia jurisprudence was largely antagonistic to the spirit of Greek civilization—including "representational sculpture and painting, drama, narrative, lyric, and political theory and practice."[156] Gouguenheim's primary research makes it plain:

> Greek texts had not been "lost," to be graciously "discovered" and "transmitted" by the Islamic empire, but in fact had been preserved, transmitted, and commented upon in the Christian Greek Roman Empire (usually referred to as the "Byzantine" Empire); that the translations of Greek scientific and philosophical texts into Arabic were done by Greek-speaking Christians from the conquered lands of the Christian Greek Roman Empire; that Aristotle had been translated in France at the abbey of Mont Saint-Michel before translations of Aristotle into Arabic (via the Syrian of the Christian scholars from the conquered lands of the Christian Greek Roman Empire) surfaced in Islamic Spain; and that there was a continuity between Greek and European civilization, via the Christian Greek Roman Empire, that did not require Islam's appearance on the historical scene.[157]

What is noteworthy about Gouguenheim is that he was willing not only to follow the facts toward whatever conclusion they might lead but also to suffer the wrath of self-loathing cultural elites. He was immediately branded Islamophobic and racist. A committee was convened to investigate his work. He was forced to stop teaching medieval history at l'Ecole Normale Superieure de Lyon pending the results of an investigation.

His research "was considered so threatening to the educational estab-lishment that 'an international collective of 56 researchers in history and philosophy' found it necessary to sign an open letter, published in the Marxist newspaper *Libération*, attacking his work."[158] And that was just the beginning.

Among the milder scholarly epithets used to describe his book have been "ignorant" (*ignare*), "a polemic disguised as scholarship," "full of conceptual incoherence," "a diatribe," "a plundering book" (*sacca-geur*), "a work scientifically dishonest," "a dishonor to its publisher," "an amateurish work based on compilation and a priori assumptions," "a sad case," "a work of fear and hatred," "cultural racism," "embar-rassing," "discredited," "a dereliction of historical deontology," "a product of retrograde Catholic ideology," "not qualified to go against the consensus of specialists regarding medieval Islam and Christianity," and, of course, "Islamophobic" and part of a contemporary "scholarly Islamophobia" (*islamophobie savante*).[159]

Not one of the fifty-six academics who signed the open letter deemed it necessary to comment on the need to demythologize the myth of an Andalusian paradise or to comment on the draconian effect sharia has had on the women of medieval and modern history. Likewise, no one thought it necessary to comment on sharia mandates that have produced fourteen centuries of Islamic warfare.

Where is the outrage over the Muslims who are being martyred for converting to Christianity or the Christians who are being martyred for criticizing Muhammad? In place of anger there is accommodation—a dispo-sition among Western elites to appease. Some, like Rowan Williams, former archbishop of Canterbury and the most powerful person in the Church of England, going as far as to suggest that British law should accommodate sharia, beginning with laws on finance and marriage.[160]

In his insightful short monograph titled *Sharia Law for the Non-Muslim*, Bill Warner summed up the dilemma facing Western civilization begin-ning with Europe: "Europe is witnessing a rise in Islamic supremacism, demands for Sharia, and violent intimidation. Laws passed by European states, and resolutions in universities and other organizations have stifled free speech." Warner continued:

> Sharia tribunals operate in the UK, run by Islamists who openly defend a man's "right" to use violence against his wife. In the UK and Denmark, "Sharia controlled zones" have been declared, and in Germany, "Sharia patrols" roam city streets attempting to impose Sharia norms. [All the while] the establishment's response shows more concern with preventing discussion of these facts, than in confronting them.[161]

While there is little likelihood that Muslims in places like Iran and Saudi Arabia will dispense with sharia, Western elites must come to their senses and insist that Muslims abdicate sharia practices that militate against Western jurisprudence. And as Ayaan Hirsi Ali has emphatically emphasized, "Under no circumstances should Western countries allow Muslims to form self-governing enclaves in which women and other supposedly second-class citizens can be treated in ways that belong in the seventh century."[162]

CHAPTER 4

LEVANT

Crossroads of World History

*Throughout the last three millennia, the Levant
has seen the emergence and assertion of world
religions, the ebb and flow of mighty empires, and
the dramatic rise and fall of strange, exceptional
little states. World powers repeatedly confronted one
another in the region, from Pharaonic Egypt and
Assyria to the United States and Soviet Russia.*[1]
—PROFESSOR WILLIAM HARRIS

In the classic volume *The Levant: A Fractured Mosaic*, William Harris
defines the expression *Levant* as "an Italian-derived word originating with traders from the medieval Italian city-states. It meant 'the point where the sun rises,' and referred to the eastern Mediterranean. It implied a source of light, possibly evoking the antiquity of civilization in the eastern Mediterranean, or the presence of the Holy Land."[2]

The modern Levant, essentially the western rim of the Fertile Crescent, is today occupied by "Israel, Syria, Lebanon, and Jordan, in addition to the Palestinian Arabs of the West Bank and the Gaza Strip, and the Republic of Turkey on the northern margins." It is "the geographical center of the Middle East and the Arab world, and from the seventh century C.E. onward it became critical for the geographical continuity of Islamic civilization between Asia and Africa."[3] As a "land bridge linking three continents— Europe, Asia, and Africa"—the Levant has been "the stage for some of the principal events of human history. The region was the source of the two great monotheistic religions—Judaism and Christianity. It therefore also supplied the foundations for the third—Islam."[4]

As the link between Eurasia and Africa, the Levant is of surpassing significance to what are commonly thought of as the three great Abrahamic religions. For the Jews, the Levant entails the region in which God promised to make Abram a great nation through which "all peoples on earth will be blessed" (Genesis 12:3). For Christians, the Levant embodies the place where the promises God made to Abraham are ultimately fulfilled in "one person, who is Christ" (Galatians 3:16). And for Muslims, the Levant encompasses the sacred stone from which Muhammad ascended through the seven rings of heaven to greet Abraham and subsequently become the first and only human to stand in the presence of Allah.

SIGNIFICANCE OF THE LEVANT TO JEWS

Two thousand years before Jesus was born in Bethlehem, God told Abram to leave his ancestral home in Basra (southern Iraq). "The LORD said to Abram, 'Go forth from your native land and from your father's house to the land that I will show you'" (Genesis 12:1).[5] God's promises to Abram as preserved in the Jewish Torah are not merely memorable but poignantly paradigmatic:

> "I will make of you a great nation,
>   and I will bless you;
> I will make your name great,
>   and you shall be a blessing.
> I will bless those who bless you,
>   and whoever curses you I will curse;

and all peoples on earth
will be blessed through you." (Genesis 12:2–3)[6]

When Abram was ninety-nine years old, God reiterated his promise:

"You shall no longer be called Abram, but your name shall be Abraham,
for I make you the father of a multitude of nations. I will make you
exceedingly fertile, and make nations of you; and kings shall come forth
from you. I will maintain My covenant between Me and you, and your
offspring to come, as an everlasting covenant throughout the ages, to be
God to you and to your offspring to come. I assign the land you sojourn
in to you and your offspring to come, all the land of Canaan, an everlasting holding. I will be their God." (Genesis 17:5–8)[7]

Ironically, the only portion of the promised land Abraham ever took
possession of was a cave in Hebron where he buried his wife Sarah. And
even then he did not assume it by virtue of the promise but through payment
of the value. Thus, when Ephraim the Hittite offered the land to Abraham as
a gift, he responded, "If only you would hear me out! Let me pay the price
of the land; accept it from me, that I may bury my dead there" (Genesis
23:13).[8] Thus, for the sum of four hundred shekels of silver "the field with
its cave passed from the Hittites to Abraham, as a burial site" (v. 20).

The promise of God regarding the land was not relegated to Abraham.
During a time of great famine, he reiterated the promise to Abraham's son
Isaac:

"I will assign all these lands to you and to your offspring, fulfilling the
oath that I swore to your father Abraham. I will make your descendants
as numerous as the stars of heaven, and give to your descendants all
these lands, so that all the nations of the earth shall bless themselves by
your offspring—inasmuch as Abraham obeyed Me and kept My charge:
My commandments, My laws, and My teachings." (Genesis 26:3–5)[9]

In like fashion, God confirmed the promise to Jacob in a riveting dream
at Bethel. Jacob, whose name God would change to Israel (Genesis 32:29),

saw a stairway that extended from earth to heaven and heard the voice of God saying,

"I am the LORD, the God of your father Abraham and the God of Isaac: the ground on which you are lying I will assign to you and to your offspring. Your descendants shall be as the dust of the earth; you shall spread out to the west and to the east, to the north and to the south. All the families of the earth shall bless themselves by you and your descendants." (Genesis 28:13–14)[10]

The land promises God made to Abraham were fulfilled when Joshua led his physical descendants into Palestine. As the book of Joshua records, "The LORD gave to Israel the whole country which He had sworn to their fathers that He would assign to them; they took possession of it and settled in it." Indeed, said Joshua, "Not *one* of the good things which the LORD had promised to the House of Israel was lacking. Everything was fulfilled" (Joshua 21:41, 43).[11] Even as the life ebbed from his body, Joshua reminded the children of Israel that the Lord had been faithful to his promises. "Acknowledge with all your heart and soul that *not one* of the good things that the LORD your God promised you has failed to happen; they have all come true for you, *not a single one has failed*" (23:14).[12]

Solomon was equally unambiguous. "Praised be the LORD who has granted a haven to His people Israel, just as He promised; not a single word has failed of all the gracious promises that He made through His servant Moses" (1 Kings 8:56).[13] At the height of the Solomonic kingdom, "Judah and Israel were *as numerous as the sands of the sea*; they ate and drank and were content. Solomon's rule extended over all the kingdoms from the Euphrates to the land of the Philistines and the boundary of Egypt" (4:20–5:1).[14]

Tragically, Solomon's peaceful and prosperous rule ended in idolatrous scandal and strife. As he grew old, "his wives turned away Solomon's heart after other gods." He "followed Ashtoreth the goddess of the Phoenicians, and Milcom the abomination of the Ammonites" (1 Kings 11:4–5)[15]. He played fast and loose with the covenants and decrees of the Almighty. Therefore, the Lord spoke to Solomon saying, "Because you are guilty of this—you have not kept My covenant and the laws which I enjoined upon you—I will tear the kingdom away from you and give it to one of your servants" (v. 11).[16]

The word of the Lord took on foreboding reality when Ahijah, the prophet of Shiloh, "took hold of the new robe he was wearing and tore it into twelve pieces. 'Take ten pieces,' he said to Jeroboam. 'For thus said the LORD, the God of Israel: I am about to tear the kingdom out of Solomon's hands, and give you ten tribes. But one tribe shall remain his—for the sake of My servant David and for the sake of Jerusalem, the city that I have chosen out of all the tribes of Israel'" (1 Kings 11:30–32).[17]

Thus, after but a century (1031–931 BC) of relative peace and prosperity, a united kingdom was torn in two. In accordance with the prophecy of Ahijah, a nation that had flourished under the rules of Saul, David, and Solomon became a divided kingdom—Israel (the ten tribes to the north) ruled by Solomon's subordinate Jeroboam, and Judah ruled by Solomon's son Rehoboam. In 722, Assyria conquered the northern kingdom of Israel and assimilated the ten tribes into Assyrian culture. Not long after, Babylon enslaved the southern kingdom of Judah (beginning in 606) and demolished Solomon's temple (586).

It wasn't until 539 BC that Cyrus, king of Persia, conquered Babylon and decreed that the Jews be permitted to "go up to Jerusalem that is in Judah and build the House of the LORD God of Israel, the God that is in Jerusalem" (Ezra 1:3).[18] As such, seventy years after its destruction, the temple was rebuilt under the leadership of Ezra and Nehemiah and later enlarged under the Roman Herod at the time of Christ. A mere ten years after the completion of its restoration, however, the second temple was destroyed by Titus and the Roman army (AD 70).[19]

The destruction of the temple brought an end to the age of sacrifice for Jews. As such, Judaism now finds expression in Torah study rather than temple sacrifice. Orthodox Judaism is today largely known for its strict dedication to the eternal and unalterable Mosaic law as reinterpreted by rabbis. Only through devotion to this complex code of Jewish law (*halakhah*) can one experience nearness to God. Orthodox Jews await a rebuilt temple, and a Jewish messiah who will restore the Levant to Israel.

As within other religious constructs there are many variations within

Judaism. In Reform Judaism human autonomy trumps the authority of *halakhah*. As a movement that arose in the eighteenth century, Reform Judaism seeks to adapt to the modern world in order to preserve Jewish identity amid pressures of assimilation. While many within the Jewish Reform movement are grateful to have a democratic ally in the Middle East, "the sanctity of Jewish life takes precedence over the sanctity of Jewish land."[20]

For its part, Conservative Judaism (historical) is a late nineteenth-century reaction to the liberal tendencies inherent in Reform Judaism. As such, Conservative Judaism forges a middle way between Orthodox Judaism and Reform Judaism. On the one hand, adherents embrace modern culture. On the other, they observe Jewish laws and customs without the fundamentalist fervor of the Orthodox.

In addition to broad categories of Judaism, such as Reform, Conservative, and Orthodox mentioned above, there are ultra-orthodox groups, such as Neturei Karta (Guardians of the City), which, as their core value, strongly oppose the Jewish resettlement of Palestine. During a speaking engagement at the Iranian University of Tehran, I spent considerable time with two such ultra-orthodox rabbis (Rabbi Weiss and Rabbi Rosenberg) who were dead set against Jewish resettlement in Palestine because the land was defiled and must be cleansed by the coming of a Jewish messiah. They passionately communicated their conviction that Zionism had perverted pure Judaism through establishment of a Jewish state in the Levant beginning in 1948. Weiss and Rosenberg pointed to the dismantlement of apartheid in South Africa as an example of how Israel must be pressured by people of conscience to transform Israel into a genuine secular democracy with equal rights for all peoples regardless of religion or race.

Contrarily, for cultural Zionists, such as Benny Morris, Jewish professor of history at Ben-Gurion University of the Negev in Be'er Sheva, the Zionist slaughter that began with the 1948 establishment of a Jewish state in the Levant is an eminently defensible cruelty. In a book titled *The Birth of the Palestinian Refugee Problem, 1947–1949*, Morris gives his perspective on the Semitic horror that unfolded on the western outskirts of Jerusalem at Deir Yassin. Before the day had ended, "some 250 Arabs, mostly non-combatants, were murdered; there were also cases of mutilation and rape. The surviving inhabitants were expelled to Arab-held East Jerusalem."[21]

In clinical fashion, Morris unmasks "the Zionist murders, terrorism, and ethnic cleansing that drove 600,000–750,000 Palestinians from their homes in 1948."[22]

While Professor Morris condemned these rapes and murders as war crimes, he expressed no moral outrage against the expulsion of hundreds of thousands of Palestinians: "There are circumstances in history that justify ethnic cleansing." Moreover, "a Jewish state would not have come into existence without the uprooting of 700,000 Palestinians." If there was a serious historical mistake in 1948, said Morris, it was that David Ben-Gurion, first and third prime minister of the state of Israel, "got cold feet" and did not complete the job of cleansing the land of Palestinian people. "He should have done a complete job."[23]

Eight years before Israel was formally founded in 1948, Joseph Weitz, director of the Jewish National Land Fund, asserted that there was not enough room in Palestine for both Jews and Arabs. "If the Arabs leave the country, it will be broad and wide open for us. If the Arabs stay, the country will remain narrow and miserable. The only solution is Israel without Arabs. There is no room for compromise on this point."[24] Israel's first prime minister, David Ben-Gurion, was equally direct when he wrote, "We will expel the Arabs and take their place."[25]

In a book titled *Whose Land? Whose Promise? What Christians Are Not Being Told about Israel and the Palestinians*, Dr. Gary Burge, professor of New Testament at Wheaton College in Chicago, recounts a story of an Arab peasant and an official at the Israel Lands Administration:

> "How do you deny my right to this land? It is my property. I inherited it from my parents and grandparents, and I have the deed of ownership." The official replied, "Ours is a more impressive deed; we have the deed for the land from Dan [in the far north] to Elat [in the far south]." Another official was paying a peasant a token sale price for his land. Holding the peasant's property deed, the official remarked, "This is not your land; it is ours, and we are paying you 'watchman's wages,' for that is what you are. You have watched our land for two thousand years, and now we are paying your fee. But the land has always been ours."[26]

Israeli Prime Minister Benjamin Netanyahu put it plainly, "Our claim to this land is based on the greatest and most incontrovertible document in creation—the Holy Bible."[27] As such, he is committed to building Jewish settlements in occupied territories of the Levant.

SIGNIFICANCE OF THE LEVANT TO CHRISTIANS

Like Netanyahu, authentic Christians appeal to the Holy Bible as the greatest and most incontrovertible document in creation. Unlike Netanyahu, however, they are strongly opposed to using the biblical text as a pretext. The Old Testament, to which Netanyahu appeals, plainly refutes the idea that the land promises God made to Abraham apply to the present Levant.

In the aftermath of Israel's exile in Babylon, Nehemiah extolled the faithfulness of God in fulfilling the land promises he made to the patriarchs. As the temple was being rebuilt, he entreated the Almighty to bless Judah and return it to its former glory. If ever there was a time to adjure God to fulfill an as yet unfulfilled promise, this would have been the time. Yet far from appealing to the Abrahamic covenant as a reason for God to restore Judah to the land, Nehemiah humbly acknowledged that the loss of the land was due to the sin of the people of Israel, not to faltering faithfulness on the part of God.

In his impassioned prayer, Nehemiah praised the Lord for faithfulness to the Abrahamic covenant. "You found [Abraham's] heart faithful to you, and you made a covenant with him to give to his descendants the land of the Canaanites, Hittites, Amorites, Perizzites, Jebusites and Girgashites. *You have kept your promise because you are righteous*" (Nehemiah 9:8).[28]

As with the Levitical law, in a thoroughly biblical worldview, the promises concerning the Levant find ultimate fulfillment in the Lord. Thus, when the disciples asked, "Lord, are you at this time going to restore the kingdom to Israel?" (Acts 1:6), Jesus reoriented their thinking from a restored Jewish state in the Levant to a kingdom that knows no borders or boundaries. "My kingdom," he reiterated before Pilate, "is not of this world" (John 18:36).

The writer of Hebrews makes clear that the rest the descendants of

Abraham experienced when they entered the land is but a type of the rest we experience when we enter an eternal relationship with the Lord. The Levant provided temporal rest for the *physical* descendants of Abraham; the Lord provides eternal rest for the *spiritual* decedents of Abraham. As such, the Levant was never the focus of our Lord; rather, our Lord is forever the focus of the Levant.[29]

As Nehemiah made plain, the promises God made to Abraham *were* fulfilled when the children of Israel took possession of the promised land, *are* typologically fulfilled in the Lord who is the locus of the land,[30] and *will be* fully consummated when paradise lost is reconstituted as paradise restored.

Canaan is thus typological of a renewed cosmos. Accordingly, Abraham, like Isaac and Jacob, viewed living in the Levant in the same way that a stranger views living in a foreign country. For, as the writer of Hebrews makes plain, "He was looking forward to the city with foundations, whose architect and builder is God" (Hebrews 11:10). As Abraham looked beyond binding borders and boundaries to a day in which the meek would "inherit the earth," so, too, do those who place their faith in Abraham's royal seed.

The quintessential point of understanding for John and the rest of the disciples began to dawn at the time of his post-resurrection appearances. They had expected Jesus to establish Jerusalem as the capital of a sovereign Jewish empire. The notion was so ingrained in their psyches that even as he was about to ascend into heaven they asked: "Lord, are you at this time going to restore the kingdom to Israel?" (Acts 1:6).

Jesus not only corrected their erroneous thinking but also expanded their horizons from a tiny strip of land on the east coast of the Mediterranean to the farthest reaches of the earth. "You will receive power when the Holy Spirit comes on you"—said Jesus, as he was about to be taken up into heaven—"and you will be my witnesses in Jerusalem, and in all Judea and Samaria, *and to the ends of the earth*" (Acts 1:8).[31]

Scripture underscores the reality that Abraham was not to be the father of *a* nation but the father of *many* nations through whom all the world would be blessed (Genesis 17:5). When God promised Abraham "I will bless those who bless you, and whoever curses you I will curse; and all peoples on earth will be blessed through you" (Genesis 12:3), such blessings and cursings pertain not simply to the faithful remnant of ethnic Israel, but to true Israel, which consists of every person who through faith has been adopted into the family of God.[32]

Just as God's promise to Abraham was fulfilled when the gospel went out from Jerusalem to all the earth, so God's promise to David that one of his descendants would sit on the throne forever (see 2 Sam 7:11–16; Isaiah 9:7) was fulfilled when Christ, the "Son of David" (Matthew 1:1; 12:23; 21:15; Luke 1:32), ascended to the throne of the heavenly Jerusalem and established his rule and reign over all the earth.[33]

Paul illustrates this heightened fulfillment when he figuratively contrasts Sarah with Hagar:

> These things are being taken figuratively: The women represent two covenants. One covenant is from Mount Sinai and bears children who are to be slaves: This is Hagar.
>
> Now Hagar stands for Mount Sinai in Arabia and corresponds to the present city of Jerusalem, because she is in slavery with her children. *But the Jerusalem that is above is free, and she is our mother.*" (Galatians 4:24–26)

In saying this, Paul emphasizes that all who fixate on Eretz Israel (the greater Levant) are in slavery to types and shadows. Conversely, all who recognize that the shadow of the land has found fulfillment in the Lord are set free to inherit the earth.[34]

There are, of course, those in the Christian community who, like Benjamin Netanyahu, remain convinced that the promises God made to Abraham, Isaac, and Jacob with respect to the land are unconditional and as yet unfulfilled. Accordingly, such Zionists are convinced that Israel will soon control not only the West Bank and Gaza but also Iraq, Jordan, Lebanon, Syria, and even the northern portion of Saudi Arabia. They contend that for God's promises to Abraham to be fully fulfilled, Israel must yet control an area of land roughly thirty times its present size.[35]

This, however, is far from true. Abraham was not promised a country thirty times its present size. He was promised the cosmos! As Paul, apostle to the Gentiles, underscores, "Abraham and his offspring received the promise that he would be *heir of the world*" (Romans 4:13). Thus, while Zionists hyperventilate over tiny areas of land, including the West Bank and Gaza, God promises true Israel the globe.[36]

What this means is that while the Levant continues to have archaeological, historical, and sentimental significance for Christians, it no longer drives the eschatological dreams of those faithful to the main and plain teachings of historic Christianity.

SIGNIFICANCE OF THE
LEVANT TO MUSLIMS

Midnight, May 14, 1948, was a watershed moment for Zionist aspirations in the Levant. What Theodor Herzl (d. 1904), the person most responsible for galvanizing Zionism into a cohesive cultural movement, and John Nelson Darby (d. 1882), the priest most responsible for growing Zionism into a cohesive Christian movement, dreamed of was finally a tangible reality. As World War I drew to a close, British statesman Arthur James Balfour (d. 1930) wrote a letter to British baron Lord Rothschild effectively committing Britain to a Jewish homeland in the epicenter of the Levant. Balfour believed the formation of a Jewish homeland, which happened to coincide with the best interests of British foreign policy, would be the key that unlocked the door of the biblical framework of prophecy.[37]

While Zionists were thrilled that the Jews had regained an anchor in the Levant, they were perplexed with respect to its borders. Even more perplexing was the fact that Jews did not control the Holy City and had not been able to reinstitute Old Testament sacrifices in a rebuilt temple on the site where the Muslim Dome of the Rock and al-Aqsa Mosque now stood. All that changed June 10, 1967. The state of Israel launched preemptive attacks on Egypt, Syria, Iraq, and Jordan, and within six days occupied the Golan Heights, Gaza, the Sinai, the West Bank, and—most importantly—Jerusalem.[38]

On Wednesday, June 7, the Israeli Defense Forces (IDF) entered the Old City through the Lion's Gate and took control of Temple Mount. They bulldozed the area fronting the Western Wall.

Three days later, two hundred thousand Jews filled the newly created plaza to celebrate the holiday of Shavuot. For even secular Jews, the recapture of Jerusalem was a religious experience. For centuries, Jews had been praying at their annual Passover Seder that it would be celebrated "next year in Jerusalem." The desire to occupy Jerusalem's Old City was seared into Jewish consciousness, for many the most powerful symbol of Jewish identity and peoplehood.[39]

Paradoxically, from the time of Jerusalem's destruction in AD 70 to the time that Constantine made Christianity the official religion of the Roman Empire, Jerusalem had lost much of its significance. It would not play a major role in world history again until the fourth century when Constantine's mother, Queen Helena, refocused the attention of the Roman world on Jerusalem as the holy site of Jesus' crucifixion, burial, and resurrection.[40]

Constantine, in concert with his mother's wishes, transformed Jerusalem into a destination point for Christian pilgrimages. He built breathtaking basilicas over the sacred sites and, in concert with Christian convictions, left the Temple Mount in ruins. "For obvious reasons, Christians had no interest in rebuilding the temple, which the death and resurrection of Jesus had superseded in importance. Under Christian auspices, then, the Temple Mount became the garbage dump for the Holy City."[41]

All of that changed with the seventh-century advent of Islam. Jerusalem was captured by Caliph Omar Ibn al-Khatab and became a major focus in the Islamic world.

Omar, the second caliph after Mohammad, asked the Christian patriarch where the temple had stood. When he arrived at the Temple Mount, he was shocked to find that it was a rubbish heap. He ordered it cleared and built a mosque at its southern end, where today's Al-Aqsa mosque now stands. In 691 Caliph Abd al-Malik ibn Marwan constructed the Dome of the Rock over the rocky outcropping believed to be the site of the two Jewish temples.[42]

The rocky outcropping on which the Dome of the Rock now stands has transcendent significance for Muslims. It is at once the place where God called Abraham to sacrifice Ishmael[43] and the place to which Buraq, a mulish beast with a human head and the tail of a peacock, transported Muhammad during the infamous night journey. With alleged swiftness Buraq carried Muhammad "from the Sacred Mosque to the Farthest Mosque" (Q 17:1). There, Muhammad ascended through seven heavens into the presence of Allah.

The Dome of the Rock, bedecked by eighty kilograms of gold, is now the most recognizable landmark of the Levant. The Muslim message reflected from its gold-gilded dome is unmistakable—Islam is the culmination of Judaism and Christianity, and Muhammad is the climax of the prophets. From its initial military advances throughout the arid wilds of the Arabian Peninsula, to its subjugation of the Levant, Islam's purpose has never varied: to bring Judaism, Christianity, and all else into the house of Islam.

No Muslim institution is more deeply committed to this global vision than the Islamic State of Iraq and al-Sham (ISIS) or the Islamic State of Iraq and the Levant (ISIL). Consequently, after Abu Bakr al-Baghdadi conquered the northern city of Raqqa, Syria, in March of 2013, he christened it the capital of a new Islamic caliphate. A year later, he ominously dropped the last two letters of the acronym. No longer would his Islamic juggernaut be known as the Islamic State of Iraq and the Levant. Henceforth, it would be the Islamic State—a caliphate bent on ruling the earth. Ayman al-Zawahiri, Egyptian-born physician and successor to Osama bin Laden's al-Qaeda terrorist network, summed up the significance of the Levant for Muslims:

> It has always been my belief that the victory of Islam will never take place until a Muslim state is established in the manner of the Prophet in the heart of the Islamic world, specifically in the Levant, Egypt, and the neighboring states of the Peninsula and Iraq; however, the center would be in the Levant.[44]

CHAPTER 5

ISLAMIC STATE

Return of the Caliphate

*It is not an accident that several thousand Saudis have
joined the Islamic State or that Arab Gulf charities
have sent ISIS donations. It is because all these Sunni
jihadist groups—ISIS, Al Qaeda, the Nusra Front—are
the ideological offspring of the Wahhabism injected by
Saudi Arabia into mosques and madrasas from Morocco
to Pakistan to Indonesia. And we, America, have never
called them on that—because we're addicted to their
oil and addicts never tell the truth to their pushers.*[1]
—THOMAS L. FRIEDMAN, PULITZER PRIZE–WINNING JOURNALIST

Hilary Clinton was adamant! "Whether you call them ISIS or ISIL, I refuse to call them the Islamic State, because they are neither Islamic or a state."[2] Barack Obama and John Kerry were of the same opinion. Why? Because, in lockstep with Clinton, they cling tenaciously to the dogma that the teachings and practices of the Islamic State—founded under the leadership of Abu Bakr al-Baghdadi, holder of a PhD in Qur'anic Sciences[3]—have nothing whatsoever to do with what they hold to be the "religion of peace."

What is more, in the considered opinion of the Obama administration, the Islamic State does not pose a particularly significant problem to Western civilization. As he famously opined in 2014, "I think there is a distinction between the capacity and reach of a bin Laden and a network that is actively planning major terrorist plots against the homeland versus jihadists who are engaged in various local power struggles and disputes, often sectarian."[4]

By way of illustration, Obama compared ISIL—his preferred acronym for the Islamic State—to a junior varsity basketball team. "The analogy we use around here sometimes, and I think is accurate," opined the former commander-in-chief, "is if a jayvee team puts on Lakers uniforms that doesn't make them Kobe Bryant."[5]

Long before Obama's condescending caricature, the twenty-first–century junior varsity of global Islamic jihadism had amassed fighters and weaponry in proximity to Syria's border with Turkey. Then, in March of 2013, they seized the northern city of Raqqa, and would make it capital of a new Islamic caliphate.[6]

While all of this was junior varsity to Obama, it has proved nothing short of a mass genocide for Middle-Eastern Christians. As noted by author and journalist Mindy Belz, "The Islamic fighters took captive those Christians who didn't flee, turning their churches into mosques and holding cells, forbidding crosses, Bible reading, and prayer in public, and demanding the Christians pay in gold a *jizya* in exchange for 'protection.'"[7]

With jaundiced viciousness, the junior varsity "constructed crosses in a central square by attaching two-by-fours to light poles, and there they hung their victims crucifixion style."[8] Yet this was but the beginning:

> The holding cells in Raqqa and Aleppo housed American hostages, too, including journalist James Foley, who would be beheaded in public videos designed to taunt the United States. Children, according to a UN fact-finding mission, were "killed or publically executed, crucified, beheaded, and stoned to death." The team also reported "the capture of young girls by [ISIS] for sexual purposes. Girls as young as twelve."[9]

Despite the widespread carnage, the message telegraphed by the Obama administration was crystal clear. The United States was not ready to engage a junior varsity terrorist organization. Thus, the Islamic State continued a rapid ascent to the apex of Islamic jihadist networks, its ominous shadow radiating from Raqqa to the far reaches of the globe.

As the Islamic State continued its ominous ascent to the apex of Islamic jihadist movements, governments around the world bitten by the political-correctness bug continued in a state of denial. Rather than own up to the reality that the Islamic State had long transcended Iraq and the Levant (ISIS), they continued to conjure up language that diminished the global reach and aspirations of the Islamic State. The foreign minister of France, Laurent Fabius, was hell-bent in his predilection for relegating the most powerful modern global Islamic jihadist network in history to the Arabic acronym Daesh (ad-Dawlat al-Islamiyah fi al-Iraq wa sh-Shams).[10] John Kerry followed suit.[11] Of one thing they were certain. Daesh had nothing to do with Islam because the former is committed to brutality; the latter to peace.

Whether some future Islamic jihadist network eclipses the Islamic State to such an extent that it appears junior varsity by comparison remains to be seen. What is not in question is that from its very beginnings, Islam has sought to create the house of Islam (dar-Islam)—an Islamic state that subjects the whole of humanity to the horrors of sharia.

What that entails are a caliphate, a caliph, and cobelligerents willing to pledge their lives and sacred fortunes to taking the seventh-century dream of a worldwide Muslim theocracy and transforming it into a twenty-first-century eschatological reality.

CALIPHATE

Had the Ottoman Empire succeeded in 1683, when it besieged the gates of Vienna, Europe today might well be Eurabia. Instead, beginning September 11 of that year, the Ottoman caliphate experienced humiliating defeat at the hands of Jan Sobieski, a king willing to abandon all that was dearest in order to halt advance of the caliphate.[12]

From that day onward, the Ottoman Empire began a precipitous decline, until on March 3, 1924, Mustafa Kemal abolished the caliphate altogether,

banishing the last remaining caliph. Kemal, who famously took on the sur-
name Atatürk (literally *"Father Turk"*), summed up all that is Islam as the
"theology of an immoral Arab"[13] and set himself to the task of founding a
secular Turkish state out of the ruins of the caliphate.

> [He] closed all religious courts and schools, prohibited the wearing of
> headscarves among public sector employees, abolished the ministry of
> canon law and pious foundations, lifted a ban on alcohol, adopted the
> Gregorian calendar in place of the Islamic calendar, made Sunday a
> day of rest instead of Friday, changed the Turkish alphabet from Arabic
> letters to Roman ones, mandated that the call to prayer be in Turkish
> rather than Arabic and even forbade the wearing of fez hats. Mustafa
> Kemal's government espoused industrialization and adopted new law
> codes based on European models. "The civilized world is far ahead of
> us," he told an audience in October 1926. "We have no choice but to
> catch up."[14]

Atatürk was certain that Islam had seen its heyday. "Islam, this theology of an immoral Arab, is a dead thing," he opined. "Possibly it might
have suited tribes of nomads in the desert. It was no good for a modern
progressive State."[15] Atatürk was right in asserting that Islam is no good for
a modern progressive state. He was dead wrong in supposing it was dead.
Islam has not only survived his abolition of the caliphate, it has thrived.

Today, Islam has surpassed Christianity as the fastest-growing religion
in the world. And as Pat Buchanan argues in the *New York Times* bestseller
Suicide of a Superpower, Islam is uniquely poised to reshape and replace
Christianity in the West.

> First, with a more robust birth rate, its population is growing, while
> that of the West is declining. Second, immigration is bringing Islam
> back to Europe, five hundred years after its expulsion from Spain and
> three centuries after the retreat from the Balkans began. Millions have
> come to fill spaces left empty by aging, dying, and aborted Europeans.
> Third, as there was once a church militant, there is today a mosque
> militant.[16]

To put it plainly, "not one post-Christian nation has a birth rate sufficient to keep it alive."[17] John Paul II summed it up succinctly, "A nation that kills its own children is a nation without hope."[18] The Christian West faces an inescapable reality. "When the faith dies, the culture dies, the civilization dies, and the people die. This appears less a bold prediction of what may happen than a depiction of what is happening now."[19]

To compound the population problem is an acute persecution problem. In the West, Christians face the specter of militant secularism. No one has depicted this reality better than the brilliant author and essayist Mary Eberstadt. In a book titled *It's Dangerous to Believe*, she soberly noted that the "C for *Christian* has become the new scarlet letter."[20] In evidence, Eberstadt cited hundreds of alarming anecdotes:

The high school football coach suspended in Washington state in 2015 for kneeling to say a prayer at the end of a game;[21] the American military chaplains who claim to have been reassigned on account of their faithfulness to traditional Christianity;[22] the small business owners working in the wedding industry at a time when vindictiveness in the name of the sexual revolution is apparently boundless;[23] the Christian staffer at a day-care center who would not address a six-year-old [girl] as a [boy], and was fired on account of it;[24] the teacher fired in New Jersey for giving a curious student a Bible;[25] and related cases in which acting on religious conviction has been punished, at times vehemently.[26]

Yet all of this is but the tip of the Muslim spear. While Christians are being marginalized in the West, they are being martyred in the East. In Iraq, a vast majority of Christians have been either executed or exiled. "In Mosul, Iraq, one of the oldest Christian communities in the world, almost every Christian in the city fled after ISIS offered exile or death, according to the *Washington Post*; churches across Iraq now stand empty."[27] The same is true in Syria. "Jean-Clément Jeanbart, the Greek Melkite Catholic archbishop of Aleppo, Syria, reports that the terrorist group ISIS has almost wiped out Christians in that country altogether."[28]

Added to the population and persecution problem is the propaganda problem. Over and over and in myriad ways, the West is being seduced into believing that Islam is a religion of peace and tolerance. Conversely, that Christianity is a crusader religion, and as such, the epitome of intolerance.

Consider, as just one example, the Hollywood movie *Kingdom of Heaven*.[29] Capitalizing on historical illiteracy, *Kingdom* portrays Muslims as benevolent and broadminded; Christians as bloodthirsty and boorish. Nowhere is there even the faintest hint that in contrast to Islam, Christianity does not sanction permanent jihad to submit all nations to Christ. Nor is there any contextualization of the crusades as a defensive response to almost half a millennium of global Islamic jihadism.[30]

Instead, cultural elites including presidents, politicians, professors, and pundits persistently position previous Islamic caliphates as exemplary periods of peace and tolerance in which Muslims lived in harmony with People of the Book. More alarmingly the collective rhetoric of social commentators is not merely Islamophilic but manifestly Christophobic. Obama's gratuitous comparison of current Islamic jihadism with "terrible deeds" committed by Christians during "the Crusades and the Inquisition" is particularly appalling.[31] What is glaringly absent from the Christophobic rhetoric is that, in contrast to Islam, such "terrible deeds" were in spite of Christian values, not because of them.

The not so subtle undertone of Obama's message, now echoing from West to East, is that culture under the caliphate clearly outshines culture under Christianity. This propaganda, in concert with previously discussed population and persecution dynamics, has created a convenient context for the reestablishment of an Islamic caliphate that Atatürk declared "a dead thing."

Lost in all of the pandering and propaganda is the inviolate truth that if Islam is anything at all it is theocratic. Qur'anic theology recognizes no separation between sharia and state. Only that sharia is state and state is sharia. Conversely, Jesus underscored separation of church and state with the words, "Give back to Caesar what is Caesar's and to God what is God's" (Matthew 22:21). When the disciples asked him if he was going to establish a Jewish theocracy, he reoriented their thinking from a restored Jewish state to the kingdom "not of this world" (John 18:36; see Acts 1:1–10).

This is hardly insignificant. In contrast to Christianity, the caliphate reborn is preeminent in Islamic theology and thinking. From the abolishment of the Ottoman caliphate by Atatürk in 1924 to the present, one Muslim group after the other has sought its reenactment by means of global Islamic jihad.

This was the message of Sayyid Qutb (1906–1966), who was convinced that Christianity had faltered in the West because it had prostituted oneness (*tawhid*) in God and government through bifurcation of the sacred and the secular. Qutb, who joined the Muslim Brotherhood founded by Hasan al-Banna a mere four years after Atatürk's abolition of the caliphate, rose to prominence as its leading ideologue. His short monograph, *Milestones*, transcended the Brotherhood to become a global field manual for jihadism the world over. In it, Qutb repeatedly underscores the inviolate Islamic mandate to reinstitute the global end-time caliphate.[32]

Of one thing Qutb was certain. Separation of sharia and state imposed by the modern Republic of Turkey was anathema. Writing after the last caliph had been unceremoniously ushered out of Istanbul, Qutb called on all true Muslims to return to the principles of a totalitarian Islamic theocracy in which mere Islamic tradition is trumped by the pure and unadulterated principles of the Qur'an. "Islam knows only two kinds of societies," scrawled Qutb from the confines of an Egyptian prison cell, "the Islamic and the *jahili*. The Islamic society is that which follows Islam in belief and ways of worship, in law and organization, in morals and manners. The *jahili* society is that which does not follow Islam."[33]

For Qutb, the only antidote to moderate Muslims were militant Muslims willing not only to keep infidels from controlling sacred Muslim territory but also to overthrow the West through violent Islamic jihadism. Qutb would not live to see his dream become reality. In 1966, he was executed for his role in a conspiracy to assassinate the second president of Egypt, Gamal Abdel Nasser. His legacy, however, lives on in the minds of Muslim militants across the globe. As ably articulated by Dr. Sebastian Gorka, internationally recognized authority on counterterrorism and author of *Defeating Jihad*, the message encapsulated in *Milestones* has not only served to shape the thinking of the Muslim Brotherhood, but has become "an essential text of Al Qaeda and other key jihadi groups."[34]

In concert with the aims of the Muslim Brotherhood, al-Qaeda—its reckless ideological descendant—has morphed into a "global terror network with cells in more than fifty countries and affiliates and sympathizers in many more. Under the millionaire bin Laden and the prestige of the Al Qaeda brand, jihad was once again redefined to fit a new mission." That of taking "the fight to the heart of the infidel, striking not military targets such as troop convoys or attack helicopters [in Muslim strongholds such as Afghanistan] but civilians in downtown New York, Washington, Fort Hood, or Boston."[35] Al-Qaeda's crowning accomplishment would be the havoc wreaked on American soil during 9/11; its overarching objective, however, has remained reestablishment of the caliphate.

Behind bin Laden's jihadi successes stood the shadowy figure of Sheikh Abdullah Azzam (d. 1949) who more than any other person in modern history was responsible for rejuvenating the concept of global Islamic jihad in the minds of the Muslim masses. "Those who met Azzam were dazzled by his spellbinding oratorical skills, his capabilities as a military strategist, his religious leadership, and his interminable energy"[36]—all of which he used effectively to galvanize myriad Muslims around the al-Qaeda brand.

In one infamous missive delivered to devotees in Kansas (1988), he spelled out his conspiratorial contention that Jews and Christians were primary obstacles to rebirth of the caliphate:

Today, humanity is being ruled by Jews and Christians. The Americans, the British and others. And behind them, the fingers of world Jewry, with their wealth, their women and their media. The Israelis have produced a coin on which it is written "we shall never allow Islam to be established in the world."[37]

In another speech appropriately called the "First Conference of Jihad" given at the Al-Farook Mosque in Brooklyn, New York, in 1988, he ominously pontificated that "every Moslim on earth should unsheathe his sword." Azzam's reasoning was unapologetic and straightforward: "Jihad means fighting. You must fight in any place you can get. Whenever jihad is mentioned in the Holy Book, it means the obligation to fight. It does not mean to fight with the pen or to write books or articles in the press or to fight by holding lectures."[38]

Little wonder, then, that by the time the Soviets gave up in Afghanistan

(1989) his terrorist network had enlisted and deployed some fifty-five thousand jihadists. Through the network—aptly codified "The Base for Holy War against the Jews and Crusaders" or more cryptically "The Base" or "al-Qaeda"—Azzam and bin Laden wreaked previously unimagined havoc on humanity, including the formidable feat of flying planes into the World Trade Center in New York. What they did not accomplish was reestablishment of the caliphate. That would be left to another illegitimate ideological child—appropriately named the Islamic State.

The Muslim Brotherhood continues to be a significant global Islamic jihadist organization, as does the Base or al-Qaeda. For the moment, however, the al-Qaeda star has been eclipsed by the Islamic State. Whatever comes of it in the long run, they have been able to do what their predecessors have not. Namely, reestablish the caliphate.

What is now dubbed the Islamic State was birthed in 1999 by Abu Musab al-Zarqawi as "the Party of Monotheism and Jihad."[39] After finding religion, Zarqawi "gave up drinking and drugs, memorized the Qur'an, and embarked upon the path that would lead him to become one of the most notorious men in the world."[40]

After joining jihadists to fight Soviet troops in Afghanistan in the late 1980s,[41] "he founded a jihad group named Jund al-Sham (Soldiers of the Levant), which foreshadowed ISIS in its dedication to overthrowing a relatively secular government (that of Jordan) and uniting a larger territory (the Levant) in a single Islamic state."[42]

> [Zarqawi] became infamous as a pioneer of the media jihad for which ISIS has now become feared and hated and was personally responsible for one of the first decapitation videos to be posted on the internet and capture the attention of the West—that of American hostage Nicholas Berg in May 2004.[43]

That same year, Zarqawi, who had become iconic to jihadists around the globe, pledged allegiance to Osama bin Laden—rechristening his terrorist network al-Qaeda in the Land of Two Rivers. Within two years (June 7, 2006), he would die in a U.S. airstrike,[44] but his terror network would remain very much alive. Following various permutations—al-Qaeda in Iraq (AQI); Islamic State of Iraq (ISI); the Islamic State of Iraq and the Levant (ISIL); the Islamic State of Iraq and al-Sham (ISIS)—the quintessential terror network ominously rebranded itself the Islamic State (IS).

In *The ISIS Apocalypse*, William McCants, who directs the Project on U.S. Relations with the Islamic World at the Brookings Institution, astutely observes that "while other rebel groups worked together to overthrow governments, the State was busy creating its own."[45] Thus the motto: "Enduring and Expanding."[46]

This, more than anything else, is what separated the Islamic State from its jihadi competitors.

> The Islamic State believes prophecy requires the conquest of every country on earth. "This religion will reach everywhere day and night reach" the Prophet had foretold, so the Islamic State determined to make it a reality. As its magazine proclaimed, "The shade of this blessed flag will expand until it covers all eastern and western extents of the Earth, filling the world with the truth and justice of Islam and putting an end to the falsehood and tyranny." [As such,] in 2014, the Islamic State set about laying the groundwork for taking over the world, beginning in Muslim-majority countries.[47]

What the Islamic State has been able to do historically is quite staggering. Said Dr. Gorka: "Latest estimates have the Islamic State at more than seventy-five thousand fighters, with half of those recruited from outside the region and coming from over a hundred nations." Gorka goes on to explain that "successful recruiting has enabled ISIS to capture territory in Syria, Iraq, and Libya. The land under ISIS control today is more extensive than Great Britain, encompassing more than six million persons and some of the biggest cities in the region."[48]

"Dozens of groups from all over the world, including the lethal Nigerian jihadi movement Boko Haram," have pledged allegiance to the Caliphate. As such,

> large swaths of land under Boko Haram's control are now de facto part of the new caliphate (and also arguably de jure from the perspective

of sharia law). The Islamic State is thus the first insurgency in human history to hold territory not only in multiple countries in one region but in multiple countries in multiple regions.[49]

Equally daunting were the financial resources at the disposal of the Islamic State. "The most successful insurgency in history is also the richest."[50] Unlike previous Islamic jihadist networks, such as the Muslim Brotherhood or al-Qaeda, the Islamic State is not solely dependent on wealthy donors.

It makes millions of dollars every day from its own criminal activities and from the caliphate's governmental operations. Its major sources of funding are illicit sales from captured oil fields, hostage taking, racketeering, the sale of rare antiquities on the black market, and the formal taxation of the population living within the caliphate.[51]

Despite coalition airstrikes on its oil infrastructure in 2015, the Islamic State still controlled a two-billion–dollar domain. As evidenced by research from the Center for the Analysis of Terrorism:

[When] oil fell from 38% to 25% of its revenue stream last year, ISIS cranked up its extortion racket. In 2015, taxes went from supplying 12% of yearly ISIS revenue to 33%. [As such,] the Islamic State's extortion of the people living inside its territory in Iraq and Syria has skyrocketed from $360 million in 2014 to $800 million in 2015.[52]

Perhaps more daunting than all else was the Islamic State rose to guru status in social media expertise:

The Islamic State has a media presence online that makes the jihadi products of Al Qaeda look like the work of high school amateurs. Whether it is the English-language jihadi magazine *Dabiq*, already on its thirteenth issue, or the videos it posts relentlessly on the web, the Islamic State is communicating in ways that perpetuate a constant stream of recruits.[53]

The message delivered through the IS's media machine continues to be clear and consistent: *We will return Islam to its glory days under the caliphate and rightly guided caliphs.*

CALIPH

Just over a hundred years ago (1914), the last Muslim caliphate issued a fatwa mandating that all Muslims massacre Christians in their midst. The fatwa, in concert with historical precedence, invoked one Qur'anic passage after another, including the sura of the sword: "Slay the idolaters wherever you find them—seize them, besiege them, and be ready to ambush them" (Q 9:5).[54]

In keeping with the mandate, "the Ottoman caliphate crucified, beheaded, tortured, mutilated, raped, enslaved, and otherwise massacred countless 'infidel' Christians. The official number of Armenians killed in the genocide is 1.5 million; hundreds of thousands of Greeks and Assyrians each were also systematically slaughtered."[55]

Henry Morgenthau, U.S. ambassador to the Ottoman Empire, somberly reflected upon a mass genocide to which he had been personally privy. "I am confident that the whole history of the human race contains no such horrible episode as this. The great massacres and persecutions of the past seem almost insignificant when compared with the sufferings of the Armenian race in 1915."[56]

In *Red Cross Magazine* (1918), Morgenthau added a penetrating question:

> Will the outrageous terrorizing, the cruel torturing, the driving of women into the harems, the debauchery of innocent girls, the sale of many of them at eighty cents each, the murdering of hundreds of thousands and the deportation to, and starvation in, the deserts of other hundreds of thousands, the destruction of hundreds of villages and cities, will the willful execution of this whole devilish scheme to annihilate the Armenian, Greek and Syrian Christians of Turkey—will all this go unpunished?[57]

We may appropriately add an equally noteworthy question: "Will it even be remembered?" One Great War later, Hitler cynically anticipated the collective amnesia of the modern world. "I have given orders to my Death Units to exterminate without mercy or pity, men, women, and children belonging to the Polish speaking race," he said. *"After all, who remembers the extermination of the Armenians?"*[58]

In 2014, ninety years after Abdulmecid II, the last Muslim caliph, boarded the Orient Express bound for exile in Switzerland, the caliphate was rebirthed in Mosul, the second largest city of Iraq. The sale price of innocent girls had risen from eighty cents to forty dollars. Little else had changed. Throughout the Muslim world, Christians once again faced the specter of persecution and genocide.[59]

The collective amnesia of the masses is breathtaking. Amid scores of crucified Christians, the caliphate has returned with nary a whimper. And with it, a brutal caliph dubbed Abu Bakr al-Baghdadi. Whether Baghdadi is an authentic caliph or just a pretender who will inevitably surrender the brand to another remains to be seen. What is indisputable is that Baghdadi was the only murderous jihadist to make a plausible claim to an end-time caliphate in the twenty-first century since the demise of the Ottoman caliphate in the twentieth.

Born Ibrahim al-Badri (1971), the self-proclaimed caliph of the Islamic State is progeny of the deeply devoted Muslim cleric Awwad al-Badri, instructor of Qur'anic recitation in a mosque in Samarra located on the eastern edge of the Sunni Triangle north of Baghdad.[60]

From childhood on, Baghdadi immersed himself in Qur'anic studies. After graduation from the University of Baghdad in 1996, he devoted himself to a master's program in Qur'anic recitation and thereafter a doctoral curriculum in Qur'anic studies. In 2007, he received an earned PhD in Qur'anic Sciences and was subsequently appointed supervisor of the Islamic State's sharia committee.[61]

Alongside Qur'anic proficiency, Baghdadi was proficient in Islamic history and geography. As such, he renamed himself Abu Bakr, in honor of the first caliph and favored father-in-law of Muhammad, as well as Baghdadi in honor of Baghdad, famed capital of the Abbasid dynasty widely considered the quintessential caliphate of the Islamic empire.[62]

Mirroring the history of his hero Abu Bakr, who fourteen hundred years earlier had commandeered Iraq from the Persians and Syria from the Romans, Baghdadi began solidifying a caliphate encompassing both lands. His plans for the future of the Islamic State began to take on an eerie resemblance to what has been variously dubbed *The Age of the Rightly Guided Caliphs* and *The Greatest Golden Age of Islam.*

Umar ibn al-Khattab, who succeeded Abu Bakr, was likewise an exemplar to Baghdadi. In the manner of Umar, Baghdadi emphasized collection of the *jizya* poll tax as a significant source of financing his caliphate. Any *dhimmi* (subject of the gangster protection racket) who dared resist faced a ghastly death.

In addition to Abu Bakr and Umar, Baghdadi idolized Uthman ibn Affan, the third rightly guided caliph, who was fastidiously committed to standardizing the Qur'anic text so that all good Muslims in every epoch of time might be fully committed to the pattern and practices of the apostle of Allah.

The history of the final caliph in the supposed golden age of Islam was likewise a role model for Baghdadi, particularly in that he did not hesitate to exact violence against fellow Muslims whom he considered heretics. Moreover, like his father-in-law Muhammad, Ali ibn Abi Talib, the fourth rightly guided caliph, distinguished himself as a ruthless warrior in the famed Battle of Badr (624).

Unsavory exemplars for the Islamic State did not end with the twenty-nine–year rule of the four rightly guided caliphs (four personal companions of Muhamad). The Umayyad caliphate that followed (661–750) added historical precedence to atrocities exemplified by the Islamic State. In evidence, Baghdadi's religiously motivated destruction of priceless artifacts, museums, books, and ancient churches were a virtual recapitulation of the "cultural cleansing" that took place during Umayyad dominance.[63]

The Abbasid caliphate (750–1258) set an equally gruesome blueprint for Baghdadi to emulate. The first Abbasid caliph, Abul Abbas, aptly nicknamed "the blood-thirsty," could hardly have been more of a prototype. Though he and Baghdadi died centuries apart, they shared the same predilection for mayhem forged in the image and likeness of Muhammad. The caliphs that followed were likewise brutal, respecting People of the Book.

The Abbasid caliph al-Mutawakkil (847–861) was so intent on making sure that Jews and Christians were thoroughly humiliated and subjugated that he ordered them to wear yellow clothing so that they could always be recognized as non-Muslims and treated accordingly. He also demanded that they put images of devils on their homes, and not ride horses, but only mules or donkeys.[64]

Baghdadi had a great deal in common with leaders of the Ottoman caliphate as well. While the Ottoman caliphate reached its zenith in the sixteenth century, its most notable atrocities are of far more recent vintage. Among a litany of horrific barbarisms was the extermination of the historic city of Smyrna. There they proceeded with house-to-house murdering, looting, pillaging, and raping.

In his inaugural speech as Caliph, Baghdadi signaled the murderous mayhem of the Ottomans had returned in full. From his pulpit in the Nuri Mosque in Mosul he spoke of the "duty upon the Muslims" to "declare the Caliphate." Dressed in a black robe and turban harkening back to the garb donned by Muhammad during his subjugation of Mecca, he declared "the establishment of the religion: a Book that guides and a sword that supports."[65]

COBELLIGERENTS

On June 28, 2016—two years following the return of the caliph and the caliphate—three suicide bombers blew themselves up in an Atatürk Airport terminal in Istanbul.[66] It was a grim reminder that the Islamic State not only had gobbled up large swaths of land in the greater Levant but also had jihadi cobelligerents who hail from far-flung places across the globe.

Robert Spencer aptly put it:

The oil-rich Middle East is full of fantastically wealthy men who read the same Qur'an that is read in the Islamic State, and they are ready to use their wealth to aid the jihad for the sake of Allah worldwide. They don't see the Islamic State as a twisting and hijacking of the peaceful tenets of their religion—that kind of talk is for Western consumption. Quietly, and with the full force of their pocketbooks, they demonstrate that—on the contrary—they see ISIS as a true and faithful embodiment of Islamic teaching.[67]

Most prominent among cobelligerents is the kingdom of Saudi Arabia, which has spent $100 billion—perhaps much, much, more—to spread their fundamentalist brand of Islamic jihadism around the globe.[68] "By comparison, the Soviets spent about $7 billion spreading communism worldwide in the 70 years from 1921 and 1991."[69]

Consider just one example. "Indian intelligence says that in India alone, from 2011 to 2013, some 25,000 Saudi clerics arrived bearing more than $250 million to build mosques and universities and hold seminars."[70] As Thomas Friedman put it, in a provocative *New York Times* piece titled "Our Radical Islamic BFF, Saudi Arabia," the "title greatest 'purveyors of radical Islam' does not belong to the Iranians. Not even close. That belongs to our putative ally Saudi Arabia."[71]

Friedman went on to observe;

> It is not an accident that several thousand Saudis have joined the Islamic State or that Arab Gulf charities have sent ISIS donations. It is because all these Sunni jihadist groups—ISIS, Al Qaeda, the Nusra Front—are the ideological offspring of the Wahhabism injected by Saudi Arabia into mosques and madrasas from Morocco to Pakistan to Indonesia. And we, America, have never called them on that—because we're addicted to their oil and addicts never tell the truth to their pushers.[72]

Instead, America enables Saudi terror lords to peddle their poisonous propaganda pills across the planet with impunity.

No less a luminary than Hilary Clinton agrees. Though the Clinton Foundation is beholden to the Saudis for upward of $25 million,[73] WikiLeaks has then–Secretary of State Hillary Clinton acknowledging that Saudi Arabia is not just *a* source of terrorist funding but *the* source. "Donors in Saudi Arabia," confessed Clinton, "constitute the most significant source of funding to Sunni terrorist groups worldwide."[74]

More alarming still is that according to the former Democratic senator from Florida, Bob Graham, Saudi Arabia had direct ties to the massacres of September 11, 2001. On July 15, 2016, following the declassification of twenty-eight pages of congressional inquiry into the 9/11 attacks, Graham averred that there was "a solid case for the position that there was significant Saudi involvement going up at least to the Saudi Ambassador to the United States Prince Bandar in the time leading up to 9/11." Graham went on to say, "I think there's enough in these pages for the families [of 9/11 victims] to establish that there was probable cause that the Saudi government and its agents and citizens were involved in assisting the 9/11 hijackers"—and, not insignificantly, fifteen of the nineteen were Saudi nationals.[75]

Against the weight of political correctness, Graham overtly dubbed ISIS "a product of Saudi ideals, Saudi money, and Saudi organizational support."[76] All of this, of course, is being whitewashed in the Western world, where sharia-subservient states, including Saudi Arabia, are consistently portrayed as peace-loving allies in the fight against terrorism. Little wonder then that when the Grand Mufti of Saudi Arabia declared it necessary to destroy every church in the whole of the Arabian Peninsula, Western governments did not so much as blink.[77]

Worse yet, Western governments, along with academic institutions and media outlets have proven themselves to be cobelligerents with the Wahhabis of Saudi Arabia in exporting a false narrative respecting the religious tenets that animate the Islamic State. As Raymond Ibrahim aptly put it in a remarkable book titled *Crucified Again*, "they employ an arsenal of semantic games, key phrases, convenient omissions, and moral relativism to uphold a narrative first forged by virulently anti-Western academics in the 1960s and 1970s: that Muslim violence and intolerance are products of anything and everything—poverty, political and historical grievances, or territorial disputes—except Islam."[78] As such, the bloodlust of global Islamic jihadist networks is "portrayed as a natural byproduct of the frustration Muslims feel as an oppressed minority, 'rightfully' angry with the 'colonial' West and its Israeli proxy."[79]

To date, the worst cobelligerent to Islamic jihadism was the eight-year Obama administration. As painful as it is to remember, the Obama juggernaut advanced the agenda of Egyptian president Muhammad Morsi, well-known for proud membership in the Muslim Brotherhood.[80] This despite Morsi's in-your-face recitation of the Muslim Brotherhood maxim:

"The Koran is our constitution, the Prophet Muhammad is our leader, jihad is our path and death for the sake of Allah is our most lofty aspiration."[81]

And who can forget the outrages of Benghazi, Libya? Said Ibrahim, "To hide the fact that the al-Qaeda rebels whom the Obama administration empowered in Libya were behind this terrorist attack, the administration tried to frame the attack as a response to a YouTube movie about the prophet of Islam."[82] All of this was aided and abetted by then Secretary of State Hilary Clinton, who deceitfully absolved Islamic jihadism under the pretense of a rogue video.[83]

If Obama was consistent in anything, it was his resolute refusal to make any association between Islam and acts of terror. The Orlando massacre provides a classic case in point. "Omar Mateen called the cops to pledge his fealty to ISIS as he was carrying out his mass murder" at an Orlando nightclub, June 12, 2016.[84] Later that day, the president of the United States declared, "We've reached no definitive judgment on the precise motivations" of Omar Mateen but "what is clear is that he was a person filled with hatred."[85] The Obama administration went so far as to release a redacted transcript of the 911 call by Mateen which had scrubbed Mateen's pledges to ISIS and other references deemed to be "propaganda."[86]

Of one thing the Obama administration was certain. All references to Islam must characterize it as a "tradition of peace, charity and justice."[87] Who can forget the chilling directive of US Attorney General Eric Holder, who categorically forbade any law enforcement training materials that impinged upon the "Islam means peace" narrative? Said US attorney Dwight C. Holton, "I want to be perfectly clear about this: training materials that portray Islam as a religion of violence or with a tendency towards violence are wrong, they are offensive, and they are contrary to everything that this president, this attorney general and Department of Justice stands for." As such, "They will not be tolerated" because "they play into the false narrative propagated by terrorists that the United States is at war with Islam."[88]

Even more telling was the following undeniable fact about assistant defense secretary for homeland defense:

[Paul Stockton] refused to associate Islamic terrorists with Islam in any way, shape, or form, regardless of "any set of qualifiers"; he would not even agree that al-Qaeda is following a "distorted" or "perverted" version of Islam. When Representative Dan Lungren repeatedly asked Stockton if he would at least concede that al-Qaeda "is acting out violent Islamist extremism," Stockton continued to refuse, insisting that the group merely consists of "murderers," as a visibly stunned Lungren and others looked on.[89]

So pervasive was Obama's repression of any materials that might as much as hint at Islamic core values being systemic to Islamic jihadism that when Boko Haram—*which overtly declared its allegiance to the Islamic State*— bombed churches and massacred tens of thousands of Christians, he resolutely refused to designate them a "Foreign Terrorist Organization (FTO)."[90]

Instead, as Raymond Ibrahim courageously and correctly communicated, the Obama administration "agreed to spend $600 million [six hundred million!] on a USAID initiative launched to ascertain the 'true causes' behind Boko Haram's jihad—as if the organization has not been perfectly clear about its goals: the enforcement of Sharia law and elimination (or at least subjugation) of all infidels, chief among them Christians."[91]

Ibrahim's *Crucified Again*, as indicated by its subtitle, is focused on exposing Islam's new war on Christians. However, as Ibrahim makes plain, there is a larger lesson to be learned: "The West must learn to connect the dots and understand the interconnectivity of Islam."[92] His words, though unnerving, must not go unheeded.

The fundamental reason for Muslim hostility to Christians is that they are non-Muslims, *infidels*, and Islam's Sharia—its way—calls for subjugating *all* infidels. To ignore this fact, or, worse, to empower Islam— whether through mainstream media dissembling or Western policies in support of the "Arab Spring"—is not only to perpetuate the sufferings of Christians and others under Islam. It is also to prepare the way for the West's own demise. Islamists around the world are still working to fulfill the Muslim mission that began nearly 1,400 years ago: global hegemony. As a Christian patriarch in Syria put it, after pointing out that the slaughter and displacement of Syria's Christian population is the work of jihadis, "The jihadis will not stop here, the war will spread to Europe. What will England be like in ten or 15 years?" Indeed, the Islamic jihad knows no bounds, nor is it a respecter of anything or anyone non-Islamic.[93]

Whether the Islamic State will succeed in its murderous mission to expand its caliphate or will be supplanted by an even more dangerous ideological child remains to be seen. What we do know is this. The caliphate that Atatürk abolished in 1924 has returned with a vengeance—and that amid a crumbling post-Christian culture. Os Guinness said it well: "The forces of barbarism are growing uglier by the day, not only externally but internally—from the rising tide of Islamic violence, the degenerating decadence of post-Christian Western secularism, and the evident impotence and disarray of the Jewish and Christian ideas and institutions that once inspired and shaped Western civilization."[94]

Make no mistake. We are at a tipping point in history. While squarely in the blind spot of the West, Christians in the Middle East face mass genocide. Concurrently, a demographic time bomb threatens a Western world seemingly blind to the polygamous rush of migrant Muslims filling the vacuum left by "aging, dying, and aborted Europeans."[95] And while the West continues to coddle an Islamic time bomb, it is simultaneously cultivating a rash of self-destructive ideals. Said Guinness:

> The legalization and then normalization of polyamory, polygamy, pedophilia and incest follow the same logic as that of abortion and homosexuality, the socially destructive consequences of these trends will reverberate throughout society until the social chaos is beyond recovery. We can only pray there will be a return to God and sanity before the terrible sentence is pronounced: "God has given them over" to the consequences of their own settled choices.[96]

Thus the question: Will Christianity once again do for the truth what Islam is even now doing for a lie? If the answer roiling up within your heart at this momentous moment in human history is yes, it is paramount to understand *major Muslim misapprehensions* and the corresponding truths that transform.

Chapter 6

Major Muslim Misapprehensions

He ['Iesa (Jesus)] was not more than a slave. We granted
Our Favour to him, and We made him an example to the
Children of Israel (i.e. his creation without a father).
—Q 43:59, Hilali–Khan

In *Islam and the Cross*, Samuel Zwemer, appropriately dubbed Apostle to Islam, correctly identifies Islam as "a composite faith, with pagan, Jewish, and Christian elements." Pagan elements borrowed from "old Arabian idolatry," the "warp and woof of the Koran" from Talmudic Judaism, and "the mystic beliefs and ascetic practices of later Islam" from Christianity.[1]

> [Islam] entrenches itself everywhere and always in animistic and pagan superstition. It fights with all the fanatic devotion of Semitic Judaism with its exaggerated nationalism. It claims at once to include and supersede all that which Jesus Christ was and did and taught. It is a religion of *compromise*, of *conservatism*, and of *conquest*.[2]

Of *compromise* in that it misapprehends the very religious systems it draws from, thus compromising the essential dogmas to which these systems adhere. With respect to the deity of Christ, for example, the Muslim asks, "If Jesus was Almighty God, with power to strike terror into all men, / Why do you believe that the Jews could make him endure the agony of the cross? / And why do you believe that God died, and was buried in the dust?"[3]

It is a religion of *conservatism* in that Muslims are committed at all costs to the conservation of the faith and practices of their prophet and revelator. The foremost thought in the Muslim mind in any given situation is: "What would Muhammad do?" When Muhammad was alive and available, those close to him sought his direction personally. Today, Muslims seek to understand the way of Muhammad through conserved tradition. In *Sahih Muslim*, two of Muhammad's warriors discuss the proper way to engage in sex with captured women:

> "We went out with Allah's Messenger (may peace be upon him) on the expedition to the Bi'l-Mustaliq and took captive some excellent Arab women; and we desired them, for we were suffering from the absence of our wives, (but at the same time) we also desired ransom for them. So we decided to have sexual intercourse with them but by observing 'azl (Withdrawing the male sexual organ before emission of semen to avoid-conception). *But we said: We are doing an act whereas Allah's Messenger is amongst us; why not ask him?* So we asked Allah's Messenger (may peace be upon him), and he said: It does not matter if you do not do it, for every soul that is to be born up to the Day of Resurrection will be born."[4]

Thus, Muslim men in the present deal with female captives in accord with the precepts and practices of Muhammad.

It is a religion of *conquest* in that its aim is to bring the whole world—including Christianity—into the house of Islam. Ironically, the final exclamation point will come not from Muhammad but from Christ. "He will break the crosses" because it is an abomination to imagine that he who prepared the way for Muhammad could have been victimized upon one. "He will kill all the pigs" because in an Islamized world there will be no need or room for them. And "he will abolish the jizya tax" because People of the Book will have been killed or converted.[5]

Perhaps more than anything else, however, Islam is a religion of *corruption*. As Robert Spencer aptly put it, "the Qur'an appropriates half-digested and sometimes dimly understood biblical traditions, generally recasting them in fundamental ways, while often leaving traces of Jewish and Christian theology that remain unexplained in their new Islamic setting."[6]

> [Moreover] its teachings on Jesus are a curious amalgam of material from the New Testament and the writings of heretical and schismatic sects. In a certain sense, there is something for everyone: a bit of orthodox Christianity (the Virgin Birth, the idea of Jesus as the Word of God, even if improperly understood), a bit of Gnosticism (the illusory crucifixion), a bit of hyper-Arianism (the denial of Christ's divinity) and Ebionism (the Qur'an calls Jesus "messiah" but rejects his divinity, as did the Judaizing Ebionite sect).[7]

Such misapprehensions are not merely minor; they are manifestly major in that they compromise, confuse, or contradict essential Christian doctrine. As such, major Muslim misapprehensions obliterate the line of demarcation between that which corresponds to reality and that which most certainly does not.

This is all the more evident when we contrast the essential doctrines of the historic Christian faith with the perversions of Islam. Os Guinness was right; "Contrast is the mother of clarity."[8] Or as has been well said, "The way to show that a stick is crooked is not to argue about it or to spend time denouncing it, but to lay a straight stick alongside it."[9]

In the case at hand, that straight stick is the Bible—a sacred masterpiece that is divine rather than qur'anically human in origin. And that is not merely a dogmatic assertion. It is a defensible argument. In my book *Has God Spoken? Memorable Proofs of the Bible's Divine Inspiration*, I demonstrate that *manuscript copies*, the *archaeologist's spade*, and *prophetic stars* in the constellation of biblical prophecy collectively underscore this salient truth.

In short, the manuscript evidence is overwhelming. The Bible has stronger manuscript support than any work of classical history—including Homer, Plato, Aristotle, Caesar, and Tacitus. Equally amazing, the Bible has been virtually unaltered since the original writing, as is attested by scholars who have compared the earliest manuscripts with those written centuries later. Additionally, the reliability of the Bible is affirmed by the testimony of its authors, who were eyewitnesses—or close associates of eyewitnesses—to the recorded events, as well as by secular historians who confirm the people, places, and particulars chronicled in Scripture.

Furthermore, archaeology is a powerful witness to the accuracy of the New Testament documents. Repeatedly, archeological fieldwork and careful biblical interpretation affirm the reliability of the Bible. Archaeological finds have, for instance, corroborated biblical details surrounding the trial that led to the fatal torment of Jesus Christ. It is telling when secular scholars must revise their biblical criticisms in light of solid archaeological evidence.

Finally, the Bible records prophecies of events that could not have been known or predicted by mere chance or common sense. For example, the book of Daniel (written before 530 BC) accurately foretold the progression of kingdoms from Babylon through the Median and Persian empires to the further persecution and suffering of the Jews under Antiochus IV Epiphanes with his desecration of the temple, his untimely death, and freedom for the Jews under Judas Maccabeus (165 BC). It is statistically preposterous that any or all of the Bible's specific, detailed prophecies could have been fulfilled by chance, good guessing, or deliberate deceit.[10]

In sharp contrast, predictive prophecies demonstrating the divine origin of the Qur'an are conspicuous by their absence. While the Qur'an contains many self-fulfilling prophecies, such as Muhammad's prediction that he would return to Mecca (48:27), this is very different from the biblical prophecy outlined above. Other prophecies, such as Muhammad's prediction that the Romans would defeat the Persians at Issus (30:2–4), are equally underwhelming. Unlike biblical examples, this prophecy is not fulfilled in the far future and, thus, can be easily explained through good guessing or an accurate apprehension of prevailing military conditions.

The Qur'anic worldview, however, has a far greater liability. When compared with the straight stick of Scripture, its crookedness is apparent. While this is clearly the case with respect to faulty ethics—such as the fact that the Qur'an allows men to "beat" their wives in order that they might "return to obedience" (4:34)—and factual errors—such as the Qur'anic denial of Christ's crucifixion (4:157)—Qur'an's crookedness is most obvious when compared with the straight stick of essential Christian DOCTRINE—let's begin with *D* for "deity."

DEITY OF CHRIST

Google "counterfeit money" and one of the first hits that pops up is a Treasury Department posting titled "How to Detect Counterfeit Money." The article goes on to say that you and I "can help guard against the threat from counterfeiters by becoming more familiar with United States money." How? "Compare a suspect note with a genuine note of the same denomination and series, paying attention to the quality of printing and paper characteristics. Look for differences, not similarities."[11] What is true with respect to counterfeit currency is likewise true with respect to counterfeit religions. Those familiar with essential Christian doctrine will recognize a counterfeit instantaneously when it looms on the horizon.

No better illustration can be given than the deity of Jesus Christ. When Jesus came to Caesarea Philippi, he asked his disciples the mother of all questions, "Who do you say I am?" (Matthew 16:15). Muslims answer by saying that though Jesus was a virgin-born,[12] sinless[13] worker of miracles[14] and a way-shower for Muhammad,[15] in the end he was only a man.[16] Jesus, however, answered the same question by claiming to be the unique Son of God.[17]

In John 8:58, Jesus went so far as to use the very words by which God revealed himself to Moses from the burning bush (Exodus 3:14). To Jews, this was the epitome of blasphemy, for they knew that by choosing these words, Jesus was clearly claiming to be God. On yet another occasion, Jesus explicitly told the Jews:

> "I and the Father are one."
>
> Again his Jewish opponents picked up stones to stone him, but Jesus said to them, "I have shown you many good works from the Father. For which of these do you stone me?"

"We are not stoning you for any good work," they replied, "but for blasphemy, because you, a mere man, claim to be God." (John 10:30–33)

Furthermore, Jesus made an unmistakable claim to deity before the chief priests and the whole Sanhedrin. Caiaphas the high priest asked him: "'Are you the Messiah, the Son of the Blessed One?' 'I am,' said Jesus. 'And you will see the Son of Man sitting at the right hand of the Mighty One and coming on the clouds of heaven'" (Mark 14:61–62). A biblically illiterate person might well have missed the import of Jesus' words. Caiaphas and the council, however, did not. They knew that in saying he was *the Son of Man* who would come *on the clouds of heaven* he was making an overt reference to the Son of Man in Daniel's prophecy (Daniel 7:13–14). And in doing so, he was not only claiming to be the preexistent sovereign of the universe but also prophesying that he would vindicate his claim by judging the very court that was now condemning him. Moreover, by combining Daniel's prophecy with David's proclamation in Psalm 110, Jesus was claiming that he would sit upon the throne of Israel's God and share God's very glory. To students of the Old Testament, this was the height of blasphemy; thus, "they all condemned him as worthy of death" (Mark 14:64).

Finally, Jesus claimed to possess the very attributes of God. For example, he claimed omniscience by telling Peter, "This very night, before the rooster crows, you will disown me three times" (Matthew 26:34). Jesus demonstrated omnipotence not only by resurrecting Lazarus (John 11:43) but also by raising himself from the dead (John 2:19); and he alluded to his omnipresence by promising he would be with his disciples "to the very end of the age" (Matthew 28:20). Not only so, but Jesus said to the paralytic in Luke 5:20, "Friend, your sins are forgiven." In doing so, he claimed a prerogative—forgiving a person's sin—reserved for God alone. In addition, when Thomas worshiped Jesus, saying, "My Lord and my God!" (John 20:28), Jesus responded with commendation rather than condemnation.[18]

Jesus not only claimed to be God but also provided many convincing proofs that he was indeed divine. To begin with, Jesus demonstrated that he was God in human flesh by manifesting the credential of sinlessness. While the Qur'an exhorts Muhammad to seek forgiveness for his sins (47:19),[19] the

Bible exonerates Messiah, saying Jesus "had no sin" (2 Corinthians 5:21). And this is not a singular statement. John declared, "in him is no sin" (1 John 3:5), and Peter said that Jesus "committed no sin, and no deceit was found in his mouth" (1 Peter 2:22). Jesus himself went so far as to challenge his antagonists asking, "Can any of you prove me guilty of sin?" (John 8:46).[20]

Furthermore, Jesus demonstrated supernatural authority over sickness, the forces of nature, fallen angels, and even death itself. Matthew 4 records that Jesus went throughout Galilee teaching, preaching, "and healing every disease and sickness among the people" (v. 23). Mark 4 documents Jesus rebuking the wind and the waves saying, "Quiet! Be still!" (v. 39). In Luke 4, Jesus encountered a man possessed by an evil spirit and commanded the demon to "Come out of him!" (v. 35). And in John 4, Jesus told a royal official whose son was close to death, "Your son will live" (v. 50). And all four Gospels record how Jesus demonstrated ultimate power over death through the immutable fact of his resurrection.[21]

Finally, the credentials of Christ's deity are seen in the lives of countless men, women, and children. Each day people of every tongue and tribe and nation experience the resurrected Christ by repenting of their sins and receiving Jesus as Lord and Savior of their lives. Thus, they not only come to know about Christ evidentially, but experientially Christ becomes more real to them than the very flesh upon their bones.

In addition to Christ's claims and credentials, the biblical text clearly claims that Jesus is God. Three texts stand out above the rest. Not only are they clear and convincing, but their "addresses" are easy to remember— John 1, Colossians 1, and Hebrews 1.

First is John 1: "In the beginning was the Word, and the Word was with God, *and the Word was God*" (v. 1). Here we see that Jesus not only was in existence before the world began, but he is differentiated from the Father and explicitly called "God," indicating that he shares the same nature as his Father.

Furthermore, Colossians 1 informs us that "in him [Jesus] all things were created" (v. 16); He is "before all things" (v. 17); and "God was pleased to have all his fullness dwell in him" (v. 19). Only deity has the prerogative of creation, preexists all things, and personifies the full essence and nature of God.

Finally, Hebrews 1 overtly tells us that—according to God the Father himself—Jesus is God: "About the Son he [the Father] says, 'Your throne, O God, will last for ever and ever'" (v. 8). Not only is the entirety of Hebrews 1 devoted to demonstrating the true deity of Jesus, but in verses ten through twelve, the inspired writer quoted a passage from Psalm 102 referring to Yahweh and directly applied it to Christ. In doing so, these verses specifically declare Jesus ontologically equal with Israel's God.[22]

Many similar texts could be added to this list. For example, in Revelation 1, the Lord God said, "I am the Alpha and the Omega, who is, and who was, and who is to come, the Almighty" (v. 8). In the last chapter of Revelation, Jesus applied these same words *Alpha* and *Omega*—to himself![23] Additionally, in 2 Peter 1, Jesus is referred to as "our God and Savior Jesus Christ" (v. 1). In these passages and a host of others, the Bible explicitly claims that Jesus *is* God.[24]

The counterfeit Christ of the Qur'an could not be more different from the crystal Christ of the Bible. Far from being God, he is rendered but the "slave of Allah" (Q 4:172; 19:30; 43:59).[25] Indeed, Allah is intensely exercised over the Christian contention that Jesus is the Son of God.

> They say: "(Allah) Most Gracious has begotten a son!" Indeed ye have put forth a thing most monstrous! As if the skies are ready to burst, the earth to split asunder, and the mountains to fall down in utter ruin. That they should invoke a son for (Allah) Most Gracious. For it is not consonant with the majesty of (Allah) Most Gracious that He should beget a son. (Q 19:88–92)

Allah rejects the notion that God could have a son on the basis that he does not have a consort. Asks Allah: "How can He have a son, when he hath no consort?" (Q 6:101). In uttering such words, Allah demonstrates utter cluelessness respecting the notion of sonship. To his way of thinking, calling God "Father" and Jesus "Son" suggests sexual procreation. Nothing, of course, could be further from the truth! When the Bible speaks of Jesus as "the only *begotten* of the Father" (John 1:14 NKJV), it quite obviously is underscoring the unique deity of Christ.

Likewise, when the Bible refers to Jesus as "the firstborn over all creation" (Colossians 1:15), it does so to emphasize Christ's preeminence or prime position as the Creator of all things (Colossians 1:16–19). This usage is firmly established in the Old Testament. For example, Ephraim is referred to as the Lord's "firstborn" (Jeremiah 31:9) even though Manasseh was born first (Genesis 41:51). Likewise, David was appointed the Lord's "firstborn, the most exalted of the kings of the earth" (Psalm 89:27) despite being the youngest of Jesse's sons (1 Samuel 16: 10–13). While neither Ephraim nor David was the first one born in his family, both were firstborn in the sense of prime position.

It is one thing for Allah to disagree with the biblical position; it is quite another for him to completely misapprehend it. As the panoply of Scripture makes plain, Jesus is the eternal Creator who spoke and the limitless galaxies leapt into existence. As noted, in John 1, he is overtly called "God" (v. 1), and in Hebrews 1, he is said to be the one who "laid the foundations of the earth" (v. 10). And in the very last chapter of the Bible, Christ referred to himself as "the Alpha and the Omega, the Beginning and the End, the First and the Last" (Revelation 22:13). Indeed, the whole of Scripture precludes the possibility that Christ is anything other than the preexistent sovereign of the universe.[26]

ORIGINAL SIN

The account of how an artist transformed the ceiling of the Sistine Chapel into a reflection of God's creative prowess is stunning.[27] It took over three years for the diminutive Michelangelo to paint the vast expanse of the Chapel vault using the tiny brushes of his craft. He persevered through the stifling heat of summer and through the bitter cold of winter, sometimes painting for weeks on end without so much as taking off his boots.

With otherworldly endurance, he persevered until the vast expanse was transformed into a biblical narrative that looked as though it might well be life itself. Yet as stunning as the pictorials of the Sistine Chapel are, they pale by comparison to God's creative handiwork. The psalmist so suitably sang,

> The heavens declare the glory of God;
> the skies proclaim the work of his hands.

Day after day they pour forth speech;
> night after night they reveal knowledge.

They have no speech, they use no words;
> no sound is heard from them.

Yet their voice goes out into all the earth,
> their words to the ends of the world." (Psalm 19:1–4)

As incomparable as Michelangelo's masterpiece is, it is but a faint reflection of God's "eternal power and divine nature—having been clearly seen, being understood from what has been made" (Romans 1:20).

Tragically, the paint of God's masterpiece had hardly dried before the crowning jewels of his creation "marred it, like a delinquent spraying graffiti on the Sistine Chapel."[28] The master painter had spoken to the apex of his creation: "You are free to eat from any tree in the garden; but you must not eat from the tree of the knowledge of good and evil, for when you eat from it you will certainly die" (Genesis 2:16–17). In reckless response, Adam sprayed the canvas of God's masterwork with the venom of his own self-will.

As the consequence, all of humanity plunged into lives of perpetual sin, terminated by death. Adam disobeyed, and the whole of humanity inherited his broken gene—an inclination toward sin—a disease leading inexorably to death. In the words of the apostle Paul, "sin entered the world through one man, and death through sin, and in this way death came to all people, because all sinned" (Romans 5:12).[29]

In the grand meta-narrative of Scripture, the doctrine of original sin looms large. The original sin led to a life of perpetual depravity, as Adam was banished from paradise—relegated to restlessness and wandering, separated from intimacy and fellowship with his Creator.

The very chapter that references the fall, however, records the divine plan for restoration (Genesis 3)—a plan that takes on definition with God's promise to make Abram a great nation through whom "all peoples on earth will be blessed" (Genesis 12:3). Abram's call, therefore, constituted the divine antidote to Adam's fall.

God's promise that Abraham's children would inherit the promised land was but a preliminary step in a progressive plan through which Abram and his heirs would inherit "a better country—a heavenly one" (Hebrews 11:16). The plan came into sharp focus when Moses led Abraham's descendants out of the four hundred–year bondage in Egypt. For forty years of wilderness wandering, God tabernacled with his people and prepared them for the land of promise. Like Abram, however, Moses saw the promise only from afar.

The plan became a tangible reality when Joshua led the children of Israel into Palestine. God's promises to Abram, however, were far from exhausted. For Palestine was but a preliminary phase in the patriarchal promise. God would make Abram the father of not only a nation, but Abram would become Abraham—"a father of *many* nations" (Genesis 17:5). Abraham "would be heir of the world" (Romans 4:13). As such, the climax of the promise would not be Palestine regained, but paradise restored.

As God promised Abraham Palestine, so, too, he promised him a royal seed.[30] Joshua led the children of Israel into the promised land; Jesus will one day lead redeemed humanity into paradise restored. There they will forever experience rest. From Adam's rebellion to Abraham's royal seed, Scripture chronicles God's one unfolding plan for the redemption of humanity.[31] In the beginning, the Tree of Life stood as the centerpiece of the Edenic garden. After Adam ate the forbidden fruit, the tree remained a memorial to paradise lost: God "placed on the east side of the Garden of Eden cherubim and a flaming sword flashing back and forth to guard the way to the tree of life" (Genesis 3:24).

Standing on the other side of history, the Tree of Life is rooted in an eternal garden, now, a memorial to paradise regained. The angel of the apocalypse showed John, the apostle of the apocalypse:

> the river of the water of life, as clear as crystal, flowing from the throne of God and of the Lamb down the middle of the great street of the city. On each side of the river stood the *tree of life*, bearing twelve crops of fruit, yielding its fruit every month. And the leaves of the tree are for the healing of the nations. No longer will there be any curse. (Revelation 22:1–3)

"To him who overcomes," said Jesus, "I will give the right to eat from the *tree of life*, which is in the paradise of God" (2:7).

Another tree stood on Golgotha's hill as the fulcrum of human history. On it, Jesus stretched one hand toward the Edenic garden, the other toward the eternal garden. The immortality the first Adam could no longer reach, the second Adam touched in his place. Thus, Jesus vanquished the power of evil, giving ultimate victory to the knowledge of good.[32]

The grand meta-narrative of Scripture is indeed a majestic master-piece. But a masterpiece obscenely vandalized by the graffiti of Islam, its crookedness ever more apparent when contrasted with the straight stick of biblical brilliance. Thomas Carlyle was right. The Qur'an is as toilsome a read as one can possibly imagine. It is "a wearisome confused jumble, crude, incondite; endless iterations, long-windedness, entanglement; most crude," written "as badly as almost any book ever was!"[33] Or as Robert Spencer commented: "Remarkably decontextualized."[34]

To begin with, in the Qur'anic account, Allah confuses the *Tree of Life* with the *Tree of the Knowledge of Good and Evil*.[35]

> Satan whispered evil to him: he said, "O Adam! Shall I lead thee to the Tree of Eternity and to a kingdom that never decays?" In the result, they both ate of the tree, and so their nakedness appeared to them: they began to sew together, for their covering, leaves from the Garden: thus did Adam disobey his Lord, and allow himself to be seduced. (Q 20:120–121)

A graver misapprehension can hardly be imagined. To confuse a tree representing life with one leading to death, disease, and destruction is the epitome of missing the point. In eating from the tree about which God said, "When you eat from it you will certainly die," Adam challenged God as the arbiter of good and evil (Genesis 2:17). As such, the Tree of Knowledge of Good and Evil was symbolic of choice—choice between obedience and dis-obedience, between majestic revelation (God's truth) and moral relativism (my truth).

Furthermore, in the Islamic account, there is no original sin—just an original act of heedlessness. Thus, while the biblical worldview highlights the severity of sin and its consequences, the Qur'anic worldview reduces the original sin to an original slip—a mere bout of forgetfulness. In short, *the* fall is reformulated *a* fall. In the words of Muslim scholars Jane Idleman Smith and Yvonne Yazbeck Haddad,

> the common Christian conception has been that Adam was expelled from paradise because of his sin, and due to this original act of disobedience the succession of humanity is tainted. While the Qur'an contains the narrative of Adam's expulsion from the Garden [Q 2:35–39], the expulsion is the result of satanic deception, immediately pardoned, rather than a progenitive act of disobedience with ramifications for the rest of humanity.[36]

Finally, according to Islam, every newborn child is born in a state of *fitrah*—or a state of original Muslim purity.[37] As Muhammad purportedly put it, "No babe is born but upon Fitra [as a Muslim]. It is his parents who make him a Jew or a Christian or a Polytheist."[38] Or, as Yusuf Ali explained in his Qur'anic commentary, "As turned out from the creative hand of Allah, man is innocent, pure, true, free, inclined to right and virtue, and endued with true understanding about his own position in the Universe and about Allah's goodness, wisdom, and power."[39]

In sum, to misapprehend the gravity of original sin is to miss the good news by which humanity may be saved.

> Judgment followed one sin and brought condemnation, but the gift followed many trespasses and brought justification. For if, by the trespass of the one man, death reigned through that one man, how much more will those who receive God's abundant provision of grace and of the gift of righteousness reign in life through the one man, Jesus Christ!
>
> Consequently, just as one trespass resulted in condemnation for all people, so also one righteous act resulted in justification and life for all people. For just as through the disobedience of the one man the many were made sinners, so also through the obedience of the one man the many will be made righteous. (Romans 5:16–19)

CANON

Both Christians and Muslims have a canon. That is, a *measuring stick* or *standard of measurement* by which to "test all things" and "hold fast what is good" (1 Thessalonians 5:21 NKJV). In the case of Christianity, that measuring stick is the Bible;[40] in Islam it is the Qur'an. Thus, the question at hand: How straight—trustworthy—is the measuring stick?

Muslims make the dogmatic assertion that the Qur'an is Allah's only credible uncorrupted revelation. As such, it is a straight stick of unalterable reliability. From the Muslim perspective, God spoke through the archangel Gabriel, who dictated the Qur'an to Muhammad over a period of about twenty-three years. Muhammad memorized the words of Gabriel and then dictated what he had memorized to his companions. "They, in turn, memorized it, wrote it down, and reviewed it with the Prophet Muhammad (peace be upon him). Moreover, the Prophet Muhammad (peace be upon him) reviewed the Qur'an with the Angel Gabriel once each year and twice in the last year of his life." As such, Muslims assert that not even "one letter of the Qur'an has been changed over the centuries."[41]

This, say the followers of Muhammad, is the miracle of the Qur'an. It "exists in its original text, without the slightest alteration of letter, syllable, jot, or tittle."[42] "No change has occurred in a single word." Not even "a single punctuation mark" has been altered during the entire fourteen-hundred-year history of Islam.[43] As the Qur'an promises, "We have, without doubt, sent down the Message; and We will assuredly guard it (from corruption)" (Q 15:9).

Conversely, say the Muslims, the biblical canon is a very crooked stick that cannot be trusted. Muslim scholar A. S. K. Joommal put it this way:

> What used to be the Word of God has been so adulterated by human hands that the Word of God is hardly distinguishable from the word of man. In some places we do still find a glimmer of the truth that Jesus taught—the gems of divine wisdom that he uttered for the good of his people—but these are few and far between in the jungles of interpolations and contradictions with which the Bible is dense.[44]

And the twentieth-century Pakistani scholar Sayyid Abul A'La Maududi wrote, "Not one of the earlier books—*Torah*, *Zabur* (Psalms of David), *Injeel* (Gospel of Jesus), etc.—exists today in its original text and even the followers of these books confess that they do not possess the *original* books."[45] As such, current versions of the Bible are but the product of contaminated copies, cleverly invented stories, and corrupt collaborators. Not even the central message of Christ's crucifixion is true. As Allah dogmatically asserts, "For of a surety they killed him not" (Q 4:157).

Solomon—no doubt the wisest man who ever lived[46]—said, "The first to plead his case *seems* right, *until* another comes and examines him" (Proverbs 18:17 NASB). His words have relevance to the matter at hand. One who contends that the biblical manuscripts are hopelessly riddled with error, that cherished biblical stories are legendary rather than legitimate, that the crucifixion of Christ and his subsequent resurrection is a cruel hoax rather than credible history "seems right, until another comes and examines him."

When reason prevails over rhetoric, a completely different perspective emerges. Far from a liability, extant manuscript copies bear eloquent testimony to the veracity of the Bible. This, unlike the contention of Muslims, is not merely a dogmatic assertion; it is an eminently defensible argument. By God's grace, the acronym COPIES turns out to be a perfect way to remember the sequential line of reasoning demonstrating that extant manuscript copies faithfully preserve the words of the original text.

Copyist Practices. Old Testament scribal luminaries ranging from Ezra to the Masorites set an unimaginable standard of excellence in their copyist practices. As *sophers*, they literally tallied the words and letters to make certain that nothing was amiss.[47] No letter could be inscribed without looking back at the original and verbalizing the text. As part of the Jewish *sopherim*, these scribes had such an exalted view of the Old Testament text that they perceived the missing of a mere tittle—a microscopic appendage at the end of a Hebrew letter—to be an affront to the holiness of their Creator.[48] New Testament counterparts, likewise, engaged in their craft with care. Guided by the admonition "do not add to it or take away from it" (Deuteronomy 12:32), New Testament copyists engaged their copyist practices with reverential awe akin to their Old Testament predecessors.[49] Did they make mistakes? Of course! While they engaged their craft with care, they were hardly infallible. Unlike preprogrammed automatons, they were subject to all the frailties that are part of the human condition. The beauty from a biblical perspective, however, is the wealth of manuscripts by which textual critics can sort out their errors, even apart from context and common sense.[50]

Oral Culture. It is often contended that biblical accounts ranging from the exodus of the Jews to the extraordinary miracles of Jesus were not only recorded long after the fact but also recklessly embellished. This, however, is hardly the case. Why? Because the biblical accounts were not only recorded early—by eyewitnesses—but they were recorded in an oral culture in which people practiced the principles of memory. As such, they left us a cultivated oral tradition communicated in memorable prose.[51] In sharp contrast to the present, past generations chose oral transmission as the principal means by which to pass along historical truths.[52] This, of course, does not imply the ancients did not employ written records. Instead, it is to put the emphasis on the right syllable: manuscript repositories augmented mental recall, not vice versa.[53]

Papyrus and Parchment. The original writings of the prophets and apostles are forever immortalized in a supernaturally preserved corpus of biblical manuscripts, some made of papyrus; others of parchment. While God could have preserved the autographs (original writings), the attendant problems would have been significant. Given the proclivities of humanity, we would no doubt have made idols out of them. In evidence, one need look no further than the Muslim veneration of Adam's white stone enshrined within the Great Mosque of Mecca—now allegedly black through the absorption of the sins of multiplied millions of pilgrims.[54]

And how would we determine the originals to be the originals? Think Shroud of Turin. Even in an age of highly advanced technology, there is no certainty that this is the original burial cloth that shrouded the face of Christ.[55] Moreover, who would control the originals—Jesuits, Rabbis, Imams? Would they be under glass in the Vatican or enshrined on Temple Mount in the Muslim Dome of the Rock?

In brief, if we had an identifiable autograph, the material paper and ink would likely replace God as the object of our worship; rancor would be palpable; and we would have no assurance that the text was indeed the text. We might well have had an autograph enshrined in Rome but we would lack the epistemic certainty of its authenticity.

Cumulatively, the sheer volume of manuscripts undergirding sacred Scripture dwarfs that of any other work of classical history. In the words of distinguished Greek scholar F. F. Bruce, "There is no body of ancient literature in the world that enjoys such a wealth of textual attestation as the New Testament."[56] Not only is there a relatively short time interval between the earliest extant papyrus and parchment copies and their autographs, but there is less than a generation between the autographs and the events they chronicle. The quantity and quality of papyrus and parchment manuscripts assure us that the message and intent of the original autographs have been passed on to the present generation without compromise.[57]

Internal Evidence. The eyewitness testimony of its authors is surpassingly powerful internal evidence to the absolute and irrevocable trustworthiness of Scripture. As Peter reminded his hearers, "We did not follow cleverly devised stories when we told you about the coming of our Lord Jesus Christ in power, but we were *eyewitnesses* of his majesty" (2 Peter 1:16). Luke, likewise, said that he gathered *eyewitness* testimony and "carefully investigated everything" (Luke 1:3). Internal evidence points to the reality that far from being inventors of internally inconsistent stories about Jesus, the gospel writers were inspired to faithfully narrate the core set of facts by which they had been radically transformed.[58] While it is conceivable that they would have faced torture, vilification, and even cruel deaths for what they fervently believed to be true, it is inconceivable that they would have been willing to die for cleverly invented stories that they knew to be lies.[59]

External Evidence. *Internal* evidence is sufficient to establish the biblical manuscripts as authentic, reliable, and complementary. *External* evidence, however, provides remarkable corroborating confirmation. From early external evidence provided by such credible historians as Tacitus[60] (the greatest first-century history historian of the ancient Roman Empire) as well as Suetonius[61] (well known for gathering historical data from eyewitnesses and citing historical accounts without prejudice or partiality[62]), it is possible to piece together highlights of Christ and New Testament Christianity wholly apart from the internal evidence.[63] It is amazing to think that even such historians as the Jewish Josephus—an eyewitness to many of the details found in the New Testament[64] —would provide ancient and authoritative attestation to the authenticity of the sacred text, but such is precisely the case.[65]

Science of Textual Criticism. Imagine writing a monograph on global Islamic jihadism and then asking five of your friends to produce handwritten copies. Suppose each of your friends asked five of their friends to produce copies of their copies. Of one thing you can be sure: your friends *will* make mistakes and so will *their* friends! By the fifth generation, three thousand *flawed* manuscript copies of the Muslim terrorism piece would exist somewhere on the planet. Moreover, imagine that during the copying process, your original monograph was discarded due to wear and tear or even destroyed. Would all have been lost? Of course not! Your five copyist friends all made mistakes, but it is unlikely that they all made the same mistakes. And that would be true of their friends and their friends' friends. Not only so, but most of the mistakes would be obvious—such as misspelled words or missed conjunctions. As such, no essential aspect of your treatise on terrorism would be tainted and even nonessential copyist errors could be resolved through what is known as the *science of textual criticism*. What is true of your monograph is true of the biblical manuscripts: the original writings are no longer available, but we can be certain that the copies accurately reflect the intent of the original writers.[66] The beauty from a biblical perspective is that the wealth of biblical manuscripts empowers textual critics to credibly ferret out copyist errors and allow the autographa to emerge unscathed.[67]

As the acronym COPIES reminds us, God has spoken, and the Bible is the infallible repository of what he has said. Likewise, the archaeologist's SPADE continues to accumulate evidence for the trustworthiness of Scripture and is an apt acronym for remembering that what is discovered in the soil corresponds to what is detailed in Scripture.[68]

Steles and Stones. In demonstrating that what was concealed in the soil corresponds to what is revealed in Scripture, the Merneptah and the Tel Dan Steles immediately come to mind, as do the Moabite and Pilate stones. With "Israel is wasted, bare of seed" etched into it, the Merneptah

Stele presents as formidable a challenge to exodus deniers as the Tel Dan Stele does to those pontificating that the biblical account of King David is no more factual than tales of King Arthur.[69] As *Time* rightly observed, "the skeptics' claim that King David never existed is now hard to defend."[70] The Moabite stone honors the victory of King Mesha of Moab over Israel, mentioning Yahweh, House of David, Omri, and Nebo and therefore making it difficult to contend that these biblical kings and places are the stuff of myth.[71] Likewise, the Pilate stone demonstrates in spades that Pilate was the Roman authority in Judea when Christ was crucified.[72]

Pools and Fools. Until quite recently, skeptics viewed the existence of the pools John referred to in his gospel to be little more than a religious conceit, a predilection on the part of Christians to believe that what they think is true *is* true solely because they *think* it's true. Only fools believed in John's pools. All of that changed in June 2004, when workers in the Old City of Jerusalem unearthed the place where Jesus cured the man born blind. Today, you can step into the very pool of Siloam in which the blind man "washed, and came *back* seeing" (John 9:7, NASB). Likewise, you can rest your arms on the guardrail overlooking the excavated ruins of the pool of Bethesda, where Jesus cared for the physical and spiritual needs of a man who suffered there for thirty-eight years (John 5). And you can stand amazed that what was once secreted in soil accurately reflects that which is scaled in Scripture.[73]

Assyrian Empire. From six hundred years before Christ until eighteen hundred years after him, Assyria and its chief city, Nineveh, lay entombed in the dustbin of history. Then the stones cried out. In 1845, Henry Austen Layard began digging along the Tigris River and unearthed Nineveh, the diamond of Assyria, embedded in the golden arc of the Fertile Crescent midway between the Mediterranean and Caspian Seas. Among the stunning archaeological gems discovered there were Sennacherib's prism, which corroborates the Bible's account of Sennacherib's assault on the Southern Kingdom of Judah (2 Kings 18–20); the black obelisk of Shalmaneser, showing archaeology's oldest depiction of an Israelite, Jehu the king of Israel, giving attribute of gold and silver to the Assyrian king; and the palace of Sargon, previously known only by a single reference in sacred Scripture (Isaiah 20:1). Together, Sennacherib's prism, Shalmaneser's black obelisk, and the ruins of Sargon's palace provide weighty testimony to the reliability of the biblical record.[74]

Dead Sea Scrolls. In 1947, the shattering of parchment-preserving pottery led to one of the greatest archaeological discoveries of modern times. With the discovery of the Dead Sea Scrolls, we now have a virtual first-century Hebrew Old Testament library available at the click of a twenty-first-century mouse. Not only so, but the Dead Sea Scrolls predate the earliest extant Hebrew text—Masoretic—by a full millennium. Thus, everyone from scholar to schoolchild can determine whether the Old Testament scriptures have been corrupted by men or miraculously preserved by God.[75] Additionally, the Dead Sea Scrolls provide significant insight into the text of the Old Testament and add considerable clarity to the text of the New Testament.[76]

Epic of Gilgamesh. Until the late nineteenth century, the masses presumed the great primordial deluge to be relegated to the text of Scripture. That began to change in 1853, when Hormuzd Rassam discovered the palace of Assurbanipal. There, among the treasures of Assyria's last king, he uncovered clay tablets on which was recorded the Epic of Gilgamesh and its independent confirmation of a vast flood in ancient Mesopotamia, complete with a Noahlike figure and an ark.[77] While the Epic views the waters of the flood through the opaque lens of paganism, it lends significant credence to the actual event. It is likewise a reminder that the reality of a great deluge is impressed on the collective consciousness of virtually every major civilization from the Sumerian epoch to the present age.[78]

Like manuscript copies and the archaeologist's spade, prophetic STARS in the constellation of biblical prophecy are powerful proofs for biblical authenticity. In the words of the Almighty, "I told you these things long ago; before they happened I announced them to you so that you could not say, 'My images brought them about; my wooden image and metal god ordained them'" (Isaiah 48:5). Or in the words of Jesus, "I have told you now before it happens, so that when it does happen you will believe" (John 14:29). Counterfeit prophecy stars are consistently wrong. In illuminated contrast, genuine STARS are infallibly correct.

Succession of Nations. As previously noted, one of the most significant demonstrations that God has spoken is the undeniable reality that

Daniel, writing six centuries before the advent of Christ, was empowered by almighty God to do what no soothsayer or astrologer could. With awe-inspiring precision, he predicted a succession of nations from Babylon through the Median and Persian empires. He also foretold the persecution and suffering of the Jews under the second-century Greco-Syrian beast Antiochus IV Epiphanes, including the despot's desecration of the Jerusalem temple, his untimely death, and freedom for the Jews under Judas Maccabaeus. Moreover, as Daniel looked down the corridor of time, he got a glimpse of a kingdom that will itself endure forever. Truly, the succession of nations immortalized by Daniel is a spectacular star in the constellation of biblical prophecy.[79]

Typological Prophecy. Predictive prophecy is fairly straightforward. Micah 5:2 immediately comes to mind. When Herod asked the chief priests where Christ was to be born, they answered that in accordance with the prophecy of Micah—Christ would be born in Bethlehem. Thus, Micah 5:2 is directly fulfilled with the birth of Christ in Bethlehem (Matthew 2:5).

As amazing as such predictive prophecies are, typological prophecies are even more mind-boggling in that they provide a structure that knits the Old Testament to the New and facilitates the understanding of each through reference to the other. In the array of spectacular typological prophecies made in the Old and fulfilled in the New, the "virgin birth" prophecy of Isaiah 7:14 shines with particular brightness: "Therefore the Lord himself will give you a sign: The virgin will conceive and give birth to a son, and will call him Immanuel."[80] This is the prototypical expression of a divinely intended pattern of events that encompasses both historical correspondence and intensification.[81]

The very first chapter of the very first book of the New Testament chronicles the birth of Jesus, as the glorious fulfillment of what the Lord had said through the prophet Isaiah—"'The virgin will conceive and give birth to a son, and they will call him Immanuel' (which means, 'God with us')" (Matthew 1:23). Matthew saw a historical pattern of events surrounding the birth of Isaiah's son that found quintessential fulfillment in a corresponding historical pattern surrounding the birth of Immanuel. While Isaiah's wife gave birth to Maher-Shalal-Hash-Baz in the fashion common to all humanity, the historical pattern reached a climax in the virgin birth of Messiah. Thus, while Isaiah's wife did not give birth as a virgin, Mary most certainly did![82]

Suffice it to say; only when the surpassing brilliance of typological prophecy is comprehended can the majesty of Scripture be fully apprehended.

Abomination of Desolation. The Olivet Discourse began with Jesus walking away from the very house that afforded the Jewish people their spiritual and sociological significance. He had pronounced seven woes on the Pharisees and then uttered the unthinkable: "Your house is left to you desolate" (Matthew 23:38). When the disciples called the Master's attention to the magnificence of the temple and its surroundings he replied, "Truly I tell you, not one stone here will be left on another; every one will be thrown down" (Matthew 24:2). Filled with apocalyptic awe and anxiety, they asked, "When will this happen, and what will be the sign of your coming and of the end of the age?"

In sober response, Jesus pointed his disciples toward the coming abomination:

> "When you see standing in the holy place 'the abomination that causes desolation,' spoken of through the prophet Daniel—let the reader understand—then let those who are in Judea flee to the mountains. Let no one on the housetop go down to take anything out of the house. Let no one in the field go back to get their cloak. How dreadful it will be in those days for pregnant women and nursing mothers! Pray that your flight will not take place in winter or on the Sabbath. For then there will be great distress, unequaled from the beginning of the world until now—and never to be equaled again. (Matthew 24:15–21)

"Then will appear," said Jesus, "the sign of the Son of Man in heaven. And then all the peoples of the earth will mourn when they see the Son of Man coming on the clouds of heaven, with power and great glory" (Matthew 24:30). So as to leave no doubt regarding the time of his coming, Jesus said, "Truly I tell you, this generation will certainly not pass away until all these things have happened. Heaven and earth will pass away, but my words will never pass away" (Matthew 24:34–35).

Like Daniel, Isaiah, Ezekiel, and a host of prophets before him, Jesus employed the language of "clouds" to warn his disciples of judgment that would befall Jerusalem within a generation.[83] Using final consummation language to characterize a near-future event, Jesus prophesied that those who saw standing in the holy place the abomination that causes desolation would likewise see his vindication and exaltation as Israel's rightful king.

"The abomination of desolation" spoken of by Jesus, had, of course, been prophesied six centuries earlier by Daniel who wrote, "His armed forces will rise up to desecrate the temple fortress and will abolish the daily sacrifice. Then they will set up the abomination that causes desolation. With flattery he will corrupt those who have violated the covenant, but the people who know their God will firmly resist him" (Daniel 11:31–32; see also 9:27; 12:31). In 167 BC, Daniel's prophecy became an unforgettable reality when Antiochus IV Epiphanes took Jerusalem by force, abolished temple sacrifices, erected an abominable altar to Zeus Olympus, and violated the Jewish covenant by outlawing Sabbath observance.[84]

Thus, when Jesus referenced the desolation spoken of by the prophet Daniel everyone knew precisely what he was talking about. The annual Hanukkah celebration ensured that they would ever remember the Syrian antichrist who desecrated the temple fortress, the pig's blood splattered on the altar, and the statue of a Greek god in the Holy of Holies. Had God not supernaturally intervened, through the agency of Judas Maccabaeus, the epicenter of their theological and sociological identity would have been destroyed, not just desecrated.

In the Olivet Discourse, Jesus took the quintessential Jewish nightmare and extended it to cosmic proportions. In the fullness of time, what Jesus declared desolate was desolated by Roman infidels. They destroyed the temple fortress and ended the daily sacrifice. This time, the blood that desolated the sacred altar did not flow from the carcasses of unclean pigs but from the corpses of unbelieving Pharisees. This time, the Holy of Holies was not merely desecrated by the defiling statue of a pagan god but was manifestly destroyed by the pathetic greed of despoiling soldiers. This time, no Judas Maccabaeus intervened. Within a generation, the temple was not just desecrated; it was destroyed! "Not one stone here," said Jesus, "will be left on another; every one will be thrown down" (Matthew 24:2). A generation later, when the disciples saw "Jerusalem being surrounded by armies" they *knew* "its desolation" was "near" (Luke 21:20). Thus, as Jesus had instructed, they fled to the mountains (Matthew 24:16; Luke 21:21). Those who rejected the prophetic message of Jesus and disregarded the abomination of desolation on the great altar of burnt offering were savagely slaughtered. Some one million fell by the sword. When they saw Jerusalem surrounded by armies, they should have known its desolation was near.[85]

The prophesied abomination of desolation by which the temple was desecrated in the Old Testament and destroyed in the New is yet another prophetic star enlightening our minds to the divine nature of the Scripture.

Resurrection. Without a doubt, resurrection is the brightest star in the constellation of biblical prophecy. While all other prophecies demonstrating the Bible to be divine rather than merely human in origin invoke the supernatural—resurrection embodies it. When the Jews demanded that Jesus prove his authority over temple, priest, and sacrifice, he responded, "Destroy this temple, and I will raise it again in three days" (John 2:19). The Jews thought he was speaking of Herod's temple, which had taken forty-six years to build. "But the temple he had spoken of was his body. After he was raised from the dead, his disciples recalled what he had said. Then they believed the scripture and the words that Jesus had spoken" (2:21–22).

Context here is crucial. Jesus had just "made a whip out of cords, and drove all from the temple courts, both sheep and cattle; he scattered the coins of the money changers and overturned their tables. To those who sold doves he said, 'Get these out of here! Stop turning my Father's house into a market!'" (John 2:15–16). The meaning of the passion of the Christ was not lost on his disciples. They had seen his miracles. They knew who he was. And did not in the least question his authority to do what he did. Collectively they remembered the prophetic words of King David, "Zeal for your house will consume me" (v. 17).

The Jewish Sanhedrists, too, knew of the miracles of Jesus. Thus, they did not immediately instruct the temple police to arrest him for civil disobedience. Instead, they asked for a miracle: "What sign can you show us to prove your authority to do all this?" (John 2:18). In place of a sign, Jesus presented a prophecy. Not just *a* prophecy—*the* prophecy. The prophecy demonstrating that the whole of the law and prophets pointed forward to him. The prophecy signifying that the Word of God cannot be broken. The prophetic star shining brightest in the constellation of biblical prophecy. "Destroy this temple," said Jesus, "and I will raise it again in three days." Dull of mind and spirit, those who heard the words of Jesus seemed incapable of comprehending them. The Sanhedrists thought the Savior referred exclusively to a sanctuary of glistening gold and luminous limestone. Sadly, the disciples fared no better. Not until Jesus had risen from the dead did they realize that the temple he had spoken of was the temple of his body.

When Jesus uttered the words *destroy this temple*, he was standing in the shadow of a sanctuary of which he himself was the substance. Instead of bowing to the substance, the temple keepers reveled in its shadow. "It has taken forty-six years to build this temple," they sneered, "and you are going to raise it in three days?" (John 2:20). Enamored by the picture, they were oblivious to the person. Sadly, they loved the type and loathed the antitype who had emerged in their midst.

In the end, their faithlessness led to the destruction of not just one, but two temples. First, they murdered Jesus. But in three days he took up his life again, thus fulfilling the prophecy: "Destroy this temple, and I will raise it again in three days." Their treachery led to the destruction of the temple as well. Thus was fulfilled the prophetic words of Jesus as he left the temple and was walking away, "Truly I tell you, not one stone here will be left on another; every one will be thrown down" (Matthew 24:2). The sun that daily refracts light from the golden dome of the Muslim mosque that has replaced the Jewish temple is an enduring reminder that God has spoken—that his Word cannot be broken.[86]

Superstar. In history there are superstars. Alexander the Great. Aristotle. Augustine. They lit the earth for a brief time but have long since disintegrated into dust. Only one superstar endures. One for whom there is no measure. He spoke and numberless stars leapt into existence. Morning stars together proclaimed his birth. One day he will flash across the eastern sky in an epic return to the planet he saved. He is the root and the offspring of David and the bright morning star.

Where there are STARS in the constellation of biblical prophecy, there is only one enduring superstar. Little wonder, then, that prophecies concerning him outnumber all others. His ancestry was marked and his birthplace foretold. Circumstances surrounding his death were prophesied before crucifixion was invented. The date of his visitation was predicted within historically narrow time parameters. He would work extraordinary miracles and fulfill the law and the prophets. It would be too small for him to bring back only those of Israel; thus, he would be a light for the Gentiles so that salvation would go out to the ends of the earth. Only the hand of God could have etched a prophetic portrait of the Christ in the Old Testament. Only God could cause it to take on flesh in the New. Only Jesus of Nazareth—the unique superstar—could emerge through the doorway of Old Testament prophecy.[87]

Together, manuscript COPIES, the archaeologist's SPADE, and prophetic STARS provide compelling proof that God has preserved the Scriptures. Moreover, as aptly noted by Dr. James White,[88] God's wisdom is evident through the way he "protected the text from the one thing we, centuries and millennia later, could never detect: wholesale change of doctrine or theology by one particular man or group who had full control over the text at any one point in its history."[89]

> [Instead,] because the New Testament books were written at various times and were quickly copied and distributed as soon as they were written, there was never a time when anyone or any group could gather up all the manuscripts and make extensive changes in the text itself, like cutting out Christ's deity or inserting some foreign doctrine or concept.[90]

In other words, no one could "gather up the texts and try to make them all say the same thing by harmonizing them." Instead, we have absolute assurance that this did not happen! "By the time anyone did obtain great ecclesiastical power in the name of Christianity, texts like P66 and P75 already were long buried in the sands of Egypt, out of the reach of any attempted alteration."[91]

Precisely the opposite is true of the Qur'an. In sharp contrast to such saliently significant texts as P66, P75, the Qur'an does not have an abundance of "freely reproduced texts from all over the Islamic state to draw upon to determine the earliest text."[92] Instead, according to the earliest authoritative Islamic account on how the Qur'an was composed (*Sahih al-Bukhari*),[93] Uthman, third rightly guided caliph after Muhammad, collated an Uthmanic version and "ordered that all the other Qur'anic materials, whether written in fragmentary manuscripts or whole copies, be burnt."[94]

Far from preserving Qur'anic fragments—whether on a stone, a palm stock, or the bleached shoulder bone of a camel—Uthman used his substantial ecclesiastical powers to produce "one compilation, then two decades later, a revision, followed by the concerted central-government effort to destroy any competing textual form."[95] Thus, the 114 surviving suras are not only infected by factual errors and faulty ethics but also constitute by design a fabricated edition that has been added to and subtracted from.[96]

Manuscript corruption, however, is far from the only Qur'anic problem. We may also know that the biblical canon is a straight measure and the Qur'an by contrast, crooked, through archaeology. Against the weight of archaeology, as well as history, the Qur'an denies the crucifixion of Christ (Q 4:157). This despite the reality that Christ's crucifixion as recorded in the biblical text is one of the best attested facts of ancient history. There is virtual consensus among New Testament scholars—both liberal and conservative—that Jesus died on a Roman cross and was buried in the tomb of Joseph of Arimathea.[97] Moreover, archaeological discoveries buttress both the biblical description of Roman crucifixion and the biblical details surrounding the religious trials that led to Christ's crucifixion.[98]

As with archaeologists, such ancient historians as Cornelius Tacitus, widely deemed the greatest first-century historian of the ancient Roman Empire, provide reliable corroborating testimony. Yet rather than rely on an authenticated biblical text or on credible ancient historians—including, Tacitus, Gaius Suetonius Tranquillus, and Flavius Josephus—Islam spurns the weight of history and evidence, contending that God made someone look like Jesus and the look-alike was crucified in place of him. This notion, popularized by a late medieval invention called *The Gospel of Barnabas*, is not only abominable but absurd.[99]

It should also be noted that while crucifixion is a major Qur'anic theme—as in Qur'an 5:33, where the penalty for disbelief in this life is "execution, or *crucifixion*, or the cutting off of hands and feet from opposite sides, or exile from the land"[100]—Allah can't so much as get the origin of crucifixion straight. Instead, he rips it out of its historical context and anachronistically places it in ancient Egypt at the time of Moses and Joseph.[101] As Muslims must surely know, this is historical revisionism at its worst. Crucifixion was invented by the Persians and later perfected by the Romans long after the time of Moses.[102] *The Study Quran* adds to this inexplicable historical blunder indicating that in accord with Muslim commentators "the first person to execute the punishment of 'cutting off hands and feet on alternate sides' and crucifixion was Pharaoh."[103]

Finally, we should add to manuscript corruptions and mistakes unearthed by the archaeologist's spade prophetic claims that simply do not correspond to reality. For example, in Qur'an 61:6, Allah allegedly claims that Jesus prophesied the coming of Ahmad (Muhammad): "And remember, Jesus, the son of Mary, said: 'O Children of Israel! I am the messenger of Allah (sent) to you, confirming the Law (which came) before me, and giving Glad Tidings of a Messenger to come after me, whose name shall be Ahmad'" (61:6).

The assertion is that the name Ahmad is derived "from the same root as Muhammad—*h-m-d*—and has long been recognized by Muslims as one of the many honorific names given to the Prophet by God Himself."[104] Thus, according to myriad Muslim scholars, when Jesus said, "I will ask the Father, and he will give you another advocate to be with you forever—the Spirit of truth" (John 14:16–17), what is really meant is that at the request of Jesus, the Father would send his disciples nothing less than Muhammad himself.

As Yusuf Ali put it,

> "Ahmad", *or* "Muhammad", the Praised One, is almost a translation of the Greek word *Periclytos* [*periklutós*]. In the present Gospel of John, 14:16, 15:26, and 16:7, the word "*Comforter*" in the English version is for the Greek word "*Paracletos*" [*parákletos*], which means "*Advocate*", "one called to the help of another, a kind friend", rather than "*Comforter*". Our doctors contend that *Paracletos* is a corrupt reading for *Periclytos*, and that in their original saying of Jesus there was a prophecy of our Holy Prophet Ahmad by name.[105]

Although many Muslims make the claim, it is, on the face of it, absurd. First, not a single biblical manuscript contains *periklutós* ("praised one") rather than *parákletos* (advocate, counselor). If such a textual corruption occurred at any point in its transmission, it could not be hidden. The beauty from a biblical perspective is that the embarrassment of riches respecting biblical manuscripts empowers textual critics to credibly sort out copyist changes so that the autograph emerges unscathed—which is precisely what scholars mean when they speak of the tenacity of the text.[106] Thus, in sharp distinction to the Qur'anic text, the science of textual criticism guarantees that the biblical text authentically recapitulates the words of the original writers.[107]

Furthermore, the immediate and broader context of the Gospel of John self-evidently precludes this Muslim invention. The counselor of whom Jesus speaks is already with them, and will be in them (14:17); and he will comfort and counsel the very disciples whom Jesus is addressing—Peter, James, John, and so forth—certainly not people living half a millennium later at the time of Muhammad (vv. 16, 18, 19, 26, and so on).

Finally, as forthrightly confessed by the Muslim scholars of *The Study Quran*, to insert Muhammad into John 14:16 is at best problematic:

Such an interpretation is, however, complicated by the next verse, 14:17, where the Advocate or Paraclete is said to be "the Spirit of truth, whom the world cannot receive, because it neither sees him nor knows him. You know him, because he abides with you, and he will be in you," and by 14:26, where the Advocate is again equated with the Holy Spirit.[108]

I conclude by repeating the maxim we began with, "Contrast is the mother of clarity." As such, "The way to show that a stick is crooked is not to argue about it or to spend time denouncing it, but to lay a straight stick alongside it." Both Christians and Muslims have their canon. That is, both religions have a standard of measurement. When we compare the Christian canon with the Muslim canon the contrast conclusively demonstrates that the Qur'anic canon is more than a little crooked.

TRINITY

Allahu Akbar! Allahu Akbar! Allahu Akbar! The Muslim cry repeated ad nauseam ad infinitum is now imprinted on the collective consciousness of humanity. It was the cry of the fanatical Muslim killer in Orlando who killed forty-nine people and injured fifty-three others on June 12, 2016, in the worst mass shooting in United States history,[109] just as it was the cry of chief hijacker Muhammad Atta on 9/11.[110] Indeed, it is the cry on the lips of every fervent Islamic believer.

And while media pundits seek to convince the gullible that "Allahu Akbar" means "God is great" (*Allahu kabir*), in actuality Allahu Akbar means Allah is *greater*—greater than all that is, including greater than the Christian God.[111] In truth, however, Allah cannot be great, much less greater than God, for at least three reasons. To begin with, the greatest of all gods would not misapprehend the Trinity. Second, he would not offer Islamic jihadists a paradise of idyllic joys as a reward for immoral jihad.[112] Third, the unitarian Allah of Islam, by definition, lacks the moral perfection of love and, thus, on the basis of logic, is morally defective.[113]

This is so because for God to be a perfect being, he must of necessity also be a loving being (1 John 4:8). This implies that there is someone to love. But there has not always been someone to love, because in accordance with modern cosmology,[114] the universe and the persons that inhabit it came into being a finite time ago.[115] Thus, independent of creation, the unitarian Allah would not have had an object on which to lavish love.[116]

While moral imperfections apply to the unitarian Allah, they do not likewise apply to the trinitarian God. Why? Because though the biblical God is a single being, there are subject-object distinctions within the Godhead. And the three centers of consciousness within the one true God have loved one another from all eternity.[117] Said C. S. Lewis:

> All sorts of people are fond of repeating the Christian statement that
> "God is love." But they seem not to notice that the words "God is love"
> have no real meaning unless God contains at least two Persons. Love is

something that one person has for another person. If God was a single person, then before the world was made, He was not love.[118]

Additionally, Christian philosopher William Lane Craig stated:

> On the Islamic view of God, God is a person who does not give himself away essentially in love for another. He is focused essentially only on himself. He cannot therefore be the most perfect being. But on the Christian view, God is a triad of persons in eternal self-giving love relationships. Thus, since God is essentially loving, the doctrine of the Trinity is more plausible than any unitarian concept of God such as Islam.[119]

The Allah of the Qur'an not only is morally imperfect but also, as previously noted, completely misapprehends trinitarian theology. Not only does Allah suppose the biblical God to be "the third of three," he supposes Mary to be the third person of the Triad.[120] This, of course, is completely wrongheaded. In concert with Jews, Christians have always been fiercely monotheistic. Moreover, there is not the slightest hint in the whole of Scripture that Mary is God.

While the Trinity is incomprehensible, the doctrine is hardly incoherent. As Professor Donald Fairbairn explained,

> Christian monotheism affirms the presence of three eternal, divine persons who are united in such a way as to be a single God and whose love for one another is the basis for all of human life. These persons are not separate—that would imply that they were different gods—but they are distinct as persons, and this distinction is what makes it possible for God to share love within himself from all eternity.[121]

In short, the trinitarian platform contains three planks. The first underscores the reality that there is only one God. The second emphasizes that in hundreds of passages the Father, Son, and Holy Spirit are each declared to be truly God. The third asserts that the Father, Son, and Holy Spirit are eternally distinct. It is likewise significant to reemphasize that when Christians speak of one God, the reference is to the nature or essence of God. And, when they speak of Persons, it is to "identity formed and completed on the basis of relationships" within the Godhead.[122] In other words—the one true God of the Bible is one *What* and three *Whos*.[123]

Early Christians, like their Old Testament counterparts, were willing to die for the unalterable truth that there is one and *only* one God. Three biblical passages persuasively highlight this foundational reality: *D*euteronomy 6:4; *I*saiah 43:10; *E*phesians 4:6.

Deuteronomy 6:4, of course, contains the Hebrew Shema—the most significant prayer of Old Testament Judaism—"Hear, O Israel: The LORD our God, the LORD is one." Isaiah 43:10 likewise codifies the Old Testament commitment to only one God. Here, as elsewhere, God called ancient Israel to "know," "believe," and "understand" this singular truth: "Before me no god was formed, nor will there be one after me." Ephesians 4:6, in the New Testament, is equally emphatic: There is "one God and Father of all, who is over all and through all and in all." As the student of Scripture knows full well, the Bible contains scores of similar passages so that "you might know that the LORD is God; *besides him there is no other*" (Deuteronomy 4:35).

Furthermore, the Bible declares that the Father is God in numerous passages including Ephesians 1:3; 1 Peter 1:3; and 2 Corinthians 1:3. The Son is declared God in the first chapters of John, Colossians, Hebrews, and Revelation. And the Spirit is unmistakably rendered God in such passages as Acts 5:3–4, in which lying to the Holy Spirit is equated with lying to God.[124]

Finally, the Bible decrees Father, Son, and Holy Spirit eternally distinct. Jesus, for example, made a distinction between himself and the Father, saying that the Father and Son are two distinct witnesses and two distinct judges (see John 8:16–18). Such self-distinctions within the Godhead are amplified through the annunciation of Christ's birth (Luke 1:35); his baptism (Luke 3:22); and his commission to baptize believers "in the name of the Father and of the Son and of the Holy Spirit" (Matthew 28:19).

For Christians, the doctrine of the Trinity is hardly theoretical; rather, it is eminently practical. For unlike Allah, who renders human beings mere servants,[125] the true and living God invites us to participate in the loving relationships that Father, Son, and Holy Spirit have enjoyed throughout eternity.[126]

RESURRECTION

The Muslim denial of Christ's resurrection strikes at the very heart of the historic Christian faith. Allah is adamant, "They killed him not, nor crucified him, but so it was made to appear to them." Adds Allah, "For of a surety they killed him not—Nay, Allah raised him up unto Himself; and Allah is Exalted in Power, Wise" (Q 4:157–58). As Yusuf Ali noted, "The Qur'anic teaching is that Christ was not crucified nor killed by the Jews, notwithstanding certain apparent circumstances which produced that illusion in the minds of some of his enemies."[127]

In forwarding the narrative that Christ's crucifixion was merely an illusion—that God made someone look like Jesus and the lookalike was crucified in place of Jesus—Muslims forward candidates ranging from Simon of Cyrene to Judas Iscariot. Some Muslims contend that one of the disciples volunteered to take on the likeness of Christ while others contend that God involuntarily caused one of Christ's enemies to take on his appearance.[128]

Perhaps most amazing of all, Yusuf Ali in his Qur'anic commentary seeks to bolster the denial of the crucifixion and subsequent resurrection of Christ through an appeal to *The Gospel of Barnabas*,[129] a late-medieval fabrication, not even concocted until the fourteenth century![130]

Muslims also disagree among themselves on what happened to Jesus subsequent to the crucifixion of his purported lookalike. A majority, however, suppose that he was taken into heaven and will one day return to earth where he will kill the antichrist and all pigs, destroy all churches and crosses, and accelerate the worldwide spread of Islam, before being buried in Medina next to the prophet Muhammad.[131]

If Muslims are right, the biblical account of the resurrection of Christ three days after his brutal death on the cross is either fiction, fantasy, or a gargantuan fraud. If, on the other hand, Christianity is factually reliable, his resurrection is the greatest feat in human history. No middle ground exists. The resurrection is history or hoax, miracle or myth, fact or fantasy.

Suffice it to say, the physical resurrection of Jesus Christ constitutes the very capstone of our faith. Without it, Christianity crumbles. As such, those who take the sacred name of Christ upon their lips must be prepared to defend its historicity. To make the process memorable, I've developed the acronym FEAT. It serves as an enduring reminder that the resurrection of Jesus Christ is the greatest feat in the annals of recorded history. Each letter will serve to remind you of an undeniable fact pertaining to the resurrection of our Lord.

Fatal Torment. The fatal suffering of Jesus Christ as recounted in the New Testament is one of the most well-attested facts of ancient history. Even in today's modern age of scientific enlightenment, there is a virtual consensus among New Testament scholars—both conservative and liberal—that Christ suffered and died upon a Roman cross and that his death drove his disciples to despair.[132] Allah overtly denies Christ's fatal torment (Q 4:157), thus demonstrating once more that he is neither wise nor all-knowing. The internal witness of the Christian Scriptures is sufficient proof that Christ died on a Roman cross; however, external evidence provides remarkable corroborating testimony. It is simply incredible to think that Tacitus, widely considered to be the greatest first-century historian of the ancient Roman Empire, would provide credible external evidence for the biblical account of Christ's crucifixion at the hands of the Roman governor Pontius Pilate.[133] Or that the Jewish Josephus, writing to please the Romans, would provide ancient authoritative attestation.[134] But such is precisely the case. Thus, Allah could not be more deluded in this matter.

Empty Tomb. As with Christ's fatal torment, liberal and conservative New Testament scholars agree that the body of Jesus was buried in the private tomb of Joseph of Arimathea. As a member of the Jewish court that convicted Jesus, Joseph of Arimathea is unlikely to be Christian fiction. And considering that females in ancient Judaism were routinely considered little more than chattel, the empty tomb accounts provide powerful evidence that the gospel writers valued truth over cultural correctness. Had the gospel accounts been legendary, males would most certainly have been heroes of the narrative. Not only so, but the earliest Jewish response to the resurrection presupposes the empty tomb; and in the centuries following the resurrection, the fact of the empty tomb was forwarded by Jesus' friends and foes alike. Christianity simply could not have survived an identifiable tomb containing the remains of Messiah.[135] As the late liberal scholar John A. T. Robinson of Cambridge conceded, the burial of Christ "is one of the earliest and best attested facts about Jesus."[136]

Appearances. One thing can be stated with ironclad certainty: the apostles did not merely propagate Christ's teachings, they were certain that he had appeared to them in the flesh after his crucifixion, death, and burial. Although two thousand years removed from the actual event, we, too, can be confident in Christ's post-resurrection appearances. In 1 Corinthians 15:3–7, the apostle Paul reiterated a Christian creed that scholars of all stripes have concluded can be dated to mere months after Messiah's murder. The short timespan between Christ's crucifixion and the composition of this early Christian creed precludes the possibility of legendary corruption. The creed is early, free from legendary contamination, unambiguous, specific, and ultimately rooted in eyewitness testimony.[137] Paul claimed that Christ appeared to hundreds of people, still alive and available for cross-examination. It would be one thing to attribute such supernatural experiences to people who had already died. It is quite another to attribute them to multitudes who were still alive.[138]

Transformation. The Twelve (minus Judas, plus Paul) were radically revolutionized by the post-resurrection appearances of Christ. After the resurrection, Peter—once afraid of being exposed as a follower of Christ by a young woman—was transformed into a lion of the faith. He, of course, was not alone. Within weeks of the resurrection, not just a few, but an entire community of thousands of Jews, willingly transformed the spiritual and sociological traditions underscoring their national identity.[139] The Sabbath was transformed into a first-day-of-the-week celebration of the rest we have through Christ, who delivers us from sin and the grave. Not only so, but after the resurrection, followers of Christ suddenly stopped making animal sacrifices. They recognized the new covenant as better than the old covenant because the blood of Jesus Christ was better than the blood of animals. The Jewish rite of Passover was radically transformed as well. In place of the Passover meal, believers began partaking of the Eucharist. In like fashion, baptism took on new meaning. Prior to the resurrection, converts to Judaism were baptized in the name of Yahweh, God of Israel. After the resurrection, converts to Christianity were baptized in the name of Jesus. In doing so, believers equated Jesus with Israel's God.[140]

Christian statesman Chuck Colson provided a poignant perspective:

> I know the resurrection is a fact, and Watergate proved it to me. How? Because 12 men testified they had seen Jesus raised from the dead, then they proclaimed that truth for 40 years, never once denying it. Every one was beaten, tortured, stoned and put in prison. They would not have endured that if it weren't true. Watergate embroiled 12 of the most powerful men in the world—and they couldn't keep a lie for three weeks. You're telling me 12 apostles could keep a lie for 40 years? Absolutely impossible.[141]

Of one thing I am certain: if twenty-first-century Christians in concert with the disciples would fully apprehend the reality of the greatest FEAT in history, they could—no, would—stem the resurgent tide of Islam by building a lighthouse in the midst of the gathering storm.

INCARNATION

The more I contemplate incarnation, the more staggered my imagination. The very thought that the One who spoke and a hundred billion galaxies leapt into existence should cloak himself in human flesh is, well, unthinkable. To imagine that the One who knit me together in my mother's womb would himself inhabit Mary's womb boggles the mind. Yet this is precisely what Christianity proffers—a Creator beyond comprehension who has revealed himself in incarnation.

Incarnation (quite literally, "coming in flesh") is the greatest of all revelations. When Germanic invaders overwhelmed the Roman Empire in the West, Christianity established a new order called Europe. And the principle undergirding the new world order was codified in a singular word—*revelation*. Indeed, Augustine believed revelation to be the necessary precondition for all knowledge.[142]

The realization that revelation is axiomatic for knowledge led medieval thinkers to crown theology queen of the sciences. Peter Paul Rubens personified this elegantly in his seventeenth-century painting *The Triumph of the Eucharist*. Seated in a chariot propelled by angelic beings is theology—queen of the sciences. Walking alongside are philosophy, the wise and grizzled veteran, and science, a newcomer in the cosmic conversation. Theology is never absent philosophy and science.[143] But philosophy and science absent revelation leads inexorably to the blind ditch of ignorance.[144]

The new world order that arose from the impotence of Greco-Roman thought was grounded in the premise that God has revealed himself as creator and sustainer of the universe through general revelation, special revelation, and the apex of all revelations—incarnation. In the words of the Beloved Apostle, "The Word became flesh, and dwelt among us, and we saw His glory, glory as of the only begotten from the Father, full of grace and truth" (John 1:14 NASB).

To the Allah of Islam, this is nothing short of blasphemous. God "begetteth not, nor is He begotten" (Q 112:3). The very notion is offensive. To Allah's way of thinking, calling God "Father" and Jesus Christ "Son" suggests sexual procreation. "It is not befitting to (the majesty of) Allah that He should beget a son" (Q 19:35). "How can He have a son when He hath no consort?" (Q 6:101). "And exalted is the majesty of our Lord: He has taken neither a wife nor a son" (Q 72:3).

What Allah fails to understand, of course, is that the Bible does not use the term *begotten* with respect to the Father and the Son in the sense of sexual reproduction but rather in the sense of special relationship. Thus, when the apostle John spoke of Jesus as "the only begotten from the Father" (John 1:14 NKJV), he was underscoring the unique deity of Christ. Likewise, when the apostle Paul referred to Jesus as "the *firstborn* over all creation" (Colossians 1:15), he was emphasizing Christ's preeminence or prime position as the Creator of all things (Colossians 1:16–19). As such, Christians are sons of God through adoption; Jesus is God the Son from all eternity.

For followers of the Muslim Allah, the incarnation of Jesus Christ entails the gravest of all sins. Why? Because the doctrine of incarnation—that

Jesus Christ is God come in flesh—is tantamount to *shirk*—the unforgivable sin of assigning partners to God. As Islamic expert Dr. James White explained, "In secular Arabic, the root *shirk* simply means 'association, to join together,' as in a secular corporation. But in religious usage, *shirk* takes on a whole different meaning as the worst possible negation of *tawhid* [Allah's absolute oneness and uniqueness], associating anyone, or anything, with Allah."[145]

Allah is direct and emphatic: "Allah forgiveth not (the sin of) joining other gods with Him; but He forgiveth whom He pleaseth other sins than this" (Q 4:116). Thus, while Muslims readily affirm the sinlessness of Christ, they dogmatically deny his incarnation as both insulting to the majesty of Allah and logically incoherent.

But is it really? While many issues surrounding the incarnation, such as the precise modes of interaction between Christ's divine nature and his human nature, may transcend human understanding, the doctrine of incarnation does not transgress the laws of logic. To understand the logical coherence of the incarnation, one must first consider the *imago Dei* (image of God). Because God created humanity in his own image (Genesis 1:27), the essential properties of human nature (rationality, will, moral character, and the like) are not inconsistent with his divine nature. Thus, while the notion of God becoming a clam would be self-evidently absurd, the reality that God became a man is not.

Moreover, it is crucial to point out that though the God-man is *truly* human, he is not *merely* human. And though the divine Son of God took on all the essential properties of human nature, he did not take on that which is nonessential (e.g., sinful inclinations). Indeed, as Adam was created without a proclivity toward sin, so the Second Adam (Jesus) was untainted by original sin. And like his moral perfection, Jesus' other divine attributes (omniscience, omnipotence, omnipresence, and so forth) were not undermined in the incarnation.

While Jesus Christ voluntarily refrained from exercising certain attributes of deity, he did not divest himself of a single divine attribute (John 1:14; Philippians 2:1–11; Colossians 1:15–20; Hebrew 2:14–18). With respect to his omniscience, for example, his human nature may have served as a filter limiting his knowledge as a man (e.g., Mark 13:32). Nonetheless, Jesus' divine omniscience was ever accessible at the will of the Father. To put it directly, there is no incoherence in the biblical teaching that the eternal Son of God added humanity to his divinity such that he will forever remain one person with two distinct natures, neither confusing his natures nor becoming two persons.

It is more than intoxicating to reflect on the reality that as Christ is incarnate in the image of humankind, so humanity in Christ is being refashioned in the image of God. As Athanasius of Alexandria, widely regarded as the greatest theologian of his time, well said, "He was made man that we might be made God."[146] Or in the words of Peter, we "participate in the divine nature" (2 Peter 1:4). This, of course, is not to say that we, though redeemed, possess God's incommunicable attributes. Who among us can claim self-existence, immutability, eternality, omnipotence, omniscience, omnipresence, and absolute sovereignty? God *is eternal*,[147] but humanity was created at a point in time[148] and has but a brief mortal existence on the earth.[149] God has life in himself,[150] but man is dependent on God to sustain him.[151] God is all-powerful,[152] but man is weak.[153] God is all-knowing,[154] but man is limited in knowledge.[155] God is everywhere present,[156] but humans are confined to a single space at a time.[157]

Thus, far from being reproductions of God, human beings are more correctly portrayed as reflections of God. That humans are created in God's image simply means that they share, in a finite and imperfect way, the communicable attributes of God. Among such attributes are personality, spirituality, rationality (including knowledge and wisdom), and morality (including goodness, holiness, righteousness, love, justice, and mercy).[158]

These attributes in turn give us the capacity to enjoy fellowship with God and to develop personal relationships with one another. Theologian Millard Erickson summed it up nicely when he wrote that the image of God in humanity comprises "those qualities of God which, reflected in man, make worship, personal interaction, and work possible."[159]

The glorious reality is this. Despite the fall, you and I continue to be image bearers of God. This reflection of the divine image in us has been blemished, yet not obliterated. James, the half-brother of Jesus, affirmed this truth when he wrote that men are "made in God's likeness" (James 3:90). Through sanctification in Christ, God is renewing an image that is blemished and broken. We have taken off the "old self" with its practices and have put on the new self, which is being renewed in knowledge in the image of its creator.[160]

Indeed, it is liberating for believers to revel in the reality that in the consummation of all things God will completely restore the *imago Dei* in fallen humanity. Had the incarnate Christ not come in the image and likeness of man, there would be no hope for humanity to be refashioned in the *imago Dei*.[161]

For Muslims, then, incarnation invokes the unforgivable sin of *shirk*. For Christians, it is entryway into new creation.

NEW CREATION

There is no higher note in the symphony of Scripture than this: "If anyone is *in Christ*, the *new creation* has come; The old has gone, the new is here!" (2 Corinthians 5:17). Such an ayah (verse) is conspicuous by its absence in the whole of the Qur'an. Indeed, it would be sheer absurdity to so much as suggest that someone could be a new creation *in Muhammad*. The very concept is rightly foreign to Islam. A Muslim might imitate Muhammad or idealize Muhammad, but the notion that they could be *in Muhammad* is self-evidently absurd.

Not so with Christ. The Father's greatest gift to those saved through the death of his Son is the impartation of a new order of life. An order of life that is of the same quality as the life of Christ. For that is precisely what it is—the ingrafting of the life of Christ. Thus, to be *in* Christ is more than a changed life; it is an exchanged life—an impartation of life by which the incarnation continues. As the apostle Paul put it, "I have been crucified with Christ and I no longer live, but Christ lives *in me*" (Galatians 2:20).

Union with the divine is God's greatest gift to humanity and the apex of human existence. It is the high peak truth of redemptive revelation— the Everest of experiential epistemology. To recapitulate the words of the apostle to the Gentiles, "If anyone is in Christ, the new creation has come: The old has gone, the new is here!" Such newness is not relegated to the felicity of forgiveness and purification—though it is most certainly that. But it encompasses the great and glorious grace by which the forgiven now live in intimate union with the triadic One. This is not merely an objective truth to be cognitively apprehended. "Life in the Trinity" is a living reality to be comprehended experientially.

No one expressed this glorious grace more eloquently than did Martin Luther in his famed Christmas sermon of 1514. "For the word becomes flesh precisely so that the flesh may become word. In other words: God becomes man so that man may become God."[162] As such, the descent of the ineffable in incarnation provides the ladder of divine ascent by which fallen humanity may rise up to union with God—*and as such become new creations in Christ*. What that means, said Luther, is nothing less than the inviolate truth "that a man helped by grace is more than a man; indeed, the grace of God gives him the form of God and deifies him, so that even the Scriptures call him 'God' and 'God's son.'"[163]

This, of course, is not so much as to hint at heresy. Luther, should he have imagined that his aphorism, "God becomes man so that man may become God," would be taken as a confusion of essences, would turn over in his grave. In like fashion, the other greats of church history. Of one thing they were certain. While redeemed humanity may partake in the energies of God, the essence of God remains inviolate. As Gregory Palamas rightly observed, "the Logos became flesh, and the flesh became Logos, even though neither abandoned its own proper nature."[164]

Thus, when the apostle Peter proclaims that those in Christ "may participate in the divine nature" (2 Peter 1:4), he is not suggesting that redeemed humanity may become what God is in essence. That is not only impossible, it is heretical. Those in Christ become by grace what the Son of God is by nature—"children of God" (John 1:12). As such, his divinity interpenetrates our humanity.

Historically, the Christian church has illustrated this scintillating truth through the thrusting of a sword into the red-hot flames of a furnace. While the steel of the sword takes on the properties of fire, such that gray steel turns fiery red, the sword never becomes the fire nor the fire the sword. Augustine elucidated the self-same verity by way of water and sponge. Though the sponge absorbs the ineffable waters of God's inexhaustible energy, it yet remains a sponge. The sponge does not become the water, nor the water the sponge.[165] Again, to be in Christ—to experience his divine life—is to experience his energies, not to partake of his essence.[166]

The "tin man," to use a C. S. Lewis illustration, is being turned into a real man. Those who are in Christ have been transformed into new creations. The image and likeness of God, once ruinously marred, is being miraculous restored. Said Lewis:

> The real Son of God is at your side. He is beginning to turn you into the same kind of thing as Himself. He is beginning, so to speak, to 'inject' His kind of life and thought, His *Zoe*, into you; beginning to turn the tin soldier into a live man.[167]

It is not a famous counselor or teacher who is changing the sensibilities of the redeemed from one thing to another. No! It is Jesus himself turning the tin man into a true man. Yes, he is God. The one who spoke and the limitless galaxies leapt into existence. But he is also very much a man. Not one who is dead, but one who is alive forevermore. Not only alive, but actively transforming you and me into a likeness of himself.

"It is a root and branch change," proffered Charles Haddon Spurgeon, the prince of preachers:

> It is not a new figuring of the visible tapestry, but a renewal of the fabric itself. Regeneration is a change of the entire nature from top to bottom in all senses and respects, and such is the new birth! Such is it to be *in* Christ and to be *renewed* by the Holy Spirit. [In Christ, we are new creatures!] It is as though the former creature were annihilated and put away, and a something altogether new were formed from the breath of the eternal God.[168]

It is rather like metamorphosis. Like the caterpillar becoming a monarch. Eyes that once could only distinguish between light and darkness are transformed into majestic orbs with an unimaginable field of vision and color acuity. Wings appear as if by magic. An indescribably complex reproductive system—wholly absent in the caterpillar—materializes mysteriously.

An unimaginable strawlike proboscis emerges, allowing the "new creation" to indulge in the nectar of a brand-new life. The new creature that emerges is simply beyond belief![169]

And so it is with those who are new creatures in Christ. We've experienced a kind of metamorphosis.

> These new creatures, fresh from the divine hand, as though just fashioned between the eternal palms, are the men and women who weep because of sin; the men and women who confess their iniquity; those who say, "God be merciful to us, sinners"; those who rest in the blood of the atonement; who love Christ Jesus, and live to the glory of the Most High—these are *new creatures*! There is freshness about them; they have just come from the hand of God; they enjoy nearness to God; they get to the fountainhead of life, and drink where the crystal stream is cool, and clear, and not muddied by distant trickling through earthly channels! There is freshness, I say, about them which is to be found nowhere else![170]

Certainly not in Islam. There, one cannot be in Christ, for Christ is not God. Nor is there any need or room for the atonement of the cross. All one can hope for is that our good deeds outweigh the bad;[171] that perhaps Muhammad may intercede on our behalf;[172] or that based on an arbitrary judgment we are granted forgiveness. A celebrated story from *Sahih al-Bukhari* amplifies the point. In the account, Muhammad speaks of a man who had murdered ninety-nine people and asked a monk whether his repentance could be accepted.

> The monk replied in the negative and so the man killed him. He kept on asking till a man advised to go to such and such village. (So he left for it) but death overtook him on the way. While dying, he turned his chest towards that village (where he had hoped his repentance would be accepted), and so the angels of mercy and the angels of punishment quarreled amongst themselves regarding him. Allah ordered the village (towards which he was going) to come closer to him, and ordered the village (whence he had come), to go far away, and then He ordered the

angels to measure the distances between his body and the two villages. So he was found to be one span closer to the village (he was going to). So he was forgiven.[173]

No justice here, merely an arbitrary judgment.

As contrast is the mother of clarity, we do well to consider an analogous account of criminality, but with a far different reckoning. Two scoundrels are crucified on either side of Christ. One reviles. The other repents. If the first had any use for Christ at all it was only as a means by which to cheat justice and perpetuate an earthly existence of wanton wickedness. Nowhere is there even a hint of remorse, much less repentance. Conversely, the second criminal had a genuine change of heart. He contrasted the innocence of Christ with the justice of his own crucifixion and humbly asked the Lord of glory to include him as a participant in his eternal kingdom. Knowing the imminence of his death, Jesus answered, "Truly I tell you, today you will be with me in paradise" (Luke 23:43). In the end, one criminal dies in rebellion. The other in repentance. Here there is no capriciousness. No arbitrary act of divine forgiveness. Instead, as on every other occasion, faith finds the sinner's prayer sufficient: *Lord Jesus Christ, Son of God, have mercy on me a sinner.*

To the account of *Sahih al-Bukhari*, Dr. White provides a perceptive response:

> From the perspective of this *hadith*, forgiveness flows not from God's actions in providing a *basis* for salvation, but from His power alone. He acts capriciously—there are many others who have done less moral evil that He does not forgive and who populate hell—and not in reference to any standard derived from His own unchanging nature.[174]

How odious the crooked stick when laid next to the straight stick of Scripture. "In Islam, forgiveness is an impersonal act of arbitrary divine power. In Christianity, forgiveness is a personal act of purposeful and powerful yet completely just divine grace."[175]

One criminal receives justice in perfect measure for his wickedness. The other is refashioned a new creation. Said Paul:

All this is from God, who reconciled us to himself through Christ and gave us the ministry of reconciliation: that God was reconciling the world to himself in Christ, not counting people's sins against them. And he has committed to us the message of reconciliation. We are therefore Christ's ambassadors, as though God were making his appeal through us. (2 Corinthians 5:18–20)

As such, we implore those trapped in the uncertainty of Islamic salvation: "Be reconciled to God." For "God made him [Jesus Christ] who had no sin to be sin for us, so that in him we might become the righteousness of God" (2 Corinthians 5:20–21).

ESCHATOLOGY

From the moment we are born, our bodies begin sowing the seeds of biological destruction. Yet death is hardly the end. The cycle of life and death is forever broken through resurrection. Four days after Lazarus died, Jesus said to Martha, "'Your brother will rise again.' Martha answered, 'I know he will rise again in the resurrection at the last day.' Jesus said to her, 'I am the resurrection and the life. The one who believes in me . . . will never die'" (John 11:23–26). In saying this Jesus pointed to himself as the very one who would overcome death and the grave and as such ensure that all who put their trust in him will experience "resurrection at the last day."

Old Testament prophet Daniel likened resurrection at the end of time to the glory of the stars: "Multitudes who sleep in the dust of the earth will awake: some to everlasting life, others to shame and everlasting contempt. Those who are wise will shine like the brightness of the heavens, and those who lead many to righteousness, like the stars for ever and ever" (Daniel 12:2–3). The resurrection envisioned is unambiguous. Daniel speaks not of the disembodied state that follows death but of the bodily resurrection following Christ's second appearing.

Jesus gave certainty to the resurrection that will occur at the consummation of history in saying, "Do not be amazed at this, for a time is coming when all who are in their graves will hear his voice and come out—those who have done what is good will rise to live, and those who have done what is evil will rise to be condemned" (John 5:28–29). All who place their trust in Jesus can be absolutely certain they will experience resurrection. Jesus promised that he would lay down his life and take it up again in three days. His fulfillment of the promise is the guarantee that there is life *after* life-after-life.

There is life after life, in that the soul continues to have awareness after the death of the body. In Luke 16, Jesus tells the parable of a rich man and a beggar who die physically yet experience conscious awareness in the intermediate state—a fact difficult to deny in that the rich man's brothers are living and final judgment has not yet occurred. After death, Jesus describes Lazarus as being conscious in the presence of God. To borrow the words of the apostle Paul, he was "away from the body and at home with the Lord" (2 Corinthians 5:8). Disembodied, he no longer experienced *whereness* (extension in space); his *awareness*, however, was greatly intensified. Thus, it may well be said that Lazarus is presently experiencing life after life. Moreover, there is life *after* life-after-life, in that just as Jesus rose bodily from the grave, so, too, at Christ's second appearing our bodies will rise immortal, imperishable, and incorruptible (1 Corinthians 15:50–56). Proof of the resurrection is so certain that martyrs willingly lay down their lives, certain that they will take them up again at the end of time.

This is the essence of eschatology—the study of end-times. Eschatology is the thread that weaves the tapestry of Scripture into a harmonious pattern. Early in Genesis, Adam and Eve fell into lives of perpetual sin terminated by death. The rest of Scripture chronicles God's unfolding plan of redemption. While Christians debate various secondary aspects of eschatology, such as the timing of the tribulation[176] or the meaning of the millennium,[177] they are united in the truth that just as Christ came to earth once to bear the sins of the world,[178] so, too, he will return to gather together those he has regenerated as new creations and to usher in the resurrection of all things.[179] In the end, the just will be resurrected to eternal life[180] and the unjust to separation from the goodness, grace, and glory of God.[181] Paradise lost will become paradise restored and the problem of sin and Satan will be fully and finally resolved.[182]

In Islam, as in Christianity, there is life after life (*barzakh*) in that the soul is said to have conscious awareness after death.[183] In classical Islam, the soul emerges through the throat, is wrapped in a foul or fragrant frock, and travels in the company of angels to the seven rings of heaven, where only those who smell good are permitted entrance—both foul and fragrant return to their bodies while washers yet attend their corpses.[184] Thereafter, the angels Munkar and Nakir invite the dead to sit up in their graves and respond to three questions: *Who is your God? Who is your prophet? What is your religion?*[185] The grave of one who correctly responds (*qwal thabit*)— Allah, Muhammad, and Islam—is made to be "an expanse of seventy cubits, and it is filled with green foliage until the Day of Resurrection."[186] The grave of one who answers otherwise "becomes so constricted that his ribs burst."[187] Moreover, Munkar and Nakir "pound him with iron hammers between his ears, and he screams a scream heard by everyone around except spirits and human beings."[188] It is largely held that both believers and infidels suffer while in the grave; however, the torment of the *kafir* far outweighs that of the Islamic devotee. What the dead engage in beyond this is in much dispute.

As there is life after life, so, too, there is life *after* life-after-life in that, in accord with Islamic eschatology, all will be recreated at the final hour. According to the renowned Qur'anic exegete Umar ibn Kathir (d.1373), two trumpet blasts signify the end of all things:

> The first blast is that of the terror (*fazac*). While people are in their marketplaces buying and selling, God commands the angel Isrāfīl, or Seraphiel, to blast the trumpet, which is heard throughout the earth. Humanity is then led to an earthly gathering place (maḥshar), followed by the swoon (ṣaq), whereby they all perish.[189]

And says the Qur'an, "the heavens will be enfolded in His right Hand" (39:67, *Study Quran*).

At the second trumpet blast, extinct humanity is recreated and regathered for a day of reckoning on a great plain where "trepidation will grip most people. The Prophet has said that people will be up to their necks in sweat."[190] They will cry out in desperation for a prophet to intercede on their behalf, but none will answer—not Adam, nor Moses, not even

Jesus. "Finally, humanity will arrive at the last messenger, the Prophet Muhammad, who will accept the task and proceed to intercede with God on behalf of humanity."[191]

Ultimately, all is a function of scrolls, scales, and *sirat*.

After the Reckoning, the receiving of the scroll of deeds occurs and individuals are each given their own book. The books, which contain all human actions, each in an individual scroll, are described as "flying" in a flurry of apparent chaos, until each arrives at its appointed person. The believers receive theirs in their right hand and rejoice, while the hypocrites and disbelievers are given theirs in the left hand from behind their backs (see [Q] 69:19–37; 84: 6–12).[192]

Everyone is forced to read their scroll and acknowledge the rightness of the record. "Read your book! On this Day, your soul suffices as a reckoner against you" (Q 17:14, *Study Quran*).

Next are the scales:

Once the records of the deeds are distributed among the resurrected, the weighing of actions on the scales takes place: *We shall set the just scales for the Day of Resurrection, and no soul shall be wronged in aught. Even if it be the weight of a mustard seed, We shall bring it. And We suffice as Reckoner* ([Q] 21:47; see also 7:8; 23:102–3; 101:6–11).[193]

In other words, for those whose good works outweighs their bad, paradise awaits. Conversely, for those whose bad deeds outweigh their good, the fires of hell await. "The Fire will burn their faces, and they will therein grin, with their lips displaced" (Q 23:104).

Following the scrolls and scales, comes the *sirat*. *Sahih Muslim* describes it as a traverse or bridge that is "finer than a hair and sharper than a sword."[194] In *The Islamic Understanding of Death and Resurrection*, Islamic scholars Smith and Haddad wrote:

[The *sirat* is] the last modality in the process that assesses the degree to which every individual has followed that [straight] path. Very probably reflecting an influence from Zoroastrian tradition in which the bridge plays a major role in the eschatological process, the ṣirāṭ in Islamic thought seems to be yet another means of verifying rather than testing the relative merit of any given individual.[195]

For hypocrites, the *sirat* is razor sharp; thus, they descend inexorably into the horror of hell. "The faithful, on the contrary, move easily and swiftly across a broad path, led by the members of the Muslim community and first of all by the Prophet himself."[196]

Following the scrolls, scales, and *sirat* is the eternal state. Believers cross an arched bridge into the bliss of the gardens, as disbelievers enter the torment of the fires. The Qur'an describes hell as having "seven gates" (Q 15:44), alluding "to the seven levels of Hell, which are a part of traditional Islamic eschatological beliefs"[197]—each level descending to intensified torment.

> The purgatorial fire [*jahannam*] for Muslims; the flaming fire [laẓā] for Christians; the raging fire [ḥuṭāma] for Jews; the blazing fire [*sa'īr*] for Sabaeans; the scorching fire [*saqar*] for the Magi; the fierce fire [jaḥīm] for idolaters; and the abyss [*hāwiya*] for hypocrites. Later traditions supplied each of the gates of the Fire with innumerable guardians who torture the damned. From the shallowest level the *mu'minun* [persons of faith] will be pardoned and taken into paradise; that layer of the Fire will then be destroyed.[198]

The Qur'anic metaphors employed to describe hell quite literally boggle the mind:

> The people of the Fire are sighing and wailing, wretched (S 11:106), their scorched skins are constantly exchanged for new ones so that they can taste the torment anew [S 4:56], they drink festering water and though death appears on all sides they cannot die (S 14:16–17), people are linked together in chains of 70 cubits (S 69:30–32) wearing pitch for clothing and fire on their faces (S 14:50), boiling water will be poured over their heads, melting their insides as well as their skins, and hooks

of iron will drag them back should they try to escape (S 22:19–21). To these terrifying details the ḥadīths could add only more elaboration and more specifics.[199]

Islamic scholars Smith and Haddad add horrifying extra-Qur'anic images that picture the damned having "black charred skins, huge long tongues, mouths vomiting pus and blood, entrails filled with fire; their bodies will be greatly enlarged so that they can more adequately experience the torture. All suffer by fire, although the degree of punishment differs according to one's sins."[200]

While descriptions of hell are beyond gruesome, descriptions of heaven by contrast are beckoningly glorious. Qur'anic images of the blessedness awaiting believers in the paradisiacal gardens are so lustrous that there has been little need to amplify expectations via extra-Qur'anic literature. In harmony with Muhammad's night journey, heaven is depicted as having seven levels—the first on which Muhammad encountered Adam; the second, John and Jesus; third, Joseph; fourth, Idris (Enoch); fifth, Aaron; sixth Moses; seventh, Abraham. The seventh and final heaven is replete with a Ka'bah around which seventy-thousand angels continuously circumambulate. In the uppermost boundary of the seventh heaven is a lote tree and beyond it is the hereafter where, during his magical mystery tour of 619, Muhammad famously found himself standing in the presence of Allah.

From the lote tree flow "rivers of water incorruptible, rivers of milk whose flavor does not change, rivers of wine delicious for those who imbibe, and rivers of purified honey" (Q 47:15).[201] Believers lounge on "embroidered couches" (56:15)[202] and are served never-ending streams of wine. "No headiness lies therein; nor are they intoxicated by it" (37:47).[203]

Smith and Haddad highlight the particular paradisiacal pleasures afforded males via the houris of heaven:

The Qur'ānic descriptions of the ḥūr [44:54; 52:20; 55:56–76; 56:22[204]], though restrained, have been sufficient to pique the imaginations of the faithful and have served as the basis for a great deal of later elaboration. In the ḥadīths details of their description differ, but they are generally said to be composed of saffron from the feet to the knees, musk from the knees to the breast, amber from the breast to the neck, and camphor from the neck to the head. Working often with multiples of seven, the traditionalists have described them as wearing seventy to 70,000 gowns, through which even the marrow of their bones can be seen because of the fineness of their flesh, reclining on seventy couches of red hyacinth encrusted with rubies and jewels, and the like. The ḥūr do not sleep, do not get pregnant, do not menstruate, spit, or blow their noses, and are never sick. References to the increased sexual process of those male believers for whose pleasure the ḥūr are intended are numerous; the reports make it clear that the ḥūr are created specifically as a reward for males of the Muslim community who have been faithful to God.[205]

The houris, who the *hadiths* carefully distinguish from female believers, "are described in the Qur'ān as chaste, with glancing eyes like pearls or guarded eggs, of equal age or contemporary with the male believers for whom they are intended as a reward, good and lovely, buxom and virginal."[206] Qur'anic descriptions of the houris are particularly intoxicating to modern-day Islamic jihadists.

In 2004, a fourteen-year-old would-be Palestinian suicide bomber told the Israeli troops who disarmed him: "Blowing myself up is the only chance I've got to have sex with seventy-two virgins in the Garden of Eden." Another fourteen-year-old explained how a jihadist recruiter enticed him to join the jihad in Iraq: "He told me about paradise, about virgins, about Islam."[207]

Tragically, most Muslims, like these young Islamic jihadists, are blithely unaware that the sensual visions of paradise that inflame and inform their lusts emanate from the fertile imaginations of a bankrupt Zoroastrian eschatology.

Finally, it should be noted that while there is general unanimity in classical Islam respecting the essentials of eschatology, there are substantive differences when it comes to secondary matters. For example, in accord with Sunni Islam, "Jesus will return before the end of time, fight the Dajjāl ('Antichrist'), and rule according to the Law of Muhammad until the world comes to an end." Said Muhammad, "No man has greater claim to Jesus than I do, because there was no prophet between us, and he will be my vicegerent over my community. He will descend, and when you see him you will know him."[208]

But how will we know him when he descends? In answer, Muhammad avers that we will know him as

> a man of medium height, reddish fair, wearing two light yellow garments, looking as if drops were falling down from his head though it will not be wet. He will fight the people for the cause of Islam. He will break the cross, kill swine, and abolish jizya. Allah will perish all religions except Islam. He will destroy the Antichrist and will live on the earth for forty years and then he will die. The Muslims will pray over him.[209]

The Shi'a have a decidedly different perspective on this matter. While Jesus plays a role in end-time Shi'a eschatology, it is subservient to that of the Muslim *Mahdi*. Dr. Samuel Shahid succinctly summarizes this secondary Shi'a distinctive:

> It is true that the Shi'ites are anticipating the second coming of Christ and they agree with some of the Sunni traditions about this historical event, but the *Mahdi*, not Jesus, is the deliverer of the world. He is the one who will make Islam the dominant religion and eradicate the non-monotheistic faiths.[210]

Most notably, it is the Mahdi, not Jesus, who, when he emerges from his great occultation, destroys the Antichrist and establishes sharia as the universal law of humanity.

While neither Sunni nor Shi'a is monolithic respecting details of their end-time scenarios, they are united in reducing Jesus to the administrative deputy of Muhammad and thoroughly human associate of the Muslim Mahdi. In either case, Jesus is demoted from the creator of all things—including Muhammad—to a mere cast member in the Muslim eschatological charade.

The end of the matter is this. We have laid the straight stick of essential Christian DOCTRINE next to the Islamic counterfeit and by contrast have observed its crookedness. The deity of Christ is denied as he is rendered the mere "slave of Allah." Original sin is recast as an original slip—a mere bout of forgetfulness. The divine canon is usurped by the factual errors, faulty ethics, and feigned eloquence of the Qur'an. The incomprehensible Trinity is commandeered by a morally defective unitarian imposter. Resurrection—the greatest feat in human history—is demoted to mere fantasy, and incarnation is demeaned as blasphemy. The scintillating truth that "if anyone is in Christ he is a new creation" is negated by a capricious Allah. And eschatology—the thread that weaves the tapestry of Scripture into a harmonious pattern—is ignominiously sullied by the sensual enticements of a largely incoherent Islamic eschatological charade.

AFTERWORD

You cannot win a war if you cannot
talk honestly about the enemy.
—Sebastian Gorka[1]

Despite its incoherence, the Muslim cult—one billion six hundred million strong and growing—is poised to fill the vacuum left by a Western culture slouching inexorably toward Gomorrah.[2] Demographics alone are alarming. While polygamous Muslims boast a robust birth rate, native Westerners are moving rapidly toward self-extinction. Filling the void are multiplied millions of Muslims who have little or no intention of assimilating into Western culture.

Equally grave is the specter of global Islamic jihadism now exacting mass genocide on Christians in the East and ever-multiplying terrorist attacks throughout the West.[3] What more can I say? We have witnessed the cobelligerency of fantastically wealthy Saudis spending billions of dollars exporting virulent Wahhabism to the West. Worse still, Western governments, academic institutions, and media outlets are bent on exporting a false narrative respecting the religious animus animating global Islamic jihadism.

While this serves to recapitulate the problem, what begs our attention are potential solutions. Some suppose that the solution lies in the aggressive use of Western military power. While this is wholly necessary, it is hardly sufficient. As Sebastian Gorka has wisely noted, "You cannot win a war if you cannot talk honestly about the enemy."[4]

Nor is the problem ultimately fixed at the ballot box. As with military might, political activism plays a necessary yet insufficient role. The despotism of militant egalitarianism, radical individualism, multiculturalism, political correctness, and religious pluralism are not magically redeemed by political victories.[5] Even during the Reagan revolution, illiberal liberalism continued to hold sway in the educational, entertainment, and environmental industries that create, manipulate, and disseminate ideological constructs that are driving Western civilization in a very dangerous direction.

The only real solution to a disintegrating West and resurgent Islam is what the prophetic pen of Os Guinness wisely designated "renaissance"— *the power of the gospel however dark the times.* The challenge, said Guinness, "is to shake ourselves free from the natural despondency of those who look only at circumstances and at the statistics of decline and gloom." We do well to realize that "the West has been won twice before, and now it appears that the West has almost been lost a second time. So now, partly in response to the courageous faith of those who achieved it twice before, but more in response to the Great Commission itself, it is time to set our minds and hearts to win back the West to our Lord again."[6]

We live in "an ABC moment ('Anything but Christianity')."[7] A moment in which Christianity is routinely ridiculed and Islam referred to with reverential tones. Yet ABC can also serve to remind us that the solution for regaining Western civilization and defeating global Islamic jihadism is ultimately grounded in answers, biblical literacy, and countering cults.

This is the task of the Christian church—a task that she and she alone can fill. Thus, it is crucial the church be awakened from a "diabetic coma" brought on by a steady diet of fast-food Christianity. Said Guinness, "The world to come will be shaped by whether the worldwide Christian church recovers its integrity and effectiveness and demonstrates a faith that can escape cultural captivity and prevail under the conditions of advanced modernity—or does not."[8]

Answers play a crucial role in that authentic Christians have been commissioned to "always be prepared to give an *answer* to everyone who asks you to give a reason for the hope that you have. But do this with gentleness and respect."[9] Just as a good attorney defends a client in a court of law by way of solid evidence and sound reasoning, so, too, authentic twenty-first-century Christians must be equipped to effectively answer ideologies such as illiberal liberalism and illicit Islam. The heart will not receive what the mind resolutely rejects.

Biblical literacy, like being equipped to provide *answers*, is a core Christian value. It is one thing to say that God has spoken—that the Bible is divine rather than merely human in origin. It is quite another to understand what God has said. A great many Muslims discount the Bible as the infallible rule for faith and practice because they mistake its meaning. When Muhammad encountered the biblical word *begotten*, he retorted, "it is not befitting to (the majesty of) Allah that He should beget a son" (Q 19:35). Of course, the Bible does not use the term *begotten* in the sense of sexual reproduction. Rather, in the sense of special relationship. Had Muhammad understood the art and science of biblical interpretation he would not have made such an elemental mistake. Reading the Bible in the sense in which it is intended is a science in that rules apply; it is an art in that the more you apply the rules, the better you get at it.[10]

Countering cults is likewise the task of the church. Wrongly apprehended, this discipline would rightly be regarded a never-ending tedium. Satan packages and repackages his lies in a wide variety of ways. Rather than attempt to absorb every deviation of every cult, we are far better served to become so familiar with the main and the plain things of Scripture that when a counterfeit looms on the horizon, we spot it instantaneously.

Cults are notorious for linguistic subversion—for pouring their own unique meanings into key words and phrases. When Muslims use the word *Jesus*, the meaning they pour into the word reduces Jesus to the merely human way-shower for Muhammad. Muslim intellectuals are also expert at taking texts out of context and using them as pretexts for theological perversions. Thus, when Jesus said, "I will ask the Father, and he will give you another advocate to help you and be with you forever" (John 14:16), Muslims contend that this advocate is Muhammad—this despite that fact that both the immediate and broader context precludes this outrageous theological perversion. Islam manifests sociological deviance as well. Devotees characteristically display displaced loyalty to Muhammad and Islam and are galvanized together through physical and psychological intimidation tactics. When Muslims convert to Christianity, they do so under Islamic threat of death.[11] Moreover, converts are cut off from family and friends.[12]

It is not enough for Christians to be intellectually equipped to communicate the truth of the gospel via answers, biblical literacy, and countering cults. We should also be internally equipped during this anything-but-Christian moment. What that means is that the church must be energized for its mission—by a power that is *in* it but not *of* it. As underscored by the apostle Paul, those who are made perfect in Christ do not labor in their own energy—rather with all Christ's energy, which so powerfully works in us (Colossians 1:29).

The Father's greatest gift to those who have been saved through the death of his Son is the impartation of a new order of life. An order of life that is of the same quality as the life of Christ. For that is precisely what it is. The impartation of the life of Christ by which the incarnation continues. The descent of the ineffable in incarnation provides the ladder of divine ascent by which fallen humanity may rise up to union with God. To "participate," as Peter put it, "in the divine nature" (2 Peter 1:4).

The explication of this divine reality is the subject of another book. For now, let me close with an illustration. The laptop on which I am writing has a limited supply of energy. In time its internal power will prove insufficient. Yet when I plug it into an inexhaustible energy supply, the screen will again radiate like the face of Moses on Mount Sinai.

The disciples got a glimpse of inexhaustible energy on the Mount of Transfiguration. There Peter, James, and John witnessed a dazzling display of uncreated power. The face of Christ "shone like the sun, and his clothes became as white as the light."[13] Moses and Elijah—who themselves had experienced divine energy—appeared as "a bright cloud covered [the disciples]."[14] They experienced the ultimate lawgiver, the archetypal prophet in "glorious splendor,"[15] and were themselves enveloped in uncreated energy.

This is the energy that alone is sufficient to empower the body of Christ in the present clash of civilizations. It is the *mysterium tremendum et fascinans*—the mystery that makes us tremble and yet attracts us. It is the mysterious energy by which we may yet reclaim the soul of the world against the forces of insistent secularism and Islamic jihad.

APPENDIX

Sunni | Shi'a Split

The split between the two major branches of Islam—Sunni and Shi'a—had its genesis in the homicide of Muhammad. The Sunnis believe Muhammad was poisoned by the Jewess Zaynab while Shi'as are convinced he was poisoned by two of his wives (Aisha, daughter of Abu Bakr, the first rightly guided caliph; and Hafsa, daughter of Umar, the second rightly guided caliph).

The Sunni scenario is rife with intrigue. Muhammad had just massacred the Jews of Khaybar, divided female booty among his men, and selected the most beautiful of the women for himself. Thereafter, the Jewess Zaynab allegedly served lamb laced with poison to him and his murderous accomplice, Bishr. Bishr died that day. Muhammad was not as fortunate. It allegedly took three to four years of horrific headaches and fever before the malicious mutton finally got the better of him. He died June 8, 632.[1]

In the Shi'a scenario, it was two of Muhammad's harem who conspired with their fathers to bring about the death of the prophet.[2] Shiites think it utterly absurd to imagine that Muhammad would eat lamb offered up by a woman who had just witnessed the murder of her husband, father, uncle, and children. Moreover, it is hard for Shi'a intellectuals to swallow the notion that it took three or four years for the poisonous mutton to do him in. Shi'a Sheikh Yasser al-Habib cogently argues that it may have taken months but could not have taken years.

Myriad theories surround Aisha's murderous motives. She may have been embittered by her father's decision to marry her off to a man as old as he was, or, perhaps, she could no longer endure the sexual oppression of a sexagenarian. She may have been intensely jealous of Muhammad's passion for the exquisitely beautiful Egyptian Coptic slave Maria or upset that Muhammad had accused her of adultery. Then again the motive may have been financial—Abu Bakr and Aisha lusting after an inheritance that Muhammad had given to his daughter Fatima and her husband Ali, who was also Muhammad's cousin.[3] Whatever the motive, the Shi'a are convinced Aisha murdered Muhammad, while the Sunni are persuaded that the Jewess Zaynab was ultimately responsible.

This is hugely significant in that immediately following the murder of Muhammad, a great controversy arose over who should succeed him. Those loyal to Aisha and Abu Bakr believed it should be the best representative of the Muslim community. Those loyal to Muhammad's daughter Fatima and her husband Ali were hell-bent on the notion that it should be a blood relative. In the end, much to the chagrin of Ali, the blood relative of Muhammad, Abu Bakr, succeeded Muhammad as the first rightly guided caliph of Islam.

Abu Bakr would be dead two years later (634) and Umar, father of Hafsa—Aisha's alleged coconspirator—would succeed him as second rightly guided caliph. Umar reigned a mere decade (634–644) and Uthman who succeeded him a meager dozen (644–656). Following Uthman's murder by a group of Muslim malcontents, Ali, son-in-law of Muhammad, finally got his turn as the fourth rightly guided caliph of Islam.[4] Ali would reign a scant five years (656–661) before being assassinated on the way to the mosque. Thus concluded the era of the four rightly guided caliphs in what is fondly commemorated as Islam's greatest golden age (632–661).

In essence, then, each of the first three rightly guided caliphs was considered to be the best representative of the way (*Sunna*) of Muhammad; while Ali, the fourth rightly guided caliph, was finally supported (*Shi'a*) as the blood relative of Muhammad. The split between Sunni and Shi'a morphed into an unbridgeable chasm with the martyrdom of Husayn (680)—son of Ali and grandson of Muhammad. Having had the temerity to oppose what he believed to be the oppressive and religiously misguided caliphate of the Umayyads and asserting his preeminence as the blood relative of the prophet, Husayn and seventy-two family and friends were martyred by an overwhelming show of Sunni military might.[5]

From then till now, the beheading of Husayn and company continues to be a passion motif inflaming Shi'a fury toward the Sunni, as well as paving their path toward paradise. Each year on the tenth day of Muharram, the first month of the Islamic calendar, Shi'a the world over commemorate the beheading of Husayn through plays and processions and by pounding their bare backs in mournful tribute to the severed head of their beloved Imam. For every tear shed, it is said that a hundred sins are forgiven. Yet with every self-flagellation, the divide between Shi'a and Sunni deepens.

Due to reverential awe for Ali and Husayn, Shi'a Islam regards the imams that followed these iconic men to be infallible interpreters of hidden meanings embedded in the text of the Qur'an. By contrast, in Sunni Islam, the imam is less like a pope and more akin to a parish priest. The majority faction within the Shi'a sect are called Twelvers in that they acknowledge twelve historical imams, the last of whom they believe went into a state of hiddenness in the year 873; while another faction dubbed Seveners await the return of a seventh imam variously believed to be either Musa or his brother Ismail.

Shi'a believe that when the Mahdi—either the twelfth or seventh Imam—emerges from his hiddenness (occultation), he will uproot the religions of the world. He will destroy the Antichrist and establish sharia as the undisputed universal law of humanity.[6] Sunnis have a very different perspective on the matter. In their view, there is an end-time Messianic Mahdi who, unlike the Shi'a Mahdi, is not presently in occultation. While this Mahdi figures prominently into Sunni eschatology, it is Jesus who will return and usher in the long-awaited messianic age.[7] "Allah's Apostle said, 'The Hour will not be established until the son of Mary (i.e., Jesus) descends amongst you as a just ruler, he will break the cross, kill the pigs, and abolish the Jizya tax. Money will be in abundance so that nobody will accept it (as charitable gifts).'"[8]

We should also note that while Sunni Islam has four schools of sharia—Hanafi, Hanbali, Maliki, and Shafii—Shi'a has only one, Jafari. Other differences include the Sunnis' belief that the Qur'an is eternal and uncreated in contrast to the Shi'a belief that the Qur'an is temporal and created;[9]

Sunnis are more geared toward predestinarianism, and the Shi'a hold more closely to a freedom of the will perspective;[10] and while Sunnis forbid pictures in mosques, Shi'a mosques are replete with pictures of holy places and holy people, most notably Ali, Husayn, and Muhammad.[11]

In terms of numbers, of the one billion, six hundred million Muslims in the world, Sunnis constitute the clear majority—in the vicinity of 80 to 90 percent. The ten countries with the largest Muslim populations are by number Indonesia, India, Pakistan, Bangladesh, Nigeria, Egypt, Iran, Turkey, Algeria, and Morocco. Shi'a have a majority in only four countries: Iran, Azerbaijan (former Soviet Republic), Bahrain, and Iraq.[12] If there is a kernel of hope for reunification among Sunni and Shi'a, it is found in the longing for the return of either Jesus or the Mahdi as a catalyst for bringing the whole of humanity into Dar al-Islam.

Despite the perpetual hatred between Sunni and Shi'a, they have remarkable unanimity when it comes to the main and the plain things of Islam. Both believe in Muhammad as God's final revelator, the Qur'an as God's final revelation, and Islam as God's final religion. Moreover, Sunnis and Shiites cling in unison to the five pillars of Islam:

- *Shahada*—"There is no god but Allah, and Muhammad is the Messenger of Allah"
- *Salat*—Prayer five times a day for Sunnis, three for Shi'a
- *Zakat*—Giving alms for the benefit of needy Muslims
- *Sawm*—Fasting during the month of Ramadan
- *Hajj*—Meccan pilgrimage, as able[13]

GLOSSARY

Abbasid caliphate (AD **750–1258**): ruling Muslim dynasty after conquering the Umayyad caliphate, claiming to be the legitimate successors of Muhammad as the descendants of the prophet's uncle al-Abbās (d. c. 653). Abbasids ruled from Baghdad until their destruction by the Mongol Empire in 1258.

bint: in Arabic names, means "daughter of."

Caliph: a religious and political successor of the prophet Muhammad. For Sunnis, the first four successors were known as rightly guided (*Rashidun*) caliphs, chosen from Muhammad's companions—Abu Bakr al-Siddiq (r. 632–34), Umar ibn al-Khattab (r. 634–44), Uthman ibn Affan (r. 644–56), and Ali ibn Abi Talib (r. 656–61). The ideal of Islam is that there is no separation of religion and state—sharia is state and state is sharia.

Caliphate: the reign of the caliph.

Dhimmis (singular, *dhimmi*): "protected people"; in Muslim lands, non-Muslims, especially Christians and Jews ("People of the Book"), live under conditions of subservience to Muslims, which includes payment of the *jizya* (poll tax).

Fatwa: an authoritative opinion or decision on a matter of Islamic law.

Hadith (plural *ahadith* or *hadiths*): Reports of what Muhammad or his companions said or did (conjoined with accounts of their train of transmission) that serve as examples for faithful Muslims to follow and form the core of Islamic tradition. According to mainstream Islam, only the Qur'an reflects the eternal and perfect word of Allah, but the words and actions of Muhammad (*Sunna*), as reported by his followers in the collected accounts (*ahadith*), and to a lesser extent the biographies (*siras*), illuminate the Qur'an. Sunni Islam recognizes six collections of *ahadith* as authoritative, with two being *sahih*, meaning most "sound" or "trustworthy": *Sahih al-Bukhari* (d. 870), *Sahih Muslim* (d. 875), *Sunan Abu-Dawud* (d. 888), *Jami' at-Tirmidhi* (d. 892), *Sunan Ibn Majah* (d. 886), and *Sunan an-Nasa'i'* (d. 915).

ibn (and *bin*): in Arabic names, means "son of."

Houris (Arabic *ḥūr*, literally, "having eyes of marked contrast of black and white"): virginal, voluptuous maidens of paradise, "with beautiful, big, and lustrous eyes—Like unto Pearls" (Q 56:22–23).

Imam: in Sunni Islam, a religious leader and authority in law and theology, analogous to a local pastor. In Shi'a Islam, highly authoritative spiritual leader of the community (perhaps analogous to the pope in Roman Catholicism), descended from Muhammad's son-in-law, Ali.

Jinn: spiritual beings with free will created by God; some jinn are good, others evil.

Jizya: poll tax that *dhimmis* are required to pay under Islamic hegemony. For a *dhimmi* to resist means death.

Ka'bah (also *Ka'ba*; literally "cube"): "The first House (of worship) appointed for mankind" (Q 3:96). The most holy shrine in Islam, the *Ka'bah* is a cube-like structure in the Grand Mosque of Mecca, toward which Muslims pray. According to Islamic tradition, Abraham and Ishmael constructed the first *Ka'bah*, placing within it the (black) stone from paradise..

Kafir (also *kuffār*): an unbeliever; one who rejects the Prophet's message from Allah.

Mahdi: The expected one—eschatological deliverer and savior in both Sunni and Shi'a Islam. Shi'a Twelvers believe that an imam, a specific descendant of Ali, is hidden (in occultation) and will return as a messianic figure at the end of time.

Mecca (in modern Saudi Arabia): Muhammad's birthplace and Islam's most holy city.

Medina (in modern Saudi Arabia): (*Medinnet el Nebi*: the city of the Prophet); formerly Yathrib, second most holy city in Islam; in AD 622 Muhammad fled from Mecca to Medina (*hijra*), initiating the Muslim era.

Ottoman Empire (AD 1299–1922): founded by Turkish tribes in Anatolia (Asia Minor) in the late thirteenth century, the Ottomans reigned for more than six hundred years. During their peak in the fifteenth and sixteenth centuries, they were among the most dominant states on the globe, controlling the rim of the Mediterranean Sea, including North Africa, large parts of the Arabian Peninsula, Middle East, and southeastern Europe. Had the Ottoman Empire succeeded in 1683 when it besieged the gates of Vienna, Europe today might well be Eurabia. While it reached its zenith in the sixteenth century, the empire's most notable atrocities are of recent vintage—the mass extermination of Armenians as well as the death of Christianity in Asia Minor—both twentieth-century Muslim mass murders. In 1924, Mustafa Kemal Atatürk, revolutionary founder of the Republic of Turkey, abolished the caliphate altogether. (However, on June 29, 2014, the Islamic State pronounced itself a caliphate.)

Quraysh (also Koreish): ruling merchant tribe of Mecca into which Muhammad was born. The Quraysh controlled the Ka'bah. According to Islamic tradition, the Quraysh descended from Ishmael, son of Abraham.

Rajab: "the honored month"; seventh month of the Islamic calendar. As one of four "sacred" months, warfare is prohibited during Rajab.

Ramadan: ninth month of the Islamic calendar. Each day of the month, Muslims around the world fast from dawn to dusk. This observance is one of the five pillars of Islam (sawm).

Rasul: "Messenger." One who recites the revelation of God. According to Islam, Muhammad was the last and greatest *rasul* of Allah.

Sahih: "authentic" or "trustworthy"; two of Sunni Islam's recognized collections of *ahadith* are deemed *sahih*, meaning most authoritative and sound: *Sahih al-Bukhari* (d. 870) and *Sahih Muslim* (d. 875).

Sallallāhu 'alayhi wa sallam: "God's blessing and peace be upon him"; or perhaps, more literally, "the prayers of Allah be upon him and peace." Abbreviated as SAW or PBHM.

Shahada: "bearing witness"; the sincere declaration of faith, in Arabic, that makes one a Muslim: *Lā ilāha illā Allāh Muhammadun rasul Allāh* ("There is no god but Allah and Muhammad is the Messenger of Allah"). One of the five pillars of Islam. (See, e.g., Q 3:18; 47:19; 48:29; and *Sahih al-Bukhari*, Volume 1, Book 2, Number 8; Volume 2, Book 24, Number 573; cf. Volume 4, Book 55, Number 644.)

Sharia: "way" or "path"; the body of Islamic sacred law, derived from the Traditions, constituting the duties that Allah has placed on the Muslim community. Sunni Islam has four schools of sharia—Shafii, Hanafi, Hanbali, and Maliki. Shi'a has one, Jafari. What the various schools have in common far outweighs their differences.

Shi'a: members of the "party" of 'Ali, who believed that as Muhammad's relative he should have been the successor of the prophet. Shi'a make up ten to twenty percent of Muslims worldwide. Shi'a have a majority in four countries: Iran, Azerbaijan (former Soviet Republic), Bahrain, and Iraq (see appendix).

Shiite: a member of the Shi'a branch of Islam.

Shirk: according to Islam, the unforgivable sin of assigning partners to Allah, negating his oneness and unity (*tawhid*). Muslims believe Christians commit *shirk* in believing the doctrines of the Trinity and that Jesus is the eternal Son of God.

Sira (plural, *siras*): biography, specifically referring to biography of Muhammad. The earliest extant biography of Muhammad is the *Sirat Rasul Allah* [Life of the Messenger of Allah] by Ibn Ishaq (d. c. 767), composed more than a century after Muhammad's death, and which survives for us in the work of Ibn Hisham (d. c. 827) and al-Tabari (d. 923).

Sunna: way of the prophet; the transmission of the prophet Muhammad's normative action, in word and deed, including unspoken consent and censures, that are followed by Muslims in living a life of submission to the will of Allah—especially as recorded in *ahadith*. The *Sunna* supplements the Qur'an as a source for Islamic theology and sharia.

Sunni: The people of the *Sunna*—followers of the way and example of Muhammad. After Muhammad's death, division occurred over who should succeed the Prophet. In contrast to the Shi'a, Sunnis believe the "rightly guided" caliphs represent the authoritative line of succession (see *caliph*). Today Sunnis constitute the clear majority—in the vicinity of 80 to 90 percent—of the world's 1.6 billion Muslims. The ten countries with the largest Sunni Muslim populations are by number Indonesia, India, Pakistan, Bangladesh, Nigeria, Egypt, Iran, Turkey, Algeria, and Morocco (see appendix).

Tawhid: the central Muslim doctrine of the absolute oneness, uniqueness, and unity of Allah. Islam denies that Allah has any partners, which

Muslims deem Jesus to be in the Christian understanding of the doctrine of the Trinity.

Umayyad caliphate (AD 661–750): the first ruling Muslim dynasty, "the Umayyads, headed by Abū Sufyān, were a largely merchant family of the Quraysh tribe centered at Mecca. They had initially resisted Islam, not converting until 627, but subsequently became prominent administrators under Muhammad and his immediate successors. In the first Muslim civil war (*fitnah*; 656–661)—the struggle for the caliphate following the murder of 'Uthmān ibn 'Affān, the third caliph (reigned 644–656)—Abū Sufyān's son Mu'āwiyah, then governor of Syria, emerged victorious over 'Alī, Muhammad's son-in-law and fourth caliph. Mu'āwiyah then established himself as the first Umayyad caliph" ("Umayyad Dynasty," Encyclopedia Britannica, www.britannica.com/topic/Umayyad-dynasty-Islamic-history).

Wahhabism: "a very strict sect of Islam founded in the eighteenth century by Muhammad ibn Abd al-Wahhab in reaction to what he perceived as Islam's adulterated original vision. It grew as a result of a religious alliance that it formed in the eighteenth century with the Saud monarchy of Saudi Arabia. Wahhabism in the twentieth century became a vast extremist fundamentalist education system, financed by Saudi petrol dollars that built mosques and schools everywhere across Saudi Arabia. (Its widespread national influence is analogous to that of the U.S. public-school system.) It teaches strict implementation of Islamic laws in religious, political, legal, moral, and private life and is shockingly anti-America and anti-Israel" (Charles Strohmer, "Submit or Die: The Geostrategic Jihad of Osama Bin Laden and Al Qaeda (Part One), *Christian Research Journal* 29, 4 (2006), www.equip.org/article/submit-or-die-the-geostrategic-jihad-of-osama-bin-laden-and-al-qaeda-part-one/). Saudis have spent multiplied billions of dollars exporting virulent Wahhabism to the West.

SUGGESTIONS FOR FURTHER READING

ANALYSIS AND CRITIQUE OF ISLAM

Ayaan Hirsi Ali, *Heretic: Why Islam Needs a Reformation Now* (Harper, 2015)

Mindy Belz, *They Say We Are Infidels: On the Run from ISIS with Persecuted Christians in the Middle East* (Tyndale Momentum, 2016)

David Cook, *Understanding Jihad* (University of California Press, 2005)

Nonie Darwish, *Cruel and Usual Punishment* (Thomas Nelson, 2008)

Darío Fernández-Morera, *The Myth of the Andalusian Paradise: Muslims, Christians, and Jews under Islamic Rule in Medieval Spain* (ISI Books, 2016)

Norman L. Geisler and Abdul Saleeb, *Answering Islam: The Crescent in Light of the Cross*, second edition (Baker Books, 2002)

Sebastian Gorka, *Defeating Jihad: The Winnable War* (Regnery Publishing, 2016)

Hank Hanegraaff, ed., *Islam: What You Must Know—The Best of the Christian Research Journal* (Christian Research Institute, 2009)

William Harris, *The Levant: A Fractured Mosaic,* fourth ed. (Markus Wiener Publishers, 2005)

Raymond Ibrahim, *Crucified Again: Exposing Islam's New War on Christians* (Regnery Publishing, 2013)

Abdu H. Murray, *Grand Central Question: Answering the Critical Concerns of the Major Worldviews* (IVP, 2014)

Nabeel Qureshi, *Answering Jihad: A Better Way Forward* (Zondervan, 2016)

Nabeel Qureshi, *No God but One: Allah or Jesus? A Former Muslim Investigates the Evidence for Islam and Christianity* (Zondervan, 2016)

Nabeel Qureshi, *Seeking Allah, Finding Jesus: A Devout Muslim Encounters Christianity* (Zondervan, 2016)

Robert Spencer, *The Politically Incorrect Guide to Islam (and the Crusades)* (Regnery Publishing, 2005)

Robert Spencer, *The Complete Infidel's Guide to the Koran* (Regnery Publishing, 2009)

Robert Spencer, *Not Peace but a Sword: The Great Chasm Between Christianity and Islam* (Catholic Answers, 2013)

Serge Trifkovic, *The Sword of the Prophet: Islam: History, Theology, Impact on the World* (Regina Orthodox Press, 2002)

Serge Trifkovic, *Defeating Jihad: How the War on Terrorism Can Be Won—In Spite of Ourselves* (Regina Orthodox Press, 2006)

Bill Warner, *Sharia Law for the Non-Muslim* (Center for the Study of Political Islam, 2010)

James R. White, *What Every Christian Needs to Know about the Qur'an* (Bethany House, 2013)

Bat Ye'or, *The Decline of Eastern Christianity under Islam: From Jihad to Dhimmitude* (Fairleigh Dickinson University Press, 1996)

ARTICLES

William Lane Craig, "The Concept of God in Islam and Christianity," Reasonable Faith, June 22, 2015, www.reasonablefaith.org/the -concept-of-god-in-islam-and-christianity

Raymond Ibrahim, "'Drip-Drip' Genocide: Muslim Persecution of Christians, February, 2017," Gatestone Institute, May 28, 2017. www.gatestoneinstitute.org/10426/christian-genocide-muslims

Charles Strohmer, "Submit or Die: The Geostrategic Jihad of Osama Bin Laden and Al Qaeda (Part One), *Christian Research Journal* 29,

4 (2006), www.equip.org/article/submit-or-die-the-geostrategic
-jihad-of-osama-bin-laden-and-al-qaeda-part-one/

Charles Strohmer, "Submit or Die: The Geostrategic Jihad of Osama
Bin Laden and Al Qaeda (Part Two), *Christian Research Journal* 29,
5 (2006), www.equip.org/article/submit-or-die-the-geostrategic
-jihad-of-osama-bin-laden-and-al-qaeda-part-two/

David Wood, "Will the Real Islam Please Stand Up?" *Christian
Research Journal* 37, 6 (2014):8–15, www.equip.org/article/will
-the-real-islam-please-stand-up/

David Wood, "Facing the Islamic Challenge: Field-Tested Responses to
Five Common Muslim Objections," *Christian Research Journal* 36,
4 (2013):10–17, www.equip.org/article/facing-islamic-challenge/

David Wood, "Jihad, Jizya, and Just War Theory," *Christian Research
Journal* 36, 1, (2013):42–47, www.equip.org/article/jihad-jizya-just
-war-theory/

David Wood, "Muhammad and the Messiah: Comparing the Central
Figures of Islam and Christianity," *Christian Research Journal* 35,
5 (2012):42–48, www.equip.org/article/muhammad-messiah
-comparing-central-figures-islam-christianity/

CHRISTIAN CRUSADES

Daniel Hoffman, "Hollywood vs. History," *Christian Research Journal*
29, 3 (2006), www.equip.org/article/hollywood-vs-history/

Thomas F. Madden, *The Concise History of the Crusades*, third student
edition (Rowman and Littlefield Publishers, 2013)

Jonathan Riley-Smith, *The Crusades, Christianity, and Islam* (Columbia
University Press, 2008)

Rodney Stark, *God's Battalions: The Case for the Crusades*
(HarperCollins, 2009)

DECLINE OF THE WEST

Robert H. Bork, *Slouching Towards Gomorrah, Modern Liberalism and
American Decline* (Regan Books, 1996)

Patrick J. Buchanan, *Suicide of a Superpower: Will America Survive to
2025?* (Thomas Dunne Books, 2011)

Mary Eberstadt, *It's Dangerous to Believe: Religious Freedom and Its Enemies* (Harper, 2016)

Os Guinness, *Renaissance: The Power of the Gospel However Dark the Times* (InterVarsity Press, 2014)

ACKNOWLEDGMENTS

I would first like to acknowledge my dear friend Jack Countryman, without whom this volume would not have become a Harper Collins publication. To be back with the team in the Thomas Nelson division is sheer delight. They have been willing to take on a project that, for many, would be simply too hot to handle.

Furthermore, I am deeply grateful for my colleagues at the Christian Research Institute—many have been with me for well over two decades. I am particularly grateful for Stephen Ross, my personal assistant, who is instrumental in helping me think through complex matters and, even more, is my treasured friend for almost twenty-eight years. I could not imagine a day in the office without him. Moreover, my beloved wife, Kathy, and blessed tribe of twelve continue to be a sanctuary amid the storms and challenges of life.

Finally, as evidenced by the notes section, I am indebted to many authors and their works. Without them, my own thinking would be greatly impoverished. I am particularly grateful to Abdu Murray for his input and insights—they have strengthened this manuscript immensely. And to Robert Spencer for contributing the foreword and for his example of telling it like it is, no matter the cost. He is as brilliant as he is brave. Other noteworthy authors and commentators include Ayaan Hirsi Ali, James M. Arlandson, Mindy Belz, Baron Bodissey, David Cook, William Lane Craig, Nonie Darwish, Mary Eberstadt, Darío Fernández-Morera, Thomas L. Friedman, Sebastian Gorka, William Harris, Daniel Hoffman, Raymond Ibrahim, Thomas F. Madden, William McCants, Nabeel Qureshi, Jonathan

Riley-Smith, Abdul Saleeb, Sam Shamoun, Charles Strohmer, Serge Trifkovic, Bill Warner, David Wood, Graeme Wood, and researchers at Answering-Islam.org, TheReligionofPeace.com, and ClarionProject.org.

Beyond any adequate thanksgiving is the Triadic One who has ordered my life around that which is divine.

NOTES

Introduction

1. From a speech by Libyan leader Mu'ammar Gadhafi that aired on Al-Jazeera TV on April 10, 2006, Middle East Media Research Institute, video clip #1121, accessed December 10, 2015, www.memritv.org/clip /en/1121.

2. In the first two sentences of this paragraph, I paraphrase Serge Trifkovic, *Defeating Jihad: How the War on Terrorism Can Be Won—In Spite of Ourselves* (Boston: Regina Orthodox Press, 2006), 57.

3. "Islam is not our adversary," Hillary Clinton, November 19, 2015, Real Clear Politics, accessed February 20, 2017, www.realclearpolitics.com/ video/2015/11/19/hillary_clinton_islam_not_adversary_muslims_peaceful _tolerant_nothing_to_do_with_terrorism.html. Clinton stated, "The bottom line is that we are in a contest of ideas against an ideology of hate, and we have to win. Let's be clear, though, Islam is not our adversary. Muslims are peaceful and tolerant people, and have nothing whatsoever to do with terrorism."

   On Facebook, Clinton posted, "Islam is not our enemy. Radical jihadists point to anti-Muslim rhetoric as a way to recruit new followers. Trump's hateful comments aren't just an affront to our values—they're a threat to our national security" (December 8, 2015, www.facebook.com /hillaryclinton/photos/a.889773484412515.1073741828.889307941125736 /1027635587292970/).

4. George W. Bush, "Address to Joint Session of Congress Following 9/11 Attacks," September 20, 2001, *American Rhetoric*, accessed February 20, 2017, www.americanrhetoric.com/speeches/gwbush911jointsessionspeech .htm.

5. Barack Obama, "Remarks by the President at Cairo University, 6-04-09," June 4, 2009, accessed February 21, 2017, obamawhitehouse.archives.gov /the-press-office/remarks-president-cairo-university-6-04-09.

6. Secretary of State John Kerry, via MRC TV video, in Brittany M. Hughes, "Kerry: 'The Real Face of Islam is a Peaceful Religion,'" CNSNEWs.com, September 3, 2014, www.cnsnews.com/news/article/brittany-m-hughes /kerry-real-face-islam-peaceful-religion.

7. "Text: National Security Adviser Condoleezza Rice," press briefing, *Washington Post*, September 19, 2001, web.archive.org/web/20020221004915 /http://www.washingtonpost.com/wp-srv/nation/specials/attacked /transcripts/ricetext_091901.html.

8. "Text of Prime Minister Tony Blair's Remarks," *New York Times*, October 7, 2001, www.nytimes.com/2001/10/07/international/07BLAIR-TEXT.html; see also video of Blair in the documentary film *Islam: What the West Needs to Know,* directed by Gregory M. Davis and Bryan Daly (Los Angeles: Quixotic Media, 2006), DVD.

9. See *Islam: What the West Needs to Know,* directed by Davis and Daly.

10. Pickthall's translation of Qur'an 3:19 is direct: "Lo! religion with Allah (is) the Surrender [*l-is'lāmu*] (to His will and guidance)," see *The Meaning of the Glorious Koran*, trans. Mohammad Marmaduke Pickthall (New York: New American Library, n.d.), 64.

The usage of the Arabic term for Islam (root *s-l-m*) within the historic religiopolitical system shows Islam means *submission* or *resignation* to the will of Allah (see Thomas Patrick Hughes, *A Dictionary of Islam* [Chicago: KAZI Publications, Inc., 1994, originally published in 1886], 220). Likewise, a Muslim is "one who submits" to the will of Allah, as revealed through Muhammad. Middle East historian and pundit Daniel Pipes explained: "Roots have a core meaning but also include unrelated words. In the case of s-l-m, *salām* means peace and *salāma* means safety. But the root also has many meanings unconnected to this core, such as *salam* (a variety of acacia), *sullam* (ladder), *sulāmā* (digital bone in the hand or foot), *sulaymāni* (mercury chloride), *aslama* (to betray) . . . and *islām* (submission). There is no connection in meaning between *salām* and *islām*, peace and submission. These are two distinct words with unrelated meanings. In brief, 'Islam = submission.'" See Daniel Pipes, "'Islam' Does Not Mean 'Peace,'" Daniel Pipes: Middle East Forum, October 9, 2005, updated February 6, 2016, accessed September 9, 2016, www.danielpipes .org/blog/2005/10/islam-does-not-mean-peace.

The Qur'an itself does not define Islam as *peace*, but rather as *submission* or *surrender*. To demonstrate this, Christian apologist Sam Shamoun cites many Qur'anic passages, including the following:

• Say (O Muslims): We believe in Allah and that which is revealed to us and that which was revealed to Abraham, and Ishmael, and Isaac, and Jacob, and the tribes, and that which Moses and Jesus received, and that which the prophets received from their Lord. We make no distinction between any of them, and to Him we have *surrendered* [Arabic *Muslimoon*] [2:136]

• Nay, but whosoever *submits (aslama)* his will to God, being a good-doer, his wage is with his Lord, and no fear shall be on them, neither shall they sorrow. [2:112]

• When his Lord said to him, '*Surrender (aslim)*,' he said, 'I have *surrendered (aslamtu)* me to the Lord of all Being.' [2:131]

• What, do they desire another religion than God's, and to Him has *surrendered (aslama)* whoso is in the heavens and the earth, willingly or unwillingly, and to Him they shall be returned? [3:83]

• And who is there that has a fairer religion than he who *submits (aslama)* his will to God being a good-doer, and who follows the creed of Abraham, a man of pure faith? And God took Abraham for a friend. [4:125]

As quoted in Sam Shamoun, "Did Jesus Command His Followers to Be Muslims?" *Answering Islam*, accessed February 10, 2016, www.answering-islam.org/Responses/Ataie/jesus_muslim.htm. See also Arthur Jeffrey, "Introduction," *Islam: Muhammad and His Religion*, ed. Arthur Jeffrey (Indianapolis: Bobbs-Merrill, 1958), xii; Bassam Darwich, "Islam and Peace," *Answering Islam*, accessed September 9, 2016, www.answering-islam.org/Hoaxes/salamislam.html; and "Myths of Islam: Islam Means 'Peace,'" What Makes Islam So Different, The Religion of Peace, accessed September 9, 2016, www.thereligionofpeace.com/pages/myths/means-peace.aspx.

11. Q stands for Qur'an in parenthetical references. Also, not all versions of the Qur'an use the same numbering system. Anytime you are given a specific sura (chapter) and verse reference that does not correspond to the version of the Qur'an you are using, check one or two verses before and after and you will likely find the reference in question.

12. See Serge Trifkovic, *The Sword of the Prophet: Islam: History, Theology, Impact on the World* (Boston: Regina Orthodox Press, 2002), chapter two, especially pp. 55, 83–86. A mainstream Muslim teaching article stated, "Islam is an all-embracing way of life. It extends over the entire spectrum of life, showing us how to conduct all human activities in a sound and wholesome manner." Thus, "When we read the Quran or the Prophetic traditions, we find instructions regarding all aspects of life: political, social, economic, material, ethical, national and international. These instructions provide us with all the details needed to perform a certain act." The implications of this comprehensive doctrine include, for example, the idea that "a spiritual belief that does not deal with social behavior, economic

relations and international organizations is as erroneous as the social doctrine that does not consider spiritual belief, morality and behavior." "Islam: A Complete Code of Life," Islamweb.net, April 8, 2014, www.islamweb.net/en/article/111867/islam-a-complete-code-of-life; and "Islam: A Comprehensive Way of Life," Islamweb.net, April 17, 2016, www.islamweb.net/en/article/158625/islam-%EF%BF%BD%EF%BF%BD -a-comprehensive-way-of-life.

13. See Ibn Ishaq, *The Life of Muhammad: A Translation of Ishaq's Sīrat Rasūl Allāh*, trans. A. Guillaume (Oxford: Oxford University Press, 1955, 2001), 675–76; 'Ali Dashti, *Twenty Three Years: A Study of the Prophetic Career of Mohammad*, trans. F. R. C. Bagley (London: Routledge, 1985, 1994), 100, online at books.google.com; cf. Al-Waqidi, *The Life of Muhammad: Al-Wāqidī's Kitāb al-Maghāzī*, ed. Rizwi Faizer, trans. Rizwi Faizer, Amal Ismail, and AbdulKader Tayob (London: Routledge, 2011), 85–86.

14. Rachael Donadio, "Provocateur's Death Haunts the Dutch," *International New York Times*, October 30, 2014, www.nytimes.com/2014/11/02/arts /provocateurs-death-haunts-the-dutch-.html.

15. As Christian apologist David Wood explained, "The earliest extant biography of Muhammad is the *Sirat Rasul Allah* [Life of the Messenger of Allah] by Muhammad Ibn Ishaq, who was born at the beginning of the eighth century AD in Medina. His grandfather, Yasar, became a Muslim shortly after being captured around AD 634. [The prophet Muhammad himself died in 632.] Yasar's son Ishaq began collecting traditions about Muhammad, and his grandson Muhammad followed in the footsteps of his father Ishaq. By age thirty, Muhammad Ibn ("son of") Ishaq was recognized as an authority on the traditions about Muhammad. He compiled the most reliable sources into the *Sirat Rasul Allah*, providing us with an early, largely accurate, and authoritative source on the life of Muhammad" (David Wood, "Murdered by Muhammad: The Brutal Deaths of Islam's Earliest Enemies," Answering Infidels, web.archive.org/web/20060929050902 /http://www.answeringinfidels.com/content/view/61/42/).

Wood elsewhere explained that the Qur'an contains very few biographical details about Muhammad. Moreover, Ibn Ishaq's biography, composed more than a century after Muhammad's death, is often criticized by modern Muslims, who have deemed that "Ishaq's methodology was defective, forcing them to turn to even later works for information concerning their prophet. Islam's most trusted collections of stories about Muhammad (e.g., *Sahih al-Bukhari, Sahih Muslim,* etc.) were written approximately two centuries (or more) after the events they report"; see David Wood, "Muhammad and the Messiah: Comparing the Central Figures of Islam and Christianity," *Christian Research Journal* 35, 5 [2012]: 44, emphasis in original, available online at equip.org.

16. Ishaq, *The Life of Muhammad*, 464 (see 461ff. for the full account); *Sahih al-Bukhari* Volume 5, Book 59, Number 447; Sahih al-Bukhari Volume 5, book 59, Number 362; Sunan Abu-Dawud Book 39, Hadith 4390. See also Al-Tabari, *The History of al-Tabari: The Victory of Islam*, vol. 8, trans. Michael Fishbein (Albany: SUNY Press, 1997), 27–41, kalamullah.com /Books/The%20History%20Of%20Tabari/Tabari_Volume_08.pdf. Cf. Al-Waqidi, *The Life of Muhammad*, 252 (244ff.).

17. The earliest extant Muslim sources report Muhammad was poisoned (see *Sahih al-Bukhari* Volume 5, Book 59, Number 713 (and Number 551); Volume 3, Book 47, Number 786; *Sahih Muslim* Book 26, Number 5430; Al-Tabari, *The History of al-Tabari: The Victory of Islam*, vol. 8, trans. Fishbein, 123–24). I discuss this in chapter 1, pp. 21–22, and in the appendix, pp. 185–88.

18. See Trifkovic, *Sword of the Prophet*, 95; Bat Ye'or, *The Decline of Eastern Christianity under Islam: From Jihad to Dhimmitude* (Madison, NJ: Fairleigh Dickinson University Press, 1996), 43–46; Robert G. Hoyland, *In God's Path: The Arab Conquest and the Creation of an Islamic Empire* (New York: Oxford University Press, 2015), 39–55; Richard Robert Madden, *The Turkish Empire: In Its Relations with Christianity and Civilizations* (London: T. Cautley Newby, 1862), 134–135.

19. Good overviews include Bat Ye'or, *The Decline of Eastern Christianity under Islam: From Jihad to Dhimmitude* (Madison, NJ: Fairleigh Dickinson University Press, 1996), 43–52; Robert Spencer, *The Complete Infidel's Guide to ISIS* (Washington, DC: Regnery Publishing, 2015), 195–214; Trifkovic, *Sword of the Prophet*, 87–96; James M. Arlandson, "Timeline of the Islamic Crusades: The Truth about Islamic Imperialism," *Answering Islam*, accessed October 2, 2016, www.answering-islam.org/Authors /Arlandson/crusades_timeline.htm.

20. The Great Schism of 1054 was the "event that precipitated the final separation between the Eastern Christian churches (led by the patriarch of Constantinople, Michael Cerularius) and the Western church (led by Pope Leo IX). The mutual excommunications by the Pope and the Patriarch that year became a watershed in church history" ("Schism of 1054," Encyclopedia Britannica, www.britannica.com/event/Schism-of-1054).

21. See Thomas F. Madden, "Crusade Myths," Ignatius Insight, n.d., accessed September 19, 2016, www.ignatiusinsight.com/features2005/tmadden _crusademyths_feb05.asp.

22. See Thomas F. Madden, *The New Concise History of the Crusades* (Lanham, MD: Rowman and Littlefield Publishers, 2006); Rodney Stark, *God's Battalions: The Case for the Crusades* (New York: HarperCollins, 2009); Jonathan Riley-Smith, *The Crusades, Christianity, and Islam* (New York: Columbia University Press, 2008).

23. Trifkovic, *Sword of the Prophet*, 112–13.
24. See Ibid., 113–25; Raymond Ibrahim, "The Forgotten Genocide: Why It Matters Today," Raymond Ibrahim, April 24, 2013, raymondibrahim. com/2013/04/24/the-forgotten-genocide-why-it-matters-today/; "The Armenian Genocide and Turkey's Attempt to Deny It," Armenian National Committee of America, July 6, 2015, web.archive.org/web/20150706045638 /http:/www.anca.org/genocide/denial.php; Taner Akcam, *A Shameful Act: The Armenian Genocide and the Question of Turkish Responsibility* (New York: Henry Holt and Company, 2006), 42–48, 105–108.
25. Trifkovic, *Sword of the Prophet*, 124–25.
26. See Reverend Father Raphael Moore, "In Memory of the 50 Million Victims of the Orthodox Christian Holocaust, Compiled by Rev. Archimandrite Nektarios Serfes," Serfes.org, October 1999, www.serfes.org/orthodox /memoryof.htm.
27. Moore, "In Memory of the 50 Million Victims;" see also "Adolf Hitler, Chancellor of Nazi Germany (1933–45)," Armenian National Institute, www.armenian-genocide.org/hitler.html; cf. Stefan Ihrig, "How the Armenian Genocide Shaped the Holocaust," *The Daily Beast*, January 24, 2016, www.thedailybeast.com/articles/2016/01/24/how-the-armenian -genocide-shaped-the-holocaust.html; Elias Maglinis, "Ataturk in the Nazi Imagination," Ekathimerini, March 7, 2016, www.ekathimerini. com/209963/article/ekathimerini/life/ataturk-in-the-nazi-imagination.
28. See "Turkish soccer fans boo moment of silence for Paris attacks victims," CBSN, November 18, 2015, www.youtube.com/watch?v=5-_dqcgirf4; for full context, see "Türkiye Yunanistan maçı öncesinde Paris saldırılarında ölenler için yapılan saygı duruşu ıslıklandı," Medyascope.tv, November 17, 2015, www.youtube.com/watch?v=dtMiwVpYAmo.
29. "Christian Workers in Syria Crucified, Beheaded," Christian Aid Mission, October 1, 2015, accessed October 1, 2016, www.christianaid.org /News/2015/mir20151001.aspx?SC=MIR; see also Nina Shea, "ISIS and Religious Genocide in the Mideast," *National Review*, October 9, 2015, accessed October 1, 2016, www.nationalreview.com/article/425288/isis -and-religious-genocide-mideast-nina-shea; Kirsten Powers, "John Kerry Should Recognize Christian Genocide," *USA Today*, December 7, 2015, accessed December 8, 2015, www.usatoday.com/story/opinion/2015/12/07 /isil-murder-christians-middle-east-recognition-genocide-column/76932274/.
30. Adam Nossiter and Hannah Olivennes, "Jacques Hamel, 85, a Beloved French Priest, Killed in His Church," *New York Times*, July 26, 2016, accessed October 1, 2016, www.nytimes.com/2016/07/27/world/europe /jacques-hamel-85-a-beloved-french-priest-killed-in-his-church.html?_r=0.
31. According to mainstream Islam, only the Qur'an is the eternal and perfect word of Allah, but the words and actions of Muhammad (*Sunna*), as

reported by his followers in the collected accounts (*ahadith*), and to a
lesser extent the biographies (*siras*), illuminate the Qur'an. Sunni Islam
recognizes six collections of *ahadith* as authoritative, with two being *sahih*,
meaning most "sound" or "trustworthy": *Sahih al-Bukhari* (d. 870), *Sahih
Muslim* (d. 875), *Sunan Abu-Dawud* (d. 888), *Jami' at-Tirmidhi* (d. 892),
Sunan Ibn Majah (d. 886), and *Sunan an-Nasa'i'* (d. 915).

"Consensus" in Islam (*ijma*) refers to agreement concerning a matter
by a specified group of Muslims pertaining, say, to sharia in particular or to
Muslims generally. I refer here to consensus pertaining to the vast majority
of Muslims, including agreement concerning the fundamentals of Islamic
doctrine and practice.

32. Serge Trifkovic wrote, "Europe is losing the ability to define and defend
itself, to the benefit of inassimilable multitudes filled with contempt for the
host society. That society is being absorbed as a python swallows its prey—
slowly, with a long digestion" (Trifkovic, *Defeating Jihad*, 74).

33. From a speech by Libyan leader Mu'ammar Gadhafi that aired on
Al-Jazeera TV on April 10, 2006, Middle East Media Research Institute,
video clip #1121, accessed December 10, 2015, www.memritv.org/clip
/en/1121.

34. "Gruesome Details of Gadhafi's Rape of Teenagers and Other Crimes
Revealed," *Haaretz*, January 26, 2014, www.haaretz.com/middle-east-news
/1.570727; "Gaddafi's Rape Chambers Revealed in BBC Documentary,"
The Clarion Project, January 29, 2014, accessed December 10, 2015, www
.clarionproject.org/news/gaddafis-rape-chambers-revealed-bbc-documentary.

35. See Ashifa Kassam, et al., "Europe Needs Many More Babies to Avert a
Population Disaster," *The Guardian*, August 22, 2015, www.theguardian.com
/world/2015/aug/23/baby-crisis-europe-brink-depopulation-disaster;
"Statistical bulletin: Births in England and Wales: 2015," Office for
National Statistics, www.ons.gov.uk/peoplepopulationandcommunity
/birthsdeathsandmarriages/livebirths/bulletins
/birthsummarytablesenglandandwales/2015; "A statistical Overview of the
Belgian Population," Belgium.be, www.belgium.be/en/about belgium
/country/Population/.

36. Karl Vick with Simon Shuster, "Person of the Year 2015: Chancellor of
the Free World," *Time*, accessed August 1, 2016, time.com/time-person
-of-the-year-2015-angela-merkel/.

37. "Germany Passes Japan to Have World's Lowest Birthrate—Study," *BBC
News*, May 29, 2015, www.bbc.com/news/world-europe-32929962.

38. Vick, Shuster, "Person of the Year 2015."

39. In Paris on November 13, 2015, a series of Islamic jihadi attacks killed 130
and injured hundreds more.

40. Total federal unfunded liabilities are at least thirty trillion. See Vance Ginn,

"You Think the Deficit Is Bad? Federal Unfunded Liabilities Exceed $127 Trillion," *Forbes*, January 17, 2014, www.forbes.com/sites /realspin/2014/01/17/you-think-the-deficit-is-bad-federal-unfunded -liabilities-exceed-127-trillion/#713f99fa10d3; Michele Ye Hee Lee, "Ben Carson's Claim That the U.S. Owes $211 Trillion Beyond the Reported Federal Debt," *The Washington Post*, May 13, 2015, www.washingtonpost. com/news/fact-checker/wp/2015/05/13/ben-carsons-claim-that-the-u-s -owes-211-trillion-beyond-the-reported-federal-debt/; Chris Cox and Bill Archer, "Cox and Archer: Why $16 Trillion Only Hints at the True U.S. Debt," *The Wall Street Journal*, November 28, 2012, www.wsj.com/articles /SB10001424127887323353204578127374039087636.

41. A nice account is offered by Baron Bodissey, "The Other September 11th," *The Gates of Vienna*, September 11, 2006, accessed October 1, 2016, gatesofvienna.blogspot.com/2006/09/other-september-11th.html.

42. Andreas Rinke, "Merkel says Islam 'belongs to Germany' ahead of Dresden rally," *Reuters*, January 12, 2015, www.reuters.com/article/us-germany -islam-merkel-idUSKBN0KL1S020150112.

43. Mark Steyn, "It's the Demography, Stupid: The Real Reason the West Is in Danger of Extinction," *The Wall Street Journal*, updated January 4, 2006, accessed September 12, 2016, www.wsj.com/articles/SB122531242161281449.

44. Steyn, "It's the Demography, Stupid."

45. David French, "The Attorney General of the United States Is Disgracing Herself," *National Review*, December 4, 2015, www.nationalreview.com /article/428048/san-bernardino-shooting-loretta-lynch-muslim-backlash, September 19, 2016; Josh Gerstein, "Lynch Warns Against Anti-Muslim Backlash," *Politico*, December 3, 2015, accessed September 19, 2016, www.politico.com/blogs/under-the-radar/2015/12/lynch-warns-against -anti-muslim-backlash-216421.

46. Bill Warner, *Sharia Law for the Non-Muslim* (n.c.: Center for the Study of Political Islam, 2010), 22, emphasis added. Warner is paraphrasing Ahmad ibn Naqib al-Misri, *Reliance of the Traveller: A Classic Manual of Islamic Sacred Law*, rev. ed., Nuh Ha Mim Keller, ed. and trans. (Beltsville, Maryland: Amana Publications, 1991, 1994), o9.8; see note 133, page 243.

47. Ibn Khaldun, *The Muqaddimah: An Introduction to History*, trans. Franz Rosenthal; ed. and abridged by N. J. Dawood (Princeton: Princeton University Press, 1967), 183, emphasis added.

48. Jihadist News, "Abu Bakr al-Baghdadi Appears in Video, Delivers Sermon in Mosul," SITE Intelligence Group, accessed July 16, 2016, news. siteintelgroup.com/Jihadist-News/abu-bakr-al-baghdadi-appears-in-video -delivers-sermon-in-mosul.html.

49. The Week Staff, "How Saudi Arabia Exports Radical Islam," *The Week*,

August 8, 2015, accessed July 16, 2016, theweek.com/articles/570297
/how-saudi-arabia-exports-radical-islam.

Chapter 1: Muhammad

1. Muhammad Iqbal, *Jāvīdnāma* (Lahore: n.p., 1932), line 608, quoted in
   Annemarie Schimmel, *And Muhammad Is His Messenger: The Veneration of
   the Prophet in Islamic Piety* (Chapel Hill, NC: University of North Carolina
   Press, 1985), 239.
2. Muhammad Iqbal, *Rumūz-i bēkhudī*, (Lahore: n.p., 1917), 190, quoted in
   Schimmel, *And Muhammad Is His Messenger*, 256.
3. Iqbal, *Jāvīdnāma*, line 608, quoted in Schimmel, *And Muhammad Is His
   Messenger*, 239.
4. See Samuel M. Zwemer, *The Moslem Christ* (Edinburgh, Scotland: Oliphant,
   Anderson, and Ferrier, 1912), chapter 7, accessed July 22, 2016, www.
   answering-islam.org/Books/Zwemer/Christ/chap7.htm; Schimmel, *And
   Muhammad Is His Messenger*, 105–122, 257–59.
5. A brief note concerning the concept of liberal Islam is in order. As Abdu
   Murray observes, "There is an effort among some who call themselves
   Muslims to moderate Islam by getting away from Muhammad's example,
   calling his deeds necessary or excusable for that place and that time, but
   not for today's culture. While they would say that they follow Muhammad
   in principle, they would not follow Muhammad in practice. Fundamentalist
   Muslims might say such people aren't really Muslims, though" (from an
   unpublished review of *Muslim*, commissioned by publisher, April 2017).
6. Ghazzali, *Ihyā' 'ulūm ad-dīn*, 2:300, quoted in Schimmel, *And Muhammad Is
   His Messenger*, 31.
7. Schimmel continued, "Only recently has this traditional world broken down
   under the onslaught of the modern technological culture. Awareness of the
   danger that now confronts Islamic tradition has certainly contributed to the
   sudden growth of Muslim fundamentalism that came as such a surprise to the
   unprepared Western world." (Schimmel, *And Muhammad Is His Messenger*, 55).
8. See Qur'an 33:21; 68:4; see also 3:31; 4:59, 80; 5:92; 24:63; 64:12. Ali ibn
   Abi Talib, the cousin and son-in-law of Muhammad and caliph from 656
   to 661, is reported to have said of Muhammad, "He was the most generous
   of people, the most truthful of the people in speech, the gentlest of them in
   temperament, and the noblest of them in social affability. If someone saw
   him unexpectedly, he was awestruck by him, and if someone associated with
   him knowingly, he loved him. . . . I have never seen the like of him, either
   before him or after him" (quoted in *The Study Quran: A New Translation and
   Commentary*, ed. Seyyed Hossein Nasr [New York: HarperOne, 2015], 1025
   note at Q 33:21).

9. The venerable Muslim translator Yusuf Ali lauds Muhammad as "the last and greatest of the Messengers of Allah" (Abdullah Yusuf Ali, *The Meaning of the Holy Qur'an*, tenth ed. [Beltsville: MD: Amana Publications, 1999, 2001], 389 [note 1127 at Q 7:157]).

10. Muhammad is called "the Messenger of Allah, and the Seal of the Prophets" (Q 33:40; see also 48:8–9). *Sahih Muslim* records, "Abu Huraira reported that the Messenger of Allah (may peace be upon him) said: I have been given superiority over the other prophets in six respects: I have been given words which are concise but comprehensive in meaning; I have been helped by terror (in the hearts of enemies): spoils have been made lawful to me: the earth has been made for me clean and a place of worship; I have been sent to all mankind and the line of prophets is closed with me" (Book 4, Number 1062, www.usc.edu/org/cmje/religious-texts/hadith/muslim/004 -smt.php#004.1062); see also *Sahih Muslim*, Book 030, Number 5673; *Sahih al-Bukhari* Vol. 4, Book 56, Hadith 735; *Sahih Muslim*, Book 004, Number 1062; *Sahih Muslim* Book 30, Number 5655.

Schimmel wrote: "Among the great messengers five are usually singled out to form the category of the *ūlū'l-'azm*, 'those with firm resolution' (Sura 46:34): Muhammad, Abraham (the father of the three 'Abrahamic religions,' Judaism, Christianity, and Islam), Moses, Jesus, and Noah. Abraham occupies the highest rank after Muhammad . . . [Muhammad's] position as *ḥabīb Allāh* ['God's beloved friend'] has been generally accepted in Muslim piety, while *khalīl Allāh* [a 'close friend of God'] is used exclusively for Abraham, as is *kalīm Allāh*, 'the one to whom God spoke,' for Moses. In fact, from Muhammad's role as *ḥabīb Allāh* one could derive the conclusion (as Ibn 'Arabi and his followers did) that Islam is 'the religion of Love,' for 'the station of perfect love is appropriated to Muhammad beyond any other prophet'" (Schimmel, *And Muhammad Is His Messenger*, 56–57).

Stephen Schwartz put it this way: "Muslims believe Muhammad to be a peer of Moses and Jesus in the constellation of Prophets, while he is also the Chief of Prophets, their Seal and Crown. It is in support of this standing that Islam reinforces the message of the earlier Prophets, that it be concentrated and focused through Muhammad" (Stephen Schwartz, *The Two Faces of Islam: The House of Sa'ud from Tradition to Terror* [New York: Doubleday, 2002], 13).

Within the contradictory traditions are also exhortations to regard Muhammad as equal to, not greater than, the other prophets (e.g., *Sahih Muslim*, Book 30, number 5854).

11. Dates in the life of Muhammad and early Islam are approximations. My brief sketch of events in the life of Muhammad draws from the traditional Muslim accounts, including Ibn Ishaq's (d. 767) *The Life of Muhammad*, Al-Waqidi's (d. circa 820) *Military Campaigns of the Prophet*, Al-Tabari's

(d. 923) *History of the Prophets and Kings*, and the highly regarded *hadiths Sahih Al-Bukhari* (d. 870) and *Sahih Muslim* (d. 875). As Serge Trifkovic explained, "Of Muhammad's life we are informed mainly from the Muslim sources: the Kuran, the *hadiths* or recorded traditions about the prophet, and the consensus of Islamic scholars. Those sources provide an account that may not be historically accurate, but is nevertheless essential because it is regarded as factual by all true Muslims and it is used as the scriptural basis for the faith, political action and the law" (Serge Trifkovic, *Defeating Jihad: How the War on Terrorism Can Be Won—In Spite of Ourselves* (Boston: Regina Orthodox Press, 2006), 21).

Middle East and Islam research specialist Raymond Ibrahim summarized the situation well: "It has been remarked, and for good reason, that there is probably no one person of late antiquity who is better documented than Mohammad. Literally thousands of pages exist consisting of what Muslims believe to be verbatim statements and deeds attributed to their prophet. These are the 'hadiths' that, after the Koran, are the second most important source for Islamic jurisprudence. There are also historical works such as Ibn Ishaq's eighth-century *Life of Mohammad*, the earliest extensive biography of Islam's prophet, as well as the voluminous histories of al-Tabari, al-Baladhuri, and al-Waki that recount the life and especially military exploits of Mohammad. . . . The question of 'what would Mohammad do?' in any given circumstance is of the utmost importance for Sunni Muslims—the word 'Sunni' denotes the need to emulate Mohammad in every possible way. It comes as no surprise, then, that the portrait of Islam's founder—his life, deeds, words, character, likes, dislikes—is very clear; only very few aspects, if any, of Mohammad's life are open to conjecture. Based solely on these sources, which, it bears repeating, Muslims themselves consider to be of great authority, one can spend pages enumerating less-than-impressive deeds attributed to Mohammad: aggressive and unprovoked warfare, mass executions, assassinations, lies, thefts, the enslavement of women and children, and marriage to a nine-year-old." (Raymond Ibrahim, "Jesus and Mohammad, Version 2.0," *National Review*, September 10, 2007, www.nationalreview.com/article/221984/jesus-and-mohammad-version-20 -raymond-ibrahim.) See also note 15 in the Introduction.

12. Concerning the growth of contemporary Islam, see Michael Lipka and Conrad Hackett, "Why Muslims are the world's fastest-growing religious group," Pew Research Center, April 23, 2015, accessed September 12, 2016, www.pewresearch.org/fact-tank/2015/04/23/why-muslims-are-the -worlds-fastest-growing-religious-group/; "The Future of World Religions: Population Growth Projections, 2010–2050," Pew Research Center, April 2, 2015, accessed September 12, 2016, www.pewforum.org/2015/04/02 /religious-projections-2010-2050/.

13. This message became Qur'an 96:1–5. Ibn Ishaq, *The Life of Muhammad: A Translation of Ishaq's Sīrat Rasūl Allāh*, trans. A. Guillaume (Oxford: Oxford University Press, 1955, 2001), 106 (see pages 104–107 for context). Arabic *Qur'an*, from *qara'a* "to read."

14. Ishaq, *The Life of Muhammad*, 106 (see 106–107), emphasis added; see also Al-Tabari, *The History of al-Tabari: Muhammad at Mecca*, vol. 6, trans. W. Montgomery Watt and M. V. McDonald (Albany: State University of New York Press, 1988), 67–77, especially 71–72, kalamullah.com /Books/The%20History%20Of%20Tabari/Tabari_Volume_06.pdf; cf. *Sahih al-Bukhari* Volume 9, Book 87, Hadith 111; Volume 1, Book 1, Hadith 3; Volume 6, Book 60, Hadith 478.

15. Ishaq, *The Life of Muhammad*, 106.

16. Ibid., 107, emphasis added.

17. See Qur'an 10:94–95 (cf. 3:60–63). The references cited in the previous note 14 in this chapter convey that Muhammad's doubts lingered. The tradition also indicates Muhammad was bewitched by magic, see *Sahih al-Bukhari*, Volume 7, Book 71, Number 660 (and Numbers 658 and 661); *Sahih al-Bukhari*, Volume 4, Book 54, Number 490.

18. Al-Tabari wrote: "The inspiration ceased to come to the Messenger of God for a while, and he was deeply grieved. He began to go to the tops of mountain crags, in order to fling himself from them; but every time he reached the summit of a mountain, Gabriel appeared to him and said to him, 'You are the Prophet of God.' Thereupon his anxiety would subside and he would come back to himself" (*The History of al-Tabari: Muhammad at Mecca*, vol. 6, trans. Watt and McDonald, 76).

19. See Al-Tabari, *The History of al-Tabari: Muhammad at Mecca*, vol. 6, trans. Watt and McDonald, 76–77, 80–86.

20. Polytheism is belief in "many gods." Most of the world's religions are polytheistic, outside of Judaism, Christianity, and Islam, which hold to forms of monotheism—the belief that there exists one and only one theistic God. Theism is the belief that there exists one and only one personal and sovereign God, who is the transcendent creator and immanent sustainer of the world. Contrast these views with pantheism ("all is God"), the belief that God and the world are ultimately identical.

21. Zamzam is the sacred well within the boundaries of the Great Mosque at Mecca. In Islamic tradition it is said to be the "identical spring from which Hagar and Ishmael drank in the wilderness. . . . The Zamzam water is held in great esteem throughout the East. It is used for drinking and ablution, but for no baser purposes; and the [Meccans] advise pilgrims to break their fast with it" (Thomas Patrick Hughes, *A Dictionary of Islam* [Chicago: KAZI Publications, Inc., 1994, originally published in 1886], 701).

22. Qur'an 94:1 is a possible reference to this story. See *Sahih Muslim*, Book 001, Number 0311; Ibn Ishaq, *The Life of Muhammad*, 71–72.
23. See Al-Tabari, *The History of al-Tabari: Muhammad at Mecca*, vol. 6, trans. Watt and McDonald, 75, 78.
24. *Masjid Al-Aqsa* means "the farthest mosque" or the most distant place of worship of the one God. The mosque stands adjacent to the Dome of the Rock in Jerusalem and is Islam's third holiest site after Mecca and Medina.
25. "The Night Journey and the Ascension (Part 3 of 6): The Ascension," The Religion of Islam, www.islamreligion.com/articles/1511/viewall /night-journey-and-ascension/.
26. See Qur'an 52:4.
27. See Qur'an 53:14.
28. The tradition agrees that Muhammad stood in the very presence of Allah, but did Muhammad see Allah? Many Muslims say that Qur'an 53:1–18 and 81:15–29 in conjunction with the accounts of the Ascent to Heaven indicate he did. The *Sahih Muslim* Collection at USC-CMJE states, "Chapter 78: THE MEANING OF THE WORDS OF ALLAH: "HE SAW HIM IN ANOTHER DESCENT" (AL-QUR'AN, LIII. 13). DID THE APOSTLE (MAY PEACE BE UPON HIM) SEE HIS LORD ON THE NIGHT OF HIS JOURNEY (TO HEAVEN)? Book 001, Number 0334: It is narrated on the authority of Ibn 'Abbas that he (the Holy Prophet) saw (Allah) with, his heart." And Book 001, Number 0335: "It is narrated on the authority of Ibn Abbas that the words: 'The heart belied not what he saw' (al-Qur'an, liii. 11) and 'Certainly he saw Him in another descent' (al-Qur'an, liii. 13) imply that he saw him twice with his heart" (www.usc.edu/org/cmje/religious -texts/hadith/muslim/001-smt.php#001.0334).

    Also, there is much dispute over the translation and meaning of *Sahih Muslim*, Book 1, Numbers 0341 and 0342, which for many imply that Muhammad saw Allah ("He is light"; "I saw light"). Others deny that Muhammad saw Allah. "Narrated Masruq: 'I said to 'Aisha, "O Mother! Did Prophet Muhammad see his Lord?" 'Aisha said, "What you have said makes my hair stand on end! Know that if somebody tells you one of the following three things, he is a liar: Whoever tells you that Muhammad saw his Lord, is a liar." Then 'Aisha recited the Verse: "No vision can grasp Him, but His grasp is over all vision. He is the Most Courteous Well-Acquainted with all things." [Q 6:103] "It is not fitting for a human being that Allah should speak to him except by inspiration or from behind a veil. [Q 42:51]'" (*Sahih al-Bukhari*, Volume 6, Book 60, Number 378, sunnah.com/bukhari/65; see also *Sahih Muslim*, Book 001, Number 0337).
29. Accounts of the Night Journey and Ascension (Miraj) include *Sahih*

al-Bukhari Volume 1, Book 8, Number 345; *Sahih al-Bukhari* Volume 4, Book 54, Number 429; *Sahih al-Bukhari* Volume 5, Book 58, Number 227; *Sahih Muslim*, Book 1, Number 309 (also 313 and 314); Ibn Ishaq, *The Life of Muhammad*, 181–87; Al-Tabari, *The History of al-Tabari: Muhammad at Mecca*, vol. 6, trans. Watt and McDonald, 78–80.

30. See Ishaq, *The Life of Muhammad*, 183.

31. "The Night Journey and the Ascension (Part 6 of 6): The Return," The Religion of Islam, www.islamreligion.com/articles/1511/viewall/night -journey-and-ascension/. Ibn Ishaq reports (per al-Hasan) that "the apostle said, 'And you, Abū Bakr, are the *Ṣiddīq*.' This was the occasion on which he got this honorific" (Ibn Ishaq, *The Life of Muhammad*, 183). In a footnote, Ishaq's translator, A. Guillaume, stated that the honorific means "Testifier to the Truth." *Encyclopedia of Islam* states that Abu Bakr's "nickname was *al-Siddiq* (the truthful) because he was the first to confirm the reality of Muhammad's Night Journey and Ascent" (Juan Eduardo Campo, *Encyclopedia of Islam* [New York: Facts on File, 2009], 9).

32. Schwartz, *Two Faces of Islam*, 11.

33. The Qur'an explicitly condemns Abu Lahab and his wife (see Q 111:1–5). See also *Sahih Muslim*, Book 001, Number 0406; *Sahih al-Bukhari*, Volume 6, Book 60, Hadith 475.

34. Al-Tabari, *The History of al-Tabari: Biographies of the Prophet's Companions and their Successors*, vol. 39, trans. Ella Landau-Tasseron (Albany: SUNY Press, 1998), 4, 161, kalamullah.com/Books/The%20 History%20Of%20Tabari/Tabari_Volume_39.pdf; Ibn Ishaq, *The Life of Muhammad*, 191.

35. Ishaq, *The Life of Muhammad*, 197–98; Al-Tabari, *The History of al-Tabari: Muhammad at Mecca*, vol. 6, trans. Watt and McDonald, 124–26.

36. Ishaq, *The Life of Muhammad*, 198–99; Al-Tabari, *The History of al-Tabari: Muhammad at Mecca*, vol. 6, trans. Watt and McDonald, 126–27.

37. "Aqaba Pledges and the Spread of Islam in Madinah," The Prophet Muhammad—The Pride of the Universe, www.resulullah.org/en/aqaba -pledges-and-spread-islam-madinah; see also Ibn Ishaq, *The Life of Muhammad*, 203–204; Al-Tabari, *The History of al-Tabari: Muhammad at Mecca*, vol. 6, trans. Watt and McDonald, 133 (130–38).

38. The Muslim calendar begins with the emigration from Mecca to Medina in AD 622 (AH 1—*Anno Hegirae*, "in the year of the Hijra"). The lunar calendar tracks 12 months comprising about 354 days in a year. Thus, over time, Ramadan and Islamic observances rotate backward through the four seasons. For accounts of the Hijra, see Ishaq, *The Life of Muhammad*, 221ff; Al-Tabari, *The History of al-Tabari: Muhammad at Mecca*, vol. 6, trans. Watt and McDonald, 142ff.

39. See, e.g, Q 2:62, revealed in Medina soon after the Hijra. See James

Arlandson, "Muhammad and the Jews," Answering Islam, www.answering
-islam.org/Authors/Arlandson/jews.htm.

40. See throughout Q 2:40–121; *Sahih al-Bukhari* Volume 3, Book 31, Number
222.

41. See Q 2:143 ("We appointed the Qibla to which thou wast used, only to
test those who followed the Messenger from those who would turn on their
heels (From the Faith)") in conjunction with *The History of al-Tabari: The
Foundation of the Community*, vol. 7, trans. M. V. McDonald (Albany:
State University of New York Press, 1987), 24–25, kalamullah.com/Books
/The%20History%20Of%20Tabari/Tabari_Volume_07.pdf. For discussion,
see Sam Shamoun, "Muhammad's Changing of the Qibla," Answering
Islam, www.answering-islam.org/Shamoun/qiblah.htm.

42. See Qur'an 4:48, 116, 171; 5:17, 72–73, 77; 9:30–31; 19:35; 98:6; 112:1–4.
Note that some passages in the Qur'an seem to affirm Christians (e.g., Q
2:62; 5:82), while many other passages condemn them. Haggai Mazuz
shows that, according to "Islamic exegetical writings dating from the earliest
period of Qur'anic commentary up to the late Middle Ages," Christians in
the view of the Qur'an can be divided into two basic categories: "Those
who did not accept Muhammad and Islam, thus remaining Christian, were
condemned. However, those who acknowledged Muhammad as a prophet
and accepted Islam were therefore not Christians, but Muslims, and were
praised" (Haggai Mazuz, "Christians in the Qur'an: Some Insights Derived
from the Classic Exegetic Approach," *Studia Orientalia* 112 [2012], 41, 51,
www.academia.edu/2540851/_Christians_in_the_Qur'ān_Some_Insights
_Derived_from_the_Classical_Exegetic_Approach_Studia_Orientalia
_112_2012_41_53).

43. See *Sahih al-Bukhari* Volume 5, Book 58, Number 227.

44. Although Q 2:142–49 does not specifically state that the direction of
prayer was changed from Jerusalem to Mecca, authoritative Muslim
sources underscore this tradition. *Sahih Muslim* reads, "Anas reported:
The Messenger of Allah (may peace be upon him) used to pray towards
Bait-ul-Maqdis [in Jerusalem], that it was revealed (to him): 'Indeed We
see the turning of the face to heaven, wherefore We shall assuredly cause
thee to turn towards Qibla which shall please thee. So turn thy face towards
the sacred Mosque (Ka'ba)' (ii. 144)" (*Sahih Muslim*, Book 004, Number
1075, www.usc.edu/org/cmje/religious-texts/hadith/muslim/004-smt.
php#004.1075). See also *Sahih al-Bukhari* Volume 1, Book 8, Number 392;
and *The History of al-Tabari: The Foundation of the Community*, vol. 7,
trans. McDonald, 24–25.

45. Schwartz, *Two Faces of Islam*, 10.

46. Ishaq, *The Life of Muhammad*, 130–31.

47. *Sahih al-Bukhari*, Volume 5, Book 57, Number 74: "Narrated Qais: I heard

Sad saying, 'I was the first amongst the 'Arabs who shot an arrow for Allah's Cause'" (www.usc.edu/org/cmje/religious-texts/hadith/bukhari/057-sbt. php#005.057.074). See also Ibn Ishaq, *The Life of Muhammad*, 281; cf. Al-Waqidi, *The Life of Muhammad: Al-Wāqidī's Kitāb al-Maghāzī*, ed. Rizwi Faizer, trans. Rizwi Faizer, Amal Ismail and AbdulKader Tayob (London: Routledge, 2011), 7.

48. Ishaq, *The Life of Muhammad*, 287.
49. Ibid., 287–88.
50. Ibid., 288.
51. See also Q 2:191 (see vv. 190–93). The word "mischief" translates "*Al-Fitnah*," which, in this context, means disbelief or the strife and commotion resulting from unbelief. Ibn Ishaq wrote that when there was much talk about the event, "God sent down to his apostle, 'They [Jews and pagan Quraysh] will ask you about the sacred month, and war in it. Say, war therein is a serious matter, but keeping people from the way of God and disbelieving in Him and in the sacred mosque and driving out His people therefrom is more serious with God.' i.e. If you have killed in the sacred month, they have kept you back from the way of God with their unbelief in Him, and from the sacred mosque, and have driven you from it when you were its people. This is a more serious matter with God than the killing of those of them whom you have slain. 'And seduction is worse than killing.' i.e. They used to seduce the Muslim in his religion until they made him return to unbelief after believing, and that is worse with God than killing. 'And they will not cease to fight you until they turn you back from your religion if they can.' i.e. They are doing more heinous acts than that contumaciously" (*The Life of Muhammad*, 288; compare the accounts in Al-Waqidi, *The Life of Muhammad*, 8–11; Al-Tabari, *The History of al-Tabari: The Foundation of the Community*, vol. 7, trans. McDonald, 18–23; and *Tafsir Ibn Kathir*, 2:217, online at Alim.org). Rather than mere defensive warfare, the Qur'anic passage in context commands fighting those who resist Muslim domination. (See "Violence" at TheReligionsofPeace.com.)
52. See Q 3:13; Schwartz, *The Two Faces of Islam*, 22.
53. Qur'an 8:9 speaks of a thousand angels. Quran 3:124 refers to at least three thousand angels, though some commentators interpret the latter passage to refer to the Battle of Uhud a year later, which is unlikely since the Muslims were defeated at Uhud. The scenario involving Gabriel and Michael is found in Ibn Kathir's revered commentary concerning Qur'an 8:9 (see *Tafsir Ibn Kathir*, 8:9, online at QTafsir.com).
54. "Abu Jahal," *Islamic Encyclopedia*, accessed July 12, 2016, islamicencyclopedia.org/public/index/topicDetail/id/59.
55. See Ishaq, *The Life of Muhammad*, 289ff.; Al-Waqidi, *The Life of*

Muhammad, 11ff.; Al-Tabari, *The History of al-Tabari: The Foundation of the Community*, vol. 7, trans. McDonald, 26ff.

56. Schwartz is quoting Q 56:17–21. Schwartz, *The Two Faces of Islam*, 23. I discuss the houris further below, see pp. 176–77.

57. See Ishaq, *The Life of Muhammad*, 131; see also *Sahih al-Bukhari*, Volume 1, Book 4, Number 241.

58. See Ibn Ishaq, *The Life of Muhammad*, 304.

59. Ali, *The Meaning of the Holy Qur'an*, 417 (note 1189 at Q 8:12).

60. Schwartz, *The Two Faces of Islam*, 24.

61. Concerning the exile of the Banu Qaynuqa, see Ibn Ishaq, *Life of Muhammad*, 260, 363–64; Al-Waqidi, *Life of Muhammad*, 87–90; Al-Tabari, *The History of al-Tabari: The Foundation of the Community*, vol. 7, trans. McDonald, 85–87 (see also xxvii–xxix).

62. See *Sahih al-Bukhari*, Volume 5, Book 59, Number 362.

63. Ishaq, *The Life of Muhammad*, 676; cf. Al-Waqidi, *Life of Muhammad*, 85–86; 'Ali Dashti, *Twenty Three Years: A Study of the Prophetic Career of Mohammad*, trans. F. R. C. Bagley (London: Routledge, 1985, 1994), 100, online at books.google.com.

64. Muhammad Husayn Haykal, *The Life of Muhammad*, trans. Isma'il Ragi A. al Faruqi (Oak Brook, IL: American Trust Publications, 1976), 235.

65. See David Wood, "Murdered by Muhammad: The Brutal Deaths of Islam's Earliest Enemies," December 16, 2011, accessed April 1, 2017, www .myislam.dk/articles/en/wood%20murdered-by-muhammad.php.

66. Concerning the exile of the Banu Nadir, see Ibn Ishaq, *Life of Muhammad*, 437ff.; Al-Waqidi, *Life of Muhammad*, 177ff.; Al-Tabari, *The History of al-Tabari: The Foundation of the Community*, vol. 7, trans. McDonald, 156ff.

67. *Sahih al-Bukhari* records, "Narrated 'Aisha: that the Prophet married her when she was six years old and he consummated his marriage when she was nine years old, and then she remained with him for nine years (i.e., till his death)" (Volume 7, Book 62, Number 64 [see also Numbers 65 and 88], www.usc.edu/org/cmje/religious-texts/hadith/bukhari/062-sbt. php). See also *Sahih al-Bukhari*, Volume 5, Book 58, Number 2346; *Sahih al-Bukhari*, Volume 9, Book 87, Number 140 (see also Number 139); *Sahih Muslim*, Book 008, Number 3309. See also *Sahih Muslim*, Book 8, Numbers 3309 and 3310 (cf. 3311). See also Sam Shamoun, "Muhammad and Aisha Revisited: An Examination of Muhammad's Marriage to a Prepubescent Girl and Its Moral Implications," *Answering Islam*, n.d., accessed September 22, 2016, www.answering-islam.org/Shamoun/prepubescent .htm.

68. Rayhana's husband was among the hundreds of Qurayza Jews Muhammad

beheaded in 627. She refused his marriage proposal, and Muhammad kept her as a concubine until her death (though traditions conflict as to whether she ultimagely married Muhammad; see Ishaq, *The Life of Muhammad*, 466; and note 81 following for this chapter).

69. See Q 33:37–38; 33:4–5; Ibn Hisham's note 918 in Ibn Ishaq, *The Life of Muhammad*, 793. The account is told in al-Tabari, *The History of al-Tabari: The Victory of Islam*, Vol. VIII, trans. Michael Fishbein (Albany: State University of New York Press, 1997), 1–4, accessed October 1, 2016, kalamullah.com/Books/The%20History%20Of%20Tabari/Tabari _Volume_08.pdf.

70. "Zaynab bint Jahsh," Islam's Women: Jewels of Islam, accessed January 12, 2016, www.islamswomen.com/articles/zaynab_bint_jahsh.php.

71. Ibid.

72. Ibid.

73. See also James R. White, *What Every Christian Needs to Know about the Qur'an* (Minneapolis: Bethany House Publishers, 2013), 45.

74. *Sahih al-Bukhari*, Volume 6, Book 60, Number 311.

75. "As for those from whom you fear misbehavior, admonish them and banish them to beds apart, and beat them. Then, if they obey you, do not be overbearing. For Allah is High, Great" (Q 4:34 *Majestic*).

76. Ali, *The Meaning of the Holy Qur'an,* 1064 (note 3704 at Q 33:26). *Muhājirs* refers to the early Muslims who migrated from Mecca to Medina.

77. Ishaq, *The Life of Muhammad*, 461. Cf. Q 2:65–66; 5:60; 7:163–66.

78. Ishaq, *The Life of Muhammad*, 464 (see 461ff. for the full account); see also the accounts in Al-Tabari, *The History of al-Tabari: The Victory of Islam*, vol. 8, trans. Fishbein, 27–41 (also 22–27); Al-Waqidi, *Life of Muhammad*, 244ff. See also the helpful analysis in James M. Arlandson, "Muhammad's Atrocity against the Qurayza Jews," *Answering Islam*, accessed January 7, 2016, answering-islam.org/Authors/Arlandson/qurayza_jews.htm.

79. Ishaq, *The Life of Muhammad*, 464.

80. Ibid., 464–65.

81. Ibid., 466. Cf. Al-Tabari, *The History of al-Tabari: The Last Years of the Prophet*, vol. 9, trans. Ismail K. Poonawala (Albany: State University of New York Press, 1990), 137 (translator's note 909), 141, at archive.org /details/TabariEnglish.

82. Ishaq, *The Life of Muhammad*, 466; see also Al-Tabari, *The History of al-Tabari: The Victory of Islam*, vol. 8, trans. Fishbein, 39.

83. Ali, *The Meaning of the Holy Qur'an*, 1336 (note 4910 at Q48:27).

84. Ibid., 1328 (note 4866 at Q48:1).

85. Cf. Yusuf Ali, *The Meaning of the Holy Qur'an*, 1326. Yusuf Ali puts the date at February 628.

86. "PA minister: PA agreements are modeled after Muhammad's Hudaybiyyah

Peace Treaty," Arafat speech in Johannesburg, May 10, 1994, Palestinian Media Watch, bracketed insertions in original, accessed April 3, 2017, palwatch.org/main.aspx?fi=157&doc_id=9401; see also Daniel Pipes, "[Al-Hudaybiya and] Lessons from the Prophet Muhammad's Diplomacy," *Middle East Quarterly*, September 1999, *Daniel Pipes Middle East Forum*, accessed January 7, 2016, www.danielpipes.org/316/al-hudaybiya-and -lessons-from-the-prophet-muhammads.

87. Mortimer B. Zuckerman, editorial in *U.S. News and World Report*, June 10, 1996, as quoted in Pipes, "[Al-Hudaybiya and] Lessons from the Prophet Muhammad's Diplomacy."

88. See Pipes, "[Al-Hudaybiya and] Lessons from the Prophet Muhammad's Diplomacy."

89. *Sahih al-Bukhari* reports that Muhammad said, "He who makes peace between the people by inventing good information or saying good things, is not a liar" (*Sahih al-Bukhari*, Volume 3, Book 49, Number 857, www.usc .edu/org/cmje/religious-texts/hadith/bukhari/049-sbt.php#003.049.857). See also Raymond Ibrahim's incisive study, "Taqiyya about Taqiyya," Raymond Ibrahim, April 12, 2014, raymondibrahim.com/2014/04/12/taqiyya-about -taqiyya/.

90. On this verse, Yusuf Ali commented, "If this part of the Surah was revealed after the autumn of the Hijrah year 7 [AD 629], it refers to the result of the Khaybar expedition of that autumn" (Yusuf Ali, *The Meaning of the Holy Qur'an*, 1064 [note 3705 at Q33:27]).

91. Edward Gibbon, Esq., *The History of the Decline and Fall of the Roman Empire*, Vol. V (1782, rev. 1845), Chapter L, Part VI, www.gutenberg.org /files/25717/25717-h/25717-h.htm.

92. Ishaq, *The Life of Muhammad*, 515. See also Al-Tabari, *The History of al - Tabari: The Victory of Islam*, vol. 8, trans. Fishbein, 122–23.

93. Ishaq, *The Life of Muhammad*, 516–17; see also pp. 241–42, 511, 514–15, 520, 793–94 [Ibn Hisham's note 918].

94. Ishaq, *The Life of Muhammad*, 511; see also *Sahih al-Bukhari* Volume 5, Book 59, Number 512.

95. Ishaq, *The Life of Muhammad*, 523. On the battle of Khaybar, see also Al-Waqidi, *The Life of Muhammad*, 311ff. (see 347–48 concerning the affair of Fadak); Al-Tabari, *The History of al-Tabari: The Victory of Islam*, vol. 8, trans. Fishbein, 116ff.

96. Ishaq, *The Life of Muhammad*, 531.

97. Trifkovic, *The Sword of the Prophet*, 48, emphasis added. Cf. Ishaq, *The Life of Muhammad*, 547; Al-Waqidi, *The Life of Muhammad*, 401–403; see also al-Tabari's account of Muhammad's order to assassinate Abu Sufyan, but the mission failed, in *The History of al-Tabari: The Foundation of the Community*, vol. 7, trans. McDonald, 147–150.

98. *Sahih al-Bukhari*, Volume 5, Book 59, Number 582; Ibn Ishaq, *The Life of Muhammad*, 550–51. Ishaq indicates that Ibn Khatal was executed for apostasy.

99. Ibn Sa'd, Kitab al-Tabaqat al-Kabir, as quoted in "Muhammad and the Ten Meccans," *Answering Islam*, accessed September 27, 2016, www.answering -islam.org/Muhammad/Enemies/meccan10.html.

100. Ishaq, *The Life of Muhammad*, 551.

101. Ibid., 550. If a Muslim abandons or renounces Islam, the penalty is death. See Q 2:217 and 4:89; see also 9:11–12, 66, 73–74. *Sahih al-Bukhari* reports, "[T]he Prophet said: 'If somebody (a Muslim) discards his religion, kill him'" (Volume 4, Book 52, Number 260, www.usc.edu/org/cmje/religious -texts/hadith/bukhari/052-sbt.php); see also Volume 4, Book 52, Number 260; Volume 9, Book 89, Number 271; Volume 9, Book 84, Number 58; Volume 9, Book 83, Numbers 17 and 37). *Reliance of the Traveller: A Classic Manual of Islamic Sacred Law* states, "When a person who has reached puberty and is sane voluntarily apostatizes from Islam, he deserves to be killed" (Ahmad ibn Naqib al-Misri, *Reliance of the Traveller: A Classic Manual of Islamic Sacred Law*, rev. ed., Nuh Ha Mim Keller, ed. and trans. [Beltsville, Maryland: Amana Publications, 1991, 1994], 595 [o8.1]). This statement and relevant law, founded on the Qur'an and the recorded words and actions of Muhammad, reflect all schools of classic Islamic jurisprudence.

102. Ishaq, *The Life of Muhammad*, 550. See also "Muhammad and the Ten Meccans," *Answering Islam*.

103. Ishaq, *The Life of Muhammad*, 552.

104. *Sahih Muslim*, Book 037, Number 6670, www.usc.edu/org/cmje/religious -texts/hadith/muslim/037-smt.php#037.6670.

105. Ibn Kathir continued, "Abu Bakr As-Siddiq used this and other honorable Ayat [verses] as proof for fighting those who refrained from paying the Zakah [obligatory alms giving]. These Ayat allowed fighting people unless, and until, they embrace Islam and implement its rulings and obligations. . . . In the Two Sahihs, it is recorded that Ibn `Umar said that the Messenger of Allah said, (I have been commanded to fight the people until they testify that there is no deity worthy of worship except Allah and that Muhammad is the Messenger of Allah, establish the prayer and pay the Zakah [*Sahih al-Bukhari* 1:33; 8:387; *Sahih Muslim* 001:0033].) This honorable Ayah (9:5) was called the Ayah of the Sword, about which Ad-Dahhak bin Muzahim said, 'It abrogated every agreement of peace between the Prophet and any idolator, every treaty, and every term.' Al-`Awfi said that Ibn `Abbas commented: 'No idolator had any more treaty or promise of safety ever since Surah Bara'ah was revealed.'" Ibn Kathir, *Tafsir Ibn Kathir* (Riyadh: Darussalam Publishers, 2000), online at QTafsir.com, www.qtafsir.com

/index.php?option=com_content&task=view&id=2581&Itemid=64. For discussion on "the Verse of the Sword" and Jihad, see Robert Spencer, *Onward Muslim Soldiers: How Jihad Still Threatens America and the West* (Washington, DC: Regnery Publishing, 2003), chap. 4.

106. *Sahih al-Bukhari*, Volume 4, Book 52, Number 175.

107. Robert Spencer, *The Politically Incorrect Guide to Islam (and the Crusades)* (Washington, DC: Regnery Publishing, 2005), 108–09.

108. *Hajj* (Arabic, "setting out") is the pilgrimage to Mecca required once during the lifetime of every able Muslim (one of the five pillars of Islam).

109. Daniel C. Peterson, *Muhammad: Prophet of God* (Grand Rapids, MI: William B. Eerdmans Publishing Co., 2007), 158, bracketed insertion "[submission]" in original. Yusuf Ali comments that this verse is "considered by many as the last verse revealed chronologically" (Yusuf Ali, *The Meaning of the Holy Qur'an*, 245 [note 696 at Q 5:3]]).

110. Ishaq, *The Life of Muhammad*, 652.

111. Al-Tabari, *The History of al- Tabari: The Victory of Islam*, vol. 8, trans. Fishbein, 123–24.

112. *Sahih al-Bukhari*, Volume 5, Book 59, Number 713 (see also Number 551), www.usc.edu/org/cmje/religious-texts/hadith/bukhari/059-sbt.php#005.059.713; see also *Sahih al-Bukhari*, Volume 3, Book 47, Number 786; *Sahih Muslim*, Book 026, Hadith Number 5430.

113. "Narrated 'Aisha, 'I never saw anybody suffering so much from sickness as Allah's Apostle'" (*Sahih al-Bukhari*, Volume 7, Book 70, Number 549 [see also Numbers 550 and 551], www.usc.edu/org/cmje/religious-texts/hadith/bukhari/070-sbt.php#007.070.549).

114. *Sahih al-Bukhari* Volume 7, Book 62, Number 144; Ibn Ishaq, *The Life of Muhammad*, 682; Haykal, *The Life of Muhammad*, 494, 497.

115. See Hank Hanegraaff, *Has God Spoken? Memorable Proofs of the Bible's Divine Inspiration* (Nashville: Thomas Nelson, 2011), 116–20.

116. Ibid., 121–25.

117. Ibid., 125–27, 153–162.

118. Within the first-century Jewish context, women were not allowed to serve as legal witnesses. But after he had risen from the dead, Jesus appeared first to women and entrusted them to announce his resurrection to the disciples (Matthew 28; John 20). Furthermore, during his ministry Christ had "invited women to accompany Him and His disciples on their journeys (Luke 8:1–3). He talked with the Samaritan woman at Jacob's Well and led her to a conversion experience (John 4). Jesus did not think it strange that Mary sat at His feet, assuming the role of a disciple; in fact, He suggested to Martha that she should do likewise (Luke 10:38–42). Although the Jews segregated the women in both temple and synagogue, the early church did not separate the congregation by sex (Acts 12:1–17; 1 Cor. 11:2–16). The

apostle Paul wrote, 'There is neither Jew nor Greek, there is neither slave nor free, there is neither male nor female; for you are all one in Jesus Christ' (Gal. 3:28)" (Ronald F. Youngblood, ed., *Nelson's New Illustrated Bible Dictionary* [Nashville: Thomas Nelson Publishers, 1995], 1318). Moreover, the preeminent Christian venerated by the historic church is a woman, not a man: Mary, called the Mother of God (*Theotokos*).

119. Concerning the principles of the kingdom of heaven, see especially the Sermon on the Mount (Matthew 5–7). That the kingdom of God is eternal, see Psalm 145:13; Isaiah 9:6–7; Daniel 2:44; 4:34; 7:14, 27; Luke 1:32–33; 2 Peter 1:11; Revelation 21–22.

120. Matthew 5:43–48; Luke 6:27–36.

121. Matthew 5:39.

122. Matthew 5:9.

123. Matthew 26:52.

124. Matthew 11:28–29 and Matthew 23.

125. See especially Mark 10:45; John 15:13; Romans 5:6; 8:32; Ephesians 5:2; Titus 2:14.

126. John 14:6.

Chapter 2: Unreliable Revelations

1. See Qur'an 43:3–4; 85:21–22; see also 3:7; 13:39. The "Mother of the Book"—the foundation of all revelation—is said to be eternally in Allah's own presence, as generally understood by Sunni Muslims. Shi'a Muslims say it is created (see appendix: Sunni | Shi'a Split). Either way, the earthly Arabic Qur'an is said to be a perfect copy.

2. Concerning "Tradition," Muhammad is said to have "received the *Waḥy ghair Matlū* ([literally] 'an unread revelation'), whereby he was enabled to give authoritative declarations on religious questions, either moral, ceremonial, or doctrinal. Muḥammad traditions are therefore supposed to be the uninspired record of inspired sayings" (Thomas Patrick Hughes, *A Dictionary of Islam* [Chicago: KAZI Publications, Inc., 1994, originally published in 1886], 639).

3. Schwartz, *Two Faces of Islam*, 4. According to Muslim scholar Aḥmad Muḥammad al-Ṭayyib, "*Sunnah* ('wont') designates the sayings and actions of the Messenger of God, whereas *Hadīth* ('tradition') specifically designates his sayings. Understanding the Quran needs the *Sunnah* to provide clarifications and specific illustrations of the former's general declarations" (Aḥmad Muḥammad al-Ṭayyib, "The Quran as Source of Islamic Law," in *The Quran Study Bible*, ed. Seyyed Hossein Nasr [New York: HarperOne, 2015], 1715).

4. W. St. Clair Tisdall, *The Original Sources of the Qur'an: Its Origin in*

Pagan Legends and Mythology (London: Society for Promoting Christian Knowledge, 1905), 25, online at www.answering-islam.org/Books/Tisdall /Sources/chap1.htm.

5. Ibid., 27.

6. See Qur'an 2:116–17; 6:100–102; 9:30; 10:68; 18:1–5; 19:35, 88–93; 23:91; 25:2; 39:3–6; 43:15, 57–65, 81; 72:3; 112:1–4. In the context of speaking of Mary and "Jesus the son of Mary," the Qur'an states, "It is not befitting to (the majesty of) Allah that He should beget a son. Glory be to Him! When He determines a matter, He only says to it, 'Be,' and it is" (19:34, 35; see 19:16–35). In 6:101 the Qur'an asks the rhetorical question, "How can He [Allah] have a son when He hath no consort?" Qur'an 2:116 states, "They say: 'Allah hath begotten a son': Glory be to Him—Nay, to Him belongs all that is in the heavens and on earth: everything renders worship to Him."

Concerning Q 2:116–17, Ibn Kathir (d. 1373) wrote, "This and the following Ayat [verse] refute the Christians, may Allah curse them, and their like among the Jews and the Arab idolators, who claimed that the angels are Allah's daughters. Allah refuted all of them in their claim that He had begotten a son." (Ibn Kathir, *Tafsir Ibn Kathir* [Riyadh: Darussalam Publishers, 2000], online at QTafsir.com, www.qtafsir.com/index.php ?option=com_content&task=view&id=319.)

Concerning Q 2:116, Yusuf Ali commented, "It is a derogation from the glory of Allah—in fact it is blasphemy—to say that Allah begets sons, like a man or an animal. The Christian doctrine is here emphatically repudiated. If words have any meaning, it would be an attribution to Allah of a material nature, and of the lower animal functions of sex" (Abdullah Yusuf Ali, *The Meaning of the Holy Qur'an*, tenth ed. [Beltsville: MD: Amana Publications, 1999, 2001], 49, note 119).

7. This special relationship between God the Father and God the Son is well-summarized in the Nicene Creed, "I believe in one God, Father Almighty, Creator of heaven and earth . . . .And in one Lord Jesus Christ, the only-begotten Son of God, begotten of the Father before all ages; Light of Light, true God of true God, begotten not created, of one essence with the Father, through Whom all things were made" (see Genesis 1:1; Psalms 2:7; Micah 5:2; Matthew 3:17; 17:5; John 1:1–3, 10, 14, 18; 3:16; 5:23; 8:12; 10:30, 33; 14:9; 17:5; 20:28, 31; 1 Corinthians 8:6; Ephesians 4:5–6; Philippians 2:6; Colossians 1:15–17, 19; 2:9; Hebrews 1:1–8; 1 John 1:1; 4:9; Revelation 1:8, 17; 21:6; 22:13 [cp. Isaiah 44:6]). For discussion, see Charles Lee Irons, "Begotten of the Father before All Ages: The Biblical Basis of Eternal Generation according to the Church Fathers," *Christian Research Journal* 40, 1 (2017): 40–47; and Charles Lee Irons, "Let's Go Back to 'Only Begotten,'" The Gospel Coalition, November 23, 2016, www.thegospelcoalition.org/article/lets-go-back-to-only-begotten.

8. See pp. 37–39.

9. See Qur'an 16:102 and 26:192–193; see also 2:87; 2:253; 5:110; 19:17–19; 78:38; 97:4. Muslim commentators typically see these verses in the Qur'an taken together as implying that the Holy Spirit is the angel Gabriel. *The Study Quran* note at 5:110 states, "The *Holy Spirit* (*rūḥ al-qudus*) is widely understood in its Quranic context and in the commentary tradition to be a reference to the Archangel Gabriel, the angel of revelation ([al-Ṭabarī]; see also 16:102; 17:85; 26:193; 42:52; 97:4)" (Nasr, *The Study Quran*, 333).

10. See Qur'an 4:157–158.

11. Ishaq, *The Life of Muhammad*, 288.

12. Qur'an 2:191 *Malik* (see vv. 190–93); and see 2:217. See also note 51, page 216.

13. "Narrated Ibn 'Umar: Allah's Apostle said: 'I have been ordered (by Allah) to fight against the people until they testify that none has the right to be worshipped but Allah and that Muhammad is Allah's Apostle, and offer the prayers perfectly and give the obligatory charity, so if they perform that, then they save their lives and property from me except for Islamic laws and then their reckoning (accounts) will be done by Allah" (*Sahih al-Bukhari* Volume 1, Book 2, Number 25, www.usc.edu/org/cmje/religious-texts /hadith/bukhari/002-sbt.php#001.002.025). Robert Spencer wrote: "This is one of the best attested statements in the Hadith. Bukhari repeats it five times; it also appears three times in *Sahih Muslim* and once in *Sunan Abu Dawud*. Muslims who study Hadith give a statement a presumption of authenticity if it appears even once in *Bukhari* or *Muslim*; the repetitions and its presence in a third respected Hadith collection make its authenticity virtually certain. The repetitions are attested by different chains of transmission, suggesting that Muhammad said this on numerous occasions, to many different people, or both" (Robert Spencer, *Onward Muslim Soldiers: How Jihad Still Threatens America and the West* [Washington, DC: Regnery Publishing, 2003], 149).

The Islamic State declares plainly, "Islam is the religion of sound principles providing the perfect foundations upon which the solid structures of justice and glory are built. One of these great principles is that all people must be fought until they accept Islam or come under a shar'i covenant. This principle establishes the prohibition of shedding Muslim and covenant-bound kafir blood as well as the permissibility of shedding the blood of all other kuffar. The Prophet [peace be upon him] said, 'I have been ordered to fight mankind until they say that there is no god except Allah and that I am the Messenger of Allah, and they establish the prayer and pay the zakah. Whoever does so, then his blood and wealth are safe from me except for a lawful reason' (reported by al-Bukhari and Muslim from Ibn 'Umar), and he [peace be upon him] said, addressing the Muslims, "For verily your blood, wealth, and honor are haram to each other" (reported by al-Bukhari and Muslim from Abu Bakrah)." ("The Kafir's Blood is Halal for You. So Shed It" *Rumiyah*, 1 (2016): 35, clarionproject.org/wp-content/uploads /Rumiyah-ISIS-Magazine-1st-issue.pdf.) See also *Sahih al-Bukhari* Volume 1, Book 8, Number 387; Volume 4, Book 52, Number 196; Volume 6, Book 60, Number 80; and *Sahih Muslim*, Book 001, Number 0030–0033, and Book 019, Number 4294.

14. See pp. 13–14.

15. See Q 2:216–18 in conjunction with note 51, page 216; see also discussion of context in Ibn Kathir's commentary (*Tafsir Ibn Kathir*) on Q 2:216–18 available online at Alim.org; and see also Ishaq, *Life of Muhammad*, 286–89.

16. Muhammad approved a form of prostitution through temporary marriage (see *Sahih al-Bukhari* Volume 6, Book 60, Number 139; *Sahih Muslim*, Book 8, Numbers 3247, 3248, 3252).

17. See Betwa Sharma, "Islam's Sex Licenses," *The Daily Beast*, April 29, 2009, accessed September 23, 2016, www.thedailybeast.com/articles/2009/04/29 /islams-sex-licenses.html. "The most important verse of the Holy Qur'an which establishes the legitimacy of Mut'ah is verse 24 of Surat an-Nisa [surah 4], known to all hadeeth commentators (Sunni and Shia) as 'the verse of Mut'ah.' This verse provides a clear and unshakeable permission for the practice of temporary marriage" ("Qur'anic Evidences for the Legitimacy of Mut'ah," *Shia Pen*, accessed September 23, 2016, www.shiapen.com/comprehensive/mutah/quranic-evidences.html.

18. See chapter 1, page 17.

19. *Sunan Abu Dawud* records, "Abu Sa'id Al Khudri said 'The Apostle of Allaah (peace be upon him) sent a military expedition to Awtas on the occasion of the battle of Hunain. They met their enemy and fought with them. They defeated them and took them captives. Some of the Companions of Apostle of Allaah (peace be upon him) were reluctant to have relations with the female captives because of their pagan husbands. So, Allaah the exalted sent down the Qur'anic verse 'And all married women (are forbidden) unto you save those (captives) whom your right hand possess.' This is to say that they are lawful for them when they complete their waiting period" (Book 11, Hadith 2150, sunnah.com/abudawud/12/110). See also *Sahih al-Bukhari*, Volume 5, Book 59, Number 459; *Sahih Muslim*, Book 008, Number 3432 (and Numbers 3371 and 3384.)

20. See chapter 1, page 13.

21. See discussion of Islamic eschatology in Major Muslim Misapprehensions on pp. 171–79.

22. "And know [O Muslims] that whatever you take as spoils of war, a fifth is for Allah and for the Messenger, and kinsmen, orphans, the needy, and the

wayfarer, if you believe in Allah and that which We sent down upon Our slave on the day of discrimination, the day when the two armies met. And Allah is able to do all things" (Q 8:41 *Majestic*).

23. "Remarks by the President at Cairo University, 6-04-09," White House Office of the Press Secretary, accessed February 21, 2017, obamawhitehouse .archives.gov/the-press-office/remarks-president-cairo-university-6-04-09. Obama is citing Q 5:32.

24. See David Wood, "Will the Real Islam Please Stand Up?" *Christian Research Journal* 37, 6 (2014): 8–15, accessed also online June 17, 2016, www.equip.org/article/will-the-real-islam-please-stand-up/.

25. "CAIR-Philadelphia's Submissions to the Inquirer: 'Not My Islam,'" CAIR Philadelphia, January 19, 2015, accessed September 23, 2016, pa.cair.com /news/inquirer-not-my-islam/.

26. See also Qur'an 13:42. Similar to others, Yusuf Ali renders 3:54 as "And (the unbelievers) plotted and planned, and Allah too planned, and the best of planners is Allah." Slightly better is *The Study Qur'an*: "And they plotted, and God plotted. And God is the best of plotters." See Sam Shamoun and David Wood, "Is Allah the 'Best of Deceivers'?" *Answering Muslims*, March 2, 2014, video, www.answeringmuslims.com/2014/03/is-allah-best -of-deceivers.html; and Sam Shamoun, "None Can Feel Safe from Allah's Schemes," *Answering Islam*, www.answering-islam.org/authors/shamoun /abu_bakr_fear.html.

27. 2 Samuel 12:1–23.

28. See chapter 1, pp. 11–13.

29. Concerning the Lord's judgment on Solomon, see 1 Kings 11.

30. See also Qur'an 4:3, 24; 33:50; 70:29–30.

31. Pickthall translation.

32. Yusuf Ali translation. *The Majestic Qur'an* rendition of this portion of Q 4:34 is "As for those from whom you fear misbehavior, admonish them and banish them to beds apart, and beat them. Then, if they obey you, do not be overbearing. For Allah is High, Great."

33. See further detail on pp. 66–68.

34. See Gary R. Habermas, *The Historical Jesus* (Joplin, MO: College Press, 1996), 143–70 (esp. 158); *Will the Real Jesus Please Stand Up? A Debate between William Lane Craig and John Dominic Crossan,* Paul Copan, ed. (Grand Rapids: Baker Books, 1998), 26–27; William Lane Craig, "Did Jesus Rise from the Dead?" in Michael J. Wilkins and J. P. Moreland, eds., *Jesus Under Fire* (Grand Rapids: Zondervan, 1995), 147–48.

35. See Luke 22:44. For medical descriptions concerning Christ's suffering and death, I draw from C. Truman Davis, "The Crucifixion of Jesus: The Passion of Christ from a Medical Point of View," *Arizona Medicine* (Arizona Medical Association), March 1965, 183–87; and William

D. Edwards, Wesley J. Gabel, and Floyd E. Hosmer, "On the Physical Death of Jesus Christ," *The Journal of the American Medical Association*, March 21, 1986, 1455–63.

36. See John McRay, *Archaeology and the New Testament* (Grand Rapids: MI: Baker Book House, 1991), 203-4; James K. Hoffmeier, *The Archaeology of the Bible* (Oxford, England: Lion Hudson, 2008), 155–56.

37. See Hoffmeier, *The Archaeology of the Bible*, 154; Paul L. Maier, "Biblical Archaeology: Factual Evidence to Support the Historicity of the Bible," *Christian Research Journal*, volume 27, number 2 (2004), accessed August 26, 2016, www.equip.org/article/biblical-archaeology-factual -evidence-to-support-the-historicity-of-the-bible/.

38. See Josephus, *Antiquities* 18:63. Historian Paul L. Maier translates and condenses *Antiquities* 18:63 as follows: "At this time there was a wise man called Jesus, and his conduct was good, and he was known to be virtuous. Many people among the Jews and the other nations became his disciples. Pilate condemned him to be crucified and to die. But those who had become his disciples did not abandon his discipleship. They reported that he had appeared to them three days after his crucifixion and that he was alive. Accordingly, he was perhaps the Messiah, concerning whom the prophets have reported wonders. And the tribe of the Christians, so named after him, has not disappeared to this day." *Josephus: The Essential Works: A Condensation of Jewish Antiquities and The Jewish War*, trans. ed. Paul L. Maier (Grand Rapids: Kregel, 1994), 269–70; see also 282n8 and 284–85 in which Maier discusses and defends the veracity of Josephus's references to Jesus.

39. See Tacitus, *Annals* 15.44.

40. See Suetonius, *Twelve Caesars*, Nero 16.2 and Claudius 25.4.

41. See note 34 in this chapter.

42. See Ali, *The Meaning of the Holy Qur'an*, 236 (note 663 at Q 4:157). For a refutation of *The Gospel of Barnabas*, see Norman L. Geisler and Abdul Saleeb, *Answering Islam: The Crescent in Light of the Cross*, second edition (Grand Rapids: MI, Baker Books, 2002), appendix 3: "The Gospel of Barnabas."

43. See Habermas, *The Historical Jesus*, 152–57; and William Lane Craig, *Reasonable Faith: Christian Truth and Apologetics*, third edition (Wheaton, IL: Crossway Books, 2008), 362ff.

44. See Mathew 13:55; Mark 3:20–21; John 7:3–5; Galatians 1:18–19; 2:9–10; 1 Corinthians 9:5; 15:7. See also Josephus, *Antiquities* 20:197 –203; Eusebius, *Ecclesiastical History* 2.23.8–18; Clement of Alexandria, *Hypotyposes*, Book 7. For analysis, see also Sean McDowell, "Did the Apostles Really Die as Martyrs for Their Faith?" *Christian Research Journal* 39, 2 (2016): 15.

45. See McDowell, "Did the Apostles Really Die as Martyrs for Their Faith?" 10–16.
46. Material in subsection "Crucifixion" is adapted from Hank Hanegraaff, *Resurrection* (Nashville: Word Publishing, 2000), chapters 2 and 5; Hank Hanegraaff, *Has God Spoken? Memorable Proofs of the Bible's Divine Inspiration* (Nashville: Thomas Nelson, 2011), chapter 5; and Hank Hanegraaff, *The Complete Bible Answer Book*, Collector's Edition, revised and updated (Nashville: Thomas Nelson, 2008, 2016), 252–53.
47. See Qur'an 96:2 (especially Yusuf Ali translation).
48. See Augustine, *The Trinity* 1.2 and books 8–15; *Confessions*, books 10–11. See also Robert Crouse, "Knowledge," in *Augustine Through the Ages: An Encyclopedia*, ed. Allan D. Fitzgerald (Grand Rapids: William B. Eerdmans Publishing Co., 1999), 486–88; R. C. Sproul, *The Consequences of Ideas: Understanding the Concepts that Shaped our World* (Wheaton, IL: Crossway, 2000), 58–59.
49. C. S. Lewis, *Beyond Personality*, in *Mere Christianity*, a revised and amplified edition, with a new introduction, of the three books *Broadcast Talks*, *Christian Behavior* and *Beyond Personality* (New York: HarperOne, 1943, HarperCollins paperback edition 2001), 164.
50. Lewis, *Beyond Personality*, 165.
51. See, e.g., Luke 3:22; John 3:35; 12:28; 14:26, 31; 15:26; 17:1–26.
52. Five previous paragraphs adapted from Hanegraaff, *The Complete Bible Answer Book*, 50–51.
53. Other passages in the Qur'an that misconstrue or denounce the Christian doctrine of the Trinity include 4:171; 5:17, 70–75; 116–117; 6:100–101; 72:3.
54. See Qur'an 43:3–4; 85:21–22; see also 3:7; 13:39.
55. Ishaq, *The Life of Muhammad*, 272. See also, taken together, Q 4:166 –72; 5:17, 68–77, 116–17; in conjunction with Q 6:100–101; 72:3. Ibn Ishaq contends that Christians, who "differered among themselves in some points," had been debating with Muhammad, "saying He is God; and He is the son of God; and He is the third person of the Trinity, which is the doctrine of Christianity. They argue that he is God because he used to raise the dead, and heal the sick, and declare the unseen; and make clay birds and then breathe into them so that they flew away [Q 3:49]; and all this was by the command of God Almighty, 'We will make him a sign to men' [Q 19:21]. They argue that he is the son of God in that they say he had no known father; and he spoke in the cradle [Q 19:29ff] and this is something that no child of Adam has ever done. They argue that he is the third of three in that God says: We have done, We have commanded, We have created and We have decreed, and they say, If He were one he would have said I have done, I have created, and soon, but He is He and Jesus and Mary.

Concerning all these assertions the Quran came down" (Ishaq, *The Life of Muhammad*, 271–72, capitalization in original).

Concerning Q 5:73, Ibn Kathir wrote, "(Surely, they have disbelieved who say: 'Allah is the third of three.') Mujahid and several others said that this *Ayah* [verse] was revealed about the Christians in particular. As-Suddi and others said that this *Ayah* was revealed about taking 'Isa [Jesus] and his mother as gods besides Allah, thus making Allah the third in a trinity. As Suddi said, 'This is similar to Allah's statement towards the end of the Surah, (And [remember] when Allah will say: "O 'Isa, son of Maryam! Did you say unto men: 'Worship me and my mother as two gods besides Allah' He will say, 'Glory be to You!'") [5:116].'" (Ibn Kathir, *Tafsir Ibn Kathir* (Riyadh: Darussalam Publishers, 2000), online at QTafsir.com, www.qtafsir.com/index.php?option=com_content&task=view&id=753&Itemid=60).

Concerning Q 4:171, E. M. Wherry wrote, "The commentators Baidhawi, Jalaluddin, and Yahya agree in interpreting the three to mean 'God, Jesus, and Mary,' in the relation of Father, Mother, and Son" (E. M. Wherry, *A Comprehensive Commentary on the Quran*, Vol. 2 [London: n.p., 1886], 116, as quoted at Answering-Islam, answering-islam.org/Books/Wherry/Commentary2/ch4.htm).

For a closely argued discussion concerning the Qur'an's representation of the Christian doctrine of the Trinity, see James R. White, *What Every Christian Needs to Know about the Qur'an* (Minneapolis: Bethany House Publishers, 2013), chapter 4.

56. The Bible contains abundant teaching concerning the personal deity of the Holy Spirit. As the "Spirit of God" (Genesis 1:2; Romans 8:9–17; 1 Corinthians 2:11, 14), the Holy Spirit is *holy, equated with God* (Acts 5:3–4; Romans 8:9–11; 2 Corinthians 3:17–18), and *shares in the work of God* (e.g., *creation*: Genesis 1:2; Job 33:4; *Incarnation*: Matthew 1:18, 20; *Resurrection*: 1 Peter 3:18; *salvation*: 1 Corinthians 6:11; *inspiration of Scripture*: 2 Timothy 3:16). The Holy Spirit is *omnipotent* (Luke 1:35), *omnipresent* (Psalm139:7–9), *omniscient* (1 Corinthians 2:10–11), *eternal* (Hebrews 9:14), and *personal* (John 14:26; 15:26; Acts 8:29; 15:28; 16:6; Romans 5:5; 8:14–16, 26–27; 15:30; Ephesians 4:30; 1 Corinthians 12:11; 2 Corinthians 13:14), yet distinct from the Father and the Son (John 14:26; 15:26; 16:13–14). As the Athanasian Creed says, "We worship one God in Trinity, and Trinity in Unity; neither confounding the persons nor dividing the substance." See articles concerning the doctrine of the Trinity available through the Christian Research Institute at www.equip.org.

57. See also Nehemiah 9:20, 30; 2 Samuel 23:2; Zechariah 7:11–12; Acts 1:16; 4:25; 11:28; 2 Timothy 3:16; 1 Peter 1:11.

58. Other examples of the Holy Spirit's empowering and leading the people of God in Acts include 2:4, 14; 7:55–56; 8:29; 11:12; 15:28; 16:6; 20:28.

59. In addition to citing Qur'an 2:97, which does not unambiguously indicate that Gabriel is the Holy Spirit, the article goes on to say, "To understand the connection between the Angel Gabriel and calling him the Spirit, the Holy Spirit and the Honest Spirit in the Quran we should also read all related verses, 16:102 and 26:192–193." Then, finally, the article brings forth Qur'an 2:87; 2:253; 5:110; 19:17–19; 78:38; 97:4 to make its case. "The Holy Spirit in Quran," *Submission.org*, accessed January 25, 2016, submission.org /Holy_Spirit.html.

60. "The Holy Spirit in Quran," *Submission.org*, emphasis added.

61. Yusuf Ali, *The Meaning of the Holy Qur'an*, 664 (note 2141 at Qur'an 16:102).

62. The Chicago Statement on Biblical Inerrancy (1978) remains an accurate statement for our time: "Being wholly and verbally God-given, Scripture is without error or fault in all its teaching, no less in what it states about God's acts in creation, about the events of world history, and about its own literary origins under God, than in its witness to God's saving grace in individual lives." The full statement is online at www.bible-researcher.com/chicago1 .html. Of course, to know what the Bible is *teaching* requires the proper application of the art and science of biblical interpretation (see Hank Hanegraaff, *Has God Spoken?*, part four).

63. See chapter 6, pp. 144–46.

64. Ishaq, *The Life of Muhammad*, 106. The words of Qur'an 96:1–5 constitute the first alleged direct divine revelation to Muhammad.

65. See *Sahih al-Bukhari*, Volume 9, Book 87, Number 111; Ishaq, *The Life of Muhammad*, 105–107.

66. Ishaq, *The Life of Muhammad*, 106.

67. See note 17, page 212.

68. According to Islamic tradition, the goddesses Lat, 'Uzza, and Manat were the three principal idols of pre-Islamic Arabia. The quotation is from Al-Tabari, *The History of al-Tabari: Muhammad at Mecca*, vol. 6, trans. W. Montgomery Watt and M. V. McDonald (Albany: State University of New York Press, 1988), 108, accessed September 25, 2016, kalamullah. com/Books/The%20History%20Of%20Tabari/Tabari_Volume_06.pdf. See also Cornelius, "Muhammad, Satan, and Muhammad's Prophetic Call," *Answering Islam*, accessed January 27, 2016, www.answering-islam.org /authors/cornelius/mo_satan.html.

69. Watt and McDonald, *The History of al-Tabari: Muhammad at Mecca*, 108.

70. Ibid., 109.

71. Qur'an 22:52 as quoted in Watt, McDonald, *The History of al-Tabari: Muhammad at Mecca*, 109.

72. Ibid., 110.

73. Ibn Ishaq, *The Life of Muhammad*, 166–67.

74. Many Muslim apologists today reject the veracity of the satanic verses account. But as W. Montgomery Watt, the highly regarded professor of Arabic and Islamic studies at the University of Edinburgh, explained in the introduction to the translation of al-Tabari quoted above, "The truth of the story cannot be doubted, since it is inconceivable that any Muslim would invent such a story, and it is inconceivable that a Muslim scholar would accept such a story from a non-Muslim." (Watt, McDonald, *The History of al-Tabari: Muhammad at Mecca*, xxxiv.) See also James M. Arlandson, "How Jesus and Muhammad Confronted Satan," *Answering Islam*, accessed September 25, 2016, www.answering-islam.org/Authors/Arlandson /confronting_satan.htm.

75. Salman Rushdie, *The Satanic Verses* (New York: Viking, 1989).

76. "*The Hunger Games* Reaches another Milestone: Top 10 Censored Books: *The Satanic Verses*," *Time*, September 28, 2008, accessed September 25, 2016, entertainment.time.com/2011/01/06/removing-the-n-word-from -huck-finn-top-10-censored-books/slide/the-satanic-verses/.

77. In his commentary note, Yusuf Ali judges that the Qur'an's language here is metaphorical and proceeds to justify the language by appealing to human anatomy, including the spinal cord and medulla oblongata (see Ali, *The Meaning of the Holy Qur'an*, 1632 [note 6071]). Muslim apologist Maurice Bucaille claims that common English translations, like the one I've quoted, "would seem to be more an interpretation than a translation" and are "hardly comprehensible." He offers his own translation: "(Man) was fashioned from a liquid poured out. It issued (as a result) of the conjunction of the sexual area of the man and the sexual area of the woman" (Maurice Bucaille, *The Bible, the Qur'an, and Science: The Holy Scriptures Examined in the Light of Modern Knowledge* [n.p., n.d.], 208).

78. See, e.g., Yusuf Ali, "Who Was Dhū al Qarnayn?" in Ali, *The Meaning of the Holy Qur'an*, 738–42.

79. See also Q 12:41; 20:71; 26:49. Concerning the history of crucifixion, see Gerald G. O'Collins, "Crucifixion," *The Anchor Bible Dictionary*, vol. 1, ed. David Noel Freedman (New York: Doubleday, 1992), 1207–1210.

80. Hans Christian Andersen, "The Emperor's New Clothes," trans. Jean Hersholt, The Hans Christen Andersen Centre, accessed September 25, 2016, www.andersen.sdu.dk/vaerk/hersholt/TheEmperorsNewClothes_e.html.

81. See also Qur'an 10:37.

82. Thomas Carlyle, "The Hero as Prophet: Mahomet: Islam" (1840) in "Thomas Carlyle on Heroes Lecture II Prophet as Hero," Muhammad Umar Chand, ed., Archive.org, 33, accessed January 27, 2016, archive.org/details /ThomasCarlyleOnHeroesLectureIIProphetAsHero.

83. Carlyle, "The Hero as Prophet: Mahomet: Islam," 34, 35.

84. Spencer, *Onward Muslim Soldiers*, 126–27.

85. Robert Spencer, *The Complete Infidel's Guide to the Koran* (Washington, DC: Regnery Publishing, 2009), 16.

86. Carlyle, "The Hero as Prophet: Mahomet: Islam," 36.

87. See Hanegraaff, *Has God Spoken?* chap. 12, "Succession of Nations."

88. See Yusuf Ali, *The Meaning of the Holy Qur'an*, 1336 (note 4910 at Q 48:27).

89. See *Sahih al-Bukhari* Volume 3, Book 50, Number 891; *Tafsir Ibn Kathir*, 48:27, online at QTafsir.com; see also Sam Shamoun, "Muhammad's False Prophecies," *Answering Islam*, accessed January 29, 2016, www.answering -islam.org/Shamoun/false_prophecies.htm.

90. Yusuf Ali, *The Meaning of the Holy Qur'an*, 1008 (note 3507 at Q 30:4).

91. Al-Tabari places the Roman victory over Persia after the Treaty of Hudaybiyah—thus, about AD 628/29, constituting approximately fourteen years between Roman loss (in Jerusalem) and victory. See Al-Tabari, *The History of al-Tabari: The Victory of Islam*, 100–101, kalamullah.com /Books/The%20History%20Of%20Tabari/Tabari_Volume_08.pdf; and see Fishbein's clarifying comments in note 436, pp. 100–101. See also Shamoun, "Muhammad's False Prophecies."

92. Shamoun, "Muhammad's False Prophecies."

93. Yusuf Ali, *The Meaning of the Holy Qur'an*, 389 (note 1127 at Q 7:157). See also note 10 in chapter 1, page 210.

94. Deuteronomy 18:18 NKJV. See Yusuf Ali, *The Meaning of the Holy Qur'an*, 389 (note 1127 at Q 7:157).

95. The context of Deuteronomy 17–18 shows that "brother" or "countryman" designates a member of the Israelite tribes in contrast with "foreigner" (17:5). Indeed, the NIV reads, "from among their fellow Israelites" (18:18; see also 18:2, 15). Muhammad was not a member of the Israelite tribes by any reckoning and, thus, would have been deemed a foreigner (see White, *What Every Christian Needs to Know about the Qur'an*, 204–205).

96. Yusuf Ali, *The Meaning of the Holy Qur'an*, 389 (note 1127 at Q 7:157).

97. See White, *What Every Christian Needs to Know about the Qur'an*, 206–211.

98. See David Wood, "Muhammad in the Bible?" *Answering Islam*, accessed September 25, 2016, www.answering-islam.org/Authors/Wood /muhammad_in_bible.htm; White, *What Every Christian Needs to Know about the Qur'an*, chapter 9.

99. Os Guinness, *Fool's Talk: Recovering the Art of Christian Persuasion* (Downers Grove, IL: InterVarsity Press, 2015), 243.

100. See *Sahih al-Bukhari* Volume 6, Book 61, Number 510.

101. James R. White, *The King James Only Controversy: Can You Trust*

Modern Translations? Second Edition (Minneapolis, MN: Bethany House Publishers, 2009), 77–78.

102. 'Ali Dashti, *Twenty Three Years: A Study of the Prophetic Career of Mohammad,* trans. F. R. C. Bagley (London: Routledge, 1985, 1994), 48–49, 50, online at books.google.com.

103. *Gnosticism* (from Greek, *gnosis*, meaning knowledge) refers to an intuitive, esoteric knowledge of spiritual truth deemed necessary for salvation. Active especially in the second century AD, Gnostics denied the incarnation and crucifixion of Christ, believing that Jesus was spirit and did not have a physical body. There is no historical evidence from the first century of anyone denying the bodily death of Christ by crucifixion (see "Gnosticism," New Advent, The Catholic Encyclopedia, www.newadvent.org/cathen /06592a.htm).

104. Infancy Gospel of Thomas, IV:1, M. R. James Translation, Gnostic Society Library, accessed September 20, 2016, gnosis.org/library/inftoma.htm.

105. Samuel M. Zwemer, *Islam and the Cross: Selections from "The Apostle to Islam"* Roger S. Greenway, ed. (Phillipsburg, NJ: P&R Publishing, 2002), 152.

Chapter 3: Sharia Is State, and State Is Sharia

1. A. Kevin Reinhart, "Introduction," in *Encyclopedia of Islamic Law: A Compendium of the Major Schools*, adapted by Laleh Bakhtiar (Chicago: KAZI Publications, 1996), xxxii–xxxiii.

2. Martin Luther, On War against Islamic Reign of Terror, 1528 (*Vom Kriege wider die Türken* WA 30 II, 107–148), (accessed June 8, 2016, www .reverendluther.org/pdfs2/On-War-Against-Islamic-Reign-of-Terror.pdf.

3. Ibid. Within the same context, said Luther:

> [Mohammad] praises and exalts himself highly and boasts that he has talked with God and the angels, and that since Christ's office of prophet is now complete, it has been commanded to him to bring the world to his faith and if the world is not willing, to compel it or punish it with the sword; and there is much glorification of the sword in [the Koran]. Therefore, the Turks think their Mohammed much higher and greater than Christ, for the office of Christ has ended and Mohammed's office is still in force.
>
> From this anyone can easily observe that Mohammed is a destroyer of our Lord Christ and His kingdom, and if anyone denies concerning Christ, that He is God's Son and has died for us, and still lives and reigns at the right hand of God, what has he left of Christ? Father, Son, Holy Ghost, Baptism, the Sacrament, Gospel, Faith and all Christian doctrine and life are gone, and there is left, instead of Christ, nothing more than Mohammed with his doctrine of works and

especially of the sword. That is the chief doctrine of the Turkish faith in which all abominations, all errors, all devils are piled up in one heap. (Ibid.)

4. Ibid.
5. Definition of *jizya* in E. W. Lane, *An Arabic-English Lexicon* (London, 1865), book 1, 422; quoted in Andrew G. Bostom, "Jihad Conquests and the Imposition of *Dhimmitude*—A Survey," *The Legacy of Jihad: Islamic Holy War and the Fate of Non-Muslims*, ed. Andrew G. Bosom (Amherst, NY: Prometheus Books, 2008), 29.
6. Jason Thompson, "An Account of the Journeys and Writings of the Indefatigable Mr. Lane," *ARAMCO World,* March/April 2008, archive. aramcoworld.com/issue/200802/the.indefatigable.mr.lane.htm.
7. Reinhart, "Introduction," xxxvi.
8. Karen Armstrong, *Islam: A Short History* (New York: Modern Library, 2002), 77.
9. Hirsi Ali, *Heretic: Why Islam Needs a Reformation Now* (New York: HarperCollins, 2015), 133.
10. Nonie Darwish, *Cruel and Usual Punishment* (Nashville: Thomas Nelson, 2008), ix.
11. Ibid., 4.
12. Ibid., ix.
13. Hirsi Ali, *Heretic*, 135.
14. Taken from Hank Hanegraaff, *Has God Spoken? Memorable Proofs of the Bible's Divine Inspiration* (Nashville: Thomas Nelson, 2011), 269.
15. See Hirsi Ali, *Heretic*, 135.
16. See note 118, page 221.
17. Barack Obama, *The Audacity of Hope: Thoughts on Reclaiming the American Dream* (New York, Vintage, 2006, 2008), 258. The same point is made in Barack Obama, "News and Speeches: Call to Renewal Keynote Address" June 28, 2006, web.archive.org/web/20080711013555/www .barackobama.com/2006/06/28/call_to_renewal_keynote_address.php.
18. Adapted from Hanegraaff, *Has God Spoken?* 268; see also 241.
19. Adapted from ibid., 275.
20. Two paragraphs adapted from Hank Hanegraaff, *The Complete Bible Answer Book*, Collector's Edition, revised and updated (Nashville: Thomas Nelson, 2008, 2016), 174–75.
21. Paragraph adapted from Hanegraaff, *Has God Spoken?*, 269.
22. Bill Ozanick, "The Implications of Brunei's Sharia Law," *The Diplomat*, May 21, 2015, accessed June 8, 2016, thediplomat.com/2015/05/the -implications-of-bruneis-sharia-law/.
23. Hirsi Ali, *Heretic*, 139.
24. "The World's Muslims: Religion, Politics, and Society: Executive Summary,"

Pew Research Center, April 30, 2013, accessed June 8, 2016,
www.pewforum.org/2013/04/30/the-worlds-muslims-religion-politics
-society-exec/.

25. "The World's Muslims: Religion, Politics, and Society: Overview," Pew
Research Center, April 30, 2013, accessed June 8, 2016, www.pewforum
.org/2013/04/30/the-worlds-muslims-religion-politics-society-overview/.
The report stateed, "Together, the 39 countries and territories included in
the survey are home to about two-thirds of all Muslims in the world."

26. Cf. Ben Shapiro, "The Myth of the Tiny Radical Muslim Minority," Reality
Check, October 15, 2014, accessed June 8, 2016, www.youtube.com
/watch?v=g7TAAw3oQvg.

27. Barack Obama, "Remarks by the President at Cairo University, 6-04-09,"
White House Office of the Press Secretary, accessed February 21, 2017,
obamawhitehouse.archives.gov/the-press-office/remarks-president-cairo
-university-6-04-09.

28. Barack Obama, "Remarks by the President at Islamic Society of Baltimore,"
White House Office of the Press Secretary, February 3, 2016, emphasis
added, obamawhitehouse.archives.gov/the-press-office/2016/02/03
/remarks-president-islamic-society-baltimore.

29. See note 10 in the Introduction, pp. 202–03.

30. Hirsi Ali, Heretic, 143.

31. Darwish, Cruel and Usual, 63.

32. Ibid., 65, 66.

33. Theodore Roosevelt, "The Influence of the Bible," 1901 address to the
Long Island Bible Society, in Christian F. Reisner, Roosevelt's Religion
(New York: Abingdon Press, 1922), 306, accessed June 9, 2016, archive.org
/stream/christianfichthor00reisrich/christianfichthor00reisrich_djvu.txt.

34. Obama, Audacity of Hope, 258.

35. Kristan Hawkins, "President Barack Obama's Shameful Legacy on
Abortion," Life News, January 13, 2016, www.lifenews.com/2016/01/13
/president-barack-obamas-shameful-legacy-on-abortion/; John McCormack,
"Video: Obama Says He's 'Pro-Choice' on Third-Trimester Abortions,"
Weekly Standard, August 22, 2012, www.weeklystandard.com/video
-obama-says-hes-pro-choice-on-third-trimester-abortions/article/650524.

36. Three paragraphs adapted from Hanegraaff, Has God Spoken?, 240–41, and
Hanegraaff, The Complete Bible Answer Book, 170, 176–77.

37. Although John 7:53–8:11 is not in the oldest extant manuscripts, there are
good reasons to hold that the passage reflects a "genuine episode from
Jesus' life, preserved in the oral tradition, and later added to the text by
Christian scribes" (Craig L. Blomberg, The Historical Reliability of John's
Gospel: Issues and Commentary [Downers Grove, Ill.: InterVarsity Press,
2001], 140).

38. *Sahih Muslim*, Book 17, Number 4206, www.usc.edu/org/cmje/religious
-texts/hadith/muslim/017-smt.php#017.4206.

39. Ishaq, *The Life of Muhammad*, 652. Other instances of Muhammad
commanding stoning for adultery, as recorded in the *ahadith*, include
Sahih al-Bukhari Volume 9, Book 83, Number 37; *Sahih Muslim*, Book 17,
Numbers 4192, 4193, and 4196.

40. *Sahih Muslim*, Book 17, Number 4194, www.usc.edu/org/cmje/religious
-texts/hadith/muslim/017-smt.php#017.4194.

41. Ahmad ibn Naqib al-Misri, *Reliance of the Traveller: A Classic Manual of
Islamic Sacred Law*, rev. ed., Nuh Ha Mim Keller, ed. and trans. (Beltsville,
Maryland: Amana Publications, 1991, 1994), 611 [o12.6].

42. See Qur'an 23:5–6; 70:29–30.

43. Hirsi Ali, *Heretic*, 149.

44. Ibid.

45. See page 17.

46. *Sahih al-Bukhari* Volume 7, Book 72, Number 715, www.usc.edu/org
/cmje/religious-texts/hadith/bukhari/072-sbt.php#007.072.715, emphasis
added. See the helpful discussion by Andrew Bostom, "'Beat My Wife—
Please!'—Mainstream Muslim Misogyny in North America, Too?"
Dr. Andrew Bostom, March 26, 2012, www.andrewbostom.org/2012/03
/beat-my-wife-please-mainstream-muslim-misogyny-in-north-america-too/.

47. *Sahih Muslim*, Book 004, Number 2127, www.usc.edu/org/cmje/religious
-texts/hadith/muslim/004-smt.php#004.2127. See also "Wife-Beating," The
Religion of Peace, accessed June 9, 2016, www.thereligionofpeace.com
/pages/quran/wife-beating.aspx.

48. See various translations at the University of Leeds: Qurany Tool, accessed
June 11, 2016, www.comp.leeds.ac.uk/nora/html/38-44.html. As the recent
ecumenical work *The Study Quran* explained, commentators report that
"Job rebuked [his wife] and vowed to punish her. God then told him to
strike her with a sprig of leaves, so that he could fulfill his vow without
harming her unjustly," citing several commentators including ibn Kathir and
al-Tabari (Nasr, *The Study Quran*, 1111, note at Quran 38:44).

49. Quoted in Bostom, "Beat My Wife—Please"; see also "Women under
Sharia Law–The Dilemma of 'Wife Beating Protocol,'" *The Qur'an
Dilemma*, July 5, 2011, thequrandilemma.com/uncategorized/women-under
-sharia-law-the-dilemma-of-wife-beating-protocol; and Silas, "Wife Beating
in Islam," *Answering-Islam*, www.answering-islam.org/Silas/wife-beating.
htm#_Toc160373814.

50. Naqib al-Misri, *Reliance of the Traveller*, 540–41 [m10.12], parenthetical
documentary information has been omitted from the quoted material.

51. See Ibid., 541 [m10.12], parenthetical documentary information has been
omitted from the quoted material.

52. Ibid., 542 [m10.12]; Step 3 states in full: "If keeping from her is ineffectual, it is permissible for him to hit her if he believes that hitting her will bring her back to the right path, though if he does not think so, it is not permissible. His hitting her may not be in a way that injures her, and is his last recourse to save the family."
53. Saint Thomas Aquinas, Commentary on the First Epistle to the Corinthians, trans. Fabian Larcher, 321, 323, dhspriory.org/thomas/SS1Cor.htm#71.
54. Ibid.
55. Rukmini Callimachi, "ISIS Enshrines a Theology of Rape," *New York Times*, August 13, 2015, accessed February 15, 2016, www.nytimes.com /2015/08/14/world/middleeast/isis-enshrines-a-theology-of-rape.html?_r=1.
56. "The Revival of Slavery Before the Hour," *Dabiq* 4 (1435 [2014]): 15, media .clarionproject.org/files/islamic-state/islamic-state-isis-magazine-Issue-4 -the-failed-crusade.pdf.
57. Callimachi, "ISIS Enshrines a Theology of Rape."
58. *Sahih al-Bukhari* continues, "the Prophet got Juwairiya [the daughter of the chief of the Banu Mustaliq] on that day" (Volume 3, Book 46, Number 717, www.usc.edu/org/cmje/religious-texts/hadith/bukhari/046-sbt.php #003.046.717); see also *Sahih Muslim*, Book 19, Number 4292; *Sahih Muslim*, Book 008, Number 3371; see also Ibn Ishaq, *The Life of Muhammad: A Translation of Ishaq's Sīrat Rasūl Allāh*, trans. A. Guillaume (Oxford: Oxford University Press, 1955), 490–93; Al-Waqidi, *The Life of Muhammad: Al-Wāqidī's Kitāb al-Maghāzī*, ed. Rizwi Faizer, trans. Rizwi Faizer, Amal Ismail, and AbdulKader Tayob (London: Routledge, 2011), 198–208.
59. Umm Sumayyah al-Muhājirah, "Slave-girls or Prostitutes?" *Dabiq* 9 (1436 [2015]): 45, accessed June 11, 2016, media.clarionproject.org/files /islamic-state/isis-isil-islamic-state-magazine-issue%2B9-they-plot-and -allah-plots sex-slavery.pdf.
60. "The Revival of Slavery Before the Hour," *Dabiq* 4, 17; the *Dabiq* article cites Qur'an 23:1–7: "Allah ta'āla said, {Successful indeed are the believers who are humble in their prayers, and who shun vain conversation, and who are payers of the zakāh, and who guard their modesty except from their wives or the [female slaves] that their right hands possess, for then they are not blameworthy, but whoever craves beyond that, such are transgressors} [Al-Mu'minūn: 1–7]." See also James M. Arlandson, "Slave-girls as sexual property in the Quran," *Answering Islam*, accessed February 13, 2015, www.answering-islam.org/Authors/Arlandson/women_slaves.htm; and Silas, "Muhammad and the Female Captives," accessed February 13, 2015, www.answering-islam.org/Silas/femalecaptives.htm.
61. *Sahih Muslim*, 8, Number 3371, www.usc.edu/org/cmje/religious-texts /hadith/muslim/008-smt.php#008.3371; see also Al-Waqidi, *The Life of*

Muhammad, 202; compare a similar occasion reported in *Sahih al-Bukhari*, Volume 3, Book 34, Number 432.

62. See also Qur'an 4:24; 23:5–6.

63. Naqib al-Misri, *Reliance of the Traveller*, 604 [o9.13].

64. *Sahih al-Bukhari* Volume 3, Book 46, Number 717; *Sahih Muslim*, Book 019, Number 4292; Ibn Ishaq, *The Life of Muhammad*, 490–93; Al-Waqidi, *The Life of Muhammad*, 198–202. See also Sam Shamoun, "Muhammad's Marriage to Safiyyah Revisited," *Answering Islam*, www.answering-islam .org/Responses/Osama/zawadi_safiyyah2.htm.

65. "The Revival of Slavery Before the Hour," *Dabiq* 4, 17.

66. See note 118, page 221.

67. Darwish, *Cruel and Usual Punishment*, 33, emphasis added.

68. Ibid., 41.

69. Ibid. Darwish cites *Reliance of the Traveller* n1.2 and n1.3; and Kitab Al-Talaq Law no. 1537 and 1538.

70. Naqib al-Misri, *Reliance of the Traveller*, 565 [n7.7]. See Qur'an 2:229–231.

71. Robert Spencer, *The Politically Incorrect Guide to Islam (and the Crusades)* (Washington, DC: Regnery Publishing, 2005), 72. See also notes 16 and 17 for chapter 2 on page 225.

72. Darwish, *Cruel and Usual Punishment*, 45.

73. Spencer, *The Politically Incorrect Guide to Islam*, 69. Hilali-Khan's translation is equally clear: "And those of your women as have passed the age of monthly courses, for them the *'Iddah* (prescribed period), if you have doubts (about their periods), is three months, and for those who have no courses [(i.e. they are still immature) their *'Iddah* (prescribed period) is three months likewise, except in case of death]. And for those who are pregnant (whether they are divorced or their husbands are dead), their *'Iddah* (prescribed period) is until they deliver (their burdens), and whosoever fears Allah and keeps his duty to Him, He will make his matter easy for him." (65:4, parenthetical and bracketed insertions in original).

74. "Gender Equality in Islam," Muslim Women's League, September 1995, www.mwlusa.org/topics/equality/gender.html.

75. El-Saadawi continues, "But what has happened is that men have sometimes used certain aspects of this religion to create a patriarchal class system in which males dominate females." Nawal El-Saadawi, quoted in Muhammad Ali Al-Hashimi, *The Ideal Muslimah: The True Islamic Personality of the Muslim Woman as Defined in the Qur'an and Sunnah*, trans. Nassrudin al-Khattab (International Publishing House, 1998), online at www. islamicbulletin.org/free_downloads/women/the_ideal_muslimah.pdf.

76. "Your wives are a tillage for you. Go, then, into your tillage as you will" (Q 2:223 *Majestic*).

77. Naqib al-Misri, *Reliance of the Traveller*, 525 [m5.0].

78. See Bill Warner, *Sharia Law for the Non-Muslim* (n.c.: Center for the Study of Political Islam, 2010), 16; *Sahih al-Bukhari* Volume 7, Book 62, Number 81.

79. *Sahih al-Bukhari* Volume 7, Book 62, Number 121 (see also Number 122), www.usc.edu/org/cmje/religious-texts/hadith/bukhari/062-sbt.php #007.062.121.

80. As noted, Islam means "submission (to the will of Allah)." See Introduction, page xiii.

81. Madeleine K. Albright, "Obama's Muslim Speech," *New York Times*, June 2, 2009, accessed August 2, 2016, www.nytimes.com/2009/06/03/opinion /03iht-edalbright.html.

82. George W. Bush, "Address to Joint Session of Congress Following 9/11 Attacks," September 20, 2001, *American Rhetoric*, accessed February 20, 2017, www.americanrhetoric.com/speeches/gwbush911jointsessionspeech. htm.

83. Abed Z. Bhuyan, "Powell Rejects Islamophobia," *On Faith*, n.d., accessed August 2, 2016, www.faithstreet.com/onfaith/2008/10/19/powell-rejects -islamophobia/103; Suhail A. Khan, "Colin Powell and My American Faith," *On Faith*, n.d., accessed August 4, 2016, www.faithstreet.com /onfaith/2008/10/22/colin-powell-and-my-american-f/5585.

84. Prime Minister Tony Blair, "Text of Prime Minister Tony Blair's Remarks," *New York Times*, October 7, 2001, accessed June 8, 2016, www.nytimes. com/2001/10/07/international/07BLAIR-TEXT.html.

85. Steven Swinford, "David Cameron: Britain to Stand with France and Tunisia against Terrorism," *The Telegraph*, June 26, 2015, accessed August 2, 2016, www.telegraph.co.uk/news/uknews/terrorism-in-the-uk/11701916/David -Cameron-Britain-to-stand-with-France-and-Tunisia-against-terrorism.html.

86. "Introduction to Islam | Belief | Oprah Winfrey Show," YouTube video (transcribed by the author), October 26, 2015, accessed August 4, 2016, www.youtube.com/watch?v=wgP_OSOS3IA; see also Leah Marieann Klett, "'Jihad' Is Simply 'Misunderstood,' Claims Muslim Scholar During Segment on Oprah Winfrey's 'Belief' Series," *The Gospel Herald*: Entertainment, November 6, 2015, accessed August 4, 2016, www.gospelherald.com/articles/59541/20151106/jihad-is-simply -misunderstood-claims-muslim-scholar-during-segment-on-oprah -winfreys-belief-series.htm.

87. Richard Burkholder, "Jihad—'Holy War,' or Internal Spiritual Struggle?" Gallup, December 3, 2002, emphasis added, accessed February 18, 2016, www.gallup.com/poll/7333/jihad-holy-war-internal-spiritual-struggle.aspx.

88. Hirsi Ali, *Heretic*, 177–178.

89. Naqib al-Misri, *Reliance of the Traveller*, 599 [o9.0].

90. Ibid.

91. *Zakat* ("purity") is obligatory almsgiving (in the amount of one fortieth of one's income) for the benefit of needy Muslims as an act purification. One of the five pillars of Islam.
92. Naqib al-Misri, *Reliance of the Traveller*, 599 [o9.0].
93. See Ibid., xiv–xxi. The Amana Publications website shows endorsements, accessed February 18, 2016, www.amana-publications.com/amana_old /amana_bestsellers.shtml, also see www.amana-publications.com /amana_old/1997_books.shtml; and see photo of Al-Azhar certification, accessed August 4, 2016, umdatalsalik.wordpress.com/introduction/, which corresponds to the copy of the Al-Azhar certification, pages xx–xxi in *Reliance of the Traveller*. See also www.sunnah.org/history/Scholars /shkeller.html, www.masud.co.uk/ISLAM/nuh/reliance.htm, and gatesofvienna.blogspot.com/2010/03/al-misri-on-circumcision.html (accessed August 4, 2016).
94. See Bill Warner, "Tears of Jihad," *Political Islam*, March 3, 2008, accessed August 4, 2016, www.politicalislam.com/tears-of-jihad/; "The Black Hole of History," *Political Islam*, November 3, 2011, accessed August 4, 2016, www .politicalislam.com/the-black-hole-of-history/; see also Pamela Geller, "270 Million Victims of Jihad? Maybe More," *Pamela Geller*, November 1, 2011, accessed August 4, 2016, pamelageller.com/2011/11/270-millions-of -jihad-maybe-more.html/; "How Many Slaughtered Millions under Jihad?" *Pamela Geller*, November 3, 2011, accessed August 4, 2016, pamelageller .com/2011/11/how-many-slaughtered-millions-under-jihad.html/#sthash .NEX7Wgps.dpuf.
95. *Sahih al-Bukhari*, Volume 1, Book 2, Number 26, www.usc.edu/org/cmje /religious-texts/hadith/bukhari/002-sbt.php#001.002.026. See also *Sahih al-Bukhari*, Volume 2, Book 26, Number 594; *Sahih Muslim*, Book 20, Hadith 4645.

As Raymond Ibrahim explained, "To many Muslims, jihad, that is, armed struggle against the non-Muslim, is the informal sixth pillar. Islam's prophet Muhammad said that 'standing in the ranks of battle [jihad] is better than standing (in prayer) for sixty years,' even though prayer is one of the Five Pillars, and he ranked jihad as the 'second best deed' after belief in Allah as the only god and he himself, Muhammad, as his prophet, the shehada, or very First Pillar of Islam" (Raymond Ibrahim, "Taqiyya about Taqiyya," Raymond Ibrahim, April 12, 2014, raymondibrahim. com/2014/04/12/taqiyya-about-taqiyya/).
96. Darwish, *Cruel and Usual Punishment*, 219. In a personal e-mail, Darwish explained, "The calculation is based on work done by Bill Warner on the amount of texts devoted to non-Muslims (the Kafir) in the Islamic Trilogy, namely, the Hadith, Sira, and Koran. According to Warner, the figures are more than 35,000—negative mentions of non-Muslims and promotion of

hatred towards them in the Islamic Trilogy." Statistics from Bill Warner come from "Kafirs in the Trilogy," Center for the Study of Political Islam, cspipublishing.com/statistical/TrilogyStats/AmtTxtDevotedKafir.html and "Statistical Islam," *Political Islam*, www.politicalislam.com/trilogy-project /statistical-islam/.

97. Thomas Patrick Hughes, *A Dictionary of Islam* (Chicago: KAZI Publications, Inc., 1994, originally published in 1886), 243.

98. David Cook, *Understanding Jihad* (Berkeley: University of California Press, 2005), 2. Cook went on to explain that "attempts to rewrite history occur solely in Western-authored presentations of jihad, or those with Western audiences as the primary focus." He concluded that "those who write in Arabic or other Muslim majority languages realize that it is pointless to present jihad as anything other than militant warfare," since early Muslim history holds a high priority in the Islamic educational curriculum (43).

99. The latter is the definition offered for English-language learners at the Merriam-Webster online dictionary; the first standard definition is "a holy war waged on behalf of Islam as a religious duty; *also*: a personal struggle in devotion to Islam especially involving spiritual discipline," emphasis in original, accessed May 20, 2017, www.merriam-webster.com/dictionary /jihad, The first and second definitions in the *Oxford Dictionary of Current English* (fourth edition) define *jihad* as "(1) a war or struggle against unbelievers. (2) (also greater jihad) the spiritual struggle within oneself against sin." Dictionary.com defines *jihad* as "(1) a holy war undertaken as a sacred duty by Muslims. (2) any vigorous, emotional crusade for an idea or principle," accessed May 20, 2017, www.dictionary.com/browse /jihad. Cf. Richard Burkholder, "Jihad—'Holy War,' or Internal Spiritual Struggle?" Gallup, December 3, 2002, accessed February 18, 2016, www.gallup.com/poll/7333/jihad-holy-war-internal-spiritual-struggle.aspx.

100. Naqib al-Misri, *Reliance of the Traveller,* 600 [o9.1].

101. Ibid., 602 [o9.8].

102. See Robert Spencer, *Onward Muslim Soldiers: How Jihad Still Threatens America and the West* (Washington, DC: Regnery Publishing, 2003), 5–11; Gregory Davis, "Islam 101," accessed September 9, 2016, www. jihadwatch.org/islam101.pdf; Darío Fernández-Morera, *The Myth of the Andalusian Paradise: Muslims, Christians, and Jews under Islamic Rule in Medieval Spain* (Wilmington, Delaware: ISI Books, 2016), 22–35; Cook, *Understanding Jihad*, chapter one, esp. pp. 21–22.

103. Khaldun continues, "Therefore, caliphate and royal authority are united in Islam, so that the person in charge can devote the available strength to both of them at the same time" (Ibn Khaldun, *The Muqaddimah: An Introduction to History*, trans. Franz Rosenthal; ed. and abridged by N. J. Dawood [Princeton: Princeton University Press, 1967], 183.

104. Fertile Crescent: A region of the Middle East that served as the seat of ancient Mesopotamian civilization. Egypt, Assyria, Babylonia, Israel, and other nations developed in this fertile land ranging from the Nile Valley to the Tigris and Euphrates rivers.
105. See Fred Donner, "Conquests of Islam," in *Dictionary of the Middle Ages*, ed. Joseph R. Strayer (New York: Charles Scribner's Sons, 1989), 568, faculty.washington.edu/brownj9/LifeoftheProphet/Summary%20of%20Islamic%20Conquests-Donner.pdf.
106. Al-Tabari, *The History of al-Tabari: The Challenge to the Empires*, vol. 11, trans. Khalid Yahya Blankinship (Albany: SUNY Press, 1993), 159–171, kalamullah.com/Books/The%20History%20Of%20Tabari/Tabari_Volume_11.pdf. See also Donner, "Conquests of Islam," 568.
107. See Eusebius, *Church History* 3, 5, 3, online at Christian Classics Ethereal Library, www.ccel.org/ccel/schaff/npnf201.iii.viii.v.html.
108. Fred M. Donner, "Muhammad and the Caliphate," in *The Oxford History of Islam*, ed. John L. Esposito (Oxford: Oxford University Press, 1999), 12, online via books.google.com.
109. Donner, "Muhammad and the Caliphate," 12.
110. Fernández-Morera, *Myth of the Andalusian Paradise*, 19–20.
111. Ibid., 21.
112. Ibid., 22.
113. Bill Warner, "Why We Are Afraid, A 1400 Year Secret," YouTube video, accessed April 21, 2016, www.youtube.com/watch?v=t_Qpy0mXg8Y.
114. See note 41, page 208.
115. In this context, Andalusia (Arabic *al-Andalus*, Muslim Iberia) is the politically correct term for Islamic Spain—the territory under Muslim theocratic domination, constituting most of what is today Spain and Portugal, from the Umayyad conquest in 711 to its significant reduction in 1248 and final demise in 1492 (see Fernández-Morera, *Myth of the Andalusian Paradise*, 48–51, 85).
116. "Remarks by the President at Cairo University, 6-04-09," White House Office of the Press Secretary, accessed February 21, 2017, obamawhitehouse.archives.gov/the-press-office/remarks-president-cairo-university-6-04-09.
117. David Levering Lewis, *God's Crucible: Islam and the Making of Europe, 570–1215* (New York: W.W. Norton, 2008), 335.
118. Fernández-Morera cites *Across the Centuries* (New York: Houghton Mifflin Company, 1994).
119. Fernández-Morera cites www.islaminourschools.com.
120. Fernández-Morera, *The Myth of the Andalusian Paradise*, 23.
121. Ibid.
122. Ibid.

123. Fernández-Morera, *The Myth of the Andalusian Paradise*, 26. See also note 102, page 241.

124. Ibn Hayyan de Córdoba, *Cronica del Califa Abdarrahman III An-Nasir entre los anos 912 y 942 (al Muqtabis V)*, trans. María Jesús Viguera and Federico Corriente (Zaragoza: Anubar, 1981), 34–35, as quoted in Fernández-Morera, *Myth of the Andalusian Paradise,* 127–28.

125. Ibn Hayyan, *Muqtabis V*, 322–23, as quoted in Fernández-Morera, *Myth of the Andalusian Paradise*, 129.

126. Fernández-Morera, *Myth of the Andalusian Paradise*, 135.

127. Ibid., 4.

128. Ibid.

129. Ibid. "The existence of a Muslim kingdom in Medieval Spain where different races and religions lived harmoniously in multicultural tolerance is one of today's most widespread myths" (Darío Fernández-Morera, "The Myth of the Andalusian Paradise," Intercollegiate Studies Institute, Fall 2006, home.isi.org/myth-andalusian-paradise).

130. Barack Obama, "Remarks by the President at National Prayer Breakfast," February 5, 2015, White House Office of the Press Secretary, obamawhitehouse.archives.gov/the-press-office/2015/02/05 /remarks-president-national-prayer-breakfast.

131. Thomas F. Madden, "Crusade Myths," Ignatius Insight, n.d., accessed September 19, 2016, www.ignatiusinsight.com/features2005/tmadden _crusademyths_feb05.asp. See also Thomas F. Madden, *The New Concise History of the Crusades* (Lanham, MD: Rowman and Littlefield Publishers, 2006), and Rodney Stark, *God's Battalions: The Case for the Crusades* (New York: HarperCollins, 2009).

132. Jonathan Riley-Smith, *The Crusades, Christianity, and Islam* (New York: Columbia University Press, 2008), 11–12.

133. Warner, *Sharia Law*, 22. To quote directly from the English translation of *Reliance of the Traveller*, under the subheading, "The Objectives of Jihad": "The caliph (o25) makes war upon Jews, Christians, and Zoroastrians (N: provided he has first invited them to enter Islam in faith and practice, and if they will not, then invited them to enter the social *order* of Islam by paying the non-Muslim poll tax (jizya . . .)—which is the significance of their paying it, not the money itself—while remaining in their ancestral religions) (O: and the war continues) until they become Muslim or else pay the non-Muslim poll tax (O: in accordance with the word of Allah Most High, 'Fight those who do not believe in Allah and the Last Day and who forbid not what Allah and His messenger have forbidden—who do not practice the religion of truth, being of those who have been given the Book—until they pay the poll tax out of hand and are humbled' (Koran 9:29)" (Naqib al-Misri, *Reliance of the Traveller*, 602 [o9.8]).

134. Ibn Khaldun, *The Muqaddimah*, 183.
135. Cyrille Aillet, *Les mozárabes: christianisme, islamisation, et arabisation en péninsule ibérique (IXe–XIIe siècle)* (Madrid: Casa de Velázquez, 2010), 122–23, as quoted in Fernández-Morera, *Myth of the Andalusian Paradise*, 41, bracketed material is Fernández-Morera's insertion.
136. Fernández-Morera, *Myth of the Andalusian Paradise*, 85.
137. See Ibid.
138. Ibid., 89. An ablution is a ritual washing, especially of the body.
139. Ibid., 107.
140. Al-Qayrawani's *Risala* stating the Maliki school's position as quoted in Fernández-Morera, *Myth of the Andalusian Paradise,* 107.
141. Fernández-Morera, *Myth of the Andalusian Paradise*, 110.
142. Information in this paragraph is drawn from Spencer, *Politically Incorrect Guide*, 93.
143. Widely used juridical manual during Andalusian Malikism, *al-Tafri*, in Soha Abboud-Haggar, El Tratado Jurídico de Al-Tafri de Ibn Al-Gallab: Manuscrito Aljamiado De Almonacid De La Sierra (Zaragoza). Edición, Estudio, Glosario y Confrontación Con El Original Árabe (Zaragoza: Institución "Fernando el Católico," 1999), 572, as quoted in Fernández-Morera, *Myth of the Andalusian Paradise*, 101.
144. Fernández-Morera, *Myth of the Andalusian Paradise*, 101.
145. Ibid., 239, emphasis in original.
146. Ibid., 240.
147. Tony Blair, "A Battle for Global Values," *Foreign Affairs*, January/February 2007, web.archive.org/web/20080621162451/http://www.foreignaffairs.org/20070101faessay86106/tony-blair/a-battle-for-global-values.html.
148. Carly Fiorina, "Technology, Business and our Way of Life: What's Next," Minneapolis, HP Speeches, September 26, 2001, accessed September 25, 2016, www.hp.com/hpinfo/execteam/speeches/fiorina/minnesota01.html.
149. "Remarks by the President at Cairo University, 6-04-09," White House, Office of the Press Secretary, emphasis added.
150. Islamophobia is the "name that has been given to a modern-day thought crime. The purpose of the suffix in the term 'Islamophobia' is to suggest that any fear associated with Islam is irrational—whether that fear stems from the fact that its prophet and current-day imams call on believers to kill infidels, or because the attacks of 9/11 were carried out to implement those calls. Worse than that, it is to suggest that such a response to those attacks reflects a bigotry that itself should be feared" (David Horowitz and Robert Spencer, "Islamophobia: Thought-Crime of the Totalitarian Future," *Frontpage Mag*, May 8, 2015, www.frontpagemag.com/fpm/256647/islamophobia-thought-crime-totalitarian-future-david-horowitz).

151. Naqib al-Misri, *Reliance of the Traveller*, 541–42, [m10.12], emphasis added.
152. Fiorina, "Technology, Business."
153. Ibid.
154. Ibid.
155. Thomas F. Bertonneau, "The West's Cultural Continuity: Aristotle at Mont Saint-Michel," *The Brussels Journal*, January 5, 2009, www.brusselsjournal.com/node/3732.
156. Fernández-Morera, *Myth of the Andalusian Paradise,* 6. Fernández-Morera cites Sylvane Gouguenheim, *Aristote au mont Saint-Michel: Les racines grecques de l'Europe chrétienne* (Paris: Seuil, 2008).
157. Fernández-Morera, *The Myth of the Andalusian Paradise*, 6.
158. Ibid.
159. Ibid., 6–7.
160. See "Archbishop's Lecture—Civil and Religious Law in England: A Religious Perspective," Dr. Rowan Williams, 104th Archbishop of Canterbury, February 7, 2008, rowanwilliams.archbishopofcanterbury.org /articles.php/1137/archbishops-lecture-civil-and-religious-law-in-england -a-religious-perspective; and "'Sharia law'—What Did the Archbishop Actually Say?" Dr. Rowan Williams, 104th Archbishop of Canterbury, February 8, 2008, rowanwilliams.archbishopofcanterbury.org/articles .php/1135/sharia-law-what-did-the-archbishop-actually-say.
161. Bill Warner, *Sharia Law for the Non-Muslim*, 1.
162. Hirsi Ali, *Heretic*, 152.

Chapter 4: Levant

1. William Harris, *The Levant: A Fractured Mosaic,* fourth ed. (Princeton: Markus Wiener Publishers, 2005), ix–x.
2. Ibid., 2.
3. Ibid., xiii.
4. Ibid., 1.
5. *TANAKH: A New Translation of the Holy Scriptures, According to the Traditional Hebrew Text* (Philadelphia: The Jewish Publication Society, 1985). Tanakh is an acronym for the Hebrew Scriptures formed from the initial Hebrew letters of each of its major sections: *Torah* ("Law"), *Nevi'im* ("Prophets"), and *Ketuvim* ("Writings").
6. Ibid.
7. Ibid.
8. Ibid.
9. Ibid.

10. Ibid.
11. Ibid.
12. Ibid.
13. Ibid.
14. Ibid.
15. Ibid.
16. Ibid.
17. Ibid.
18. Ibid.
19. The materal thus far presented in this subsection ("Significance of the Levant to the Jews") is adapted from Hank Hanegraaff, *The Apocalypse Code: Find Out What the Bible Really Says about the End Times . . . and Why It Matters Today* (Nashville: Thomas Nelson, 2007), 175–79, 205–206. The next three paragraphs in this subsection are adapted from Hank Hanegraaff, *The Complete Bible Answer Book*, Collector's Edition (Nashville: Thomas Nelson, 2008, 2016), 320–21. The final five paragraphs in this subsection are adapted from Hanegraaff, *The Apocalypse Code*, xxiii, xxv–xxvi, 162–63.
20. "Accepted by the Central Conference of American Rabbis," June 24, 1997, accessed June 8, 2016, ccarnet.org/rabbis-speak/platforms/reform -judaism-zionism-centenary-platform/.
21. Benny Morris, *The Birth of the Palestinian Refugee Problem, 1947–1949* (Cambridge: Cambridge University Press, 1987), 113. After further documents were released by the Israeli government, Morris revised his estimate of those who were murdered at Deir Yassin to 100–110. In a revealing, provocative interview, Morris was asked, "How many acts of Israeli massacre were perpetrated in 1948?" He responded: "Twenty-four. In some cases four or five people were executed, in others the numbers were 70, 80, 100. . . . The worst cases were Saliha (70–80 killed), Deir Yassin (100–110), Lod (250), Dawayima (hundreds) and perhaps Abu Shusha (70). There is no unequivocal proof of a large-scale massacre at Tantura, but war crimes were perpetrated there. At Jaffa there was a massacre about which nothing had been known until now. The same at Arab al Muwassi, in the north. About half the acts of massacre were part of Operation Hiram [in the north, in October 1948]: at Safsaf, Saliha, Jish, Eilaboun, Arab, al Muwasi, Deir al Asad, Majdal Krum, Sasa. In Operation Hiram there was an unusually high concentration of executions of people against a wall or next to a well in an orderly fashion. That can't be chance. It's a pattern. Apparently, various officers who took part in the operation understood that the expulsion order they received permitted them to do these deeds in order to encourage the population to take to the roads. The fact is that no one was punished for these acts of murder. Ben-Gurion silenced the matter. He

covered up for the officers who did the massacres" (Ari Shavit, "Survival of the Fittest? An Interview with Benny Morris," *Haaretz*, January 9, 2004, accessed December 2, 2006, www.haaretz.com/hasen/pages/ShArt .jhtml?itemNo=380986&contrassID=2; also available in PDF, accessed June 8, 2016, www.logosjournal.com/morris.pdf.

22. Jim Holstun, prefatory note in Ari Shavit, "An Interview with Benny Morris," *Counterpunch*, January 16, 2004, accessed June 8, 2016, www.counterpunch.org/2004/01/16/an-interview-with-benny-morris/.

23. Shavit, "Survival of the Fittest?"

24. Joseph Weitz, *Yomani Ve'igrotai Labanim* (*My Diary and Letters to the Children*), entry for December 20, 1940; as quoted in Gary M. Burge, *Whose Land? Whose Promise? What Christians Are Not Being Told about Israel and the Palestinians* (Cleveland, OH: The Pilgrim Press, 2003), 39 (cf. 130). See also Morris, *Birth of the Palestinian Refugee*, 27; Benny Morris, "Falsifying the Record: A Fresh Look at Zionist Documentation of 1948," *Journal of Palestine Studies*, vol. 24, no. 3, 1995, pp. 44–62, www.jstor.org/stable/2537879.

25. A letter from D. Ben-Gurion to A. Ben-Gurion, October 5, 1937. Quoted in Burge, *Whose Land? Whose Promise?* 39. See also Morris, *Birth of the Palestinian Refugee*, 25.

26. Burge, *Whose Land? Whose Promise?*, 92.

27. "Address by Prime Minister Benjamin Netanyahu," The Feast of Tabernacles Conference, October 5, 1998, National Christian Leadership Conference for Israel, accessed December 26, 2006, www.nclci.org /NETANYAHU-Tabernacles.htm; also quoted in Timothy P. Weber, *On the Road to Armageddon: How Evangelicals Became Israel's Best Friend* (Grand Rapids, MI: Baker Academic, 2004), 217.

28. Two paragraphs adapted from Hanegraaff, *Apocalypse Code*, 179.

29. Two paragraphs adapted from ibid, 182.

30. I discuss typological prophecy below, see pp. 147–48.

31. Four paragraphs adapted from Hanegraaff, *Apocalypse Code*, 182–83, 198–99.

32. Those who presumptuously appeal to the words of Moses—"I will bless those who bless you, and whoever curses you I will curse" (Genesis 12:3)—as a pretext for unconditionally supporting the secular modern state of Israel, which prohibits the advance of the gospel while simultaneously disregarding the plight of the Palestinians, should, according to their own hermeneutical standard, heed the words of the prophet Jeremiah: "This is what the LORD Almighty, the God of Israel, says: Reform your ways and your actions, and I will let you live in this place. Do not trust in deceptive words and say, 'This is the temple of the LORD, the temple of the LORD, the temple of the LORD!' If you really change your ways and your actions and deal with each other justly, *if you do not oppress the foreigner*, the fatherless

or the widow and do not shed innocent blood in this place, and if you do not follow other gods to your own harm, then I will let you live in this place, in the land I gave your ancestors for ever and ever" (Jeremiah 7:3–8). Adapted from Hanegraaff, *Apocalypse Code*, 226.

33. Two paragraphs adapted from Hanegraaff, *Apocalypse Code*, 200.

34. Adapted from Hanegraaff, *Apocalypse Code*, 202–203.

35. See Ronald B. Allen, "The Land of Israel," in H. Wayne House, ed., *Israel: The Land and the People: An Evangelical Affirmation of God's Promises* (Grand Rapids: Kregel, 1998), 24.

36. Two paragraphs adapted from Hanegraaff, *Apocalypse Code*, 177–78, see 178ff.

37. See Weber, *On the Road to Armageddon*, 155–86, esp. 156–60, 166–71; and Stephen Sizer, *Christian Zionism: Road-map to Armageddon?* (Leicester, England: Inter-Varsity Press, 2004), 63–66. Adapted from Hanegraaff, *Apocalypse Code*, 183.

38. Adapted from Hanegraaff, *Apocalypse Code*, 186.

39. Weber, *On the Road to Armageddon*, 182–83.

40. Adapted from Hanegraaff, *Apocalypse Code*, 195.

41. Weber, *On the Road to Armageddon*, 162.

42. Ibid. Above paragraph adapted from Hanegraaff, *Apocalypse Code*, 195.

43. Although the Qur'an is less than clear on this point, most Muslims hold that Allah commanded Abraham to sacrifice Ishmael, not Isaac.

44. "Zawahiri's Letter to Zarqawi (English Translation)," letter dated July 9, 2005, Combating Terrorism Center at West Point, www.ctc.usma.edu/posts /zawahiris-letter-to-zarqawi-english-translation-2.

Chapter 5: Islamic State

1. Thomas L. Friedman, "Our Radical Islamic BFF, Saudi Arabia," *New York Times*, Opinion, September 2, 2015, accessed July 16, 2016, www.nytimes. com/2015/09/02/opinion/thomas-friedman-our-radical-islamic-bff-saudi -arabia.html?_r=0.

2. Dan Merica, "ISIS Is Neither Islamic nor a State, Says Hillary Clinton," CNN, October 7, 2014, accessed June 20, 2016, www.cnn.com/2014/10/06 /politics/hillary-clinton-isis/; see also Robert Spencer, *The Complete Infidel's Guide to ISIS* (Washington, DC: Regnery Publishing, 2015), xxiv.

3. William McCants, "The Believer: How an Introvert with a Passion for Religion and Soccer Became Abu Bakr Al-Baghdadi Leader of the Islamic State," Brookings, September 1, 2015, csweb.brookings.edu/content/ research/essays/2015/thebeliever.html; cf. William McCants, "Who Is Islamic State Leader Abu Bakr al-Baghdadi?" BBC News, March 8, 2016, accessed June 17, 2016, www.bbc.com/news/world-middle-east-35694311.

4. David Remnick, "Going the Distance: On and Off the Road with Barack

Obama," *New Yorker*, January 27, 2014, accessed June 20, 2016, www
.newyorker.com/magazine/2014/01/27/going-the-distance-david-remnick;
see also Spencer, *Complete Infidel'sGuide to ISIS*, xxiv.

5. Remnick, "Going the Distance."

6. David Remnick, "Telling the Truth about ISIS and Raqqa," *New Yorker*,
November 22, 2015, www.newyorker.com/news/news-desk/telling-the
-truth-about-isis-and-raqqa. Caliphate was declared June 29, 2014 (Cole
Bunzel, "From Paper State to Caliphate: The Ideology of the Islamic State,"
Brookings Institution, March 2015, 31, www.brookings.edu/wp-content
/uploads/2016/06/The-ideology-of-the-Islamic-State.pdf).

7. Mindy Belz, *They Say We Are Infidels: On the Run from ISIS with
Persecuted Christians in the Middle East* (Carol Stream, IL: Tyndale
Momentum, 2016), 199.

8. Ibid.

9. Belz, *They Say We Are Infidels,* 199; Belz cites Salma Abdelaziz, "Death
and Destruction in Syria: Jihadist Group 'Crucifies' Bodies to Send
Message," CNN, May 2, 2014, www.cnn.com/2014/05/01/world/meast
/syria-bodies-crucifixions/; Nick Cumming-Bruce, "Beheadings in Syria
Now Routine, U.N. Panel Says," *New York Times*, August 27, 2014,
www.nytimes.com/2014/08/28/world/middleeast/syria-conflict.html?_
re=0; see also "Under-Secretary-General for Humanitarian Affairs and
Emergency Relief Coordinator, Valerie Amos, Security Council Briefing on
Syria," United Nations Office for the Coordination of Humanitarian Affairs,
December 15, 2014, reliefweb.int/report/syrian-arab-republic/under
-secretary-general-humanitarian-affairs-and-emergency-relief-13.

10. "French Govt to Use Arabic 'Daesh' for Islamic State Group," France 24,
September 18, 2014; cited in Spencer, *Complete Infidel's Guide to ISIS,* 223.

11. Spencer, *Complete Infidel's Guide to ISIS,* 223. Spencer cites Adam Taylor,
"'Daesh': John Kerry Starts Calling the Islamic State a Name They Hate,"
Washington Post, December 5, 2014, www.washingtonpost.com/news
/worldviews/wp/2014/12/05/daesh-john-kerry-starts-calling-the-islamic
-state-a-name-they-hate/.

12. See note 41 in Introduction, page 208.

13. H. C. Armstrong, *Gray Wolf: The Life of Kemal Atatürk* (New York:
Capricorn Books, 1933, 1961 edition), 200.

14. "Kemal Atatürk," History.com, 2009, accessed July 2, 2016, www.history.
com/topics/kemal-Atatürk; see also Norman Itzkowitz, "Kemal Atatürk:
President of Turkey," *Encyclopedia Britannica Online*, accessed July 2,
2016, www.britannica.com/biography/Kemal-Atatürk.

15. Armstrong, *Gray Wolf*, 200.

16. Patrick J. Buchanan, *Suicide of a Superpower: Will America Survive to
2025?* (New York: Thomas Dunne Books, 2011), 83.

17. Ibid., 86.
18. "John Paul II in His Own Words," *BBC News*, October 14, 2003, news.bbc
    .co.uk/2/hi/europe/3112868.stm.
19. Buchanan, *Suicide of a Superpower*, 87.
20. Mary Eberstadt, *It's Dangerous to Believe: Religious Freedom and Its
    Enemies* (New York: HarperCollins, 2016), xi.
21. Eberstadt cites Jason Hanna and Steve Almasy, "Washington High School
    Coach Placed on Leave for Praying on Field," CNN, October 30, 2015,
    accessed September 11, 2016, www.cnn.com/2015/10/29/us
    /washington-football-coach-joe-kennedy-prays/.
22. Eberstadt cites Chuck Holton, "Military Chaplains the New 'Don't Ask,
    Don't Tell?," CBN News, February 4, 2015, accessed September 13, 2016,
    www1.cbn.com/cbnnews/us/2015/February/Military-Chaplains-the
    -New-Dont-Ask-Dont-Tell.
23. Eberstadt cites Todd Starnes, "Costly Beliefs: State Squeezes Last Penny
    from Bakers who Defied Lesbian-Wedding Cake Order," FoxNews,
    December 29, 2015, accessed September 13, 2016, www.foxnews.com
    /opinion/2015/12/29/bakers-forced-to-pay-more-than-135g-in-lesbian-cake
    -battle.html.
24. Eberstadt cites Emily Foxhall, "Attorneys: Katy-Area Teacher Fired for
    Refusing to Address Girl, 6, as Transgender Boy," *Houston Chronicle*,
    November 10, 2015, accessed September 13, 2016, www.chron.com
    /neighborhood/katy/news/article/Attorneys-Katy-area-teacher-fired-for
    -refusing-6622339.php.
25. Eberstadt cites Samuel Smith, "Evangelical Teacher Fired for Giving Bible
    to Student Supported by Gov't Commission," *Christian Post*, January 8,
    2015, accessed September 13, 2016, www.christianpost.com/news
    /evangelical-teacher-fired-for-giving-bible-to-student-supported-by-eeoc
    -ruling-132293/.
26. Eberstadt, *It's Dangerous to Believe*, xii.
27. Ibid., xvii. Eberstadt cites Sarah Kaplan, "Has the World 'Looked the
    Other Way' While Christians Are Killed'?" *Washington Post*, April 7, 2015,
    accessed September 13, 2016, www.washingtonpost.com/news
    /morning-mix/wp/2015/04/07/has-the-world-looked-the-other-way
    -while-christians-are-killed/.
28. Eberstadt, *It's Dangerous to Believe*, xvii. Eberstadt cites Tom Batchelor,
    "Christians Almost Completely Destroyed by ISIS Fanatics in Syria, Says
    Aleppo Archbishop," *Express*, October 21, 2015, accessed September 13,
    2016, www.express.co.uk/news/world/613514/Islamic-State-Christians
    -Syria-wiped-out-jihadi-militants.
29. *Kingdom of Heaven*, directed by Ridley Scott (2005; Los Angeles: 20th
    Century Fox, 2005), DVD.

30. Thomas Madden wrote, "The crusades were in every way a *defensive war*. They were the West's belated response to the Muslim conquest of fully two-thirds of the Christian world" (Thomas F. Madden, "Crusade Propaganda: The Abuse of Christianity's Holy Wars," *National Review*, November 2, 2001, emphasis in original, www.nationalreview.com/article/220747/crusade-propaganda-thomas-f-madden).

31. "Remarks by the President at National Prayer Breakfast," February 5, 2015, White House Office of the Press Secretary, obamawhitehouse.archives.gov/the-press-office/2015/02/05/remarks-president-national-prayer-breakfast.

32. For discussion, see Charles Strohmer, "Submit or Die: The Geostrategic Jihad of Osama bin Laden and al-Qaeda (Part 1): Its Ideological Roots in the Theology and Politics of Sayyid Qutb," *Christian Research Journal*, volume 29, number 04 (2006); Charles Strohmer, "Submit or Die: The Geostrategic Jihad of Osama bin Laden and al-Qaeda (Part 2): The Totalitarian Vision of the Future in the Writings of Sayyid Qutb," *Christian Research Journal*, volume 29, number 05 (2006), both online at www.equip.org.

33. Sayyid Qutb, *Milestones*, in *SIME Journal* (majalla.org) (2005). 64, online at web.archive.org/web/20160910033311/http://thegorkabriefing.com/wp-content/uploads/2015/04/qutb-milestones.pdf.

34. Sebastian Gorka, *Defeating Jihad: The Winnable War* (Washington, DC: Regnery Publishing, 2016), 66.

35. Ibid., 71.

36. Steve Emerson, "Abdullah Assam: The Man before Osama Bin Laden," International Association for Counterterrorism and Security Professionals, n.d., accessed July 12, 2016, www.iacsp.com/itobli3.html.

37. As quoted in Emerson, "Abdullah Assam: The Man before Osama Bin Laden."

38. Ibid.

39. Spencer, *Complete Infidel's Guide to ISIS*, 1.

40. Ibid., 2.

41. Craig Whitlock, "Al-Zarqawi's Biography," *Washington Post*, June 8, 2006, accessed July 14, 2016, www.washingtonpost.com/wp-dyn/content/article/2006/06/08/AR2006060800299_2.html?nav=rss_world/Africa.

42. Spencer, *Complete Infidel's Guide to ISIS*, 2.

43. Ibid., 3.

44. Ellen Knickmeyer and Jonathan Finer, "Insurgent Leader Al-Zarqawi Killed in Iraq," *Washington Post*, June 8, 2006, accessed June 18, 2016, www.washingtonpost.com/wp-dyn/content/article/2006/06/08/AR2006060800114.html.

45. William McCants, *The ISIS Apocalypse: The History, Strategy, and Doomsday Vision of the Islamic State* (New York: St. Martin's Press, 2015), 126.

46. Ibid., 139.

47. Ibid., 139–40.

48. Gorka, *Defeating Jihad*, 113.

49. Ibid.

50. Ibid.

51. Ibid., 113–14.

52. Jose Pagliery, "Exclusive: ISIS Makes Up for Lost Oil Cash with Rising Taxes and Fees," *CNN*, May 31, 2016, accessed July 13, 2016, money.cnn.com/2016/05/31/news/isis-oil-taxes; see also "ISIS Financing: 2015," Center for the Analysis of Terrorism, May 2016, accessed, July 13, 2016, cat-int.org/wp-content/uploads/2016/06/ISIS-Financing-2015-Report.pdf.

53. Gorka, *Defeating Jihad*, 117–18.

54. Translation by Raymond Ibrahim, in *The Al Qaeda Reader*, Raymond Ibrahim, ed. (New York: Doubleday, 2007), 11, at books.google.com.

55. Raymond Ibrahim, "The Islamic Genocide of Christians: Past and Present," April 26, 2015, Raymond Ibrahim, accessed July 14, 2016, www.raymondibrahim.com/2015/04/26/the-islamic-genocide-of-christians -past-and-present/. See "Notes on the Genocides of Christian Populations of the Ottoman Empire," www.genocidetext.net/iags_resolution_supporting _documentation.htm.

56. "Henry Morgenthau, U.S. Ambassador to the Ottoman Empire (1913-16)," Armenian National Institute, accessed July 14, 2016, www.armenian -genocide.org/statement_morgenthau.html.

57. Quoted in Raymond Ibrahim, "The Islamic Genocide of Christians: Past and Present."

58. See note 27, page 206.

59. See Tom Heneghan, "About 100 Million Christians Persecuted Around the World: Report," Reuters, January 8, 2013, www.reuters.com/article /us-religion-christianity-persecution-idUSBRE9070TB20130108; and "World Watch List 2017," Open Doors, www.opendoorsusa.org/christian -persecution/world-watch-list/. Terry Scambray, "Islam: Victors Vanquishing Victims," *New Oxford Review*, October 2014, accessed July 15, 2016, victorhanson.com/wordpress/?p=7989.

60. Graeme Wood, "What ISIS's Leader Really Wants," *New Republic*, September 1, 2014, accessed July 15, 2016, newrepublic.com/article/119259 /isis-history-islamic-states-new-caliphate-syria-and-iraq.

61. William McCants, "Who Exactly Is Abu Bakr al-Baghdadi, Leader of ISIS?" *Newsweek*, September 6, 2015, accessed June 18, 2016, www.newsweek .com/who-exactly-abu-bakr-al-baghdadi-leader-isis-368907; McCants, "Who Is Islamic State Leader Abu Bakr al-Baghdadi?"

62. McCants, "Who Exactly Is Abu Bakr al-Baghdadi, Leader of ISIS?"

63. Regarding the erasure of non-Islamic culture by the Umayyad caliphate, see

Darío Fernández-Morera, *The Myth of the Andalusian Paradise: Muslims, Christians, and Jews under Islamic Rule in Medieval Spain* (Wilmington, Delaware: ISI Books, 2016), 78–81; Spencer, *Complete Infidel's Guide to ISIS*, 209. Regarding the same practice by the Islamic State, see "Erasing the Legacy of a Ruined Nation," *Dabiq* 8 (2015):22–24, accessed June 22, 2016, media.clarionproject.org/files/islamic-state/isis-isil-islamic-state-magazine -issue+8-sharia-alone-will-rule-africa.pdf.

64. Spencer, *Complete Infidel's Guide to ISIS*, 212–13.
65. Jihadist News, "Abu Bakr al-Baghdadi Appears in Video, Delivers Sermon in Mosul," SITE Intelligence Group, July 5, 2014, accessed July 16, 2016, news.siteintelgroup.com/Jihadist-News/abu-bakr-al-baghdadi-appears-in -video-delivers-sermon-in-mosul.html.
66. Constance Letsch and Emma Graham-Harrison, "Istanbul Airport Attack: Turkey Blames ISIS as New Details Emerge of Assault," *The Guardian*, June 30, 2016, www.theguardian.com/world/2016/jun/29/istanbul-ataturk -airport-attack-turkcy-declares-day-of-mourning.
67. Spencer, *Complete Infidel's Guide to ISIS*, 110–111.
68. Ibid., 26; see also Yousaf Butt, "How Saudi Wahhabism Is the Fountainhead of Islamist Terrorism," *The World Post*, January 20, 2015, updated March 22, 2015, accessed July 15, 2016, www.huffingtonpost.com /dr-yousaf-butt-/saudi-wahhabism-islam-terrorism_b_6501916.html.
69. Butt, "How Saudi Wahhabism."
70. "How Saudi Arabia Exports Radical Islam," *The Week*, August 8, 2015, accessed July 16, 2016, theweek.com/articles/570297/how-saudi-arabia -exports-radical-islam.
71. Friedman, "Our Radical Islamic BFF."
72. Ibid.
73. Anthony Cave, "Did Hillary Clinton Take Money from Countries that Treat Women, Gays Poorly?" *PolitiFact*, July 11, 2016, accessed July 16, 2016, www.politifact.com/arizona/statements/2016/jul/11/donald-trump /did-hillary-clinton-take-money-countries-treat-wom/; Jon Greenberg, "Fact-checking Donations to the Clinton Foundation," July 7, 2016, *PolitiFact*, accessed July 16, 2016, www.politifact.com/truth-o-meter /article/2016/jul/07/fact-checking-donations-clinton-foundation/. *PolitiFact* reports that Clinton "played no role in the foundation while she was secretary of state" and that "Saudi Arabia did not give to the foundation while Secretary Clinton was at the State Department" (Cave, "Did Hillary Clinton Take Money").
74. "US Embassy Cables: Hillary Clinton Says Saudi Arabia 'A Critical Source of Terrorist Funding,'" *The Guardian*, December 5, 2010, accessed July 16, 2016, www.theguardian.com/world/us-embassy-cables-documents/242073. See also Butt, "How Saudi Wahhabism."

75. Bob Graham, interview with Stephanie Sy on *Yahoo! News Now*, July 15, 2016, accessed July 16, 2016, www.yahoo.com/katiecouric/911-28-pages -get-declassified-sen-bob-graham-reacts-203040454.html.

76. "How Saudi Arabia Exports Radical Islam," *The Week*.

77. See Raymond Ibrahim, "Saudi Grand Mufti Calls for 'Destruction of All Churches in Region,'" *Jihad Watch*, March 14, 2012, accessed July 19, 2016, www.jihadwatch.org/2012/03/raymond-ibrahim-saudi-grand-mufti-calls -for-destruction-of-all-churches-in-region.

78. Raymond Ibrahim, *Crucified Again: Exposing Islam's New War on Christians* (Washington, DC: Regnery Publishing, 2013), 231.

79. Ibid., 232.

80. Ibid., 234; see also Spencer Case, "How Obama Sided with the Muslim Brotherhood," *National Review*, July 3, 2014, accessed July 20, 2016, www.nationalreview.com/article/381947/how-obama-sided-muslim -brotherhood-spencer-case.

81. "Mohamed Morsi During Election Campaign," The Middle East Media Research Institute, May 13, 2012, web.archive.org/web/20130323033308 /http://www.memri.org/clip_transcript/en/3476.htm.

82. Ibrahim, *Crucified Again*, 235.

83. See Pamela K. Browne, Catherine Herridge, "Diary entry from Benghazi victim's dad: 'I gave Hillary a hug,' she blamed filmmaker," Fox News, October 23, 2015, www.foxnews.com/politics/2015/10/23/diary-entry-from -benghazi-victims-dad-gave-hillary-hug-blamed-filmmaker.html; Eugene Kiely, "The Benghazi Timeline, Clinton Edition, FactCheck.org, July 1, 2016, www.factcheck.org/2016/06/the-benghazi-timeline-clinton-edition/; Hillary Rodham Clinton, "Statement on the Attack in Benghazi," U.S. Department of State, Press Statement, September 11, 2012, web.archive.org /web/20140111230112/https:/www.state.gov/secretary/20092013clinton /rm/2012/09/197628.htm; Hillary Rodham Clinton, "Remarks on the Deaths of American Personnel in Benghazi, Libya," U. S. Department of State, September 12, 2012, web.archive.org/web/20140111230104/https:/www .state.gov/secretary/20092013clinton/rm/2012/09/197654.htm.

84. John Podhoretz, "Obama: 'We' Are to Blame, Not Islamic Terrorism, for Massacre," *New York Post*, June 12, 2016, accessed July 19, 2016, nypost.com/2016/06/12/ obama-says-we-are-to-blame-not-islamic-terrorism-for-orlando-massacre/.

85. "President Obama's Statement about the Orlando Shootings," *Boston Globe* on YouTube, June 12, 2016, accessed July 19, 2016, see time mark 1:00ff., www.youtube.com/watch?v=vog1AoeX840; see also Podhoretz, "Obama."

86. Ian Schwartz, "Loretta Lynch: References to Islam from Orlando Terrorist 911 Call Removed 'To Avoid Revictimizing'" *Real Clear Politics*, June 19,

2016, accessed July 19, 2016, www.realclearpolitics.com/video/2016/06/19
/loretta_lynch_references_to_islam_from_orlando_terrorist_911_call
_removed_to_avoid_revictimizing.html. After criticism the Obama
administration released a less redacted transcript (still missing Arabic
including "Allah") ("Joint Statement from Justice Department and FBI
Regarding Transcript Related to the Orlando Terror Attack," June 20, 2016,
Department of Justice Office of Public Affairs, accessed July 20, 2016,
www.justice.gov/opa/pr/joint-statement-justice-department-and-fbi
-regarding-transcript-related-orlando-terror-attack.

87. Barack Obama, "President Obama: Religious Freedom Keeps Us
Strong," *Religion News Service*, February 6, 2016, accessed July 19, 2016,
religionnews.com/2016/02/06/president-obama-religious-freedom-keeps-us
-strong-rns-exclusive-commentary.

88. Ryan J. Reilly, "DOJ Official: Holder 'Firmly Committed' to Eliminating
Anti-Muslim Training," *Talking Points Memo* (TPM), October 19, 2011,
accessed July 19, 2016, talkingpointsmemo.com/muckraker/doj-official
-holder-firmly-committed-to-eliminating-anti-muslim-training; see also
Ibrahim, *Crucified Again*, 237.

89. Ibrahim, *Crucified Again*, 238; see RepLungrenCA03, "Dan Lungren
Questions Paul Stockton—Assistant Defense Secretary for Homeland
Defense," YouTube video, December 13, 2011, accessed July 19, 2016,
www.youtube.com/watch?v=WU6n1mrpAGY.

90. Ibrahim, *Crucified Again*, 240; see Julian Pecquet, "Obama Administration
Pressed to Do More on Boko Haram Terror Designations," *The Hill*, June 21,
2012, accessed July 19, 2016, thehill.com/policy/international/234193
-obama-administration-pressed-to-do-more-on-boko-haram-terror
-designations.

91. Ibrahim, *Crucified Again*, 240; see Steve Peacock, "Obama: Slaughter of
Christians a Misunderstanding," *WND*, May 20, 2012, accessed July 19,
2016, www.wnd.com/2012/05/obama-slaughter-of-christians-a
-misunderstanding/.

92. Ibrahim, *Crucified Again*, 246.

93. Ibid., 246, emphasis in original; Ibrahim quotes Ken Sengupta, "The plight
of Syria's Christians: 'We left Homs because they were trying to kill us,"
Independent, November 1, 2012, accessed July 19, 2016, www.independent.
co.uk/news/world/middle-east/the-plight-of-syrias-christians-we-left-homs
-because-they-were-trying-to-kill-us-8274710.html.

94. Os Guinness, *Renaissance: The Power of the Gospel However Dark the
Times* (Downers Grove, IL: InterVarsity Press, 2014), 16.

95. Buchanan, *Suicide of a Superpower*, 83.

96. Guinness, *Renaissance*, 20.

Chapter 6: Major Muslim Misapprehensions

1. Samuel M. Zwemer, *Islam and the Cross: Selections from "The Apostle to Islam"* Roger S. Greenway, ed. (Phillipsburg, NJ: P&R Publishing, 2002), 69.
2. Ibid., 70, emphasis added.
3. J. Gordon Logan, "Islam Defies Your King!" Egypt General Mission leaflet, quoted in Zwemer, *Islam and the Cross*, 6.
4. *Sahih Muslim* Book 008, Number 3371, www.usc.edu/org/cmje/religious -texts/hadith/muslim/008-smt.php#008.3371; see also Al-Waqidi, *The Life of Muhammad: Al-Wāqidī's Kitāb al-Maghāzī*, ed. Rizwi Faizer, trans. Rizwi Faizer, Amal Ismail, and AbdulKader Tayob (London: Routledge, 2011), 202; compare a similar occasion reported in *Sahih al-Bukhari*, Volume 3, Book 34, Number 432.
5. See Robert Spencer, *Not Peace but a Sword: The Great Chasm Between Christianity and Islam* (San Diego: Catholic Answers, 2013), 100, 101. *Sahih al-Bukhari* reports, "Narrated Abu Huraira: Allah's Apostle said, 'The Hour will not be established until the son of Mary (i.e. Jesus) descends amongst you as a just ruler, he will break the cross, kill the pigs, and abolish the Jizya tax. Money will be in abundance so that nobody will accept it (as charitable gifts)'" (*Sahih al-Bukhari*, Volume 3, Book 43, Number 656, www.usc.edu /org/cmje/religious-texts/hadith/bukhari/043-sbt.php#003.043.656).
6. Spencer, *Not Peace but a Sword*, 91.
7. Ibid., 93.
8. Os Guinness, *Fool's Talk: Recovering the Art of Christian Persuasion* (Downers Grove, IL: InterVarsity Press, 2015), 243.
9. Popularly attributed to D. L. Moody.
10. Text concerning manuscript evidence, archaeology, and prophecy adapted from Hank Hanegraaff, *The Complete Bible Answer Book*, Collector's Edition (Nashville: Thomas Nelson, 2008, 2016), 140–41.
11. "How to Detect Counterfeit Money," *Los Angeles Times*, August 9, 1999, accessed August 22, 2016, articles.latimes.com/1999/aug/09/local/me-64066; see also "How to Protect Yourself from Counterfeiting," University of Florida Police Department, accessed August 23, 2016, www.police.ufl.edu /community-services/how-to-protect-yourself-from-counterfeiting/.
12. See Qur'an 3:45–47 (and v. 59); 19:16–22; 21:91; 66:12.
13. The Qur'an refers to Jesus as "faultless" (19:19) and "blessed" (19:31) and never implies that Jesus sinned (whereas the Qur'an requires Muhammad to seek forgiveness for his sin; see 40:55; 47:19; cf. 48:2). The Qur'an also says Allah protected Jesus from Satan (see 3:35–36). *Sahih al-Bukhari* reports: "The Prophet said: When any human being is born, Satan touches

him at both sides of the body with his two fingers, except Jesus, the son of
Mary, whom Satan tried to touch (but failed), so he touched the placenta-
cover (instead)" (*Sahih al-Bukhari*, Volume 4, Book 54, Number 506, see
www.sunnah.com/urn/30700). See also *Sahih al-Bukhari*, Volume 4, Book
55, Number 641; *Sahih Muslim* Book 30, Number 5838. See also David
Wood, "Jesus in Islam," *Christian Research Journal* 40, 1 (2017): 15.

14. See Qur'an 3:49; 19:29–31; 5:110–15.

15. Qur'an 61:6. See discussion that follows, pp. 134–35.

16. See Qur'an 2:116; 3:59, 64; 4:171–72; 5:17, 72–75, 116–17; 6:101; 9:31;
17:111; 18:1–5; 19:30–31, 35, 88–93; 23:91; 25:2; 39:3–6; 43:15, 57–65, 81;
72:3–4; 112:1–4. Note that the Qur'an exhorts Muslims to read about Jesus
(Isa) in the Bible (Q 5:46–48 [see context vv. 44–50]; 10:94–95). *Isa* is the
Islamic Arabic name for Jesus (Arabic-speaking Christians call Jesus *Yasua*,
not *Isa*). For helpful discussion, see Wood, "Jesus in Islam," 10–17.

17. When Jesus asked, "Who do you say I am?" Simon Peter answered, "You
are the Messiah, the Son of the living God." Then Jesus said, "Blessed
are you, Simon son of Jonah, for this was not revealed to you by flesh and
blood, but by my Father in heaven" (see Matthew 16:15–17). See also Mark
12:1–12; John 1:14, 18; 3:16–18; 5:18–23, 24–26; 10:36; 11:4; 20:31.

18. Anyone reading through the Gospel of John with a truly open mind sees
Christ repeatedly identified as God. After Jesus demonstrated the power
to lay down his life and to take it up again, the disciple Thomas did not
identify him as "a god" but as "my God" (John 20:28). The Greek of John
20:28 is unambiguous and definitive. Literally, Thomas said to the risen
Christ, "the Lord of me and the God of me." As the eminent New Testament
scholar N. T. Wright explained, "Thomas, who was not present that first
evening, acquires his now perpetual nickname by declaring his doubt that
the Lord had truly risen, and is then confronted by the risen Jesus inviting
him to touch and see for himself. Thomas refuses the invitation, coming out
instead with the fullest confession of faith anywhere in the whole gospel"
(N. T. Wright, *The Resurrection of the Son of God* [Minneapolis: Fortress,
2003], 664). Note adapted from Hank Hanegraaff, *Has God Spoken?:
Memorable Proofs of the Bible's Divine Inspiration* (Nashville: Thomas
Nelson, 2011), 232, 336.

19. See also Q 40:55; cf. 48:2. *Sahih al-Bukhari* reports that Muhammad said,
"By Allah! I ask for forgiveness from Allah and turn to Him in repentance
more than seventy times a day" (Volume 8, Book 75, Number 319, sunnah.
com/bukhari/80/4). See also Wood, "Jesus in Islam," 15.

20. The author of Hebrews wrote, "We do not have a high priest who is unable
to empathize with our weaknesses, but we have one who has been tempted
in every way, just as we are—yet he did not sin" (4:15). See also Isaiah

53:9; Matthew 12:18; 17:5; Luke 2:40; 3:22; 4:1–13; 23:41, 47; John 8:29; 10:36–38; Hebrews 7:26; 9:14; 1 Peter 1:19; 2 Peter 1:17.

21. See Matthew 27:45ff; Mark 15:33ff; Luke 23:44ff; John 19:28ff; see also 1 Corinthians 15:1–11.

22. Additionally, in Romans 10:13, Paul equates calling on Christ with calling on Yahweh (Joel 2:32); and in Philippians 2:9–11, he equates bowing to and confessing the name of Jesus with bowing to and confessing the name of Yahweh (Isaiah 45:22–25), further demonstrating that Jesus is himself almighty God. The name *Yahweh* was derived by adding the vowel points of the Hebrew title Adonai (King of Kings and Lord of Lords) to the four Hebrew letter word *YHWH*, which represents the unspeakable personal holy name of God and conveys eternality and self-existence.

23. Particularly compelling is the way John presents in Revelation a set of two corresponding divine declarations of God and Christ:

   • God: "I am the Alpha and the Omega" (1:8; cp. Isaiah 44:6).
   • Christ: "I am the First and the Last" (1:17).
   • God: "I am the Alpha and the Omega, the Beginning and the End" (21:6).
   • Christ: "I am the Alpha and the Omega, the Beginning and the End, the First and the Last," (22:13)

   See Richard Bauckham, *The Theology of the Book of Revelation* (Cambridge, United Kingdom: Cambridge University Press, 1993), 26 (see chapters 2–3).

24. In his comprehensive study of the New Testament use of the term θεός (*theos*, God), New Testament scholar Murray J. Harris concludes, "While the [New Testament] customarily reserves the term θεός for the Father, occasionally it is applied to Jesus in his preincarnate, incarnate, or postresurrection state. As used of the Father, θεός is virtually a proper name. As used of Jesus, θεός is a generic title, being an appellation descriptive of his *genus* as one who inherently belongs to the category of Deity. In this usage θεός points not to Christ's function or office but to his nature." See John 1:1, 18; 20:28; Romans 9:5; Titus 2:13; Hebrews 1:8; 2 Peter 1:1. (Murray J. Harris, *Jesus as God: The New Testament Use of the Term Theos in Reference to Jesus* [Grand Rapids: Baker Book House, 1992], 298.)

25. *Hilali-Khan* and *Pickthall*.

26. In addition to the passages referenced in this section that establish the deity of Christ—that Jesus of Nazareth is God the Son—see also Isaiah 9:6; Mark 2:5–10; John 12:44–45; 13:3; 14:1, 7, 9; Romans 9:5; 2 Corinthians 4:4; 1 Timothy 3:16; Titus 2:13; 1 John 5:20; see also note 7, page 223.

   Moreover, Christ receives worship due to God alone: Matthew 2:11; 14:33; 28:9, 17; John 9:37–38; Philippians 2:9–11 (cf. Isaiah 45:23–24);

Hebrews 1:6; Revelation 5:6, 8, 13–14; 22:1–3 (cf. Exodus 20:3–6; Deuteronomy 4:35, 6:4, 6:13–16; 32:39; Matthew 4:10; John 4:24; Acts 10:25–26; 14:11–15; Revelation 19:9–10; 22:8–9).

Body text in subsection "Deity of Christ" concerning the biblical data is taken or adapted from Hanegraaff, *The Complete Bible Answer Book*, 244–45, 246–50, 275–76.

27. The following account of Michelangelo's work in the Sistine Chapel draws from *The Student Bible*, notes by Philip Yancey and Tim Stafford (Grand Rapids: Zondervan Bible Publishers, 1986), 23–24.

28. *The Student Bible*, 23.

29. See also Romans 5:14–21; 1 Corinthians 15:21–22, 45–49; Ephesians 2:3; Psalm 51:5; also Romans 3:9ff.

30. The apostle Paul wrote, "Now the promises were spoken to Abraham and to his seed. He does not say, 'And to seeds,' as *referring* to many, but *rather* to one, 'And to your seed,' that is, Christ" (Galatians 3:16 NASB).

31. Previous six paragraphs adapted from Hanegraaff, *Has God Spoken?*, 243, and Hank Hanegraaff, *The Apocalypse Code: Find Out What the Bible Really Says about the End Times . . . and Why It Matters Today* (Nashville: Thomas Nelson, 2007), 51–52, 53.

32. Three paragraphs concerning the Tree of Life adapted from Hank Hanegraaff, *The Creation Answer Book* (Nashville: Thomas Nelson, 2012), 57–58.

33. Thomas Carlyle, "The Hero as Prophet: Mahomet: Islam" (1840) in "Thomas Carlyle on Heroes Lecture II Prophet as Hero," Muhammad Umar Chand, ed., Archive.org, 34, 35, accessed January 27, 2016, archive.org /details/ThomasCarlyleOnHeroesLectureIIProphetAsHero.

34. Robert Spencer, *Onward Muslim Soldiers: How Jihad Still Threatens America and the West* (Washington, DC: Regnery Publishing, 2003), 126.

35. Spencer, *Not Peace but a Sword*, 46; contra Norman L. Geisler and Abdul Saleeb, *Answering Islam: The Crescent in Light of the Cross*, second edition (Grand Rapids, MI: Baker Books, 2002), 42.

36. Jane Idleman Smith and Yvonne Yazbeck Haddad, *The Islamic Understanding of Death and Resurrection* (Oxford: Oxford University Press, 2002), 14.

37. See Ibid., 12; Salaam Corniche, "*Fitrah* and Fig Leaves: Islamic and Christian Teachings on Sin," *St. Francis* magazine, Vol. 9, No. 5, 2013, accessed September 1, 2016, www.stfrancismagazine.info/ja/images/stories /islamic-and-christian-teachings-on-sin.pdf.

38. *Sahih Muslim*, Book 033, Number 6426, bracketed insertion in original, www.usc.edu/org/cmje/religious-texts/hadith/muslim/033-smt. php#033.6426. See also Corniche, "*Fitrah* and Fig Leaves."

39. Abdullah Yusuf Ali, *The Meaning of the Holy Qur'an*, tenth ed. (Beltsville: MD: Amana Publications, 1999, 2001), 1016 (note 3541 at Q 30:30).

Although humankind has been created weak (Q 4:28) and inclines toward
forgetfulness, there is "nothing inherently debased about man; he has been
given every natural opportunity to live a life of well-being and honor"
(Smith, Haddad, *Islamic Understanding*, 14, 15).

40. All three branches of historic Christianity (Orthodox, Roman Catholic,
and Protestant) hold as canonical (from the Greek word *kanon*, meaning
"measuring rod" or "rule") the same twenty-seven books of the Greek New
Testament officially recognized as inspired Holy Scripture by the early
Christian church. Protestants hold to thirty-nine received books constituting
the Old Testament (Hebrew Canon). Orthodox and Roman Catholic
Christians include these thirty-nine received books of the Old Testament in
the canon of inspired Holy Scipture, but each of these two branches of the
church also include various other books as deuterocanonical ("belonging to
the second canon"). For discussion, see F. F. Bruce, *The Canon of Scripture*
(Downers Grove, IL: IVP Academic, 1988) and "The Old Testament
Books Listed and Compared," *The Orthodox Study Bible*, ed. Metropolitan
Maximos, et al. (Nashville: Thomas Nelson, 2008).

41. I. A. Ibrahim, *A Brief Illustrated Guide to Understanding Islam*, second
edition (Houston: Darussalam, 1997), 5.

42. Sayyid Abul A'La Maududi, *Towards Understanding Islam*, 2nd edition
(n.c.: International Islamic Federation of Student Organizations, 1989), 60.

43. Mazhar Kazi, *130 Evident Miracles in the Qur'an* (Richmond Hill:
Crescent, 1997), 42–43, as quoted in James R. White, *What Every Christian
Needs to Know about the Qur'an* (Minneapolis: Bethany House Publishers,
2013), 250.

44. A. S. K. Joommal, *The Bible: Word of God or Word of Man?*
(n.c.: Tolu-e-Islam Trust at Aftab Alam Press, 2000), accessed
August 25, 2016, www.scribd.com/document/150077178/
THE-BIBLE-WORD-OF-GOD-OR-WORD-OF-MAN-By-A-S-K-Joommal.

45. Maududi, *Towards Understanding Islam*, emphasis in original, 60.

46. See 1 Kings 4:29–31. Excepting the Lord Jesus, of course.

47. *Sopher* (plural, *sopherim*) from Hebrew, literally, a counter; a scribe.

48. Kenneth L. Barker, "Copying the Old and New Testament Manuscripts,"
accessed March 17, 2011, helpmewithbiblestudy.org/5Bible
/TransCopyingTheOTNTManuscripts_Barker.aspx.

49. See Hanegraaff, *Has God Spoken?* chapter 1.

50. Three previous paragraphs adapted from ibid. and 6–7.

51. Rainer Riesner, "Jesus as Preacher and Teacher," in *Jesus and the Oral
Gospel Tradition*, ed., Henry Wansbrough (Sheffield: JSOT, 1991), 203.

52. See Hanegraaff, *Has God Spoken?* chapter 2.

53. Subsection "Oral Culture" taken from Hanegraaff, *The Complete Bible
Answer Book*, Collector's Edition, 152.

54. "According to Ibn ʻAbbās, Muḥammad said the black stone came down from Paradise, and at the time of its descent it was whiter than milk, but that the sins of the children of Adam have caused it to be black, by their touching it" (Thomas Patrick Hughes, *A Dictionary of Islam* [Chicago: KAZI Publications, Inc., 1994, originally published in 1886], 154–155).

55. See the fascinating work in this area by Gary Habermas, "The Shroud of Turin, Could It Be Real? (Gary Habermas)," Documentary Heaven, published March 20, 2017, www.youtube.com/watch?v=g95F5PXlI1U.

56. F. F. Bruce, *The Books and the Parchments: How We Got Our English Bible* (Grand Rapids: Revell, 1950), 178; for a more recent discussion, see Clay Jones, "The Bibliographical Test Updated," *Christian Research Journal*, vol. 35, no. 03 (2012), www.equip.org/article/the-bibliographical-test-updated/.

57. Subsection "Papyrus and Parchment" adapted from Hanegraaff, *Has God Spoken?*, 55 and chapter 3.

58. See Hanegraaff, *Has God Spoken?* chapter 4.

59. Subsection "Internal Evidence" taken from Hanegraaff, *The Complete Bible Answer Book*, Collector's Edition, 153.

60. See Tacitus, *Annals* 15.44.

61. See Suetonius, *Twelve Caesars*, Nero 16.2 and Claudius 25.4.

62. See Darrel L. Bock, *Studying the Historical Jesus: A Guide to Sources and Methods* (Grand Rapids: Baker Academic, 2002), 47–49.

63. See Gary R. Habermas, *The Historical Jesus* (Joplin, MO: College Press, 1996), 187–228 (esp. 224–28); Hanegraaff, *Has God Spoken?* chapter 5.

64. See Josephus, *Antiquities* 18:63. See note 38, page 227.

65. Subsection "External Evidence" taken from Hanegraaff, *The Complete Bible Answer Book*, Collector's Edition, 153–54.

66. See Hanegraaff, *Has God Spoken?*, chapter 6.

67. Subsection "Science of Textual Criticism" adapted from Hanegraaff, *The Complete Bible Answer Book*, Collector's Edition, 154–55.

68. The following material under the acronym S-P-A-D-E is adapted from Hanegraaff, *Has God Spoken?*, 104–106, and part three.

69. See James K. Hoffmeier, *The Archaeology of the Bible* (Oxford, England: Lion Hudson, 2008), 50, 87ff; Paul L. Maier, "Biblical Archaeology: Factual Evidence to Support the Historicity of the Bible" *Christian Research Journal*, volume 27, number 2 (2004), accessed August 26, 2016, www.equip.org/article/biblical-archaeology-factual-evidence-to-support-the-historicity-of-the-bible/.

70. Michael D. Lemonick, "Are the Bible's Stories True?" *Time*, June 24, 2001, accessed August 18, 2016, www.time.com/time/printout/0,8816,133539,00.html.

71. Alfred J. Hoerth, *Archaeology and the Old Testament* (Grand Rapids: Baker Books, 1998), 306–310.

72. For discussion of these steles and stones, see Hanegraaff, *Has God Spoken?*, chapter 7.

73. For discussion of these pools, see Hanegraaff, *Has God Spoken?*, chapter 8.

74. For discussion of Sennacherib's prism, Shalmaneser's black obelisk, and the ruins of Sargon's palace, see Hanegraaff, *Has God Spoken?*, chapter 9.

75. See Hanegraaff, *Has God Spoken?*, chapter 10.

76. Craig A. Evans, *Holman QuickSource Guide to the Dead Sea Scrolls* (Nashville: Holman Reference, 2010).

77. David Damrosch, "Epic Hero: How a Self-taught British Genius Rediscovered the Mesopotamian Saga of Gilgamesh—after 2,500 Years," *Smithsonian*, May 2007, www.smithsonianmag.com/history-archaeology /gilgamesh.html.

78. For discussion of the significance of the ancient flood accounts, see Hanegraaff, *Has God Spoken?*, chapter 11.

79. Subsection "Succession of Nations" and previous paragraph adapted from Hanegraaff, *The Complete Bible Answer Book*, Collector's Edition, 160–61 and Hanegraaff, *Has God Spoken?*, 112 (see 113ff. for discussion).

80. I am indebted to two excellent articles concerning typological prophecy in general and the nature of the relationship between Isaiah 7:14 and Matthew 1:22–23 in particular: James M. Hamilton, Jr., "The Virgin Will Conceive: Typology in Isaiah and Fulfillment in Matthew, the Use of Isaiah 7:14 in Matthew 1:18–23," Tyndale Fellowship Biblical Theology Study Group July 6–8, 2005, accessed March 23, 2011, www.swbts.edu/resources /SWBTS/Resources/FacultyDocuments/Hamilton/TheVirginWillConceive .7_19_05.pdf; and Duane A. Garrett, "Type, Typology," in *Evangelical Dictionary of Biblical Theology*, ed. Walter A. Elwell (Grand Rapids: Baker Book House, 1996), 785–87.

81. See E. Earle Ellis, "Foreword" to Leonhard Goppelt, *Typos: the Typological Interpretation of the Old Testament in the New*, Donald H. Madvid, trans. (Grand Rapids: Eerdmans, 1982), x.

82. Subsection "Typological Prophecy" adapted from Hanegraaff, *Has God Spoken?*, chapter 13.

83. See Daniel 7:13; Isaiah 19:1; Ezekiel 1:4; 30:3; Joel 2:1–2.

84. See 1 Maccabees 1–4; 2 Maccabees 4–5; Josephus, *Antiquities of the Jews* (XII.5.4), www.ccel.org/j/josephus/works/ant-12.htm.

85. Subsection "Abomination of Desolation" adapted from Hanegraaff, *Has God Spoken?*, 149–52, 162.

86. Subsection "Resurrection" adapted from ibid., 168–70.

87. Previous two paragraphs taken from ibid., 186–87 (see 186ff.).

88. I am indebted to James White for his excellent summary and critique concerning the transmission of the Bible and of the Qur'an. See James R. White, *The King James Only Controversy: Can You Trust Modern*

Translations? Second Edition (Minneapolis, MN: Bethany House Publishers, 2009) and *What Every Christian.*

89. White, *King James Only,* 77.
90. Ibid., 78.
91. Ibid., 77.
92. White, *What Every Christian,* 263.
93. See *Sahih al-Bukhari* Volume 6, Book 61, Numbers 509 and 510. White explained: "Without question, and thankfully, the most important set of *ahadith* for our study here is found in the most authoritative collection of such materials, *Sahih al-Bukhari.*" He goes on to comment that these passages, which constitute the earliest authoritative Islamic account of how the Qur'an was collected, are "more directly honest and frank than one might expect from a few centuries after the fact" (White, *What Every Christian,* 254).
94. *Sahih al-Bukhari* Volume 6, Book 61, Number 510, www.usc.edu/org/cmje /religious-texts/hadith/bukhari/061-sbt.php#006.061.510.
95. White, *What Every Christian,* 262. See also Sam Shamoun, "The Compilation of the Qur'an," *Answering Islam,* www.answering-islam.org /authors/shamoun/quran_compilation.html.
96. Christian apologist Abdu Murray (a former Muslim) adds that emerging evidence shows "the Qur'an we have today does not match the earliest copies we have, including the manuscripts uncovered at the mosque in Sana, Yemen. Those manuscripts are among the earliest we have and contain variants from today's Qur'an in terms of vowelization and diacritical marks. Also, the manuscripts contain palimpsests showing that an original writing was washed off and corrected. Additionally, the manuscripts Muslims have traditionally relied on to say that the Qur'an is perfectly preserved reveal exactly the opposite. Dr. Jay Smith, a well-known Christian polemicist, makes an excellent case in this regard in a widely-viewed debate against Dr. Shabir Ally, who is recognized as one of the best Muslim debaters on the planet. Interestingly, Dr. Ally did not respond to Dr. Smith's manuscript critiques, choosing instead to rely on faulty numerology. The debate can be viewed at youtu.be/fWHV9VnOJtc." (Excerpt from unpublished review of *Muslim,* commissioned by publisher, April 2017.)
97. William Lane Craig's opening speech in *Will the Real Jesus Please Stand Up? A Debate between William Lane Craig and John Dominic Crossan,* ed. Paul Copan (Grand Rapids: Baker Books, 1998), 26–27; William Lane Craig, "Did Jesus Rise from the Dead?" in Michael J. Wilkins and J. P. Moreland, eds., *Jesus Under Fire* (Grand Rapids: Zondervan, 1995), 147–48.
98. See subsection "Crucifixion," pp. 33–36.
99. See note 42, page 227.

100. Qur'an 5:33 Yusuf Ali.

101. See Qur'an 7:124; 12:41; 20:71; 26:49.

102. See note 79, page 231.

103. *The Study Quran: A New Translation and Commentary*, ed. Seyyed Hossein Nasr (New York: HarperOne, 2015), 447 (note for Q 7:124).

104. Ibid., 1366 (note for Q 61:6).

105. Ali, *Meaning of the Holy Qur'an*, 1461 (note 5438 at Q 61:6), emphasis and bracketed text added.

106. See White, *King James Only*, 47–48; J. Ed Komoszewski, M. James Sawyer, Daniel B. Wallace, *Reinventing Jesus: What the* Da Vinci Code *and Other Novel Speculations Don't Tell You* (Grand Rapids: Kregel, 2006), Part 2.

107. See Hanegraaff, *Has God Spoken?*, chapter 6.

108. Nasr, ed., *The Study Quran*, 1366 [note for Q 61:6].

109. "49 Killed in Shooting at Florida Nightclub in Possible Act of Islamic Terror," *Fox News*, June 12, 2016, www.foxnews.com/us/2016/06/12/florida-authorities-say-multiple-people-have-been-shot-at-orlando-nightclub.html; Karen Yourish, Derek Watkins, Tom Giratikanon, and Jasmine C. Lee, "How Many People Have Been Killed in ISIS Attacks Around the World," *New York Times*, July 16, 2016, www.nytimes.com/interactive/2016/03/25/world/map-isis-attacks-around-the-world.html?_r=0; cf. Special Agent Dave Couvertier, "Investigative Update Regarding Pulse Nightclub Shooting," FBI Tampa, June 20, 2016, www.fbi.gov/contact-us/field-offices/tampa/news/press-releases/investigative-update-regarding-pulse-nightclub-shooting.

110. "Last Words of a Terrorist," *The Guardian*, September 30, 2001, www.theguardian.com/world/2001/sep/30/terrorism.september113; Hans G. Kippenberg, "Consider That It Is a Raid on the Path of God': The Spiritual Manual of the Attackers of 9/11," *Numen*, Vol. 52, Iss. 1 (2005), www.researchgate.net/publication/240682153_Consider_that_it_is_a_Raid_on_the_Path_of_God_The_Spiritual_Manual_of_the_Attackers_of_911.

111. Ayman S. Ibrahim, "Why Do They Shout 'Allahu Akbar'?" *First Things*, September 20, 2016, www.firstthings.com/blogs/firstthoughts/2016/09/why-do-they-shout-allahu-akbar; Robert Spencer, "Robert Spencer at Breitbart: 'Allahu Akbar' Doesn't Mean What Media Says It Means," *Jihad Watch*, December 25, 2015, www.jihadwatch.org/2015/12/robert-spencer-at-breitbart-allahu-akbar-doesnt-mean-what-media-says-it-means; "The Meaning of 'Allah Akbar!'" *Investor's Business Daily*, January 5, 2011, www.investors.com/politics/editorials/the-meaning-of-allah-akbar/.

112. See Qur'an 9:29, 30, 73, 111, 123; 47:35; *Sahih al-Bukhari* 1:2:25; 4:52:63; 4:53:386; 5:59:377; *Sahih Muslim* 20:4645.

113. The word *Allah* possibly stems from the Arabic *al-Ilāh*, "the God." Although Arabic-speaking Christians (and Jews) use the same word "Allah"

to refer to God, the triune God of Christianity and the unitarian God of Islam are decidedly not the same God.

114. See Alexander Vilenkin, "The Beginning of the Universe," *Inference*, vol. 1, no. 4 (2015), inference-review.com/article/the-beginning-of-the-universe.

115. See Genesis 1, especially verse 1; Psalm 33:6–9; Psalm 148:1–6; Proverbs 8:22–29; John 1:3; Romans 4:17; Colossians 1:16–17; Hebrews 1:2–3; 11:3.

116. This state of affairs follows directly from the central doctrine of Islam, tawhid. Islamic scholar Abu Ameenah Bilal Philips wrote, "It is common knowledge that *Tawḥīd* is the basis of the religion of Islam and that it is most precisely expressed in the formula, "*Lā ilāha illallāh*" (There is no god but Allah), which states that there is only one true God and that He alone deserves to be worshipped. This seemingly simple formula forms the dividing line between *Eemān* (true belief in God) and *Kufr* (disbelief), according to the tenets of Islam. Because of this principle of *Tawḥīd*, the Islamic belief in God is considered to be unitarian and Islam is counted among the world's monotheistic religions along with Judaism and Christianity. Yet, according to the Islamic concept (*Tawḥīd*), Christianity is classified as polytheism and Judaism is considered a subtle form of idolatry" (Abu Ameenah Bilal Philips, *The Fundamentals of Tawheed (Islamic Monotheism)* (Riyadh: International Islamic Publishing House, 2005), 11, www.kalamullah.com/Books/Fundamentals%20Of%20Tawheed.pdf).

117. See John 3:35; 5:20; 14:31; Romans 5:5; 1 John 4:8, 16. For a helpful discussion, see Donald Fairbairn, *Life in the Trinity: An Introduction to Theology with the Help of the Church Fathers* (Downers Grove, IL: IVP Academic, 2009), chapters 2–4.

118. C. S. Lewis, *Mere Christianity* (New York: HarperOne, 2001), 174.

119. Craig goes on to show that, "according to the Qur'an, God's love is reserved for the God-fearing and the good-doers [see Q 19:96; see also 2:277, 281]; but he has no love for sinners and unbelievers [see Q 2:98, 276; 3:32, 57; 4:36; 5:87; 6:141; 8:58]. Thus, in the Islamic conception of God, God is not all-loving. His love is partial and has to be earned. The Muslim God only loves those who first love him. His love thus rises no higher than the sort of love that Jesus said even tax-collectors and sinners exhibit. . . . But as the greatest conceivable being, as the most perfect being, the source of all goodness and love, God's love must be unconditional, impartial, and universal. Therefore, it seems to me that the Islamic conception of God is simply morally defective." William Lane Craig, "The Concept of God in Islam and Christianity," *Reasonable Faith*, June 22, 2015, www .reasonablefaith.org/the-concept-of-god-in-islam-and-christianity, bracketed insertions added based on Qur'an passages quoted by Craig in his speech.

120. See pages 37–39.

121. Fairbairn, *Life in the Trinity*, 54.

122. Leonardo Boff, *Trinity and Society* (New York: Orbis Books, 1988), 89; see also Millard J. Erickson, *God in Three Persons* (Grand Rapids: Baker Books, 1995), 233.

123. Norman L. Geisler, *Baker Encyclopedia of Christian Apologetics* (Grand Rapids: Baker Books, 1999), 732. This paragraph and subsequent four paragraphs concerning the three planks of the trinitariam platform are adapted from Hanegraaff, *The Complete Bible Answer Book*, 50–51.

124. See note 56, page 229.

125. Qur'an 19:88–93 reads, "And they say, 'The Most Merciful has taken [for Himself] a son.' You have done an atrocious thing. The heavens almost rupture therefrom and the earth splits open and the mountains collapse in devastation that they attribute to the Most Merciful a son. And it is not appropriate for the Most Merciful that He should take a son. There is no one in the heavens and earth but that he comes to the Most Merciful as a servant" (*Sahih International*). See also Qur'an 5:18; 10:68.

126. See John 1:12; 14:16–17, 19–20; 16:13–15; 20:31; Romans 8:15–16; 2 Peter 1:4. See Fairbairn, *Life in the Trinity*, chapter 9.

127. Ali, *The Meaning of the Holy Qur'an*, 236 (note 663 at Q 4:157).

128. See Norman L. Geisler and Abdul Saleeb, *Answering Islam: The Crescent in Light of the Cross*, second edition (Grand Rapids, MI: Baker Books, 2002), 67.

129. See Ali, *The Meaning of the Holy Qur'an*, 236 (note 663 at Q 4:157).

130. See Geisler, Saleeb, *Answering Islam*, appendix 3: "The Gospel of Barnabas."

131. See page 171ff.

132. See Habermas, *Historical Jesus*, 143–170 (esp. 158); Copan, ed., *Will the Real Jesus*, 26–27.

133. See Tacitus, *Annals* 15.44.

134. See Josephus, *Antiquities* 18:63. See note 38, page 227. Two paragraphs adapted from Hanegraaff, *The Complete Bible Answer Book*, 251, and Hanegraaff, *Has God Spoken?*, 46–47.

135. Information and points in this paragraph come from William Lane Craig's opening address in Copan, ed., *Will the Real Jesus*, 26–27; William Lane Craig, "Did Jesus Rise from the Dead?" in Wilkins, Moreland, eds., *Jesus Under Fire*, 146–49; see also William Lane Craig, *Reasonable Faith: Christian Truth and Apologetics*, third edition (Wheaton, IL: Crossway Books, 2008), 367–69. The wording of this paragraph is adapted from Hanegraaff, *The Complete Bible Answer Book*, 252, and Hanegraaff, *Has God Spoken?*, 179.

136. John A. T. Robinson, *The Human Face of God* (Philadelphia: Westminster, 1973), 131, quoted in William Lane Craig's opening address in Copan, ed., *Will the Real Jesus*, 27. And as scholar D. H. van Daalen has noted, "it is extremely difficult to object to the empty tomb on historical grounds; those

who deny it do so on the basis of theological or philosophical assumptions" (William Lane Craig, "Contemporary Scholarship and the Historical Evidence for the Resurrection of Jesus Christ," *Truth* 1 [1985]: 89–95, from the Leadership University website, accessed September 5, 2016, www.leaderu.com/truth/1truth22.html; see also William Lane Craig, "Did Jesus Rise from the Dead?" in Wilkins, Moreland, eds., *Jesus Under Fire*, 152).

137. This sentence paraphrases Gary R. Habermas as interviewed by Lee Strobel in Strobel, *Case for Christ*, 233.

138. Information and points in this paragraph come from Habermas, *Historical Jesus*, 152–57; and William Lane Craig, *Reasonable Faith*, 362ff. The wording in this paragraph adapted from Hanegraaff, *The Complete Bible Answer Book*, 252, and Hanegraaff, *Has God Spoken?*, 180.

139. Christian philosopher and apologist J. P. Moreland explained that temple sacrifices, keeping the Law, the Sabbath, non-trinitarian monotheism, and the view of a human messianic political king who would deliver Jews from Gentile oppression and establish the Davidic kingdom without concept of a crucified (let alone rising) messiah formed the core beliefs of first-century Judaism, which were radically altered by the early Jewish church in the wake of the incomparable life, death, and resurrection of Jesus of Nazareth (J. P. Moreland, *Scaling the Secular City: A Defense of Christianity* [Grand Rapids: Baker Book House, 1987], 179–180; see also J. P. Moreland as interviewed in Strobel, *Case for Christ*, 250–54).

140. Adapted from Hanegraaff, *The Complete Bible Answer Book*, 253, and Hanegraaff, *Has God Spoken?*, 183.

141. Charles Colson, "The Paradox of Power," Power to Change, web.archive.org/web/20070704044611/http://www.powertochange.ie:80/changed/ccolson.html; cf. Charles Colson and Nancy Pearcey, *How Now Shall We Live?* (Wheaton, IL: Tyndale House Publishers, 1999), 275–76.

142. See Augustine, *The Trinity* 1.2 and books 8–15; *Confessions*, books 10–11. See also Robert Crouse, "Knowledge," in *Augustine Through the Ages: An Encyclopedia*, ed. Allan D. Fitzgerald (Grand Rapids: William B. Eerdmans Publishing Co., 1999), 486–88; R. C. Sproul, *The Consequences of Ideas: Understanding the Concepts that Shaped our World* (Wheaton, IL: Crossway, 2000), 58–59.

143. J. P. Moreland, "A Philosophical Examination of Hugh Ross's Natural Theology," *Philosophia Christi*, 21, 1 (1998): 33, accessed September 5, 2016, www.reasons.org/articles/philosophia-christi#heading4.

144. See Rodney Stark, *The Victory of Reason: How Christianity Led to Freedom, Capitalism, and Western Success* (New York: Random House, 2005), 22–23; Vishal Mangalwadi, *The Book That Made Your World: How the Bible Created the Soul of Western Civilization* (Nashville: Thomas Nelson, 2011), 220–45.

145. White, *What Every Christian*, 66.
146. Athanasius, "The Incarnation of the Word of God," 54.3, accessed September 5, 2014, www.ccel.org/ccel/schaff/npnf204.vii.ii.liv.html.
147. Psalms 90:2; 93:2; 102:12; Ephesians 3:21; Hebrews 9:14.
148. Genesis 1:26–31; see also Job 3; 38:4, 21.
149. Job 7; see also Job chapters 9; 10; 14; 34:20; Psalms 90; 102:11–12; 103:15; Isaiah 40:6–8; James 1:10–11; 1 Peter 1:24–25.
150. John 5:26; see also Isaiah 43:10; 41:4; 44:6; 48:12; Revelation 1:8, 17; 2:8; 3:14; 21:6; 22:13; and Exodus 3:14 with John 8:58.
151. Acts 17:28.
152. Job 42:2; see also Jeremiah 32:17; Matthew 19:26; Mark 10:27; Luke 1:37; 18:27.
153. 1 Corinthians 1:25; see also 2 Corinthians 12:9; Hebrews 4:15; Job 23.
154. Job 37:16; Psalm 147:5; Isaiah 40:13–14; 41:22–23; 42:9; 44:7; Jeremiah 17:10.
155. Isaiah 55:8–9; see also Job 11:7–12; 21:22; 36:22–33; 37:5–24; 38:4.
156. Jeremiah 23:23–24; see also Psalm 139:7–12; Ephesians 1:23; 4:10; Colossians 3:11.
157. Psalm 139:1–12. See also Job 23; 37:23; 38–41.
158. For a sampling of passages highlighting communicable attributes of God, see Leviticus 19:2; Matthew 5:48; John 4:24; 13:34; Ephesians 4:24; Colossians 3:10; Hebrews 12:7–11. For a clear and concise study of the attributes of God, see "The Attributes of God" at CRI's website, www .equip.org/articles/the-attributes-of-god-what-are-the-attributes-of-god.
159. Millard J. Erickson, *Christian Theology* (Grand Rapids: Baker Book House, 1985), 514.
160. Colossians 3:9–10.
161. Some text in subsection "Incarnation" adapted from my book Hanegraaff, *Has God Spoken?*, 281–82, and Hanegraaff, *The Complete Bible Answer Book*, 269–71.
162. Martin Luther, *Weimarer Ausgabe* (WA) 1, 28, 25–32, quoted in Mannermaa, "Theosis," 43, quoted in Veli-Matti Kärkkäinen, *One with God: Salvation as Deification and Justification* (Collegeville: MN: Liturgical Press, 2004), 47; see also discussion and a slightly different translation of the same quote in Kurt E. Marquart, "Luther and Theosis," *Concordia Theological Quarterly* 64, 3 (2000): 186–87, www.ctsfw.net /media/pdfs/marquartlutherandtheosis.pdf.
163. Martin Luther, *Weimarer Ausgabe* (WA) 2, 247–48 and *Luther's Works* (LW) 51, 58, quoted in Veli-Matti Kärkkäinen, *One with God: Salvation as Deification and Justification* (Collegeville: Minn.: Liturgical Press, 2004), 47.
164. Quoted in Daniel B. Clendenin, "Partakers of Divinity: The Orthodox

Doctrine of Theosis," *Journal of the Evangelical Theological Society* 37, 3 (September 1994), 374. See also G. Mantzaridis, *The Deification of Man* (Crestwood, NY: St Vladimir's Seminary, 1984), 29. *Logos* is "the most common Greek term for 'word,' and the source of the words 'logic' and 'wisdom.' In ordinary Greek, *logos* means 'reason,' though John used 'Word' at the beginning of his gospel to refer to Jesus: 'In the beginning was the Word, and the word was with God and the Word was God. He was in the beginning with God' (John 1:1–2). John is saying that Jesus was and is God, the 'Logic of God' or the 'Wisdom of God' incarnate. See John 1:9, 14." (Terry L. Miethe, *The Compact Dictionary of Doctrinal Words* [Minneapolis: Bethany House Publishers, 1988], 129.)

165. See Augustine, *Confessions*, VII.5.

166. Eastern Orthodox theology emphasizes the Greek *energeia* family of words in speaking about God's active presence within the physical world. Frederica Mathewes-Green explained that *energeia* and its cognates appear many times in the New Testament, especially in the writings of Paul, although for historical linguistic reasons these words are usually translated in terms of work or action. Using literal translation, she cited several examples in which Paul spoke of "God 'energizing' within us," including,

- "'God is energizing in you, both to will and to energize for his good pleasure' (Phil. 2:13).
- "'The Word of God . . . is energizing in you believers' (1 Thess. 2:13).
- "'For this I toil, striving according to the energy of him energizing in me with *dynamis* [power]' (Col. 1:29)."

Said Mathewes-Green: "There is an essence to God, an *ousia*, that we can never grasp, but his energies surround and fill us in natural and supernatural ways." God's "energy is what gives us bodies and breath, and also makes us *more* than bodies and breath: it gives us awareness and individuality, and enables us to see others and love them. 'In him was life, and the life was the light of all people' (John 1:4 NRSV)." But she emphasizes that "God's energies, by which we experience him in this world, are not all there is to God. In his essence, his unknowable inner reality, God is beyond anything we could sense or think" (Frederica Mathewes-Green, *Welcome to the Orthodox Church: An Introduction to Eastern Christianity* [Brewster, MA: Paraclete Press, 2015], 118–19, emphasis in original).

167. C. S. Lewis, *Mere Christianity: A revised and amplified edition, with a new introduction, of the three books* Broadcast Talks, Christian Behaviour *and* Beyond Personality (New York: HarperOne, 2001), 189.

168. C. H. Spurgeon, "The Believer a New Creature," Sermon no. 881, delivered July 18, 1869, Spurgeon Gems, www.spurgeongems.org/vols13-15/chs881 .pdf. (This version has been lightly edited to conform to modern-day

language; compare original at Christian Classics Ethereal Library, www.ccel.org/ccel/spurgeon/sermons15.i_1.html.)

169. See the illustrative presentation and discussion of this miraculous process in the remarkable documentary film on DVD, *Metamorphosis: The Beauty and Design of Butterflies*, directed by Lad Allen (La Mirada, CA: Illustra Media, 2011), available through Christian Research Institute at equip.org.

170. Spurgeon, "The Believer a New Creature," emphasis in original.

171. See Q 18:47–49; also 10:61; 17:13–14; 34:3–4; 45:27–35; 69:19–31; 84:6–12; 99:6–8. See discussion in Jane Idleman Smith and Yvonne Yazbeck Haddad, *The Islamic Understanding of Death and Resurrection* (Oxford: Oxford University Press, 2002), 11–17, 76ff.

172. See, possibly, Q 17:79 in conjunction with 20:109; 43:86; 47:19; see also 21:28; 34:23; 53:26. Contrast these verses with others that denounce the efficacy of intercession, such as Q 2:48; 6:51; 32:4; 39:44; 74:48; 82:19. See discussion in Smith and Haddad, *Islamic Understanding of Death and Resurrection*, 25–27, 80–82.

173. *Sahih al-Bukhari* Volume 4, Book 56, Number 676, www.usc.edu/org/cmje/religious-texts/hadith/bukhari/056-sbt.php#004.056.676.

174. White, *What Every Christian*, 158.

175. Ibid., 159.

176. See Matthew 24; Mark 13; Luke 21. In general, however, the Lord Jesus promises, "In this world you will have trouble. But take heart! I have overcome the world" (John 16:33 NIV).

177. See Revelation 20:1–6.

178. "We have been made holy through the sacrifice of the body of Jesus Christ once for all" (Hebrews 10:10). "He is the propitiation for our sins, and not for ours only but also for the sins of the whole world" (1 John 2:2 ESV). "In this is love, not that we have loved God but that he loved us and sent his Son to be the propitiation for our sins" (1 John 4:10 ESV). See also Isaiah 52:13–53:12; Matthew 20:28; 26:28; John 1:29; Romans 3:21–26; 5:6–9, 18–19; 8:3; 1 Corinthians 15:3; 2 Corinthians 5:15, 19–21; Ephesians 1:7; Colossians 1:22; Hebrews 2:17; 9:11–28; 10:1–18; 1 Peter 1:18–19; 2:21–25; 3:18.

179. As the Nicene Creed states, the Lord Jesus Christ "ascended into heaven and is seated at the right hand of the Father. He will come again with glory to judge the living and the dead; His kingdom will have no end. . . . We look for the resurrection of the dead, and the life of the age to come." See Matthew 19:28; John 14:1–3; Acts 1:9–11; 3:19–21; Romans 8:18–27; 1 Corinthians 3:13; 15:23–27, 51–54; 16:22; 2 Corinthians 5:10; Ephesians 1:9–10; Philippians 3:20–21; Colossians 3:4; 1 Thessalonians 4:16–17; Titus 2:13; 2 Timothy 4:8; Hebrews 9:28; 11:13–16; 2 Peter 3:5–13; 1 John 2:28; 3:2; Revelation 3:12; 21:1–27; 22:1–5 (cf. Isaiah 65:17–25; 66:22–24).

180. See Job 19:25–27; Psalm 16:9–11; Isaiah 26:19; Daniel 12:2, 13; Matthew

8:10–11; 19:28–29; Mark 12:26–27; Luke 14:12–14; John 3:16–18, 36; 5:21–29; 6:39–40; 11:21–26; 14:2–3; 17:3, 24; Acts 24:14–15; Romans 4:17; 6:23; 8:11; 1 Corinthians 15:12–23; 35–56; 2 Corinthians 4:14; 5:1–10; Philippians 3:11, 20–21; 1 Thessalonians 4:13–17; Revelation 21:1–27; 22:1–5, 14.

181. See Daniel 12:2; Isaiah 66:22–24; Matthew 3:10–12; 5:22; 5:29–30; 7:13–14, 19, 21–23; 8:10–12; 10:28; 12:32; 13:24–30, 42, 50; 18:8–9; 22:13, 33; 25:29–30, 31–33, 41, 46; Mark 9:42–48; Luke 16:19–31; John 3:18, 36; 5:28–29; Acts 24:14–15; Romans 2:6–8; 1 Corinthians 6:9–10; Galatians 5:19–21; 2 Thessalonians 1:5–10; Hebrews 10:26–27, 30–31; Jude 1:4–7, 11–15; Revelation 14:9–11; 19:20; 20:10–15; 21:8, 27; 22:14–15.

182. Subsection "Eschatology" text thus far presented adapted from Hank Hanegraaff, *AfterLife: What You Need to Know about Heaven, the Hereafter and Near-Death Experiences* (Brentwood, TN: Worthy Publishing, 2013), and Hanegraaff, *The Complete Bible Answer Book*, 10–11.

183. In the following discussion of death and the afterlife according to Islam, I follow Hamza Yusuf, "Death, Dying, and the Afterlife in the Quran," in Nasr, ed., *Study Quran*, 1819–1855; and Smith, Haddad, *Islamic Understanding of Death*.

184. See Smith, Haddad, *Islamic Understanding of Death*, 37–41.

185. See Ibid., 41–42.

186. Al-Bukhārī 23.67 (no. 1351), 23.86 (no. 1389); Muslim 54.18 (no. 7395), as quoted in Yusuf, "Death, Dying, and the Afterlife in the Quran," 1829.

187. Ibid.

188. Ibid.

189. Ismāʿīl ibn ʿUmar ibn Kathīr, *Tafsīr al-Qurʾān al-caẓīm*, ed. Sāmī ibn Muḥammad al-Salāmah, 8 vols. (Riyadh: Dār Ṭibah, 1999), 6:581 (on 36:48–54); as quoted in Yusuf, "Death, Dying, and the Afterlife in the Quran," 1830–31.

190. Yusuf, "Death, Dying, and the Afterlife in the Quran," 1833.

191. Ibid., 1834.

192. Ibid., 1840.

193. Ibid., 1842, emphasis in original.

194. Sahih Muslim 2.83 (no. 473), Aḥmad 10 (no. 25432), as quoted in Yusuf, "Death, Dying, and the Afterlife in the Quran," 1844.

195. Smith, Haddad, *Islamic Understanding of Death*, 78–79.

196. Ibid., 79.

197. Nasr, ed., *Study Quran*, 648, note for Qurʾan 15:43–44.

198. Smith, Haddad, *Islamic Understanding of Death*, 85, Arabic inserts in original.

199. Ibid., 85–86, parenthetical references are to the Qurʾan (S stands for sura, meaning chapter).

200. Smith, Haddad, *Islamic Understanding of Death*, 86–87.

201. Nasr, ed., *The Study Quran*.

202. Ibid.

203. Ibid.

204. Smith and Haddad explain that all references to houris are early Meccan, including Qur'an 37:48–49; 56:35–38, 78:33, in which the actual word does not appear but context implies *ḥūr*. Smith, Haddad, *Islamic Understanding of Death*, 164, 236n24.

205. Smith, Haddad, *Islamic Understanding of Death*, 164.

206. Ibid., 165.

207. Robert Spencer, *The Politically Incorrect Guide to Islam (and the Crusades)* (Washington, DC: Regnery Publishing, 2005), 104.

208. Nasr, ed., *The Study Quran*, 146, note for Q 3:55.

209. *Sunan Abu-Dawud* Book 37, Number 4310, www.usc.edu/org/cmje /religious-texts/hadith/abudawud/037-sat.php; see also *Sahih al-Bukhari* Volume 3, Book 34, Number 425; and *Sahib al-Bukhari* Volume 3, Book 43, Number 656.

210. Samuel Shahid, *The Last Trumpet: A Comparative Study in Christian-Islamic Eschatology* (n.c.: Xulon Press, 2005), 131–32.

Afterword

1. Gorka, *Defeating Jihad: The Winnable War* (Regnery Publishing, 2016), 129.

2. See Robert H. Bork, *Slouching Towards Gomorrah, Modern Liberalism and American Decline* (New York: Regan Books, 1996); Patrick J. Buchanan, *Suicide of a Superpower: Will America Survive to 2025?* (New York: Thomas Dunne Books, 2011).

3. See Raymond Ibrahim, "ISIS Massacre of Christians 'Not Genocide,' Obama Administration Insists," Gatestone Institute, March 17, 2016, accessed September 13, 2016, www.gatestoneinstitute.org/7623/isis-genocide-christians; Raymond Ibrahim, *Crucified Again: Exposing Islam's New War on Christians* (Washington, DC: Regnery Publishing, 2013); John L. Allen, Jr., *The Global War on Christians: Dispatches from the Front Lines of Anti-Christian Persecution* (New York: Image, 2013).

4. Gorka, *Defeating Jihad*, 129.

5. Specifically, militant egalitarianism as equality of outcomes as opposed to opportunities; radical individualism as unbridled craving for self-gratification; multiculturalism as mandating that one set of cultural values may not be deemed inferior to another; political correctness as repression of honest dialogue and tolerant disagreement; religious pluralism as all religions being equally true and valid ways to God.

6. Os Guinness, *Renaissance: The Power of the Gospel However Dark the Times* (Downers Grove, IL: InterVarsity Press, 2014), 47.

7. Ibid., 67.
8. Ibid., 25–26.
9. 1 Peter 3:15.
10. For further study concerning the art and science of biblical interpretation, see Hanegraaff, *Has God Spoken?*, 209–279; and Hank Hanegraaff, "L-I-G-H-T-S on Your Path to Reading the Bible for All It's Worth," a pocket-sized laminated flip-chart, available through the Christian Research Institute at www.equip.org.
11. See note 101, page 220.
12. See Q 9:23; 53:29; see also 3:118; 5:51, 80; *Sahih al-Bukhari* Volume 5, Book 59, Number 572.
13. Matthew 17:2.
14. Matthew 17:5.
15. Luke 9:31 NIV, 1984.

Appendix

1. See page 22.
2. I draw from Mohammad A. Khan, "Why Aisha Likely Poisoned Muhammad, Not a Jewish Woman, Part 1," *Islam Watch*, accessed September 17, 2016, www.islam-watch.org/home/112-mohammad/660 -why-aisha-poisoned-muhammad-not-jewish-woman-1.html; "Fadak," *Shia Pen*, accessed September 17, 2016, www.shiapen.com/comprehensive /fadak.html; Shaykh Yasser Al-Habib, "Scandal: Aisha killed the Prophet Muhammad!!" YouTube series begins, accessed September 17, 2016, www.youtube.com/watch?v=_HiMgW9yd7w.
3. Ali ibn Abi Talib was the son of Muhammad's uncle, Abu Talib. Ali married Muhammad's youngest daughter, Fatimah (daughter of Muhammad's first wife Khadija). Ali was, thus, Muhammad's first cousin and son-in-law.
4. Fred M. Donner, *Muhammad and the Believers: At the Origins of Islam* (Cambridge: Belknap Press, 2010), 156–57.
5. See Donner, *Muhammad and the Believers*, 177ff.; Stephen Schwartz, *The Two Faces of Islam: The House of Sa'ud from Tradition to Terror* (New York: Doubleday, 2002), 37–38.
6. See Samuel Shahid, *The Last Trumpet: A Comparative Study in Christian-Islamic Eschatology* (n.c.: Xulon Press, 2005), chapter 6.
7. David Cook of Rice University wrote, "Jesus' arrival will usher in a messianic age; he will kill the Antichrist and afterward convert the Christians to Islam. Traditions about this messianic period are very confused: many hold that the alternative messianic figure (the Mahdi) will appear during the previous period of apocalyptic wars with the Byzantines and even that the Mahdi will be the one to emerge victorious. A sharp

conflict exists between the Jesus and Mahdi traditions, signaling the intense discomfort of many Muslims with the Jesus scenario. Since Jesus is so revered by the Christians, it was apparently dangerous to leave him alone in control of the Muslim messianic future. Thus in many traditions he is made subordinate to the Mahdi, a purely Muslim messianic figure, to whom is assigned the more traditional roles of conquest and subjection of enemy countries." (David Cook, *Contemporary Muslim Apocalyptic Literature* [Syracuse, NY: Syracuse University Press, 2005], 9.)

8. *Sahih al-Bukhari*, Volume 3, Book 43, Number 656, www.usc.edu/org/cmje /religious-texts/hadith/bukhari/043-sbt.php#003.043.656.

9. Cyril Glassé, "Koran," in *The New Encyclopedia of Islam*, rev. ed. (Walnut Creek, CA: Altamira Press, 2001, 2002), 268, at Google Books, books. google.com/books?id=focLrox-frUC&lpg=PA268&dq=Uncreatedness%20 of%20the%20Quran&pg=PA268#v=onepage&q=Uncreatedness%20 of%20the%20Quran&f=false.

10. Cf. Jane Idleman Smith and Yvonne Yazbeck Haddad, *The Islamic Understanding of Death and Resurrection* (Oxford: Oxford University Press, 2002), 11ff.; "The Issue of Predestination and Free Will," Al-Islam. org, www.al-islam.org/justice-of-god-ayatullah-makarim-shirazi /issue-predestination-and-free-will.

11. See the internet version of the exhibition, "Devotion in Pictures: Muslim Popular Iconography," presented at Bryggens Museum in April 2000, Muslim Devotional Posters, www.webcitation.org/63BsneOUJ?url=http ://www.hf.uib.no/religion/popularikonografi/devotion04.html.

12. See "The World's Muslims: Unity and Diversity," Chapter 1 Religious Affiliation, Pew Research Center, August 9, 2012, www.pewforum. org/2012/08/09/the-worlds-muslims-unity-and-diversity-1-religious -affiliation/; and "The Future of the Global Muslim Population: Sunni and Shia Muslims," Pew Research Center, January 27, 2011, www.pewforum. org/2011/01/27/future-of-the-global-muslim-population-sunni-and-shia/.

13. See *Sahih al-Bukhari*, Volume 1, Book 2, Number 8; *Sahih Muslim*, Book 001, Number 0001. Shia Muslims categorize these foundations of Muslim life as Practices or Branches of Religion, and add others, including Jihad, Tawalla (friendship toward friends of Allah), and Tabarra (enmity toward enemies of Allah).

GENERAL INDEX

SCRIPTURE INDEX

1:8 102
3:22–23 49
5:3–4 . . . . 37, 39, 158
8:14–17 40
11:26 20
13:2 40

Romans
1:20 136
4:13 . . . . 104, 137
5:12 136
5:16–19 139
8:27 40
10:13 . . . . 258n22

1 Corinthians
2:12 40
7:3–4 68
8:6 37
15:3 34
15:3–7 . . . . 35, 161
15:50–56 172

2 Corinthians
book of 172
5:8 172
5:17 166
5:20–21 171
5:21 133

Galatians
2:20 166
3:16 . . . . 95, 259n30
3:28–29 72

Ephesians
4:6 158
5:25–27 68
5:29 68

Colossians
1:15 . . . . 135, 163

1:15–17 38
1:16, 17, 19 133
1:16–19 . . . . 135, 163
1:29 184

1 Thessalonians
5:21 140

Hebrews
book of 101–102
1:8 . . . . 37, 134
1:10, ... 135
4:15 . . . . 257n20
11:10 102
11:16 137

1 Timothy
1:10 64

James
3:90 165

1 Peter
2:22 133

2 Peter
1:1 134
1:4 . . . . 165, 167, 184
1:16 143
1:20–21 39

1 John
3:5 133
4:8 156

Revelation
book of 258n23
1:8 134
2:7 138
22:1–3 137
22:13 135

QUR'AN INDEX

QUR'AN INDEX

ABOUT THE AUTHOR

Hank Hanegraaff serves as president of the Christian Research Institute (CRI) and hosts the internationally syndicated *Bible Answer Man* broadcast and the *Hank Unplugged* podcast. He is author of more than twenty books and widely regarded as one of the world's leading Christian thinkers. Hank and his wife, Kathy, live in Charlotte, North Carolina, and are parents to twelve children.

www.equip.org
facebook.com/BibleAnswerMan